THE VULGAR TONGUE

THE PENNSYLVANIA STATE UNIVERSITY PRESS
UNIVERSITY PARK, PENNSYLVANIA

THE VULGAR TONGUE

MEDIEVAL AND POSTMEDIEVAL VERNACULARITY

EDITED BY

Fiona Somerset and Nicholas Watson

Library of Congress Cataloging-in-Publication Data

The vulgar tongue : medieval and postmedieval vernacularity /
edited by Fiona Somerset and Nicholas Watson.

    p.   cm.

ISBN 0-271-02310-4 (cloth : alk. paper)

1. Colloquial language.   2. Europe—Languages—History.

I. Somerset, Fiona.   II. Watson, Nicholas.

P408 .V85   2003

409'.4—dc21   2003010253

The Pennsylvania State University Press is a member of the
Association of American University Presses.

It is the policy of The Pennsylvania State University Press
to use acid-free paper. Publications on uncoated stock satisfy
the minimum requirements of American National Standard
for Information Sciences—Permanence of Paper for Printed
Library Material, ANSI Z39.48-1992.

For to this day touchyng the grete myht

Off this tour, which Babel yit men call,

Men fro ful ferr may han therof a syht,

For it surmountith othir touris all.

Off whiche werk thus it is befall,

Off serpentis and many a gret dragoun

It is now callid cheeff habitacioun,

That no man dar, as ferr as thei it see,

For wikkid heir and for corrupcioun,

Bi a gret space and bi a gret contre

Approche no neer that merueilous dongoun,

So venymous is that mansioun

And so horrible, no man dar approche,

Lik to a mounteyn bilt off a craggi roche.

—JOHN LYDGATE,
The Fall of Princes, I.1135–48

CONTENTS

PREFACE: ON "VERNACULAR"

Fiona Somerset and Nicholas Watson

The term "vernacular" and its synonyms have long been used to talk about at least three apparently different kinds of language or language situation. One of the useful things about the term is, indeed, its capacity for suggesting links that might otherwise be hard to see. First, as its derivation from the Latin *vernacularis* (of a slave) suggests, the term describes a subaltern or local language or style, one accessible to a particular, generally nonelite group. In this sense, "vernacular" is often associated (negatively or positively) with the vulgar, the provincial, the rustic, the rudimentary, the natural, or the carnal, and sometimes more specifically with a social underclass, or with women. English, which has had a rich lexis for describing the vernacular since the fourteenth century at the latest, might originally have termed this the "vulgar," "lewd," or "fleshly" tongue, or, more positively, the "kynde" (natural) tongue.[1]

Because many languages have developed in competition with one another, or with a prestigious classical or learned language such as Latin or Greek, this first sense of the term shades into a second one, describing a national language that acts as a focus for the cultural and political aspirations of a people and their rulers, for underprivileged and privileged alike: in Middle and Modern English, the *mother* tongue. Used in this sense, the condition of *vernacularity* is, on one level, something a national language aspires to transcend, whether by standardizing and codifying its phonology, morphology, and spelling or by generating a literature worthy to stand comparison with the classics. This is so even though apologists for a vernacular also stress its distinctiveness and independence from the languages and literatures with which it is in competition.

The same dichotomy between classical and vernacular often also gives rise to a third sense, only tenuously connected with the word's etymology, in which the term denotes, neither the local nor the national, but the universal: in Middle and Modern English, the *common* tongue. Claims to this status can be particularly volatile. On the one hand, the vernacular is what the unlearned share with each other, as well as with those who have access to classical or learned language: it is what people all around the world have in common regardless of any one vernacular's more limited range. But on the other, the learned language, or at the very least its rudiments, can also (counterintuitively) be perceived as vernacular in this sense, forming as it does a means of communication between groups far removed geographically or historically. While the lord in Trevisa's *Dialogue Between a Lord and a Clerk* (written in Middle English in the 1380s) rejects this second understanding of the phrase "common tongue" with scorn (since speakers of Latin are few), and while it can be especially controversial in postcolonial cultures, where this common tongue is the language of the former colonizers, such a language still holds value for many who rely upon it.[2]

In all three cases (with the possible exception of the last), the term describes, not a language as such, but a relation between one language situation and another, with the vernacular at least notionally in the more embattled, or at least the less clear-cut, position. But despite the overlap between these uses, and the slippage that occurs between them, they remain in theory startlingly distinct, if not mutually contradictory.

So mixed a set of meanings is possible because the relations "vernacular" describes are often emotionally and culturally fraught, so that the term itself carries as much affective as intellectual freight. It can have a defensive air, standing as it does in implied opposition to a term suggestive of superior status: "classical," "elite," "learned," "noble," "metropolitan," "polite," and so on. Or it can encode different kinds of claim for prestige: either the prestige of authenticity or integrity conferred upon the subaltern or popular through their very marginalization, or the more assertive prestige that comes with the successful displacement of the husk of the old by the vigorous growth of the new. Typically, indeed, the term is apologetic and assertive at the same time: for "vernacular" nearly always connotes a language situation in which something important is at stake for the user. Nor are modern scholarly users of the term as immune to these connotations as they might want to seem. As often with academic terminology, the apparently irreproachable credentials of "vernacular" can act as a cover for a more interested agenda: the process by which, as Larry Scanlon puts it later in this book, "disciplines allow themselves to become a bit less than systematic . . . to speak of what lies beyond them, the unlearned, the predisciplinary, or nondisciplinary, or antidisciplinary, and not only to speak of it but to speak for it" (220). In this sense, the term can function (for better or worse) not only as a marker of a linguistic or cultural relationship but also as a bridge, a relatively informal place of meeting and mediation, between scholars and their material.

Although it has venerable vernacular equivalents of its own, "vernacular" as academic terminology comes to us most immediately from the field of contemporary sociolinguistics, where it remains essential to analysis of the politics of language.[3] However, in recent years, the term has also gained ground among literary historians, particularly in medieval studies, and now offers serious challenge to partial synonyms such as "oral" and "popular," around which large bodies of work have also clustered.[4] "The rise of the European vernaculars" has long been a theme in nationalist literary histories, but the triumphalist emphasis of these histories has too often been on a few canonical writers and their role in creating or "ennobling" language.[5] More recently, vernacular studies has been instrumental in breaking down the divide between high-literary and other kinds of text, analyzing ways in which very different kinds of vernacular writing show an awareness of the need to articulate and defend their cultural role.

For Middle English scholars in particular, vernacular studies is demanding more attention be paid to the multilingual nature of English society (especially to reassess the roles of Latin and Anglo-Norman) and to a variety of emergent textualities (whether merchant, bureaucratic, or dissident) at the end of the medieval period. More broadly, vernacular studies is opening up new ways of comparing cultural situations that seem analogous but have never previously been organized within the same frame of reference: for example, to take a case from this book, comparison between the cultural situation of *Ormulum,* a twelfth-century English didactic poem that Meg Worley argues was aimed at easing the mediation of knowledge between priests and parishioners who had grown up speaking different vernaculars, and that of Ramon Llull's pan-Mediterranean plan for the conversion of Jews and Muslims, described by Harvey Hames. As such, vernacular studies is becoming a force within comparative literature. In a potentially still more significant recontextualization of medieval studies, since the perennial importance of language politics is well recognized by postcolonial and African-American studies in particular, vernacular studies has the potential to provide medievalists with new ways to configure their relation to other, later fields as well. As this book argues, "medievalism" (a word that denotes both postmedieval ideological constructions of the Middle Ages and the study of those constructions) is only one of the forms this relation takes. There are striking parallels between medieval and postmedieval language theories and practices, and long traditions whose relevance to postmedieval vernacular politics often go unnoticed.

While medievalists have much to learn from scholars of the modern, here the intellectual traffic between medievalists and modernists may, indeed, be two-way.

This book draws together nine essays reflective of the considerable variety in current scholarship on medieval vernaculars, together with a selection of four papers on postmedieval topics, in order to foster interdisciplinary discussion between students and specialists in the different languages and fields covered here. The essays have been written and revised in dialogue with one another, and authors have worked to provide adequate contextualization of their material for readers who are not specialists in their areas. The arrangement of the essays is chronological, not because we aim to demonstrate some overall historical progression, but in order to provide a simple frame of reference within which analogies between the different cases presented, as well as the recursive appeals to tradition common in assertions about the vernacular, will be easy to see. As a whole, the volume demonstrates the variety of linguistic situations in which the term "vernacular" has relevance, and traces relationships made newly visible by comparisons between the sometimes very different uses of the concept. The essays offer specific investigations of the vernacular in a variety of literary, religious, and other discourses, while also serving, collectively and individually, as reflections on the idea of the vernacular itself.

The book began life at an interdisciplinary conference, "Vernacularity: The Politics of Language and Style," organized by the editors and hosted by the Medieval and Renaissance Seminar of the University of Western Ontario in March 1999. Here, nearly eighty people heard forty-five papers that covered more than twenty languages, twelve centuries, and four continents. Like the book, the conference was at once an intensive and an extensive examination of its subject: intensive, in that it had a clear focus on medieval European language politics; extensive, in that (as in the book) a third of the papers were based outside this core area.

The thirteen papers included here have all since then been revised and updated in response to the newest work in their fields, as well as the intellectual interchanges that the conference fostered. Thus, Middle English scholars may turn to this book first because of its contribution to their field's current interest in vernacular politics in England from the period 1380–1420 (though extending back to the twelfth century and forward to the sixteenth), when the implications of vernacular writing and preaching were debated with especial vigor and awareness of the issues. Yet a distinctive feature of this book is that even the essays that participate in this discussion (by Worley, Somerset, Waters, Briggs, Taylor) take a comparative approach. And these forays beyond the bounds of Middle English are given extra texture by a series of equally wide-ranging essays that deal directly with German, French, Italian, or Spanish texts: Poor, Angelo, Robins, Hames. The four postmedieval essays provide further comparisons: two (Jansen, Fairey) with specific sociolinguistic situations; two (Bhatia, Scanlon) with haunting relationships between the twentieth century and the medieval and early modern past. Read in conjunction with one another, these papers bring together textual situations that have not been compared before, and gain complexity from their relations with one another.

   If medievalists, perhaps of all scholarly groups in the humanities, are the most interested in pursuing conversations with their colleagues in other fields (as the recent burgeoning of work on "the medieval postcolonial" would suggest),[6] this volume, then, aims to provide a point of departure for many such conversations over vernacularity.

NOTES

   1. See Jocelyn Wogan-Browne's glossary in *The Idea of the Vernacular,* ed. Wogan-Browne et al. (see Further Reading, page 257).

   2. For Trevisa's *Dialogue Between a Lord and A Clerk,* see *Idea of the Vernacular,* excerpt 2.2.

   3. See, e.g., Ronald Wardhaugh, *An Introduction to Sociolinguistics,* 3d ed. (Oxford: Blackwell, 1998).

   4. For "vernacular" as a term in Middle English studies, see many chapters of *The Cambridge History of Medieval English Literature,* ed. David Wallace (see Further Reading), and a review article by Sarah Stanbury, "Vernacular Nostalgia and *The Cambridge History of Medieval English Literature,*" *Texas Studies in Literature and Language* 44 (2002): 92–107. Increasing attention has come to focus on vernacular literary theory and hermeneutics: see, e.g., *Idea of the Vernacular; Alastair J. Minnis, Magister Amoris* (see Further Reading); Kantik Ghosh, *The Wycliffite Heresy: Authority and the Interpretation of Texts,* Cambridge Studies in Medieval Literature 45 (Cambridge: Cambridge University Press, 2002).

   5. For the early history of the rhetoric of "triumph" used of English, see Richard Foster Jones, *The Triumph of the English Language* (see Further Reading).

   6. See, for example, *The Postcolonial Middle Ages,* ed. Jeffrey Jerome Cohen (see Further Reading).

ACKNOWLEDGMENTS

The conference at which the essays in this book began life, "Vernacularity: The Politics of Language and Style," organized at the University of Western Ontario in March 1999, received a $10,000 conference award from the Social Sciences and Humanities Research Council of Canada (SSHRC), whose help we gratefully acknowledge. At the University of Western Ontario, we thank the Department of Visual Arts, the Department of English, the Department of Modern Languages, and the graduate program in Comparative Literature, as well as the Dean of Arts, all of whom provided further funding or other assistance. For the smooth running of the event, we are grateful to Kathleen Fraser and a team of graduate-student helpers; for design of a website that greatly aided publicity as well as subsequent contact between the participants, we thank Khoa Tran.

The book that emerged from the conference has been a collaborative effort on every level not only between the two editors but between editors, contributors, and, indeed, the other conference participants whose essays we were not able to include. Many of the book's larger arguments first emerged at the conference and were then developed in dialogue between the editors or between the editors and the contributors. The editors worked on all aspects of the project together, from conference to book, and are both responsible for the Preface. Nicholas Watson wrote the introductions to the individual parts, and thanks Fiona Somerset for her many helpful rereadings of their various incarnations. He also thanks Amy Appleford and Jocelyn Wogan-Browne. For the further development of the book, we are grateful to Peter Potter and the rest of the staff at Penn State Press, especially our copy editor, Keith Monley; our anonymous readers, for their comments on the initial prospectus and later on the volume and its individual essays; and our assistant and first copy editor, Margaret Toye. We thank *JMEMS* for permission to print a variant version of Sara Poor's essay, and *Callaloo,* which published a much-shortened version of Larry Scanlon's essay. Last of all, we thank the contributors to the volume for their patience with (even enthusiasm for) the lengthy process of discussion and revision in which we asked them to engage.

Fiona Somerset, Duke University
Nicholas Watson, Harvard University

Introduction

King Solomon's Tablets

NICHOLAS WATSON

In modern usage, "vernacular" differs from many theoretical terms, partly for its flexibility in referring equally well to seemingly unrelated phenomena (languages, styles of architecture, music, cuisine), but even more because it always brings with it the weight of the history that made the mother tongue, building, song, or dish the nonclassical, nonstandard, or folk thing that it is. Rather than describe either a thing or even a relationship in an abstract sense, it does so through time, place, and culture. The word "vernacular" itself also, of course, contains a history, which can be traced back to Rome—the great slave state that haunts modern African-American uses of the word—but is perhaps richest for the Middle Ages, the period considered by most of the essays in this book. Yet the mythical structures that define and endlessly complicate the conceptual, and sometimes the actual, lives of European vernaculars (especially in their written forms) draw us back to still earlier times and, from the western European perspective, farther-away places: back before Rome or Greece, to the great early empires of the Babylonians and Egyptians, and beyond them to the imagined past of the Tower of Babel and the Garden of Eden themselves. From Augustine to the Enlightenment, these last two loci are the twin focuses of most linguistic theory: their implications pondered again and again, by Christian intellectuals and their rationalist successors, as well as by Jews and Muslims. Perhaps the vernacular is born at the moment Adam says his first word, his speech surely not the same (or was it?) as the speech (or was it speech?) God uses to say *Lux fiat,* "Let there be light." Perhaps the expulsion from the Garden was also an expulsion from the first language into that of the Fall? (Which of the two would we count *vernacular?*) Or did that happen only at Babel? And whenever it happened, what survived? All are theoretical as well as mythological questions, and their answers have had real consequences in the real world.

The history of premodern linguistic theory, and its fascination with linguistic origins, have been written about a good deal, recently and notably by Umberto Eco.[1] This introduction takes as its starting point a more particular *translation = deformation*

way into the myths that may still in some sense structure European-influenced attitudes toward language: a single text whose purpose is not theoretical but mainly practical. In addition to meditating on the lost words of Eden and their relationships to Edenic reality, this text strives to bring the power of those words back into the world and make it accessible to users. Hence its protagonist is not Adam, the unworldly first man whose power lay in his innocence and fell with him, but another hero: one whose reputation for wisdom was so powerful, even sinister, that Jewish and Christian theologians were sometimes unsure of his eternal destiny: King Solomon.[2]

The Names of Angels

"Theos Megale patyr ymas heth heldya hebeath heleotezygel Salatyel salus telh samel zadaziel zadan Sadiz leogio yemegas mengas omchon Myenoym Ezel Ezely yegrogamal Salmeldach Someltasanay Geltonama hanns Simon salte patyr osyon hate haylos, Amen."[3] On golden tablets written in Greek, Chaldean, and Hebrew and placed on the altar of the temple by the angel Pamphilus in the secret night, the angelic names, prayers, and diagrams that in briefest time give wisdom to the one who uses them aright were sent from the most high Creator to King Solomon. Taught to utter the prayers and study the figures at the proper times, Solomon quickly understood all knowledge: not only the seven liberal arts, with philosophy and theology, but the seven mechanical and magical arts (*artes exceptive*) as well. Even so did he fulfill the dignity God intended for all humankind, becoming the most worthy of all sublunary creatures since the time of Adam, created in the divine image by the hand of the *Summus Plasmator* to be invested with virtue and instructed in wisdom and philosophy.[4]

Yet the words on the tablets were incomprehensible to most; even Solomon, who knew their literal meanings, could not grasp how they contained such power. So it fell to a successor, Apollonius, to translate fragments of the prayers into Latin and (so the story goes) become part of the slow expansion of the prayers, instructions, and figures into the glossed treatise, called the *Ars notoria*, that tells this fabulous tale about its own origins.[5] Fragments only: for to translate was, hopelessly, to dilate and dilute. If Daniel took twenty-three words to expound the writing on the wall (*Mene, Tekel, Phares*), then the Latin needed to render adequately the Greek, Chaldean, and Hebrew names of angels would be beyond human power either to grasp or to utter in the short periods in which they were efficacious.[6] Apollonius offers minimal translations of single words of the invocation *Theos, Megale,* in a long prayer ("Lux mundi, Deus immense, pater aeternitatis, largitor sapientiae et scientiae").[7] But we have the authority of Solomon, Apollonius, and the angel for the certainty that, for all the wisdom the text unlocks, no human understanding can fully expound anything found here.

The *Ars notoria,* whose historical origins are still unknown, survives in a variety of forms and at least a hundred manuscripts, many of them (as the text demands) including careful, sometimes lavish, figures and diagrams. (Spain has been tentatively suggested as a place where Christian intellectuals might have been susceptible to the Jewish mystical influence some scholars find in the text.) It is potentially a rich mine, not only for the study of medieval mysticism and magic, but for students of the politics of language, full as it is of unfamiliar ideas, or familiar ones seen in unfamiliar ways (that Latin is this text's nearest equivalent to a vernacular language is only the beginning). The fact that the *Ars* remains almost unanalyzed, despite the survival of lavish copies in famous libraries, may testify to the awkwardness of the fit between the text and the categories within which the Middle Ages have been studied.[8] For despite its modern obscurity, and despite the ecclesiastical condemnations (from the thirteenth century on) that make this obscurity so peculiar, the text had multitudes of users, from the late twelfth century down at least to the seventeenth. These users had to contend with a heteroglossic, multimedia text that was at its most powerful when least comprehensible and that demonstrated in its words and diagrams the mysterious otherness of divine lucidity, at the same time as it offered those words and diagrams as keys to the unlocking of all knowledge.[9]

In utilitarian terms, if the text worked, its incomprehensibility need not have mattered. Properly used by an angelically selected practitioner, the words and diagrams were meant to function like zipped computer files, infusing the complex structures of the arts and sciences into the mind in a series of instants: an act of multiple translation (God to angel, to angelic name, to human utterance, to human mind) that could bypass expensive years of study at the initial outlay of a few months of prayer, fasting, and purity. Yet for all the text's insistence on *utilitas,* this spiritual technology was too hubristic to be used casually, or for merely practical reasons. There was the danger that the unknown names of angels included fallen angels, who, it might be, had successfully inserted themselves into the textual tradition of the *Ars* to seduce humanity. (This danger looms large in condemnations of the text by Aquinas and others, and proved frighteningly true for two fourteenth-century users, John of Morigny and his sister Gurgeta, before they set out to create their own, purified text with the aid of the Virgin Mary, queen of angels and empress of hell.)[10] Besides this danger, the fact that the prayers and figures could be used to gain formal knowledge but could not be reduced to Latin was itself proof of how much more than knowledge inhered in them: at very least, the spiritual source of knowledge and the power that comes from knowledge. To learn with the *Ars* was to learn not only from Greek, Chaldean, and Hebrew antiquity but from the fecund mind of God.

Language, in the *Ars notoria,* is thus a multifaceted and ambiguous entity, compact of power and meaning: carrying the burden of the divine, yet lowering itself to the demands of the human; in some senses devolving and evolving through time, yet also preserving the fullness of an authoritative, unchanging body of knowledge. Consistently or not, the language politics of the *Ars* understands human languages hierarchically, while also acknowledging an underlying similarity in their ultimate capacity to apprehend wisdom. God's revelation of all knowledge to Solomon takes place in three languages incomprehensible to readers of the *Ars,* who have to rely on Apollonius's Latin, and the Latin of the gloss, to reach a prolix understanding of what the text offers: an understanding in which meaning is gained at the direct expense of power. Latin, then, is a weakened tongue, fallen from the divine triunity of the languages in which God writes the invocations to the powers that govern or correspond to all learning. Greek, Chaldean, and Hebrew, on the other hand, are worthy to be used in communication between the creator and his wisest creature, Solomon: the man who fulfills the project of creation initiated by Adam.

This dichotomizing of languages is a variant on the medieval theory that holds ancient Hebrew to be Adamic language (invented before the Fall and in which, according to Dante in the *De vulgari eloquentia,* sign and signified are in a natural, not arbitrary, relation), while Latin and the European vernaculars are products of the confusion following the destruction of Babel.[11] The *Ars* avoids mention of Babel and Fall and insists on three (occasionally four) divine languages, not one: perhaps an act of self-distancing from Judaism.[12] But although Latin is never explicitly described in such terms, it is still evident through much of the text that, instead of being the language of learning and spiritual authority, it is here no more than another post-Babelian vernacular. Indeed, since the knowledge infused in users of the *Ars* by angelic means is nonetheless apprehended in Latin, we could read the text as articulating a frustration with the diminished state of formally acquired Latin knowledge. Rather than simply offer a back door into Latinity, the *Ars,* in other words, implies that Latin learning is so fallen from its angelic source into multiplicity that it is only efficacious if gained directly from the spiritual entities who govern it. Otherwise, it may lack the power that makes wisdom worth having and that God's worthiest sublunary creatures need to fulfill their natures.

Yet, as this formulation suggests, the *Ars notoria* remains deeply invested

Ars Notoria mele Latin a fallen langue [handwritten annotation]

in Latinity and in the potentiality of the present moment in which its users live and learn. In its long form, the multilingual prayers are surrounded by Latin instructions ostensibly derived from Solomon or Apollonius, which are in turn surrounded by a gloss. This gloss did not always circulate with the text, initially, but seems integral to it, offering information about Solomon's relationship with his angelic visitor that is not found in the text, and unceasingly commenting on matters of language and translation. In a fascinatingly literal exemplification of the text's implied notion of Latin as a vernacular, nine of the Latin prayers are said to have been translated by Solomon himself from Greek, Chaldean, and Hebrew originals. Defying medieval historical linguistics as well as modern, the *Ars* "de-Judaizes" Solomon, making Latin the language in which he thought, wrote his own contributions to the text, and communicated with the angel.[13] The attribution of the text to Virgil by the earliest witness to its existence, Gervase of Tilbury, is perhaps not so strange after all.[14]

Admittedly, much of the post-Solomonic Latin in the *Ars* acts to compensate for the later reader's failure to understand Greek, Chaldean, and Hebrew: a function that is given narrative expression in the text's account of Apollonius's delicately partial mediations of meaning. But in general terms, Latin here performs the role fulfilled by the angel's oral instructions to Solomon, who begins his acquaintance with the *Ars* as the angel's pupil and whose contributions to the *Ars* consist of his articulation and elaboration of what he has learned. These instructions, which are given extended coverage in the gloss, not only make the prayers and diagrams usable but serve to advertise the work and explain its strategies, especially its reliance on powerful unknown words and names. (Defenses of the text's resistance to the lucidity of Latinity are crucial, not only because the unknown words were the main cause of the text's condemnations, but because it is vital to the text's efficacy that these words be taken seriously enough to be accurately copied.)[15] The gloss sticks to its claim that loss of lucidity is more than compensated by gain in power, repeating this claim in a variety of forms and going so far as to forbid attempts to work out, for example, which words of the *Theos, Megale* prayer Apollonius's partial Latin paraphrase renders. But by the very act of explanation, it also goes a good way toward subordinating power to meaning, angelic mystery to modern need, divine Chaldean to vernacular Latin. In the end, Solomon's incomprehensible tablets are less the authoritative source of a text than a conduit by which a practice whose proof lies in its performance is brought into the world.

If the dispersal and dissipation of meaning symbolized by Babel plays a role in the language theory of the *Ars notoria*, then, the text is as significantly an expression of another narrative about the origins of Christian western Europe ("Christendom"), that of *translatio studii et imperii*. This narrative tells the story of the passage, not of Babel's confusion and linguistic multiplicity, but of culture and empire, from East to West, Jew to Christian, past to present. Behind the story the *Ars* tells of its own production there indeed lies a specific *translatio* topos, one succinctly outlined in, to take one example from a multitude, the prologue to a fifteenth-century treatise on palmistry by the East Anglian writer John Metham:

> Tales Milesias, the wiche was the first philosophere in the citee of Atene [Athens], by the answere of God Appollo first dede write the Syence of Cyromancye in the longgage of Parce [in the Persian language]. And maister Aristotell translated it out of Parce into Grue [Greek]. And out of Grue doctor Aurelian, the wiche was born in Italy, translated this science into Latin. And out of Latyn, John Metham, scimple scoler in philosophy, translated it into Englissh, the twenty-fifth winter of his age, praying all the reders of pacience for the rude enditing [composition]. For as min auctor enditeth plainly in Latin, so is my purpose pleinly to endite in Englisshe.[16]

Here is the same combination of prestigious heavenly and ancient origins, and the same process of transmission, as the text moves westward and forward in time, suffering stylistic loss and a gradual decrease in the prestige of those translating it, but retaining the heart of its meaning.

The *Ars* complicates the narrative of *translatio studii* in the same way it does the Babel story, especially in its antihistorical colonization of the ancient East with Latin—presumably in order to preserve the mystical complexity it ascribes to Greek, Chaldean, and Hebrew. Where Metham associates each new interpreter of his text with a separate language, the *Ars* claims that all of the languages it contains were present at the moment of its initial reception. Despite the text's elaborate account of its composition, there is a kind of denial of history and of geography here: in this text any qualified user has, after all, the opportunity to become Solomon, and the *auctoritas* ascribed to the past is in service to *experimenta* that can only be performed in the present.

Yet, again as with its use of the Babel story, the idiosyncrasies here should not be overstressed. As a discourse, *translatio imperii* itself contains just this same mix of reverence and displacement, anxiety about decline and cultural triumphalism; it is never quite forgotten that Nimrod, the perpetrator of Babel, was also the world's first emperor. For all the text's surpassing oddness from a modern point of view, the conceptual space compounded of East and

Ars as exemplary
text for
vernacular-
ity

West, Jew and Christian, past and present, divine and earthly, loss through time and realization in time, in which the *Ars notoria* moves is a space traversed by much medieval and postmedieval European writing. It would not be completely untrue, indeed, to suggest that this is the space that defines much Christian European writing as European. And as the eager appropriations of the topos of *translatio studii* and the Babel myth by writers in many late medieval mother tongues suggest, this space is also one of those in which the idea of the vernacular comes into being.

Translations Through Time

Though largely a Latin text, the *Ars notoria* makes a good point of entry into the issues considered in this book, because it at once suggests the deeply rooted cultural particularity of European language politics and the variety of assumptions, conceptual structures, and affects for which the term "vernacular" can still, within this European context, be a bearer. The *Ars* is, of course, and in many different ways, hardly a "typical" production. But partly for that very reason it can still furnish an exemplary introduction to a book that, above all, aims to further recognition of the heterogeneity, yet also the integration, of European and European-influenced linguistic politics from the Middle Ages on. (In analogous circumstances, medieval sermon exempla likewise tend to invoke the extreme case, rather than the common one.) In the Preface, Fiona Somerset and I in effect suggest that "vernacular" (or a medieval equivalent, like Middle English "mother," "vulgar," "common," or "kynde" tongue) can be thought of as a collection point for a diversity of sociolinguistic issues, one whose usefulness for scholars lies in its multiform ability to bridge time and distance, discovering intellectual relationships between widely separated cultural situations in the process. This view of the term is what makes this book's range so blatantly extensive, rather than intensive, spanning eight centuries and a dozen languages and looking skeptically as it goes at some of the narrower assumptions that have nurtured the recent flowering of vernacular studies: that language politics can be analyzed satisfactorily within a system of binaries (in medieval studies, usually the binary Latin/vernacular); that Latin is inherently the language of cultural authority; that vernacularization is inherently progressive; and so on.

The *Ars notoria*'s mythical history likewise spans East and West, ancient and modern, heaven and earth, old and new covenants, while its actual reception history is five centuries long and a continent wide. The presence of one or both of the founding European cultural narratives in which the *Ars*'s language

7

politics are intertwined (i.e., Babel and *translatio studii et imperii*) is felt behind many of the texts discussed in this book. They hover in the background of the handbooks of essential information compiled in Latin and vernacular languages by the fourteenth-century scholars discussed by Charles Briggs, where lucid pedagogy seems almost an end in itself. They urge the process in which clerics began to write Old and Middle French texts for their own consumption: those texts that Gretchen Angelo argues protect their cultural capital from lay, especially women readers by the deployment of tropes of misogyny. Figuratively recolonizing or colonized by part of the "East," they even lie behind the bitter debates between speech communities in "British India" over "Indian Shakespeare," explored by Nandi Bhatia.

Indeed, the *Ars*'s Janus-like attitude toward its common tongue, Latin, and toward the activity of translation into that language evokes the same binary division over the meaning of *translatio* that is a presence in Ernst Robert Curtius's *European Literature and the Latin Middle Ages* and is analyzed, from its classical roots up to the fourteenth century, in Rita Copeland's *Rhetoric, Hermeneutics, and Translation in the Middle Ages*.[17] Copeland distinguishes between a translation theory indebted to the discipline of grammar, that sees translation as an activity inevitably involving loss, in which the translated text remains subordinate to the original, and a theory indebted to rhetoric, where emphasis falls on the displacement of a source language by a target language. Vernacular texts, in this model, introduce themselves either as imitations or as inventions, as old or as new. As Jeroen Jansen's essay on early modern Dutch helps us see, vernacular language reformers also construct literary languages around either term of this dichotomy, either seeking to "enrich" a language (a practice derived from rhetorical theory) or to "purify" it (a practice derived from the discipline of grammar) (see the introduction to Part III). Larry Scanlon's analysis of the phrase "laureate of the Negro race" (applied to Langston Hughes), the oxymoronic power of which lies in the historical tug-of-war the phrase precipitates—between twentieth-century African-American New York and the Petrarchan laurel wreath—offers testimony to the reach of Copeland's model. Even in our own times, translation and cultural authority continue to be intimately linked concerns.

The *Ars notoria* occupies just this double ground and, like Copeland, explains itself by appealing to history. Solomon, embodiment of wisdom and interpreter of texts in Adamic languages, is a figure from the mythical past, an *auctor* whose inspired text has suffered loss from its reception on. Yet Solomon, embodiment of error and speaker of the Latin vernacular, is also a figure for the contemporary reader, whose negotiations with angels and laborious studies make him exemplary, not authoritative: a role to be played, not a power

Model of revelation vs *translation*

to be feared. The *Ars* bends to the strong pressure toward meaning common to both traditions of *translatio studii,* not only in its narrative framework, but in its gloss-heavy academic structure and the goal of the exercises it describes. Thus Solomon must be translated from the highly colored past into the light of modern-day utility, bearing that past's meaning while also violently displacing it. To this extent, the text's language politics can, indeed, be considered "typical" of the long European traditions of theorizing about translation described by Curtius and Copeland.

The Adamic Vernacular

Yet in its careful custodianship of the Adamic words inscribed on their golden tablets, the *Ars notoria* ultimately stakes everything on a quite different view of the relations between language, history, power, and meaning. For the *Ars* also argues not only that translation of certain words is neither possible nor desirable but also that there is a more potent route between authoritative truth and vernacular language: revelation. Revelation neither displaces the archaic texts whose preservation allows each prepared user to experience it, nor submits to the loss of meaning that results every time these texts are translated. For although the results of revelation include access to the same meaning available to those who learned the arts and sciences by conventional methods and in Latin, in this text revelation actually inheres in the Adamic words and angelic diagrams themselves. Because these words in some sense evidently coinhere with (are in Adamically "natural" relation with) the angels they name and the power/meaning to which these angels in their turn correspond, it is these words and diagrams, not translation or formal study, that best unlock the power of meaning. Time, cultural and linguistic difference, and the gulf that separates the earthly and the heavenly orders are suspended in the process. The angelic powers, here, in the form of words and images, are almost literally on the page.

The linguistic models that work outward from the Babel narrative tend to function differently from those organized around the less theologically intricate narrative of *translatio studii;* Babel levels vernacular languages and can reduce Latin to the status of a vernacular (as in the *Ars notoria*) unless provision is made for its "constructed" grammatical nature—as was done not only by Dante in the *De vulgari eloquentia* but by the fifteenth-century Oxford theologians discussed here by Somerset.[18] Adamic language was not always a factor, since Christian theorists (even those who identified it with Hebrew) often assumed it to have disappeared, perhaps as a result of the Jewish diaspora of

69 C.E. (Jewish views of this matter were interestingly mixed.)[19] What makes the *Ars* radical in its linguistic theory is that, here, in a Christian text, Adamic language not only still exists but is loose in the world in such a fashion that, for those who have access to it, Babel itself becomes incidental. The idea of an unfallen primal language always has some of the same imaginative aura as the Earthly Paradise, lost to humanity but still existing in some place far to the east, haunting the earth like an ineffective ghost. Yet for the *Ars,* this primal language is not lost, and though incomprehensible it is not ineffective. Rather, all knowledge, in whatever language it takes verbal form, may depend for its potency on the Adamic.

In its presentation of a holy language in which the relationship between power and meaning (or, at least, power and lucidity) is the reverse of that it attributes to Latin, the *Ars notoria* is far from any model of *translatio* envisaged by Curtius or Copeland and might seem as idiosyncratic as the Adamic words it preserves are weird. Yet while few medieval Christian texts are as literal in their presentation of Adamic language as the *Ars,* the presence of that language is felt in many contexts. Latin can pose as a reconstituted version of Adamic language because of its lucidity, its distance from ordinary speakers, and the way it had to be acquired through formal study aided by grace. (A standard first text for schoolchildren learning their letters was "O Lord, open thou my lips, that my mouth may show forth thy praise.") Thus opponents of Bible translation argue that the minds of Latinate clerics remain unclouded by the eruption of irrationality into the world at the Fall, making Latin learning a precious reserve of wisdom not lightly to be shared with the laity.[20] In the same vein, liturgy and prayer in Latin are said to be powerful whether or not they are understood by the participant: both because power inheres in the words themselves and because the Latin language is closer to heaven than the vernacular. The final refusal of Bible translation by the Catholic Church at the Council of Trent (1545–63) sealed Latin's reputation as the language of authority and revelation, as carefully separated (in theory) from the flux of the local, the temporary, and the vulgar as Eden.

To imply that Latin is Adamic is to reaffirm its absolute difference from and superiority to any common tongue. For lay intellectuals, however, it is the vernacular, not Latin, that has the better claim to represent or substitute for Adamic language. In the *De vulgari eloquentia,* Dante proclaims an "illustrious vernacular" (the language of the *Comedy*) as the only language worthy of comparison with the Adamic, insisting that any vernacular is superior to Latin because of its intimate relation to land, people, and history. For Dante, what links Adamic and vernacular languages is the concept of the "natural," which he holds up against the artificiality he ascribes to Latin.[21] Dante may not be as unusual here as he is often assumed to be. According to Sara Poor, Mechthild von Magdeburg likewise holds that, as a vehicle of revelation, her vernacular, Low German, is superior to Latin. Mechthild's linguistic theory is incarnational but also rests on the assumption that a language of revelation has a natural relationship between words, their speakers, and what they name. Taking a different tack, Ramon Llull argues (as Harvey Hames shows) that language has a natural relationship not so much to the world as to the triune God, whose immanence in language he deduces by way of the deep grammatical structures of Arabic, Hebrew, and Catalan, as well as Latin: as though vestiges of the Adamic lay behind all languages. In all these cases, the vernacular's status as what Middle English calls a "kynde" or "mother" tongue (the language, Dante says, that you drink with your nurse's milk) makes it possible to claim for it an originary status, thus potentially a power, that otherwise inheres only in the Adamic. If such associations seem tied to medieval religious contexts, at least one of the ideas carried by the Adamic myth—an idea immediately derived from Romanticism that many believe even today, that a vernacular has deep geographical, psychic, and spiritual affinity with the "genius" of a people—has translated itself into a nationalist form with a long postmedieval history. *Mutatis mutandis,* attempts to create a "pure" early modern Dutch (as described by Jeroen Jansen) or to construct Serbian and Romanian as national vernaculars (as described by Jack Fairey) subscribe to a clearly related belief in the primal power of a mother tongue.

The strange case of the *Ars notoria* suggests some of the possibilities latent in the idea of holy or powerful or natural language when it is made the subject of a really determined myth. It urges us to look again at the power that inheres within holy or binding words in other contexts (where, for example, this power meets with the power inhering in word as bond).[22] Its careful separation of power and meaning also offers us another way of thinking about revelatory texts in the broadest sense: texts whose power (whether or not a visionary or mystical experience lies behind them) resides less in what is narrated than in the words through which it is expressed. Middle English scholars, for example, might use the notion of Adamic/natural language to reflect on how, for vernacular theologians like William Langland or Julian of Norwich, theology inheres in, rather than is expressed through, language. For both these writers, it is less that "poetry does theology" than that poetic or meditative vernacular language *is* theology.[23]

Finally, as a portal to this book in particular, the *Ars* serves as an exemplum of the length, fluidity, and capaciousness of the intellectual traditions with which medieval and postmedieval vernacular theorists, writers, and readers thought. Its surprising obscurity invites us to broaden our analysis of these traditions—as do many of the essays in this book—to include other equally neglected texts and ideas. In *Paradiso,* Adam tells Dante that, because it is a work of nature that people speak ("Opera naturale è ch'uom favella"), all languages are tied to nature and eventually die. Contrary to what Dante had thought when he wrote *De vulgari eloquentia,* even the language Adam spoke with Eve in Eden was so vernacular that it was gone before Babel ("l'ovra inconsummabile . . . di Nemrot")—the city whose sin lay in its very attempt at fixity—was built. "Ché l'uso d'i mortali è come fronda / in ramo, che sen va e altra vene" (For the usage of mortals is as a leaf on a branch, which goes away and another comes).[24] Whatever Adam is saying about the power of words and texts here, their final death is, of course, assured. Yet the traditions within which we think about words, holy or otherwise, remain.

NOTES

I wish to thank Amy Appleford, Claire Fanger, and Jocelyn Wogan-Browne for their help with this essay.

1. See Umberto Eco, *The Search for the Perfect Language* (see Further Reading, page 257).

2. See David J. Halperin, "The *Book of Remedies,* the Canonization of the Solomonic Writings, and the Riddle of Pseudo-Eusebius," *Jewish Quarterly Review* 72 (1982): 269–92.

3. *ARS NOTORIA, QUAM CREATOR ALTISSIMVS Salomoni revelavit,* in Cornelius Agrippa, *Opera* (Lyons: Beringos Fratres, [1620]; republished Landmarks of Science [New York: Readex Microprint, 1964]), 603–60, at 647. Although quotations are from this edition, my account of the *Ars notoria* is based on Paris, Bibliothèque nationale, manuscrit latin 9336, as transcribed by Julian Veronese, in "L'*Ars notoria:* Une tradition théorgico-magico au Moyen Âge (XII–XVIe siècle)" (master's diss., Université de Paris X—Nanterre, 1999). This manuscript distinguishes text and gloss as Agrippa's substantially reduced edition does not. Where possible, however, I also give page references to Agrippa. The only translation of the *Ars* to date, based on Agrippa, is *Ars Notoria: The Notory Art of Solomon,* trans. Robert Turner (London: J. Cottrel, 1657).

4. The Latin phrases are taken from the opening gloss on fol. 1r of the Paris MS, which this paragraph paraphrases. Compare Agrippa, 603.

5. Paris MS, fol. 1r. Agrippa and Turner omit this, and tend to elide Apollonius's contributions with those of the gloss.

6. Paris MS, fol. 2v, gloss; see Daniel, chap. 5 (esp. 5:25).

7. Quoted from Agrippa, 605; see Paris MS, fol. 2v. The gloss in the Paris MS is particularly concerned that the original words retain their full mystery, despite Apollonius's partial rendering.

8. Only recently has there begun to be a resurgence of interest in this text. Several studies written in the last few years offer substantial correctives to the tentative trailblazing of Lynn Thorndike in his *History of Magic and Experimental Science,* 8 vols. (New York: Columbia University Press, 1923–58), 2:279–89. These studies are (1) several essays in *Conjuring Spirits: Texts and Traditions of Medieval Ritual Magic,* ed. Claire Fanger, Magic in History (University Park: Pennsylvania State University Press, 1998): Michael Camille, "Visual Art in Two Manuscripts of the Ars Notoria" (110–39); Claire Fanger, "Plundering the Egyptian Treasure: John the Monk's *Book of Visions* and Its Relation to the Ars Notoria of Solomon" (216–49); Richard Kieckhefer, "The Devil's Contemplatives: The *Liber Iuratus,* the *Liber Visionum,* and the Christian Appropriation of Jewish Occultism" (250–65); (2) a pair

of essays on the intellectual roots of the *Ars:* J. DuPèbe, "L'"ars notoria' et la polémique sur la divination et la magie," in *Divination et controverse religieuse en France au XVIe siècle,* Cahiers V.-L. Saulnier, 4 (Paris: L'É.N.S. de Jeunes Filles, 1987), 123–34, and Jean-Patrice Boudet, "L'Ars Notoria au Moyen Âge: Une résurgence de la théurgie antique?" in *La magie: Actes du Colloque international de Montpellier, 25–27 Mars 1999 (Tome III: Du monde latin au monde contemporain)* Séminaire d'étude des mentalités antiques (Montpellier: Université Paul Valéry, 2000), 173–91. Boudet disagrees with Kieckhefer's view that the text has a proven connection with Jewish mysticism. Julian Veronese's doctoral thesis on the *Ars notoria* (still in progress) will be of fundamental importance for further research.

9. For references to condemnations of the text, see Frank Klaassen, "English Manuscripts of Magic, 1350–1500," in Fanger, *Conjuring Spirits,* 3–31, at 30 n. 44.

10. See Thomas Aquinas, *Summa theologica,* Secunda secundae 96, art. 1, in vols. 4–12 of *Opera omnia,* ed. T. M. Zagliara (Rome: Ad Sanctae Sabinae, 1888–1906). For John and Gurgeta, see Claire Fanger and Nicholas Watson, "John of Morigny, Prologue to *Liber Visionum* [c. 1304–17]," *Esoterica* 3 (2001): 108–217.

11. See Warman Welliver, *Dante in Hell* (see Further Reading), 1.1–8 (esp. 6–7).

12. Arabic is mentioned occasionally in the Paris MS, and more often by Agrippa, although the notion that the holy languages are three (perhaps alluding to the "Sanctae & Individuae Trinitatis" the text begins by invoking) seems relatively established in the text as a whole (Agrippa, 603; see Paris MS, fol. 1r).

13. Paris MS, fols. 13v–14r.

14. According to Gervase, writing in the late twelfth century: when the bones of Virgil were exhumed near Naples, the dead poet's head was found resting on a copy of the *Ars notoria,* described as "the fruit of his researches." See Boudet, "L'Ars Notoria au Moyen Âge," 174.

15. Needless to say, the divine words are not actually the same in, for example, the Paris MS and Agrippa(s edition, although the opening phrases of the prayers are often fairly stable.

16. *The Works of John Metham,* ed. Hardin Craig, Early English Text Society, Original Series 132 (London: Early English Text Society, 1916), 85, lines 1–11; spellings somewhat regularized.

17. See Ernest Robert Curtius, *European Literature and the Latin Middle Ages* (see Further Reading); Rita Copeland, *Rhetoric, Hermeneutics, and Translation* (see Further Reading).

18. For the Oxford scholars, see also my "Censorship and Cultural Change" (see Further Reading), esp. 840–46, where the grammatical structure of Latin is sometimes cited as a sign of its superiority.

19. See Dante, *De vulgari eloquentia,* 1.7, which suggests that the dispersal of the Jews brought their possession of Adamic language to an end. For Jewish views regarding the status of Hebrew, see Gershom Scholem, *Major Trends in Jewish Mysticism* (New York: Schocken, 1946), and Michael D. Swartz, *Scholastic Magic: Ritual and Revelation in Early Jewish Mysticism* (Princeton: Princeton University Press, 1996).

20. See references in my "Censorship and Cultural Change."

21. For the argument that Dante's "illustrious vernacular" is a re-creation of Adamic language, see Umberto Eco, "Languages in Paradise," in *Serendipities: Language and Lunacy* (San Diego: Harcourt Brace, 1998), 23–51. Dante establishes the connection between the vernacular and the natural in his long survey of the peoples of Italy and their dialects, *De vulgari eloquentia,* 1.9–15.

22. See, e.g., Richard Firth Green, *A Crisis of Truth* (see Further Reading).

23. See Jim Rhodes, *Poetry Does Theology: Chaucer, Grosseteste, and the Pearl Poet* (Notre Dame, Ind.: University of Notre Dame Press, 2001). I would make the same claim for vernacular theology that Rhodes makes for poetry. For Julian's language, see esp. Vincent Gillespie and Maggie Ross, "The Apophatic Image," in *The Medieval Mystical Tradition in England: V,* ed. Marion Glasscoe (Cambridge: D. S. Brewer, 1992), 53–77.

24. *Paradiso,* vol. 5 of *The Divine Comedy,* ed. and trans. Charles S. Singleton, Bollingen Series 80, 6 vols. (Princeton: Princeton University Press), XXVI.124–38.

PART I: 1100–1300
The Evangelical Vernacular

The first four essays in this book involve religious texts that take an evangelical attitude toward the vernacular. Written during a period when the power of words to persuade and enlighten was felt with a confidence unequaled before the Victorian era, these texts can be seen as parts of a concerted program of universal outreach, which demanded reflection on language as a means of access to knowledge and on the nature of useful (salvific) knowledge itself. Whether the targets of conversion are Lincolnshire peasants, South German townsfolk, or the Jews and Muslims of Spain and northern Africa, utility and persuasiveness are a concern to all five writers discussed here: Orm, Thomas of Chobham, Humbert of Romans, Mechthild von Magdeburg, and Ramon Llull. However different their approaches—a gulf yawns not only between the three Latin prose writers and the vernacular poets but also between Orm's practical metrics and Mechthild's poetic pyrotechnics—such a concern also demands careful attention to register and audience.

There resemblances end: these writers come from different cultural and linguistic backgrounds and pursue their agendas in different ways. If Humbert and Thomas, one the director of the Dominican friars, the other a noted pastoral theologian, wrote Latin analyses of preachers and preaching that influenced the church as a whole, the beguine Mechthild and the layman Llull had more difficulty gaining institutional acceptance, while Orm was a local figure. Some of Llull's works were widely read, but the heyday of his long campaign to further the conversion of Jews and Muslims was his appearance at the Council of Vienne in 1311, as an old man. In some ways, as Harvey Hames argues, Llull thought more clearly than anyone about the barriers to communication between Christians and their neighbors, and the need for a common tongue (the set of rational principles, based on grammar and pointing to the inevitable truth of Christianity, that Llull called his *Ars*) to bridge those barriers. The distance from Christian intellectual traditions given him by his status as autodidact and visionary must, indeed, have helped him arrive at this clarity: where the thirteenth-century clerics who engaged in what passed for interfaith dialogue relied partly on proof texts, partly on force, Llull's faith was explicitly a matter of personal (visionary) experience, while much of his life was lived in the multicultural, multilingual milieu of the Mediterranean. Yet in a more poignant sense, his place on the edge of clerical culture was a disadvantage for anyone who wanted to affect what happened at the center. As he struggled to convert not only Jews and Muslims but Christian theologians to his ideas, Llull wrote and rewrote his system all through his long life. Calling for a change in the church's praxis, Llull found himself tinkering, more than he can have wanted, with theory. The influence of this deeply individualistic thinker was real (not just among Christians) but scattered.

The same can be said of Mechthild, who shared Llull's desire to effect real change to the ways in which the church acted. Mechthild's call was for a collective return to a state of purity, a call she issued in what Sara Poor argues is a carefully chosen Low German but that for the most part found its readers in Latin and High German translation, often in excerpt. Her book, *Das fließende Licht der Gottheit,* was intended to be (as its title implies) a vehicle for the flowing out of the divine light over all. If its choice of Low German represents its aspiration to universality, then its poetic form represents the claim to inspiration that justifies that aspiration. Yet in the centuries after its composition, this spiritual effluence was almost blocked up by translation, anthologization, or anxious editing: all activities we must attribute, not to critics, but admirers. These transformations of Mechthild's text suggest disagreement between her and her editors and translators regarding the best medium for her message. Her struggle to reach the broad readership she aspired to, in either the language or the form she had chosen, speaks to a gulf of comprehension, as well as power, between a woman whose inner sense of possibility remained unconstrained and the masculine intellectual world of her editors.

Llull and Mechthild worked for transformations of the world whose ambition was in proportion to their distance from the institution responsible for making change happen. Their attitude toward language suggests that they thought of their respective vernaculars in "Adamic" terms: as instruments of revelation powerful enough to overcome any institutional disadvantage from which they suffered (see the Introduction). Visionary or prophetic thought like theirs is perennially associated with such distance (even the names are evocative: Julian of Norwich, William Blake, Simone Weil), and the intimate association between the vernacular, the cultural margin, and the prophetic is easily romanticized.

Claire Waters's account of how preaching manuals theorize the relationship between language and Christian community offers an antidote to this danger by focusing on how two thirteenth-century churchmen, both in some sense mouthpieces for the ecclesiastical institution, conceptualized these issues. Recent work by literary historians on the medieval clerisy's attitude toward community focuses on the fourteenth and fifteenth centuries, sometimes taking Lollard critiques of the clergy, which emphasize the latter's elitism and lack of concern for the laity, at face value. Waters shows how, for the thirteenth century, the actual situation was not only different from the picture drawn by later polemic but did not even work within the same categories. Distance between clergy and laity might be promoted (as by Thomas of Chobham), but only because ordinary parish priests had their work cut out to establish that distance. Language politics revolve not around abstract linguistic hierarchies but around the practical matter of register. How to popularize in the proper way—how to conform, not just to the needs of an audience, but to the cultural idioms of a region—is what matters here. Further, as Waters argues, popularization itself (or at least its most important manifestation, the exemplum) need not drive a wedge between clergy and laity; rather, it can act to reinforce a common sense of community. Here, Latin, the language of authority, and the vernacular, the language of communication, were not in opposition for the preachers who deployed them, but in a mutually supportive relation.

The gap is real, then, between the prophetic proposals of a Llull or a Mechthild and the detailed pastoral programs of a Thomas or a Humbert (Waters's other case study), but it is not the gap our attraction to the voice of prophecy makes it. Thomas and Humbert are in their way as ambitious as visionaries in their desire for transformation, and as aware that transformation begins at home, in the center of the ecclesiastical institution; it is opportunity that makes them pragmatists. The twelfth-century Lincolnshire poet Orm emerges from Meg Worley's essay as part pragmatist, part (in a figurative sense) visionary. On the one hand, Orm exemplifies the same concern with the comprehensibility of Christian teaching expressed by Humbert three generations later, writing his long homiletic poem in a standardized version of his local dialect, going so far as to invent new spelling rules, even letter forms, to establish pronunciation. Patriotic British philologists have often seen his efforts (with mingled respect and condescension) as a desperate response to the fluidity of Early Middle English. Dismissing this explanation (which makes Orm a philologist *avant la lettre*), Worley proposes that Orm's official motives were practical and pastoral: as one of the few native speakers in the canonry at Bourne, his text was written to help Francophone colleagues as they preached and taught in the parishes around. On the other hand, this project may have been grounded in a sense of the local (growing out of Orm's concern for his land and its traditions) that ran deeper than pragmatism. Not only does the *Ormulum* show a marked preference for English, not continental, source material. The self-regarding title of the book casts Orm as a native informant—a cleric posing as a member of the local congregation—who treats his vernacular as a mother tongue, not a utilitarian common language. If Orm shares a homiletic ecclesiastical agenda with his colleagues, on a political level he constructs the *Ormulum* as a subaltern text.

Collectively, then, these four essays explore the reach of the idea of the vernacular as a common tongue, and suggest the heterogeneity of that idea. If Llull's proposal of a universal common tongue, a religious Esperanto, represents one extreme, Orm's creation of a late-twelfth-century Lincolnshire Standard (whose obsolescence within a generation is built into this written dialect's precision) represents the other. Mechthild, reaching out to a general audience through the local medium of Low German, is caught in the middle, using a vernacular that is symbolically appropriate as a means of universal access but that in practical terms puts her at the mercy of translators. (Not that symbolic appropriateness is nothing: from the perspective either of the nineteenth-century German scholars who saw Mechthild's writing as an early monument to their "mother tongue" or of modern feminist scholars of spirituality, the poetic and theological gains for Mechthild are as significant as all her losses.) It is the pastoral theologians, Thomas and Humbert, who have the opportunity to think flexibly about two kinds of common tongue and the different possibilities offered by each for acting as instruments of divine revelation: the common tongue of the vernacular, which the friars for whom Humbert writes must adapt as they move from region to region; and the common tongue of Latin, in which the educated can theorize and draw conclusions about the local. For those in possession of both, the divide between educated and vernacular common tongues has nothing but advantages.

Using the *Ormulum* to Redefine Vernacularity

MEG WORLEY

Scholars tend to use "vernacular" as if it referred to a class of languages, but its meaning shifts according to temporal and geographical situation. Clearly, if English can be vernacular in one setting—say, tenth-century Europe—and just the opposite in another setting—twenty-first-century Dominica—vernacularity is not a quality but a relationship. The key to understanding vernacularity is its opposite: the closest (though still imperfect) descriptor we have for the languages that sit in contrast to vernacular is "standard," which suggests that the organizing principle of the relationship is the power to standardize. Usually this relationship is framed in terms of education, literacy, or high culture versus pop culture. Yet the history of European vernacularity does not always bear this out: sometimes, for example, the vernacular must be defined as that which deviates from the language of power, even when it is also the language of education or literacy. Few texts better exemplify the issues embedded in this linguistic relationship than the twelfth-century *Ormulum*.

Those who have taken a class in Middle English have probably encountered the *Ormulum,* a collection of homilies composed and written out by a monk named Orm. Because, or although, scholars, even after two centuries of intense scrutiny, still cannot agree on what to make of it, the *Ormulum* appears in nearly every handbook and reader of Middle English, from the first edition of Henry Sweet to the last printing of Charles Jones.[1] The manuscript, Bodley MS Junius 1, is an unfinished first draft hastily written with badly cut pens on scraps of parchment. Due to its physical presentation, it is always described as a curiosity, and scholars take great delight in repeating the insults heaped upon it by previous scholars: J. A. W. Bennett, G. V. Smithers, and Norman Davis's *Early Middle English Verse and Prose* is often quoted for calling it "singularly ugly and untidy,"[2] while Malcolm Parkes is famous for having said that the *Ormulum* looks as though it was written with a stick.[3]

But the aesthetic appeal, or appall, of the manuscript is not the primary reason for the *Ormulum*'s reputation among medievalists. Nor is it the content, for that too comes in for its share of abuse in the literature: John Edwin

Wells's *Manual of the Writings in Middle English* describes it as "intolerably monotonous," and C. M. Millward notes that, "[a]s literature, the result is worthless."[4] Even Orm himself inspires insult rarely cast back at medieval writers: Albert Baugh writes, "The author tells us that he has attempted with what little wit that the Lord has lent him—unfortunately not an understatement—to explain . . ."; and David Lawton describes Orm as "close to ridiculous, a White Knight of exegesis."[5] These deprecations largely miss the point, but everyone agrees on one thing: the manuscript is worth studying for the orthography.

Orm is the first individual whose name we know to attempt English spelling reform, on the basis of his consistent and idiosyncratic orthographic system, in which certain long and short vowels are marked with breves and macrons and consonants are doubled after a short vowel either at the end of the word or when followed by another consonant. Thus, he writes, in lines 7–8 of his introduction, "þurrh þatt he Godess bŏdeword / Forrlĕt for lĭtell nede" (Because he forsook God's message, for little reason). In addition, Orm uses the continental style of writing *g* to denote the palatal [ʒ], while continuing to use the traditional *g* for the velar [g]. Less famously, his orthographic system substitutes *t* for þ under certain circumstances and simplifies the diphthong *eo* into *e*.[6]

Since the early nineteenth century, scholars have proposed various explanations of what I like to call Orm's "Ormography," and most of them cast Orm in the role of spelling reformer observing recent local changes in pronunciation. The debate generally centers on what those changes in pronunciation were: Betty Phillips, Myungsook Kim, Hans Kurath, and others link Orm's spelling system to Middle English Open Syllable Lengthening (MEOSL); Robert Stevick, Richard Jordan, Karl Luick, and a number of nineteenth-century scholars argue that it signaled consonant, rather than vowel, length; others, led by Robert Fulk, see syllabification as the guiding principle behind Ormography.[7]

I feel dissatisfaction with these accounts, however, because they give short shrift to Orm's self-appointed role as a preacher and sermonist, instead imagining him as the first to insist that text should be the mirror of speech, down to the letter. Orm himself is a constant didactic presence both in the front matter and in the body of the text: he expressly names his work after himself, writing, "Þis boc is nemmned Ormulum / forrþi þat Orm it wrohhte" (This book is called the Ormulum, because Orm made it) (1–2), which is startlingly self-referential. This title, not much examined by scholars, bears further study. It is generally assumed that Orm was modeling it on "Speculum," but, as Kenneth Sisam observes, that was not a common book title until the thirteenth century. The implications of Orm's own claims to *auctoritas* in entitling a biblical retelling "Little Orm" would not have gone unnoticed by any literate twelfth-century person.

His authorial voice repeatedly inserts itself into his narrative too, as when, in his homily on the Gospel of Luke, he writes, "Here I show you how Saint John the Baptist was born of father and mother" (105–8). Orm is also particularly enamored of the word "ormete," meaning vast or imponderable, a word that, according to the *Middle English Dictionary,* is only recorded here (many times) and in the *Peterborough Chronicle* (twice). In nearly every reference to himself, Orm makes a point of positioning himself as the teacher, giving instructions to the reader. He also gives instructions to any future scribe to copy the text *exactly* as he has written it, with the same rhymes, the same number of words, and with the Ormography intact.[8] Orm may be the bossiest writer in Middle English literature.

Orm's self-referentiality and preachiness strike me as inconsistent with the phoneticist suggested by the various linguistic models of the *Ormulum*. He is not a faithful recorder of the way language is written; rather, he is an evangelist for the way language should be spoken. John Anderson and Derek Britton, interestingly, leave the question of Orm's agenda open by routinely using the word pair "reflect/project" to characterize the intent behind Orm's orthographic policies.[9] More pointedly, Kenneth Sisam, maintains that Orm's spelling and diacritic efforts were normative, aimed at improving the pronunciation of preachers reading the homilies aloud.[10] Sisam was writing in the 1930s, and his argument has been ignored by many subsequent scholars of the *Ormulum* and criticized by others,[11] but it is a compelling one. According to Sisam, Orm's inconsistent application of diacritical marks and geminate consonants conflicts with his role as a phoneticist. The textual evidence, however, fits very well with a notion of Orm as a creator, trying to dictate the way that his work should be read aloud. Orm was a member of the Augustinian order, whose primary charge was the pastoral care of commoners, and his vowel-quantity distinctions are made only in cases of potential confusion to the audience, such as between *writenn* (past participle of "write") and *wrítenn* (infinitive of "write"). Sisam sees no need to construe the orthography as phonetic positivism and every reason to construe it as audience-oriented normativism.

The manuscript holds other clues in support of Sisam's claim. For a start, Orm was fastidious in punctuating his text, in comparison with such sibling texts as the *Peterborough Chronicle* and the dialogue "Vices and Virtues." A brief analysis of a hundred lines from each of these three texts yields striking results: the *Ormulum* has a punctuation mark every fifth word, on average, whereas the *Peterborough Chronicle* has one every twelfth word, and "Vices and Virtues" every fifteenth.[12] In addition, Orm uses light pen strokes between individual words, to make the phrasing completely clear. His generosity with punctuation reflects his purpose: he is writing these homilies to be read aloud, and by chopping them up into short phrases, he is making them oratable, a system similar to, if more parchment-frugal than, Saint Jerome's *per cola et commata,* where each phrase began on a new line. Moreover, such care for pronunciation of sermons was entirely in line with the homiletic undertaking and with the express encouragement of no less an authority than Augustine himself, who devotes a section of the *De doctrina Christiana* to the importance of pronunciation.[13] We have no way of knowing whether Orm had direct access to the *De doctrina Christiana,* but it was an extremely influential work in the twelfth century, and Hrabanus Maurus, to whom Orm probably did have access,[14] certainly drew on it heavily. Given the emphasis placed on correct pronunciation by the guiding light of his own order, it is hardly surprising that Orm would turn to orthography to enforce the saint's injunction.

Another point in support of Sisam turns on the question of the *Ormulum*'s intended audience. Sisam's normative argument takes Orm as gearing his work toward a listening audience rather than a readership. Given the rhythmic pattern of the *Ormulum,* as well as its homiletic theme, scholars are generally agreed that the text was meant to be read aloud in church services. Orm excuses himself for adding words to the gospel, claiming that it is necessary for those who would preach: "Forr whase mot to læwedd follc / Larspell off Goddspell tellen, / He mot wel ekenn maniȝ word / Amang Goddspelless wordess" (For whoever must preach the gospel to unlettered folk must indeed add many words to the words of the gospel) (55–58). The pulpit seems a peculiar venue in which to work out a new orthographic system. If Orm's primary concern was spelling reform, a monastic text, which would come into contact with more actual readers, would have been a much more likely canvas on which to elaborate it than a set of populist homilies read aloud by the few monks chosen to give the homily in church services.

The one point on which I differ from Sisam is in regard to the makeup of that intended audience. Sisam presumes that both audience and readers were English, as indicated by his criticism of phonetic models: "It is hard to see how an Englishman reading his own language aloud could attach practical importance to marking the niceties of consonant-length; or why his mind should be directed to it at all as a matter of theory or tradition."[15] I want to consider more closely the differences between the listening audience—"the people who would have listened to these homilies"—and those who would have handled the text, reading it aloud *to* the audience.[16] In the secondary literature on the *Ormulum,* there is surprisingly little mention of Anglo-Norman, a term that one might expect in any discussion of a twelfth-century English text. Few scholars who have studied the *Ormulum* in depth give any serious consideration to the fact that England was not homogeneously Anglophone in 1180, around the time Orm was writing.[17] This omission is understandable, since Orm himself never mentions French but uses the word "English" over and over in the dedication, preface, and editorial asides. The fact is, however, that nearly half the clergy in England at the time were probably Francophones, either born in France or of Norman or Angevin extraction.[18] In light of this, I propose a variation on Kenneth Sisam's interpretation of the *Ormulum.*

While Sisam pictured Orm's idiosyncratic writing system as slowing down English priests who were inclined to rush through the reading of the homilies, it seems more likely that Orm was trying to guide the pronunciation of non-native speakers reading to a congregation of English-speaking laypeople. There is substantial reason to think that most of the priests at Orm's house were Francophones: Malcolm Parkes believes that Orm was located at the Augustinian abbey of Bourne, in southern Lincolnshire.[19] Bourne was founded in 1138 by Augustinians brought to England in the first century after the conquest, and this so-called alien priory was almost certainly a French-speaking community, under the direct authority not of an English house but of Saint Nicholas of Arrouaise, in northern France.[20] By Orm's time, the monks of Bourne may have begun to consider themselves English; there are no records to document the nature of the relationship with the mother house in Normandy. But they must have been Anglo-Norman speakers, given both the nature of Anglo-Angevin society and the recent establishment of the priory. Furthermore, the 1164 Constitutions of Clarendon had for the most part closed the priesthood to villeins—a group that included nearly all English speakers.[21] The name "Orm," of course, is Norse-English in the extreme, but Orm alludes to his advanced age (meaning that he probably entered the order before Clarendon) and marks himself as different from his fellow canons, particularly in his Englishness, so we are justified as seeing him as an exception to the French rule at Bourne.[22] If that is the case, then who better than the solitary Anglophone to teach Francophone priests how best to communicate to their English flock?

To return to the text of the *Ormulum,* we can see solid phonetic reasons to think that Orm was trying to improve the pronunciation of Francophone preachers. His system is most striking in the last consonant of words, as in "broþerr," and of closed syllables, as in "Wallter." It is worth noting that in the late twelfth century, Middle English consonants were not undergoing much evolution; aside from regional differences in voicing the [t] sound, nearly all the phonetic transformations were occurring in vowels, not consonants. That was not the case in Old French, however. The twelfth century was a period of great flux in the pronunciation of French consonants, possibly fueled by the interactions between very different linguistic communities brought into contact by the consolidation of power under the French monarchy.[23]

Moreover, the French consonant system was changing in exactly those places in the word that Orm emphasizes by doubling the letters. There were two main areas of evolution in twelfth-century French: one was in consonant clusters, where the Gallo-Roman *festa* gradually became the modern *fête* and *pulverum* became *poudre,* and the other was in final consonants after a vowel, which first became unvoiced and then often disappeared altogether, as in the move from *grandem* to *grant* to the modern *grand.*[24] One example sums up these changes perfectly: the Vulgar Latin *salvum* became *salv,* and then quickly *salf,* and then, with assimilation of the *l, sauf,* which we now pronounce [so:f]. In addition, Old French was in the process of dropping off the final syllable of many Gallo-Roman words, as in the move from *grandem* to *grand,* but Middle English did not make a similar move.[25] The doubled consonants in the *Ormulum* seem rather clearly addressed to these consonant changes: if we look at Orm's dedication to his "broþerr Wallter," we see that the *rr* defeats any attempt to elide the last syllable, and the *ll* counteracts the French tendency to vocalize /l/, both of which can be seen in the transformation from *alterum* to *autre.*[26] Similarly, the *ss* in "crisstenndom" may well be aimed at the same tendency that changed *Christianus* into *Chrêtien.* The links between Orm's spelling system and contemporary Anglo-Norman/Anglo-Angevin pronunciation bear much more study, but I believe that there is evidence Orm geared his text toward French speakers.

We should thus see Orm not as a herald of change in Middle English phonetics but as an Anglophone helping Francophones acquire much-needed communication skills—exactly what Robert Grosseteste was calling for a century later.[27] But he is more than just a *collaborateur,* showing the conquerors a few tricks for getting through to the villeins; he is teaching them about English as a literary language as part of a shared pastoral mission. The preeminence of English as a European literary vernacular has been a testing ground for scholars for centuries—perhaps since Bede's century—and the language's role in preserving learning in western Europe during the early Middle Ages is rarely contested. Michael Clanchy even suggests that France only gained a concept of vernacular literature (if not literacy) with the Norman Conquest.[28] Orm is the heir to this tradition of insular didactic erudition; the material he is promulgating draws from the homilies of Ælfric (sometimes referred to as the greatest teacher of the Benedictine Renaissance) and Wulfstan.[29]

The *Ormulum* has been construed by scholars as both rhythmic prose and as septenary verse, and a good case may be made for both. Without a doubt, Orm's text conforms closely to the meter of the septenarius, and when read aloud it has the singsong quality that characterizes much Middle English poetry. On the other hand, it is unrhymed and sounds very much like Ælfric's rhythmic prose (which is itself often metrical).[30] Compare, for example, the two excerpts below, the first from Orm, the second from Ælfric.

Γ ta sextene þat Ele-
    -azar her haffde strenedd,
Þa hirdess þatt, witt tu full well,
    Haffdenn an hird onn hæfedd
Haffdenn an hæfedd hird tatt wass
    Abufenn all þoþre,
Alls iff itt wære laferrdflocc
    Offr alle þoþre flockess.

            (583–90)

Se Hælend that sæt þær, of þam siþ fæte werig,
Wiþ þone wæterpytt, and hit wæs þa middæg,
And his discipuli eodon into þære byrig,
Þat Hi him mete bohton, and he abad þær hwile.[31]

[And the sixteen that Eleazar / had begotten here, / the households that, know this full well, / had one chief for one household, / They had a chief household that was / above all the others, / As if it were the royal family / over all the other families.]

[Christ sat there against the well, weary from the journey, and it was midday, and his disciples went into the city to buy him meat, and he bade there awhile.]

Both homilists take pains to maintain the rhythm in the text, making the semantic units coincide with the metrical phrasing. Orm's bridging of the caesura, sometimes within a word, and Ælfric's careful observance of the caesura highlight the similarities between their prosodic styles. It is not within the scope of this essay to rethink the classification of Orm's work as verse (or of Ælfric's as prose), but clearly both draw on a literary tradition that is sharply English. Orm may have been in an Anglo-Norman religious house, but his writing has nothing of the French—or Franco-Latin—about it. In composing distinctively native homilies, Orm was making a clear statement about the worthiness of native literature as a whole.

Orm only plays a small part in English literary culture under the Normans, but insular influence is particularly strong in the European homiletic tradition. As James Murphy has noted, the rise of the genre of preaching manuals in the twelfth and thirteenth centuries was spurred primarily by Englishmen.[32] Neither English nor French was the main literary language, of course; Latin unified the conquerors and conquered in a single literacy. English Latinity, however, was as developed as its French counterpart, and the differences between them came out most strongly in the pulpit, where clerics trained to Franco-Latin literacy had to step into the vernacular and learn literary conventions that hardly existed in France. The *Ormulum,* particularly, suggests a picture in which one group dominates and the other educates: political imperialism leads not merely to conquest but to the acceptance, by the conquerors, of new cultural influences, flowing in the opposite direction.

Such an account flies in the face of our postcolonial experiences with imperialism. Since the Enlightenment, the group that dominates has also been the group that educates, disregarding questions of relative merit. Our notions of vernacularity have grown out of this model, so that in any encounter between two languages (and I should repeat that vernacularity is a relationship, not an essence), the more "low-culture" one is called the vernacular, and the more "high-culture" one is generously considered "standard." We apply this to medieval European languages as well: Old French, Middle High German, and Middle English are vernaculars, and Latin, Greek, and Hebrew are the default languages of literacy.

But the example of the *Ormulum,* with its literary sophistication, is an indication of how erratically our shorthand notion of vernacularity fits onto the Middle Ages and, for that matter, the classical world. Literacy may be the dividing line between vernacular and standard language in the colonial and postcolonial world, but the historical record reminds us of other possibilities. The Norman Conquest is hardly the only case where a highly literate people were conquered and ruled by a group with a shorter tradition of literacy, who then gained not only labor but also learning: the Romans acquired a large part of their culture, including literacy, by annexing the Greek lands in southern Italy and enslaving the inhabitants. The earliest Roman writers were, in fact, the Greek slaves Livius Andronicus and Quintus Ennius (the latter is, coincidentally, credited with spelling reform in Latin, specifically the use of double letters to indicate consonant length), and Rome continued to depend on slave labor for scribal tasks until the late Republic.[33] They even created a class of sophisticated administrative slaves, the *familia Caesaris,* similar to the class of ministerials in Ottonian times.[34]

This harking back to Rome is also useful in that it returns our attention to the etymology of our theme word: a *vernacula* was a slave, but particularly a house slave, and *vernacular* was the language spoken by these slaves within the owner's home. We can profit in several ways by shifting from the notion of vernacular as a less literate (or perhaps completely oral) language to vernacular as enslaved and necessarily intimate—but not necessarily uneducated— language. For one thing, it permits modern-day vernaculars to avoid the essentializing politics of literacy versus orality. Instead, it recasts the relationship between languages as a function not only of power but also of proximity: Vernacularity is born when one language is invited into the home of another. Viewing it from this angle opens up possibilities for assessing the role of literature in the acquisition of power. Edward Kamau Brathwaite's *History of the Voice* advocates the institutionalization of Creoles into what he calls "nation-languages," which he considers an important part of the move to use hybridity as a means of transcending colonialism.[35] Thorlac Turville-Petre's study of medieval English literacy traces the success story of just such a move,[36] but its object lesson remains hidden from Brathwaite's audience due to narrow interpretations of the vernacular.

There can be little doubt that Middle English is an excellent example of what Édouard Glissant calls forced poetics—the creation of language under the constraint of a historically imposed idiom;[37] without the Norman Conquest, Middle English would never have existed in the shape it did. Glissant's comments on the nature of free and forced poetics (or counterpoetics) are provocative, but one in particular stands out: taking his cue from Ernst Curtius's notion of epic landscape,[38] he raises the question of territorial metaphors as the shaping force of language (and thus literature). But under conditions of forced poetics—where self-expression is enslaved, as in the case of Glissant's Martinique and Orm's England—vernacular speakers can make no legal claim to a landscape of their own. Instead, they must reverse the process: make counterpoetics the shaping force of the landscape. When the vernacular can be used to shape political and social realities, then we come closer to being able to synthesize all the oppositions Glissant proposes and condemns: the oral and the written, self-expression and language, solidarity and solitude. Orm's integration of all these is a text Glissant might be proud of.

NOTES

1. Henry Sweet, *First Middle English Primer: Extracts from the Ancren riwle and Ormulum* (Oxford: Clarendon Press, 1891), and Charles Jones, *An Introduction to Middle English* (New York: Holt, Rinehart & Winston 1972). The main editions of the *Ormulum* are Robert Meadows White's *Ormulum, now first edited from the original manuscript in the Bodleian* (Oxford: Oxford University Press, 1852), and its revision, Robert Holt's *Ormulum* (Oxford: Clarendon Press, 1878). All citations here are from the earlier volume, and all translations are my own.

2. J. A. W. Bennett, G. V. Smithers, and Norman Davis, *Early Middle English Verse and Prose* (Oxford: Clarendon Press, 1966), 174.

3. According to several former students of Professor Parkes, in conversation with the author, Oxford, July 1997.

4. John Edwin Wells, *A Manual of the Writings in Middle English* (New Haven: Yale University Press, 1926), 283. C. M. Millward, *Biography of the English Language* (Fort Worth: Harcourt Brace, 1996), 204.

5. Albert C. Baugh, *A Literary History of England,* 2d ed. (New York: Appleton-Century-Crofts, 1967), 159. David Lawton, "Englishing the Bible," in David Wallace, ed., *The Cambridge History of Medieval English Literature* (see Further Reading), 464.

6. For details on the individual graphs used in the *Ormulum,* see Daniel Brink, "Variation Between <þ-> and <t-> in the *Ormulum,*" in Irmengard Rauch, Gerald F. Carr, and Robert L. Kyes, eds., *On Germanic Linguistics* (Berlin: Mouton de Gruyter, 1992), 20–33; Arthur S. Napier, *History of the Holy Rood-Tree,* Early English Text Society, Original Series 103 (London: Early English Text Society, 1894), 71–74; and J. E. Turville-Petre, "Studies on the Ormulum Ms.," *JEGP* 46 (1947): 1–27.

7. Betty Phillips, "Open Syllable Lengthening and the *Ormulum,*" *Word* 43 (1992): 375–82; Myungsook Kim, "On Lengthening in the Open Syllables of Middle English," *Lingua* 91 (1993): 261–77; Hans Kurath, "The Loss of Long Consonants and the Rise of Voiced Fricatives in Middle English," *Language* 32 (1956): 434–45; Robert D. Stevick, "Plus Juncture and the Spelling of the *Ormulum,*" *JEGP* 64 (1965): 84–89; Richard Jordan, *Handbook of Middle English Grammar: Phonology* (Heidelberg: C. Winter, 1934); Karl Luick, "Über die Entwicklung von æ-, u-, i-, und die Dehnung in offener Silber überhaupt," *Archiv für das Studium der neueren Sprachen* 102 (1899): 43–84, and 103 (1899): 55–90; Robert D. Fulk, "Consonant Doubling and Open Syllable Lengthening in the *Ormulum,*" *Anglia* 114 (1996): 481–513.

8. Hans Kurath and Sherman Kuhn, *Middle English Dictionary* (Ann Arbor: University of Michigan Press, 1954), 296.

9. John Anderson and Derek Britton, "Double Trouble: Geminate Versus Simplex Graphs in the *Ormulum,*" in Jacek Fisiak, ed., *Studies in Middle English Linguistics* (Berlin: Mouton de Gruyter, 1997), 23–58.

10. Kenneth Sisam, *Studies in the History of Old English Literature* (see Further Reading, page 257), 185–95.

11. Anderson and Britton, particularly, refer to Sisam's account as an "erroneous view" ("Double Trouble," 24), and they criticize Fernand Mossé and G. V. Smithers for perpetuating his misreading.

12. Cecily Clark, *The Peterborough Chronicle, 1170–1154* (Oxford: Oxford University Press, 1958); Ferdinand Holthausen, ed., *Vices and Virtues: being a soul's confession of its sins with reason's description of the virtues: a Middle-English dialogue of about 1200 A.D.,* 2 vols., Early English Text Society, Original Series 89, 159 (London: Early English Text Society, 1888, 1921).

13. Augustine, *De doctrina christiana,* trans. D. W. Robertson Jr. (Upper Saddle River, N.J.: Library of Liberal Arts, 1958), 79–80.

14. Stephen Morrison, "New Sources for the *Ormulum,*" *Neophilologus* 68 (1984): 444; Heinrich

Christoph Matthes, *Die Einheitlichkeit des Orrmulum: Studien zur Textkritik, zu den Quellen und zur sprachlichen Form von Orrmins Evangelienbuch, Germanische Bibliothek* (Heidelberg: C. Winter, 1933), 140.

15. It seems safe to assume that Junius 1 was never used for its intended purpose, since it would be nearly impossible to orate from coherently, being composed of more addenda and corrigenda (jotted vertically in the margins and tipped in on shreds of parchment) than original text. If any working copies were made, they left no trace on the historical record.

16. Sisam, *Studies in the History of Old English Literature,* 190.

17. Barbara Strang, in *A History of English* (London: Methuen & Co., 1970), gives what I consider the most accurate account of Orm's purpose, but as a sidenote, saying only this: "What Orm seems to have done is to have hit upon a method for converting a priest who did not speak English (or a kind of English understood by his congregation) into a 'megaphone' for the Bible's message—an instrument whereby it could reach the people, even if the instrument remained uncomprehending" (242).

18. Ann Williams, *The English and the Norman Conquest* (Woodbridge: Boydell & Brewer, 1995), 126.

19. M. B. Parkes, "On the Presumed Date and Possible Origin of the Manuscript of the 'Orrmulum': Oxford, Bodleian Library, MS. Junius 1," in E. G. Stanley and Douglas Gray, eds., *Five Hundred Years of Words and Sounds* (Cambridge: D. S. Brewer, 1983), 115–27. Parkes's argument hinges on the dedication of the manuscript to Saints Peter and Paul, to whom Bourne was the only abbey dedicated, among those in Orm's area.

20. On the relationship between English daughters of French mother abbeys, see Marjorie Chibnall, "Monastic Foundations in England and Normandy, 1066–1189," in David Bates and Anne Curry, eds., *England and Normandy in the Middle Ages* (London: Hambledon Press, 1994), 43–44.

21. Albert Beebe White and Wallace Notestein, eds., *Source Problems in English History* (New York: Harper, 1915).

22. J. A. W. Bennett, *Middle English Literature* (Oxford: Clarendon Press, 1986), 30; *Ormulum,* lines 149–56 and 322–30, among others.

23. E. C. Einhorn, *Old French* (Cambridge: Cambridge University Press, 1974), 135–41; John Fox and Robin Wood, *A Concise History of the French Language* (London: Basil Blackwell, 1968), 37, 50, 72; R. Anthony Lodge, *French: From Dialect to Standard* (see Further Reading), 115; Wendy Ayres-Bennett, *A History of the French Language Through Texts* (London: Routledge, 1996), 62–63.

24. Glanville Price, *The French Language: Present and Past* (London: Grant & Cutler, 1998), 46.

25. Gaston Zink, *Phonétique historique du français* (Paris: Presses Universitaires de France, 1991), 76.

26. Price, *French Language,* 69.

27. John R. H. Moorman, *Church Life in England in the Thirteenth Century* (Cambridge: Cambridge University Press, 1945), 80.

28. M. T. Clanchy, *From Memory to Written Record* (1979; see Further Reading), 215–16.

29. Stephen Morrison has shown that Ælfric and his fellow homilist Wulfstan were important sources for Orm. Morrison, "New Sources"; idem, "A Reminiscence of Wulfstan in the Twelfth Century," *Neuphilologische Mitteilungen* 96 (1995): 229–34.

30. Ælfric, *Homilies of Aelfric,* ed. John C. Pope, Early English Text Society, Original Series 259 (Oxford: Early English Text Society, 1967), 111–12.

31. Ibid., 288.

32. James J. Murphy, *Rhetoric in the Middle Ages* (Berkeley and Los Angeles: University of California Press, 1974), 80.

33. Moses Hadas, *Ancilla to Classical Reading* (New York: Columbia University Press, 1954), 68–70; Joseph Vogt, *Ancient Slavery and the Ideal of Man* (Cambridge, Mass.: Harvard University Press, 1975), 124–26.

34. Interested readers are referred to P. R. C. Weaver's *Familia Cæsaris* (Cambridge: Cambridge University Press, 1972).

35. Edward Kamau Brathwaite, *History of the Voice: The Development of Nation Language in Anglophone Caribbean Poetry* (London: New Beacon Books, 1984).

36. Thorlac Turville-Petre, *England the Nation* (see Further Reading).

37. Édouard Glissant, *Caribbean Discourse* (Charlottesville: University Press of Virginia, 1989).

38. Ernst Robert Curtius, *European Literature and the Latin Middle Ages* (see Further Reading), 200–202.

Talking the Talk

Access to the Vernacular in Medieval Preaching

CLAIRE M. WATERS

The tower of Babel and the multiplication of languages that attended its fall
are a source of fascination for modern scholars intrigued by linguistic difference and hierarchy. For medieval preachers, however, language was only a
means to an end, and their attention focused not on Babel but on its New
Testament companion, Pentecost, where the "confusion of languages" is
resolved by the apostles' miraculous ability to speak to each in his own language.[1] The apostles' speaking in tongues was regarded less as a matter of
language per se than as a matter of *access,* a concept central to the interaction
of Latin and vernacular in medieval preaching.

Preaching in the Middle Ages is often assumed to have been a hierarchical,
top-down activity through which the clergy controlled the laity's access to the
Bible and to Christian doctrine.[2] But a consideration of how medieval preachers discussed their own task and the role played in it by language shows us a
more complicated picture. In the late twelfth and early thirteenth centuries,
there was a great revival of formal interest in preaching, including a concern
with the preacher's role and his relationship to his flock. Works written by
and for preachers in this period show them engaged in a delicate balancing
act. Standing between the church hierarchy and the laity in both a mediatory
and a liminal sense, preachers needed access to both of those worlds in order
to make them accessible to one another.

Preachers' discussions of their own language illustrate how shifting and
uncertain the supposed divide between Latin and vernacular was in this context. The very term most frequently used to refer to the vernacular, *vulgaris*
(common or popular), itself points to the social, rather than linguistic, implications of the concept.[3] It can be impossible to tell whether a writer is referring, for example, to a story *in the vernacular* or merely a *popular* story, a
vernacular saying or a *common* saying. The distinction, or lack thereof, is important, because it suggests that what a preacher really sought in using a vernacular was not, or not only, linguistic comprehensibility, but access and
connection to his audience.

Like many of the sermons they left behind, most preachers, and some of their audiences, must have been linguistic and cultural hybrids. Indeed, we often cannot tell for certain in what language sermons would have been preached, though recent scholarship has suggested that the long-standing notion that Latin sermons were always preached to the clergy, vernacular sermons to the laity, with little or no overlap, may be too simple.[4] Thinking about vernacularity as access allows us to move beyond the insoluble question of the exact language of preaching and toward questions of more interest to medieval preachers themselves. Looking particularly at thirteenth-century preaching handbooks by Thomas of Chobham and Humbert of Romans and at discussions of narrative exempla, we see the preacher's need both to distinguish himself from and to resemble his flock, and hence the importance of the vernacular in establishing a clerical identity often seen in opposition to it.[5]

Vernacular preaching to "the people," or the laity, was associated throughout most of Christian history with the lower clergy, as Michel Zink has noted, because it was the lower clergy—below the bishop, that is—who were able to communicate with their flocks in the native, "common" language of the region.[6] It was perhaps a lack of sufficiently prepared lower clergy that led to a growing perception, in the eleventh and twelfth centuries, that the clerical hierarchy was not fulfilling its preaching duties; instead, independent, charismatic preachers—some more orthodox than others—sprang up to fill the gap. The records of preaching for the twelfth century, for instance, often discuss preachers, like Bernard of Clairvaux or Robert of Arbrissel, whose charismatic gifts were so great that it was said they could preach in an unknown language and still move their audiences.

Bernard, Robert, and their ilk are exceptional cases, however; not everyone who preaches to the people is a popular preacher. Faced with the need for more and better "ordinary" preaching, the church in the late twelfth and early thirteenth centuries pulled itself together and began trying to train its clergy. The preachers of the thirteenth century needed both Latinity (knowledge of their institutional position and the scriptural founts of their vocation) and vernacularity (the techniques that would enable them to reach varied audiences). In learning to balance Latin and vernacular, preachers were in effect learning to establish their own role in a community.

Preachers' mediatory role as "translators" of literate, Latin, clerical culture for an unlearned, lay, "vernacular" audience can certainly be seen as one that denied the laity full or independent access to Scripture and to theological material usually produced in Latin. Opposition to vernacular translation of Scripture was already an issue in this period, and the famous, or infamous, image that the laity are to be presented with truth in simple form as infants are given milk, because they are not strong enough for solid food, appears frequently in preaching manuals.[7] Considered from the point of view of doctrine, that is, the Latin-vernacular relationship in thirteenth-century preaching seems to recapitulate a hierarchy in which the laity—*rudes, simplices, illiterati*—were always on the bottom, accorded no independent will or ability. The preaching manuals themselves, however, make it clear that the cultural difference between clergy and laity was one that had to be constructed and carefully maintained.

Thomas of Chobham, writing primarily for parish priests in the early thirteenth century, is more concerned with establishing the preacher's differences from his audience than telling him how to overcome those differences—an emphasis that no doubt reflects the state of the parish clergy, many of whom were probably hardly more educated than those they were supposed to instruct.[8] Thomas's text, which shows a careful attention to the problems of pastoral care, has little to say about the linguistic vernacular. His discussion of the preacher's communication with his audience focuses instead on the preacher's need to maintain his position—to establish and present an appropriate persona to his congregation and to keep up the distinctions between himself and them. This is a matter of responsibility as much as privilege: the preacher owes his audience a good example and good teaching and must work to provide it. But he should also be conscious of, and maintain, his authority.[9] Thomas's attitude and discussion reflect, it seems, both the popularity of lay and itinerant preaching—in which the preacher's status was not always clearly distinguished from that of his audience—and the beginning of a trend in parochial priesthood in the thirteenth century, whereby the priest became increasingly the representative of a larger, diocesan authority, of the church as a whole rather than simply of his own local jurisdiction.[10] In the context Thomas addresses, the priest would have been part of the community to which he preached. He would have been known to them—perhaps all too well—and so would not have needed Thomas's, or anyone's, instructions on how to approach them. Instead, he needed to consider how he could establish and display his access to the clerical world of learning and authority in order to make his role in the "popular" world, of which he was clearly a part, effective.

The thirteenth century, however, saw the development of new modes of preaching, distinct from both the charismatic and the parochial. The Franciscan and Dominican orders produced a new group of preachers in a position very different from that of Thomas's imagined audience. The friars, as itinerant preachers, would not necessarily be acquainted with the language, customs, style—with the vernacular—of their intended audiences. It is to such preachers that Humbert's text is primarily directed. His approach to the cultural and linguistic translations required of the preacher reflects the interdependence of lay and clerical, vernacular and Latin, cultures in the spoken, interactive context of preaching.

In a chapter entitled "On the Speech of the Preacher" (*De loquela praedicatoris*), Humbert addresses, obliquely, the relationship of Latin and vernacular. Having noted the importance of speaking clearly, he next emphasizes the preacher's need for an "abundance" of language, making reference to Pentecost. "If the early preachers were given many languages for the purpose of preaching, so that they might have abundant words for everyone," he asks, "how unbecoming is it when a preacher is lacking in words, whether on account of a lack of memory, or a lack of Latinity, or a lack of vernacular speech [or "common speech," *vulgaris loquutionis*]?"[11] Here Latin and vernacular appear as equally necessary to the work of preaching; the lack of either handicaps the preacher. This brief indication that "speaking in tongues" is the job of the preacher is, however, the only direct mention of linguistic issues in this passage. Humbert is interested in the preacher's *language* only as an element of the preacher's *speech*. Other desirable qualities he goes on to discuss, apparently equivalent in importance to ease in various languages, include sonority of voice, a manner of speaking that is easy to follow and well paced, a simple style, and, finally, "prudence in speaking of diverse things to diverse people" (*prudentiam in loquendo diversa diversis*).[12] While such "prudence" is often cited as the reason for speaking simply to the simple, it turns out that what Humbert has in mind is simply an appropriate message; the audiences he envisions are defined not as lay or clerical but as the good, the wicked, the timid, the wrathful, and so forth. For Humbert, that is, linguistic matters are a subsidiary aspect of the need to make your speech attractive to and appropriate for your audience, whoever that audience may be.

Thus, while Thomas imagines preachers who are already connected to their audiences by language and community—and who may therefore need to maintain more distance in order to shore up their institutional authority—Humbert is writing for those who have the advantage and authority of distance but lack the immediate connection of a parish priest to his flock. In neither case are purely linguistic issues much in evidence. What we do see in both texts is an awareness of vernacularity as part of a balance between different kinds of access that are equally necessary to the preacher's task.

The connection between preacher and audience created by vernacularity, and the problems this could raise, are particularly evident in discussions of the preacher's use of exempla, exemplary stories used to make a point, or similitudes, comparisons from the natural world.[13] It is often noted in preaching manuals and collections of exempla that such "concrete" means of persuasion are particularly appropriate for laypeople.[14] As Jean-Claude Schmitt says, the use of exempla "rested on a veritable anthropology, or at least on the sense that the clergy had of a certain specificity of 'popular' culture. This awareness is the condition of effective preaching: to people who for the most part were considered 'rural,' 'lesser,' 'simple,' 'unlearned,' one had to speak of concrete things, 'physicalities,' 'external things,' 'deeds,' without using the subtleties of speculative language."[15] This audience is usually distinguished with clerical loftiness from a more learned audience to whom one may speak directly of higher things.

Some modern readings of the cultural role of exempla strongly emphasize the depth of the divide that the use of example supposedly illustrates. Larry Scanlon has argued that the exemplum was "a narrative enactment of cultural authority" that reflected "virtually no social permeability between . . . the clerical (*scientes, erudites*), on one side, and the lay (*rudes, simplices*), on the other."[16] Schmitt seems to agree, claiming that the "furtive complicity" created by the use of exempla is only a "momentary rupture that . . . reinforces again the ideological function of the sermon, the speech of authority."[17] The admission of connection between preacher and audience is subordinated to an assertion of difference that echoes the *rudes, simplices* rhetoric of exempla collections and sermon manuals.

Other scholarly readings, however, remind us that the repeated references in preaching texts to the simple, the unlearned, or the rustic—terms that emphasize the divide between the clergy and their audiences—ignore the fact that exempla, like vernacularity more generally, did reflect a certain connection between the supposedly learned preacher and his supposedly unlearned flock.[18] Schmitt acknowledges that the medieval preacher "finds himself constrained in a sense by the necessities of his 'exemplary' pedagogy to involve himself in the multiple networks of oral narrativity," and David d'Avray points out that the use of "extended comparisons or analogies . . . is one of the mental habits or customs which most influenced the directions which the thinking of preachers followed in the thirteenth century and after."[19] Works directed to preachers, who were of necessity clerics, are certainly not above using concrete instances to make their points; both Thomas's and Humbert's texts are filled with such comparisons. It is worth remembering in this context that not all the clergy were equally learned and that some of them shared their audiences' cultural interests. Indeed, Caesarius of Heisterbach's famous anecdote about the preacher who woke his drowsing flock with the teaser "There was a certain king, called Arthur," is told of a monastic audience (in fact, the monks of Heisterbach).[20] Here, the ultimate symbol of *roman*—a worldly genre named for the worldly language in which it was created—is shown to appeal to the "learned" just as it might to the "simple." Such instances suggest that the gap between *simplices* and *clerici,* like that between the vernacular and Latin, was not always so wide as it might appear, and that exempla and similitudes were at least as much a way to cross as a way to maintain it.

If the clergy's own use and appreciation of exempla could suggest one important area of convergence between themselves and the laity, the need for verisimilitude in exempla fostered a further connection. While, on the one hand, the preacher's ability to guarantee his story merely by telling it was a sign of his authoritative status, the story also had to have verisimilitude, a recognizable relation to experience. As Humbert puts it, "care should be taken that exempla be of sufficient authority [*competentis auctoritatis*], lest they be scorned, and realistic [*verisimilia*], so that they will be believed, and that they contain something instructive [*aliquam aedificationem*], lest they be put forth in vain."[21] Like the preacher, these tales owe a dual allegiance: to the authority that validates them, but also to the experience that makes them acceptably "realistic" examples. The former demonstrates the preacher's claim to the learned culture of books and tradition; the latter shows his participation in the culture his audience shares. The authority of experience is not divorced from the world of learning, any more than the authority of learning is divorced from the world of experience. The preacher is the medium for both, personifying for his congregation the institutional knowledge and authority that must work through an individual—and through a vernacular.

In addition to the theoretical issues raised by exempla, there was the simple issue of performance. The preacher, unlike most of his congregation, had access to exempla in their "abstracted," usually Latin, form—that is, as elements of collections without any context.[22] It was he who made the transition from the universal to the particular, and from Latin to vernacular, a transition that demanded his participation in "networks of oral narrativity," his ability not merely to convey doctrine but to make that doctrine live. For an exemplum to be effective, various authors assert, it must be put across well. As Jacques de Vitry says, "proverbs, similitudes, and everyday examples [*vulgar(ia) exempl(a)*] . . . cannot be expressed in writing as they can by gesture and word and the manner of speaking, nor do they move or rouse the audience in the mouth of one person as they do in the mouth of another."[23] And Humbert, in his work *De habundancia exemplorum,* notes that exempla require a style all their own, and politely hints that not every preacher is equally gifted at presenting them: those who "may perhaps not have a pleasing narrative style," he says, "should not give up a means [of teaching] in which they are gifted for one in which they are not."[24] More than some other forms of instruction, the exemplum was a kind of dead letter until the preacher brought it to life.[25] Despite his access to the abstracted exemplum, he participated crucially in its transformation into a concrete, embodied form of instruction, and that transformation, if successfully enacted, demonstrated his ability to assimilate to his audience in some way, to speak to them with "verisimilitude." Like his exempla, he must appear real.[26]

Thus, although the "rupture" that the exemplum represents in a sermon may ultimately reinforce the ideological import of the rest of the sermon, it exacts a price for doing so. By marking a point of "complicity," as Schmitt puts it, a point of connection between preacher and audience, the use of exempla implicitly addresses the preacher's relationship to his own authority and raises the question of how, and indeed whether, he is set apart from his audience. The same is true of vernacularity more generally: the preacher's ability to address his congregation in the "common language" meant not only his ability to speak French, Italian, English, but also his ability to use exempla, proverbs, and so forth—"common speech"—to get his message across. Making a connection with his hearers involved, to a certain extent, making himself like them—or, rather, acknowledging and exploiting his existing likenesses to them.

The ambiguous relationship of the preacher's two allegiances can be seen also in Humbert's *De eruditione,* in a section not on formal preaching but on how to make "private conversation" edifying. In the previous chapter, Humbert has been holding forth on the wickedness of "worldly speech" (*linguam mundi*). It is clear that "worldly" here does not equate with the vernacular. While one of Humbert's arguments against worldly speech is that just as schoolboys who lapse out of Latin into the vernacular are punished, so preachers who lapse into worldly speech will be still more severely punished, another notes that just as preachers "should not abandon heavenly language for earthly [*non debent dimittere linguam caelestem propter linguam mundi*], so a Frenchman, wherever he may go, does not easily abandon his own language for another, on account of the nobility of his language and his fatherland."[27] Vernacular speech, then, can be either earthly or heavenly, just as Latin can. The schoolboy simile, moreover, implies that worldly speech is the "vernacular" of the clergy, who must be trained into the practice of heavenly speech—a perhaps unintentional equation that acknowledges both the preacher's human fallibility and the constructed, learned quality of his role as preacher.[28]

Although Humbert criticizes "worldly speech," however, he recognizes that it can be useful at times. The section following the one discussed above emphasizes again the need to consider what, when, to whom, and how one speaks, and admits that "sometimes one should speak holy words, sometimes recite some good exempla, and sometimes even use some secular words." Later Humbert clarifies this need, saying that secular words may sometimes be used "for the purpose of a certain conformity" (*propter quamdam . . . conformitatem*) with the people addressed.[29] If even secular speech is occasionally permitted for good ends, surely the "conformity" with an audience marked by the vernacular—like the "furtive complicity" created by exempla—is one of the preacher's strengths.

This is not to deny that a strong distinction remained, and was promoted, between clergy and laity, Latin and vernacular, learned and unlearned, in many cases, or that there was a cultural investment in regarding the laity as simple and unlearned by comparison with the clergy. But it is possible to lean too far in that direction; if some examples seem to concede the use of exempla or the vernacular or other means of connection as a regrettable necessity, there are other descriptions that actively valorize them. One of these is the repeated story of the unlearned preacher whose similitudes or exempla are persuasive where the words of a learned preacher are not. Christoph Maier relates one version of this exemplum, about the preaching of the Crusade in a village. A papal legate, unsuccessful in persuading the populace, eventually calls on the unlearned village priest (*sacerdos simplicissimus scripture et litterature*), who reluctantly agrees to take his place and proceeds to convince almost everyone, without use of scriptural authority, "with simplicity by showing a good example" (*simplicitate boni exempli ostencio*). This simple preacher uses the familiar image of threshing and winnowing to tell, as it were, an exemplum involving himself and the other clerics present: the papal legate, he says, has threshed the crowd like grain and prepared them; it is now his own job to winnow them and find who is chaff and who will go on Crusade.[30] As the story shows, the priest does a masterful job of including himself and his parishioners in a framework of recognizable experience that is also a manifestation of theological truth. The papal legate may use the vernacular, but clearly he does not speak the audience's language. This story also reflects the desire for holy simplicity that is a persistent thread in medieval Christianity and that mitigates the negative aspect of the repeated reference to lay audiences as *simplices*.

Conceptions of a preacher's contact with "the people," then, involve style and genre as much as language—the preacher's need not just to speak in the vernacular but to talk the talk with his audience. Other advice offered to preachers extends this need to understand and use vernacular, or "common," modes of communication to the preacher's behavior in the world, his ability to walk the walk as well as talk the talk. In these contexts, as in those that address language and genre, nonclerical culture and nonclerical people are understood to be shrewd and deserving of respect: they may be *simplices,* but they are not stupid. In this context, the insistence that a preacher should maintain a high moral standard in his behavior and avoid excessively theatrical gestures or dress is justified by the assumption that an audience will see through such behavior and reject his preaching.[31] The preacher's personal morality reflects well on the church and maintains his institutional position, but it also gains him the personal respect of his audience, without which all the institutional backing in the world is useless.

Such attention to and respect for the audience seem to be the point of an entertaining passage in an anonymous appendix to Humbert of Romans' work on the offices of the Dominican order. The unknown Dominican, writing his instructions for traveling preachers, notes that a preacher should "conform himself [*conformet se*] in good customs to those with whom he spends time [*conversatur*]." The first verb here, *conformare,* is the same word Humbert used in discussing the occasional need for a preacher to use secular words in private communication. What this author has in mind is, more precisely, the table manners of various regions. "In some areas," he writes, "it is rude to drink out of the bowl; to look over the cup while drinking; to slurp soup noisily from your spoon; to lean your elbows on the table; and so on."[32] Such things are not sins, he says, but should be avoided among those who regard them as inappropriate; it is one of the preacher's responsibilities to make himself similar to his audience in whatever ways are compatible with his office and with good behavior.

If we consider, then, the role of the common, the well-known, the shared or popular aspects of culture, we can begin to see what medieval preachers might have thought about when they thought about the vernacular. What we may regard as primarily a linguistic aspect of sermon literature was clearly, in its original, lived context, bound up with many other things. The result is that clerical attempts to present Latin and vernacular, clergy and laity, as opposed categories are continually undermined by the writers' obvious recognition of the fact that they deal with a situation, preaching, whose very function was to integrate those realms.[33] Indeed, considering vernacularity not as a purely linguistic issue but as a matter of the preacher's access to his audience can help us to see that preachers themselves did not so much traverse the imagined space between laity and clergy as embody it; the preacher's very identity as a cleric relied on his ability to participate in the vernacular.

NOTES

1. See Gen. 11:1–9 and Acts 2:1–6. Beryl Smalley, *The Study of the Bible in the Middle Ages* (Notre Dame, Ind.: University of Notre Dame Press, 1964), 34, discusses the origins of biblical interpretation by means of "types."

2. This view becomes much more central to medieval discussions with the rise of Wycliffism in fourteenth-century England, a movement also, of course, heavily invested in language politics. See, for example, the article by Fiona Somerset in this volume and, on preaching in fourteenth- and fifteenth-century England generally, Helen Leith Spencer, *English Preaching in the Late Middle Ages* (see Further Reading, page 257).

3. That "popular" does *not* necessarily mean vernacular is implied, for example, by Thomas of Chobham's observation that "dicitur uulgariter *omne rarum carum*" (it is commonly said, "everything rare is precious"). The fact that *uulgariter* here refers to a rhyming Latin proverb (*omne rarum carum*) suggests that the term can point to a "common" culture that is not linguistically vernacular, or not exclusively so. *Summa de arte praedicandi,* ed. Franco Morenzoni, Corpus Christianorum Continuatio Mediaevalis 82 (Turnhout: Brepols, 1988), 75.

4. This is an old debate, going back to Alfred Lecoy de la Marche and Barthélemy Hauréau in the nineteenth century. Their opposing viewpoints—that all preaching to the laity was entirely in the vernacular, all preaching to the clergy in Latin (Lecoy), or that some bilingualism would have characterized many, if not most, sermons (Hauréau)—are still under discussion. For instance, Jean Longère, *La prédication médiévale* (Paris: Études Augustiniennes, 1983), says that "Lecoy de la Marche a sûrement raison" (162), while Giles Constable suggests that recent scholarship would tend to support Hauréau's long-disregarded thesis; see "The Language of Preaching in the Twelfth Century" (see Further Reading).

5. Thomas, a pastoral theologian, wrote his manual around 1220, though the date is rather uncertain; see *Summa de arte praedicandi,* xxxvi–xxxviii. Humbert of Romans, master-general of the Dominicans from 1254 to 1263, probably wrote his text sometime in the third quarter of the thirteenth century.

6. Michel Zink, *La prédication en langue romane avant 1300* (see Further Reading), 89. See his full discussion of this issue, 85–113.

7. The Waldensians' attention to Scripture in the vernacular, for instance, provoked the wrath of many clerics—not least because their vernacular translation and Bible study often led to preaching. See Malcolm Lambert, *Medieval Heresy: Popular Movements from the Gregorian Reform to the Reformation* (Oxford: Blackwell, 1992), 72–74. Humbert of Romans, among many others, uses the "milk for the little ones" metaphor. His discussion is quoted in J.-Th. Welter, *L'exemplum dans la littérature religieuse et didactique du Moyen Âge* (Paris: Occitania, 1927), 73 n. 13 (cont. from 72).

8. Jean-Claude Schmitt speaks of "poor secular clerics [who were] in reaction against the monastic orders, and whose culture was at least as close to that of the laity as to the Latin culture of the Church." C. Bremond, Jacques Le Goff, and Jean-Claude Schmitt, *L'exemplum,* Typologie des sources du Moyen Âge occidental 40 (Turnhout: Brepols, 1982), 162.

9. Thomas discusses, for example, the dangers of excessive humility toward those one has wronged, which can diminish the preacher's authority, and warns against preaching in scruffy clothes, or in a "habitu laicali." *Summa de arte praedicandi,* 68–69.

10. See Joseph W. Goering, "The Changing Face of the Village Parish II: The Thirteenth Century," in *Pathways to Medieval Peasants,* ed. J. A. Raftis (Toronto: Pontifical Institute of Mediaeval Studies, 1981), 323–33. Thomas himself, a former student of Peter the Chanter's in Paris, was in a sense a conduit of this larger structure to the lower clergy, just as the preacher was supposed to become a conduit of doctrine to his flock. Franco Morenzoni discusses this movement in *Des écoles aux paroisses: Thomas de Chobham et la promotion de la prédication au début du XIIIe siècle* (Paris: Institut d'Études Augustiniennes, 1995).

11. "Item, copiam verborum. Si enim propter praedicationem primitivis praedicatoribus data sunt genera linguarum, ut abundarent verbis ad omnes, quam indecens est cum praedicator habet interdum defectum in verbis, vel propter defectum memoriae, vel propter defectum latinitatis, vel propter defectum vulgaris loquutionis, et hujusmodi?" Humbert of Romans, *De eruditione praedica-*

torum, in *B. Humberti de Romanis Opera de vita regulari,* vol. 2, ed. Joachim Joseph Berthier (Rome: Marietti, 1888–89), 402. Thomas of Chobham, too, turns to Pentecost not for its linguistic imagery but for its assertion that the Holy Spirit gave *eloquium,* speech or eloquence, to the apostles. *Summa de arte praedicandi,* 299.

12. Humbert, *De eruditione,* 403.

13. The boundaries between exempla and similitudes were somewhat blurry; see, for instance, Welter, *L'exemplum,* 79. David L. d'Avray, sensibly, treats the various types of illustrations as a coherent group, rather than try artificially to separate them: *The Preaching of the Friars: Sermons Diffused from Paris Before 1300* (Oxford: Clarendon, 1985), 225–235.

14. See, for example, Jacques de Vitry: "Per experienciam noverunt quantus fructus proveniet ex hujusmodi fabulosis exemplis laicis et simplicibus personis non solum ad edificacionem sed ad recreacionem." Welter, *L'exemplum,* 69.

15. Bremond, Le Goff, and Schmitt, *L'exemplum,* 85.

16. Larry Scanlon, *Narrative, Authority, and Power: The Medieval Exemplum and the Chaucerian Tradition,* Cambridge Studies in Medieval Literature 20 (Cambridge: Cambridge University Press, 1994), 34, 67.

17. Bremond, Le Goff, and Schmitt, *L'exemplum,* 164.

18. Siegfried Wenzel makes a similar point with regard to the snippets of vernacular songs inserted into many sermons: "Rather than prove a point or formulate the preacher's message, these round out a picture or add color to a story. Undoubtedly they kept the audience awake and created an atmosphere of common experience shared by the preacher and his congregation, much as some preachers today strive for popularity by quoting snippets from *Reader's Digest* or *Godspell.*" Wenzel, *Preachers, Poets, and the Early English Lyric* (Princeton: Princeton University Press, 1986), 227–28.

19. Bremond, Le Goff, and Schmitt, *L'exemplum,* 86. D'Avray, *Preaching,* 227.

20. "Audite, fratres, audite, rem vobis novam et magnam proponam. Rex quidam fuit, qui Artus vocabatur." The abbot then broke off and rebuked his newly attentive audience for their greater interest in secular than in spiritual matters. Caesarius of Heisterbach, *Caesarii Heisterbacensis monachi ordinis cisterciensis Dialogus miraculorum,* ed. Joseph Strange, 2 vols. (Cologne: H. Lempertz & Co., 1851), 1:205.

21. "Circa exempla vero attendendum est ut sint competentis auctoritatis, ne contemnantur; et verisimilia, ut credantur; et aliquam aedificationem continentia, ne inutiliter proferantur." Humbert, *De eruditione,* 467.

22. This translation from the "universal" Latin into the more "particular" vernacular is another instance of the preacher's mediatory status. On Latin and vernacular as universal and particular, see, for example, Kevin Brownlee, "Commentary and the Rhetoric of Exemplarity: Griseldis in Petrarch, Philippe de Mézières, and the *Estoire,*" *South Atlantic Quarterly* 91 (1992): 870–71. Nicholas Watson, in "Visions of Inclusion: Universal Salvation and Vernacular Theology in Pre-Reformation England," *Journal of Medieval and Early Modern Studies* 27 (1997): 145–87, suggests that it is rather the vernacular that is universal. See also the essay by Sara S. Poor in this volume.

23. "in . . . proverbiis similitudinibus et vulgaribus exemplis adtendendum est, quod non possunt ita exprimi scripto, sicut gestu et verbo atque pronuntiandi modo, nec ita movent vel incitant auditores in ore unius, sicut in ore alterius." Thomas Frederick Crane, ed., *The Exempla or Illustrative Stories from the Sermones Vulgares of Jacques de Vitry* (London: David Nutt for the Folk-Lore Society, 1890), xiii n (continued from previous pages).

24. Welter, *L'exemplum,* 72–73 n. 13: "Sunt enim multi quibus data est major gracia loquendi per auctoritates, raciones vel interpretationes vel aliis modis quam per exempla, circa que forte non habet graciosam narracionem et non expedit istis relinquere modum [docendi], in quo habent graciam propter illum in quo non habent."

25. Jacques Le Goff also notes the strongly oral quality of exempla and their link to performance. Bremond, Le Goff, and Schmitt, *L'exemplum,* 82.

26. This transformation from abstract to particular was an inevitable feature of all preaching, but perhaps especially that in the vernacular. There are many instances where scriptural and other Latin texts in the third person are translated in surviving sermons not only into the vernacular but also into the second person, reminding us of the personal immediacy of preaching. See, e.g., Zink, *Prédication*, 97: "Tunc convertitur . . . Adonc es trastornaz vas Deu," where the last words are a direct address in Provençal.

27. "Et ideo cum [praedicatores] vadunt per mundum, non debent dimittere linguam caelestem propter linguam mundi, sicut Gallicus, quocumque vadat, non de facili dimittit linguam propter aliam, et propter nobilitatem linguae suae, et patriae suae." The schoolboy image mentioned above immediately follows: "Item, pueri in scholis, quibus imposita est lex loquendi latinum et non romantium, quando incidunt etiam casualiter in verbum romantium, statim puniuntur cum ferula in confusionem suam: quanto magis digni sunt confusione et poena, illi quorum interest loqui utilia, quando loquuntur vana!" Humbert, *De eruditione,* 465.

28. A later vernacular work, the *Pore Caitif,* makes a similar point from a different angle. As Nicholas Watson puts it, one of the lessons of this text is that "the 'clergy' that really needs to be learned (whether by vernacular readers or clerics) is not Latin, but holiness." "Conceptions of the Word" (see Further Reading), esp. 108.

29. "quandoque dicenda sunt verba sancta, quandoque exempla aliqua bona recitanda, quandoque etiam aliqua verba saecularia referenda. . . . Circa verba vero saecularia, si quandoque dicantur, propter quamdam cum hominibus conformitatem, tamen cavendum est ne talia dicantur quae sint longe a verbis Dei." Humbert, *De eruditione,* 466–67.

30. Christoph Maier, *Preaching the Crusades: Mendicant Friars and the Cross in the Thirteenth Century* (Cambridge: Cambridge University Press, 1994), 122. This story is a variant of a popular type, whose history is discussed by Scanlon; see *Narrative,* 31–32.

31. The foundational statement of this theme comes from Gregory the Great: "Cujus vita despicitur, restat ut ejus praedicatio contemnatur." *Homilia in Evangelio,* hom. 12, n. 1, PL 76, 1119A.

32. "Item, in bonis consuetudinibus conformet se his cum quibus conversatur. Verbi gratia, in aliquibus regionibus indecens est de scutella bibere; ultra scyphum, dum quis bibit, respicere; potagium de cochleari ut sonus audiatur sorbere; mensae cubitis incumbere, et similia. Quae quamvis peccata non sint, tamen vitanda sunt propter honestatem, apud eos qui talia reputant indecora." Humbert, *B. Humberti . . . Opera,* 370.

33. As Giles Constable says, "the very term Latin was used more broadly in the Middle Ages than it is today. . . . It should be used in apposition, not in opposition, to vernacular, which it frequently resembled." "Language of Preaching" (1994), 136–37.

The Language of Conversion

Ramon Llull's Art as a Vernacular

HARVEY HAMES

When discussing the perfect vernacular in the *De vulgari eloquentia,* Dante writes: "That it is exalted in power is plain. And what greater power could there be than that which can melt the hearts of human beings, so as to make the unwilling willing and the willing unwilling, as it has done and still does?"[1] According to Dante, the illustrious vernacular has the power to reunite all that has been torn asunder and made imperfect by the hubristic attempt to build the tower of Babel. This perfect vernacular is, therefore, the universal language that will provide man with the tools to return to a state of perfection like that of Adam and Eve in the Garden of Eden.[2] A contemporary of Dante's, the Catalan philosopher and mystic Ramon Llull (c. 1232–1315) developed an *Ars,* or science, that he perceived to be the perfect vehicle for breaking through the intellectual boundaries between Christians, Jews, and Muslims. The *Ars*'s function was to provide members of the three faiths with tools for true dialogue based on a terminology acceptable to all, with the intention of establishing one united faith: Christianity. Paraphrasing Dante, the *Ars* was supposed to be that universal language which can melt the heart of human beings, so as to make the unwilling willing—a perfect vernacular for conversion. Although it is unlikely that Llull thought of the *Ars* as a vernacular, it is clear he was aware of the innovation of his approach. Thinking of Llull's *Ars* as a vernacular, or a "common tongue," which facilitates the formation of a new textual community for dialogue, may illuminate the differences between his and other approaches to conversion.

Llull sometimes made a more direct use of a vernacular, Catalan, as a language for dialogue. Unlike Dante, he did not think of the vernacular as a literary tool, but as an instrument of access to the framework of his *Ars.* Catalan was the lingua franca for Christians, Jews, and Muslims living in the parts of the Kingdom of Aragon bordering the Mediterranean. But Llull also wrote in Latin (mainly) and in Arabic. The question to be considered here is whether Llull's discussion of theological issues changes when he uses Catalan instead of the language of the literati. Does Llull in fact create a "vernacular theology" in the same manner as the vernacular writers of late medieval England?[3] Or is Llull's use of the Catalan vernacular incidental to his real purpose, that of propagating the *Ars*?

From the twelfth century onward, there was a marked growth in attempts by Christians to convert the Jews. Indicators of this trend are the proliferation of polemical tracts written against the Jews and, particularly in the thirteenth century, records of public and private disputations. Suffice it to mention the public disputations of Paris in 1240 and Barcelona in 1263, the more private disputation of Majorca in 1286, and the conversations between clerics of both faiths recorded in their respective works.[4] Many of these Jewish-Christian encounters have received attention from scholars, who have noted the growing sophistication and use of philosophical reasoning in these debates, along with the use of a greater pool of sources, particularly rabbinical, which could be trawled by Christians for proof of the falsity of Judaism and the truth of Christianity.[5] From the point of view of most of these scholars, the high point was reached with the completion of the Dominican Ramon Martí's *Pugio fidei* (Dagger of faith) in 1278, which not only used many Jewish sources but cited the texts in Hebrew, translated them into Latin, and incorporated them into a sustained and organized attack on Judaism.[6]

Yet what has not been noticed is that there was rarely any true dialogue between Jews and Christians; nor was there a real attempt to create a framework for that dialogue. If conversion of another from the other's religion to one's own is a process of convincing the other of one's own truth claims, then this is not what was happening here.[7] Even when a representative of Judaism stood face-to-face with his Christian interlocutor, they talked at each other, rather than with each other. From the Christian viewpoint, the disputation should rather be seen as an attempt to bolster Christian belief by proving the absurdity of Judaism.[8] The penetration of Aristotle and his commentators into the Latin intellectual world and the adoption of their philosophical method brought to the fore the difficulties of subjecting religious truth to philosophical investigation.[9] The result was a two-tier system of reason and faith within Christianity, in which reason could be treated as authoritative only up to a certain point. In practice, this meant that while Judaism, and by extension Islam, might be proved wrong, the doctrines of Christianity demanded belief, that is, certitude concerning their verity, but they were not regarded as provable.[10]

From the Jewish viewpoint, the balance of power in the Latin world dictated that the Christian majority, rather than the Jewish minority, instigate polemic. In the main, Jews were forced to partake in the disputation and reply to the Christian attack, and could rarely, if ever, force the Christians to examine their own beliefs. As dialogue, this was an exercise in futility, for neither party truly came to grips with the doctrines or the person of the other. Instead, debate centered on how the common sacred texts should be interpreted: a focus that allowed both sides to refrain from arguing the central issues or reaching firm conclusions, since each side, especially the Jewish underdog, could retreat into its own hermeneutical approach. Because the disputation was not based on a shared set of assumptions or concepts, both Christian and Jew could claim victory because they had not really engaged with one another.

Suffice it here to give one example from the Barcelona disputation, in which a convert to Christianity, Friar Paul, disputed with Nahmanides, the leader of the Jewish community in Catalonia, in the presence of the king, James I.[11] In this case, we are lucky to have a Hebrew and a Latin account of the debate, written by the protagonists themselves for their respective communities, which when read together give a good idea of what actually occurred. Friar Paul, wanting to prove that the Messiah had already come, cited Genesis 49:10, "The sceptre shall not pass away from Judah . . . until he comes to whom it belongs," then stated that "since it is certain that in Judah there is [now] neither sceptre nor leader, it is certain that the Messiah who was to be sent has come." Nahmanides had no difficulty in refuting this claim; he simply explained that the verse did not mean "that the kingdom of Judah would continue without any interruption, but that it would never pass away from him and cease for ever" and that whenever there was a king, he would be from the tribe of Judah. Paul goes on to cite from rabbinical texts that show that till the time of Jesus there had always been rulers from the tribe of Judah, and with the coming of Jesus, "the sceptre had departed."[12] Again Nahmanides is not hard-pressed to read the texts in a way that does not presume the Christological reading, even where he himself disagrees with the cited rabbinical text.[13] As can be seen from the two reports, each side was writing for his own textual community: Paul to show how he confounded the Jew and revealed his perfidy, and Nahmanides to illustrate that the Jewish understanding of the text did not admit the Christian claims.[14]

The problems of interreligious disputation for the purpose of conversion were thus, first, that debate involved reading of texts using incommensurate hermeneutical assumptions and, second, that engagement with the opponent only through the medium of a text, however sophisticated, meant the parties involved had no reason to learn anything real about each other's beliefs and opinions. Over and above these problems, given the unequal situation in which the disputations took place, one side was always at a disadvantage. This was not something Llull could hope to change; nor, if it ever occurred to him, would he have wanted to. However, he was very aware of the futility of polemic based on the interpretation of authoritative texts and so conceived of a different framework, within which each side would have to engage with the beliefs of the other.

Llull's understanding of the futility of disputation based on the combined use of reason and authority is expressed in a story he recounts a number of times in his literary corpus.[15] The version in his *Liber de acquisitione Terrae Sanctae* is significant because it highlights the difficulties faced by his contemporaries in creating dialogue; although the account deals primarily with Christian-Muslim encounters, its ending brings the difficulties of Christian-Jewish encounters into focus. The incident described probably refers to the Dominican Ramon Martí (author of the *Pugio fidei*), who, on a mission in Tunis in 1268–69, was able to prove to the sultan, Al-Mustansir, the falsehood of Islam. The sultan said to the friar, "I no longer want to be a Muslim; prove to me the truth of your faith so that I can become a Christian along with all my subjects." The friar replied: "It is impossible to prove the Christian faith; however, I have here the creed in Arabic; believe in it." Al-Mustansir was furious, because he was not willing to convert from Islam to Christianity without definitive proof. The sultan now felt that he had become a man with no faith, and he had the Dominican expelled from his territories. Llull goes on to recount that the same friar knew Hebrew and used to dispute frequently in Barcelona with a learned rabbi.[16] The latter told Llull he had said to the friar that, if he could prove what he preached, he, the rabbi, would convert to Christianity. Martí, of course, could not prove the doctrines of his own faith, and so the rabbi steadfastly remained a Jew.[17]

The point Llull was trying to make was that his Christian contemporaries were unsuccessful evangelists because they did not have the tools to construct an acceptable framework for dialogue, whether the opponent was Jew or Muslim. The use of reason along with authority to demolish the theological base of the other's faith was useless if reason could not also be applied to Christian dogmas. Llull proposed that the use of his *Ars* allowed all parties to start from the same vantage point and employ the same conceptual tools. Starting from these general premises, they would be able to examine the tenets of their faiths and come to conclusions regarding which was true.

From the outset, however, it is important to stress that if Llull was set on creating a "common tongue" for dialogue, it was a heavily slanted one, in that the end result was preconceived. If a language is made up of vocabulary, syntax, and grammar that allow one to express a broad variety of ideas, including even those illogical or contradictory in nature, the principles and conditions governing Llull's *Ars* create a framework in which the seemingly endless propositions and questions that can be formed are, in reality, so contrived as to lead eventually to a preconceived truth. The *Ars* prohibits the formation of any statements that, although apparently logical, contradict a particular Neo-platonic conception of being and reality necessary for demonstrating the truth of Christianity.[18]

Llull differed from many of his contemporaries involved in conversion work. He was an autodidact, and his formative learning was mainly from the book of life rather than the books of the theologians and universities. Born into the noble classes in Majorca (c. 1232), which had recently been recon-quered from the Muslims by James I, he grew up in an important port city with a multicultural and multireligious population. Jews, Christians, and Muslims mingled in the streets and marketplaces, and someone with Llull's acute sense of observation could not have helped learning much about the beliefs and habits of members of the other faiths.[19]

Llull's conversion from the worldly life to the religious was a result of recur-rent visions of Christ on the cross in the corner of his room; his creation of his "new" framework for religious debate was the result of another revelation some nine years later.[20] The visions, which occurred when he was in his thir-ties, led him to understand that he must devote his life to three things: the conversion of unbelievers, for which he was prepared to lay down his life; the establishment of monasteries where the necessary languages could be taught; and the writing of a book against the errors of unbelievers.[21]

This book was the framework of the *Ars,* which was divinely revealed to Llull and with which he was certain he would convince unbelievers of the truth of Christianity.[22] The development of this "common tongue" also led to Llull's excursions into almost all the fields of knowledge to show how every-thing was reducible to the most simple and general principle: God. The *Ars* was a language whose grammar and syntax were the dynamic structure of creation, true knowledge of which revealed the internal and eternal structure of the divine. Using general principles, conditions, and rules acceptable to all three monotheistic faiths, the Artist would discover the inherent nature of the supreme being. According to Llull, the religion revealed to be truly compati-ble with this divinely inspired *Ars* was Christianity. In other words, it is not that the other faiths are based on false premises but that they do not fully understand the language of reality. Disputation based on the framework of the *Ars* would allow members of each faith to explore their own religious doc-trines and those of the other faiths and to reach the necessary conclusions.

In effect, Llull was trying to create a new textual community in which religious disputation could take place in a common tongue and the disputants would have to engage with each other rather than with an authoritative text.[23]

By agreeing to dispute according to the principles, rules, and conditions of the *Ars,* with which they could have little reason to disagree, the interlocutors were forced to question and prove central doctrines of their faiths rather than engage in hermeneutical sophistry. They were also asked to examine their conceptions and understanding of the essence of God and the divine nature and the relationship between God and creation. At least in his early works, Llull also envisioned a more mystical aspect to the debate: as the sides progressed toward (Christian) truth, they would transcend sense and rational knowledge, and truth would be comprehended through direct cognition of God. Correct use of the *Ars* would lead to mystical knowledge of the triune structure of the divine essence.

The first exposition of the "form and method" of the *Ars* was the *Ars compendiosa inveniendi veritatem,* or the *Brief Art of Finding Truth,* probably written in 1274. Before this, Llull had written the *Libre de contemplació en Deu,* a mammoth encyclopedia that surveys the whole of being, sensible and intelligible, human and divine, visible and invisible, intermingling logical exposition with ecstatic outcries of joy and happiness. In this work are to be found the seeds of all his later thought, but without the organization and terminology that will provide the framework for disputation.[24] The divine revelation on Mount Randa provided Llull with the tools for organizing his broad-ranging ideas into a coherent structure. This structure would be continually edited, refined, and improved over the next thirty years, the last redactions being the *Ars generalis ultima,* written 1305–8, and its shorter and popular companion, the *Ars brevis.*

Llull was well aware that questions regarding the nature of the divine and God's relation with creation were taxing the minds of his religious contemporaries. He felt certain that if Muslims and Jews could be convinced that the divine essence must be internally and eternally triune and that the incarnation was necessary, then they would have to admit the truth of Christianity and convert. Thus, Llull based his *Ars* on the fundamental belief of all three monotheistic faiths that there exists one God who is the cause of all things and who created the world. The *Ars* revolves around the figure A, a circle with a series of letters equally spaced around the circumference representing, in the quaternary phase of the *Ars,* the divine attributes and, in the ternary phase, principles that in their perfection represent God.[25] Whether called *Dignitates, Sefirot,* or *Hadras,* Llull proposed that all discussion start from these most general principles believed by all to exist in God in concordance and without any contrariety. Given that the world is created in the image of God, and playing on the Neoplatonic maxim *Bonum est diffusivum sui* (Goodness necessarily diffuses itself), Llull suggested that creation is a likeness of these perfect divine dignities. As Anthony Bonner puts it, for Llull, "each of the dignities has its effect in the world in accordance with the individual creature's capacity to receive the likeness of God, and the degree of the creature's concordance with the dignities."[26] Hence, all of being reflects the divine structure, and by demonstrating the structure of being, one will have knowledge of the divine.

Using what Llull refers to as "necessary reason," which is the form of the *Ars,* it is possible to descend from the most general principle, God, to the most particular or to ascend from the most particular to that most general principle. Thus, nature, or creation, becomes a *scala,* a ladder of being, by which man could ascend from sense to rational knowledge and from rational knowledge to the discovery of "the supreme being in whom all the divine names coincide or fall together."[27] The other figures of the *Ars,* especially figure T, allow the intellect to examine multifarious propositions, affirming or negating them using the elements of creation as metaphors or analogies. What emerges is that the intellect realizes that the dynamic activity of the dignities in creation can only be understood in a triune structure, and what is true of creation must be true of God. The mature form of this thought is referred to as the theory of the correlatives of action.[28]

The latter is best explained by quoting a passage from Llull's selective biography, recounted to "certain monks who were friends of his," that exemplifies Llull's use of the *Ars* for conversion purposes. The dialogue described here took place in Tunis 1292, after Llull had recovered from a serious psychological crisis in Genoa, which almost led him to abandon his mission altogether. Upon arriving in Tunis, Llull, according to his account, proclaimed his willingness to convert to Islam if the Muslim scholars were able to prove conclusively the foundations of their faith. Over the course of the next few days, numerous scholars tried their luck, but Llull was able to overcome them, saying:

> It is proper for every wise man to hold to that faith which attributes to the eternal God, in whom all the wise men of the world believe, the greatest goodness, wisdom, virtue, truth, glory, perfection, etc., and all these things in the greatest equality and concordance. And most praiseworthy is that faith in God which places the greatest concordance or agreement between God, who is the highest and first cause, and His effect.
>
> However, as a result of what you have set before me, I see that all you Saracens who belong to the religion of Mohammed do not understand that in the above and other similar Divine Dignities there are proper, intrinsic and eternal acts, without which the dignities

49

would be idle, and this from all eternity. The acts of goodness, I call bonificative [*bonificativum*], bonifiable [*bonificabile*], and bonifying [*bonificar*], while those of greatness are magnificative, magnifiable, and magnifying, and so on for the other aforesaid dignities.

But since, as I already see, you attribute those acts only to two divine dignities or reasons, that is to wisdom and will,[29] it is thus clear that you leave the other above-mentioned dignities in a state of idleness, consequently placing inequality as well as discord between them, which is not right. For by means of the substantial, intrinsic, and eternal acts of the Dignities, Reasons or Attributes, taken equally and concordantly, as they should be, Christians clearly prove that in one complete simple Divine essence and nature, there exists a Trinity of persons, namely the Father, the Son and the Holy Ghost.[30]

Llull was lucky to escape this encounter with his life, since important Muslims called for his execution. Finally he was shipped out of Tunis with express orders never to return. However, what is immediately apparent from this dispute is Llull's willingness to engage with the mysteries of the Christian faith and prove them conclusively. He starts from what is common to all the faiths, the divine dignities, and is able to show both Jew and Muslim that their own understanding of the existence of dignities in God must imply a trinitarian structure. For if one wants to avoid change in the Godhead, then there is no alternative but to admit the existence of a triad of agent-patient-action within the dignities, which are the divine essence. These correlatives of action are imperative in order to explain how creation could take place without implying change at a particular moment in the Godhead. In other words, for creation to come about without change in the Godhead, the dignities would have had to be active eternally, and this action can only exist without implying plurality if it is triune.[31]

From what we have seen so far, it is possible to observe how the *Ars* functions as a vernacular, in the sense that it creates a "common tongue" for dialogue between the three faiths. Instead of being confrontational, the *Ars* provides a jumping-off point for debate and also the framework and tools to be used for that debate. Essentially, there is nothing in the basic premises that is problematic for any of the three faiths, and if all the sides agree to the rules, the interlocutors can range over a wide series of issues, progressing to a realization of the necessary truth of the Christian faith.

One of Llull's earliest works shows, almost too successfully, how this can be put into practice. The *Book of the Gentile and the Three Wise Men,* written between 1274 and 1276, describes an imaginary debate between a Jew, a

Christian, and a Muslim in rural surroundings. The use of the framework and conditions of the *Ars* by the wise men allows each one of them to prove the doctrines of their respective faiths. In this work, we do not yet find the developed theory of the correlatives, and here, a naïve Llull relies to a much greater extent on the active participation of the reader. He envisions the book as a map for progressing along the mystical path to revelation and cognition of the trinitarian God. In other words, the narrative as a whole and its metaphors take on a figurative meaning. For someone capable of comprehending what they encode, they articulate how to progress toward and achieve knowledge of the divine being. This was an experiment that Llull did not repeat; the far more structural approach of the correlatives did not rely solely on mystical states of realization.[32]

The *Book of the Gentile* leads us to the issue of language in Llull's literary corpus. This work, like many of Llull's others, was written in Catalan, though he also wrote in Latin and Arabic. One of his claims to fame, and a source of pride for modern Catalans, is that he was the first to write prose novels as well as theological, philosophical, and scientific works in a Romance language.[33] However, Llull's choice of languages was as pragmatic as the way he chose to portray certain issues, and depended only on the target audience. Latin was the language of the literate, the language of politics and power, and Llull, in order to further his mission, worked hard to achieve international recognition of the *Ars*'s potential. He was a frequent visitor at the courts of kings and popes, and he lectured on the *Ars* at the university of Paris and Montpellier with varying degrees of success. He wrote many works in Latin, expounding the framework of the *Ars* and showing how it could be used to prove the doctrines of the faith and how it could be applied to other fields of knowledge as well. He also compiled preaching manuals for missionaries and for the church and clearly hoped to place his *Ars* at the center of intellectual pursuits.

On the other hand, Llull realized that success of any campaign of conversion hinged on knowledge of the other's language. He was a strong supporter and propagandist for the foundation of language schools, and perhaps one of his singular achievements was Canon 24 of the Council of Vienne in 1312, which advocated the foundation of schools for the study of Arabic, Hebrew, and Syriac in Paris, Oxford, Bologna, Avignon, and Salamanca.[34] Llull's use of Catalan and Arabic is reflective of his recognition of language's importance, since within the borders of the Mediterranean world in which he was active as a missionary these two languages gave him the freedom to converse with both Jews and Muslims. First and foremost, use of the vernacular allowed him to reach his target audience and to do away with one of the formidable barriers to cross-cultural dialogue, the problem of a common language. Nevertheless, although Llull was really innovative in writing theology and philosophy in the vernacular, he viewed Catalan as no more than a formal tool to aid him in achieving his stated purpose: the conversion of the nonbelievers.

Far more important for Llull was the language of the *Ars,* for it was here that he created something new. He tried to speak a language that transcended religious and cultural borders and that sounded familiar to his interlocutors, forcing them to have to deal with its implications. This vernacular was very different from anything spoken or written in the Latin world, and Llull needed to provide continual justification for its use as well as to remind his Christian contemporaries that he, too, was an orthodox Catholic.[35] The justification took the form of claiming divine revelation for the *Ars.* If the *Ars* was revealed to Llull by God, then he had authority on his side.[36] Avowing divine authorship was also important for the work of conversion, because Llull could claim to be speaking a divine language. Revelation legitimized his shift of interreligious dialogue away from authoritative texts and toward the *Ars.* This can be seen from the continuation of the passage quoted above, where Llull says he can definitively prove the Trinity and Incarnation "with the help of God, using clear arguments based on a certain Art divinely revealed, as it is believed, to a Christian hermit [i.e., Llull] not long ago."[37]

Llull was acutely aware of the problems raised by the figures and terms of the *Ars.* His first trip to Paris in 1288 to teach the *Ars* at the university was a disaster because of what was referred to as his *modus loquendi arabicus,* "Arabic mode of speech."[38] One result of this fiasco was a redaction of the *Ars* that simplified it by reducing the number of figures and the alphabet and giving it a much more recognizable Christological form. This change has been described as the move from a quaternary phase, where the alphabet of the *Ars* revolved around sixteen letters (multiples of four), to a ternary phase of nine letters (multiples of three). Llull also abandoned his analogical and exemplary method of demonstration for a more recognizable form of scholastic logic using propositions and syllogisms. Yet, while these changes resolved the issue of the framework and the method of argumentation, the problem of the Arabic mode of speech remained and could not so easily be changed.

In his first book dealing with the Articles of Faith (written in Latin between 1283 and 1285), Llull writes, "Great is the necessity that we should search for the appropriate vocabulary by way of which we will be able to declare and prove the intrinsic activity that is in our Lord God," and he then lists each of the divine dignities with the infinitive form of the verb that expresses its dynamic activity—*bonitate, bonificare; magnitudine, magnificar,* etc.—as the appropriate language for talking about God. He continues, "However, since this vocabulary is necessary for proving the acts of the divine dignities, none should wonder if this vocabulary transcends the usual rules of grammar."[39] At the end of a commentary on the *Ars demonstrativa* that Llull wrote and lectured on in Paris in 1288, he reiterated this, begging that the scholars of the university pay more attention to the contents of the *Ars* and not reject it because of its unusual grammatical forms.[40] The problem was that Llull was trying to translate the theological language of his Muslim and Jewish contemporaries into Latin and Catalan. What makes sense in Hebrew and Arabic, deriving transitive and passive verb forms from a noun in order to express agent and patient (i.e., the object doing good and the subject receiving that good), did not work very well in Latin and Romance languages. However, this was a fundamental and central feature of the *Ars* as a vernacular, crucial for demonstrating the inherent truth of the Trinity and Incarnation. The "Arabic mode of speech" of the correlatives of action was the key for a Christian reading of God and the creation and would force Jews and Muslims to reexamine their beliefs.[41]

Llull's success at defending the integrity of the *Ars* can be seen from his third teaching experience in Paris, from 1309 to 1311. This time, the masters and students of the Faculties of Arts came to hear his lectures on the *Ars brevis* and approved of them.[42] However, the masters of theology, whom Llull most wanted to impress and persuade of the value of his *Ars,* were notable in their absence. It is perhaps not surprising that a second condemnation of Llull's *Ars,* critical of his involuted language, emanated from the Faculty of Theology in Paris at the instigation of Jean Gerson in 1390.[43]

Seeing the *Ars* as a vernacular for conversion has helped establish and sharpen the differences between Llull and his mendicant contemporaries also engaged in the conversion effort. The latter worked on the assumption that the mysteries of Christianity were beyond proof and that therefore the focus should be on disproving the faith of the other. This could be done using a combination of reason and authority. During the thirteenth century, knowledge and criticism of Islam were based on a small number of translated works.[44] Christian knowledge of the Jewish sources, on the other hand, was greater than at any other time, and this reservoir was trawled for the purpose of proving that the rabbis secretly knew and admitted the truth of Christianity. As we have seen, this was superb Christian sophistry but not a very good conversion tactic, since Jewish scholars brushed aside these claims with their own, alternative hermeneutics. Llull's *Ars,* however, in theory, did not allow escape by any of the sides in the dispute, forcing them to engage with the foundations of their beliefs. If the term "vernacular" can mean more than just a spoken or written language, if it can be a mode of expression, a form or system, that attempts to create greater understanding between disparate cultural or religious entities, then the *Ars,* with its figures, rules, and terminology, created a vernacular, a divinely revealed language, a common tongue, a textual community, for religious debate.

NOTES

1. Dante, *De vulgari eloquentia,* ed. and trans. S. Botterill (Cambridge: Cambridge University Press, 1996), 40.

2. This is a theme developed in *De vulgari eloquentia,* where Dante suggests that the *forma locutionis* given by God to Adam resulted in the birth of Hebrew. In the *Paradiso,* Adam is made to imply that even the Hebrew spoken before the events of the Tower of Babel does not reflect the perfect language with which Adam addressed God (see the Introduction to this volume).

3. See, e.g., Nicholas Watson, "Conceptions of the Word" (see Further Reading, page 257).

4. For English translations of the disputations of 1240 and 1263, see Hyam Maccoby, ed., *Judaism on Trial: Jewish-Christian Disputations in the Middle Ages* (Rutherford, N.J.: Fairleigh Dickinson University Press; London: Associated University Presses, 1982). For the Majorca disputation, see Ora Limor, *Die Disputationen zu Ceuta (1179) und Mallorca (1286): Zwei antijüdische Schriften aus dem mittelalterichen Genua,* Monumenta Germaniae Historica: Quellen zur Geistesgeschichte des Mittelalters, vol. 15 (Munich: Monumenta Germaniae Historica, 1994).

5. See Jeremy Cohen, *The Friars and the Jews: The Evolution of Medieval Anti-Judaism* (Ithaca: Cornell University Press, 1982); Robert Chazan, *Daggers of Faith: Thirteenth-Century Christian Missionizing and Jewish Response* (Berkeley and Los Angeles: University of California Press, 1989).

6. See, most recently, Jeremy Cohen, *Living Letters of the Law: Ideas of the Jew in Medieval Christianity* (Berkeley and Los Angeles: University of California Press, 1999), 342–63.

7. Forced conversion is totally different and was not normally supported by the church hierarchy. Ramon de Penyafort, the thirteenth-century minister-general of the Dominicans and confessor to King James I, wrote in his *Summa de poenitentia,* ed. Javier Ochoa Sanz and Aloisio Diez (Rome: Commentarium pro Religiosis, 1976), 309: "Tam iudaei quam sarraceni auctoritatibus, rationibus et blandimentis, potius quam asperitatibus, ad fidem christianam de novo suscipiendam provocari, non autem compelli, quia coacta servitia non placet Deo." On conversion as a process, see Karl F. Morrison, *Understanding Conversion* (Charlottesville: University Press of Virginia, 1992).

8. I argue elsewhere that the public disputations and works like *Pugio fidei* were more a reflection of Christian internal needs than an attempt to convert the Jews. See Anna Sapir Abulafia, *Christians and Jews in the Twelfth-Century Renaissance* (London: Routledge, 1995).

9. See Marie-Dominique Chenu, *Nature, Man, and Society in the Twelfth Century: Essays on New Theological Perspectives in the Latin West* (Chicago: Chicago University Press, 1968). For the correlation between the infiltration of these teachings and a growing lack of tolerance in Christian society, see R. I. Moore, *The Formation of a Persecuting Society: Power and Deviance in Western Europe, 950–1250* (Oxford: Blackwell, 1987).

10. "Articuli fidei demonstrative probari non possunt," Ramon Martí, *Pugio fidei adversus Mauros et Judaeos* (Leipzig, 1687; facs., Farnborough, Hants: Gregg Press, 1967), 229. See Harvey Hames, "Approaches to Conversion in the Late Thirteenth-Century Church," *Studia Lulliana* 35 (1995): 75–84.

11. On Friar Paul, see, most recently, J. Shatzmiller, "Paulus Christiani un aspect de son activité anti-juive," in Gérard Nahon and Charles Touati, eds., *Hommage a Georges Vajda: Études d'histoire et de pensée juives* (Louvain: Peeters, 1980), 203–17, and citations given in note 5 above.

12. For an English translation of both versions of the disputation, see Maccoby, *Judaism on Trial,*

102–46, 147–50. For the parts cited here, see 105–11 and 148–49. See also Carlos del Valle Rodriguez, "La disputa de Barcelona de 1263," in Carlos de Valle Rodriquez, ed., *La controversia judeocristiana en España (Desde el orígenes hasta el siglo XIII)* (Madrid: Consejo Superior de Investigaciones Científicas, Instituto de Filología, 1998), 277–91.

13. See, e.g, M. Fox, "Nahmanides on the Status of Aggadot: Perspectives on the Disputation of Barcelona, 1263," *Journal of Jewish Studies* 40 (1989): 95–109, and E. Wolfson, "By the Way of Truth: Aspects of Nahmanides Kabbalistic Hermeneutic," *AJS Review* 14 (1989): 153–78.

14. See further Robert Chazan, *Barcelona and Beyond: The Disputation of 1263 and Its Aftermath* (Berkeley and Los Angeles: University of California Press, 1992), 100–141.

15. That Llull recounts this one story seven times in his corpus is clear demonstration of its importance to him. See, for example, his Catalan didactic novel *Felix,* bk. 1:7, translated in Anthony Bonner, *Selected Works of Ramon Llull (1232–1316),* 2 vols. (Princeton: Princeton University Press, 1985), 2:693–94 (henceforth SWRL).

16. For the identification of the rabbi, see Jeremy Cohen, "The Christian Adversary of Solomon ibn Adret," *Jewish Quarterly Review* 71 (1980–81): 48–55.

17. *De acquisitione Terrae Sanctae,* in Eugenio Kamar, ed., *Projet de Raymond Lull "De acquisitione Terrae Sanctae" (introduction et édition critique du texte),* Studia Orientalia Christiana, Collectanea 6 (Cairo: Centro Francescano di Studi Orientali Christiani, 1961), 3.1, 126–27.

18. For a demonstration of the limitations of the *Ars,* see a passage from the *Ars demonstrativa* in SWRL 1:339, dealing with the conditions of the *Ars.* See J. M. Ruiz Simon, *L'art de Ramon Llull i la teoria escolàstica de la ciència* (Barcelona: Quaderns Crema, 1999).

19. See, e.g., David Abulafia, *A Mediterranean Emporium: The Catalan Kingdom of Majorca* (Cambridge: Cambridge University Press, 1994), 75–99. On the Jewish community in Majorca, see, e.g., J. N. Hillgarth, "Sources for the History of the Jews of Majorca," *Traditio* 50 (1995): 334–41.

20. Llull himself often used the adjective "new" to describe what he was doing: see, e.g., his *Lògica nova* and its companion *Liber de modo applicandi novam logicam ad scientiam juris et medicinae,* or *Tractatus novus de astronomia, Rhetorica nova.*

21. Llull dictated a selective biography, the *Vita coetanea,* just before he set off for the Council of Vienne in 1311; see SRWL 1:3–52. For his life, see J. N. Hillgarth, *Ramon Lull and Lullism in Fourteenth-Century France* (Oxford: Clarendon, 1971).

22. See the *Vita coetanea,* SWRL 1:22–23. Llull's claim to revelation is similar to that of the Kabbalists also spreading new and revolutionary (although portrayed as ancient) ideas in the communities of southern France and the Crown of Aragon at the same time. See Harvey Hames, *The Art of Conversion* (see Further Reading), 31–82.

23. I have borrowed the term "textual community" from Brian Stock, *The Implications of Literacy: Written Language and Models of Interpretation in the Eleventh and Twelfth Centuries* (Princeton: Princeton University Press, 1983). See Anthony Bonner, "L'art lulliana com a autoritat alternativa," *Studia Lulliana* 33 (1993): 15–32.

24. On this mammoth work, see J. E. Rubio, *Les bases del pensament de Ramon Llull* (Valencia: Institut de Filologia Valenciana, 1997).

25. The quaternary phase of the Art runs from c. 1274 to 1289, the ternary from 1290 to 1308; SWRL 1:55–56.

26. See SWRL 1:60.

27. See C. Lohr, "Metaphysics," in C. B. Schmitt et al., *The Cambridge History of Renaissance Philosophy* (Cambridge: Cambridge University Press, 1988), 541.

28. On the theory of the correlatives, see Jordi Gayà Estelrich, *La teoria Luliana de los correlativos: Historia de su formacion conceptual* (Palma, 1979).

29. These triads are found in Judaism and Islam. See Maimonides, *Guide of the Perplexed,* ed. and trans. Shlomo Pines (Chicago: University of Chicago Press, 1963), 163–66, where the triad *maskil*

muskal haskalah is used. See also W. C. Chittick, *The Sufi Path of Knowledge: Ibn al-'Arabi's Metaphysics of Imagination* (Albany: State University of New York Press, 1989), 106. See C. Lohr, "Christianus arabicus cuius nomen Raimundus Lullus," *Freiburger Zeitschrift für Philosophie und Theologie* 31 (1984): 84–86.

30. SWRL 1:34–35.

31. See further Hames, *Art of Conversion*, 190–245.

32. See Harvey Hames, "Conversion via Ecstatic Experience in Ramon Llull's *Llibre del gentil e dels tres savis*," *Viator* 30 (1999): 181–200.

33. The two famous didactic novels are *Blanquerna* (written in 1283, published as *Libre de Evast e Blanquerna,* 3 vols., Els nostres classics [Barcelona: Barcelona Editorial Barcino, 1935–54], and translated into English by A. E. Peers, *Blanquerna* [London: Jarrolds, 1926]) and *Felix* (written in 1288–89 [see note 15 above]).

34. See B. Altaner, "Raimundus Lullus und der Sprachenkanon des Konzils von Vienne," *Historisches Jahrbuch* 52 (1933): 190–219. On the issue of the *studium Arabicum,* see R. I. Burns, "Christian-Islamic Confrontation in the West: The Thirteenth-Century Dream of Conversion," *American Historical Review* 76 (1971): 386–411; R. W. Southern, *Western Views of Islam in the Middle Ages* (Cambridge, Mass.: Harvard University Press, 1962).

35. See, for example, the *Liber praedicationis contra Iudaeos,* in *Raimundi Lulli Opera Latina,* vol. 12, *Corpus Christianorum Continuatio Mediaevalis* (Turnhout: Brepols, 1984), 14: "Et si forte in isto libro erraverimus contra sanctam fidem catholicam, aut improprie locuti erimus, submittimus ipsum ad correctionem sanctae fidei catholicae, tamquam fidelis catholicus, qui sum." For other examples, see *Liber de quattuordecim articulis sacrosanctae Romanae Catholicae Fidei,* in *Raymundi Lulli Opera omnia,* ed. I. Salzinger, 8 vols. (1–6, 9–10) (Mainz, 1721–42), vi, pp. 2, 190 [henceforth MOG]; *Disputatio fidelis et infidelis,* in MOG 4, vi, p. 2; *Liber de novo modo demonstrandi,* in MOG 4, xvi, p. 16.

36. On this tactic, see R. Lerner, "Ecstatic Dissent," *Speculum* 67 (1992): 33–57.

37. SWRL 1:35.

38. Llull lectured on the Art using his *Compendium seu Commentum Artis demonstrativae,* in MOG 3, vi, pp. 1–160, and in this work he apologizes for the Arabic mode of speech (160). Llull also briefly recounts his experience in Paris in the *Vita.* See SWRL 1:29.

39. *Liber de quattuordecim articulis sacrosanctae Romana Catholicae Fidei,* in MOG 2, vi, pp. 1–190.

40. *Compendium seu Commentum Artis demonstrativae,* 159–60 (see note 38 above). See also Bonner, "L'art lulliana com a autoritat alternativa," 15–32, and his "Ramon Llull: Autor, autoritat i illuminat" (see Further Reading).

41. On this issue, see R. D. F. Pring-Mill, "The Trinitarian World Picture of Ramon Lull," *Romanistisches Jahrbuch* 7 (1955–56): 229–56, and his "Ramón Llull y las tres potencias del alma," *Estudios Lulianos* 12 (1968): 101–30.

42. There are three documents that attest to Llull's success. They are found in Heinrich Denifle and Emile Châtelain, *Chartularium universitatis Parisiensis,* 4 vols (Paris: H. Didier, 1889–97), 2:140–41, 144, 148–49. These documents have been discussed by Hillgarth, *Ramon Lull and Lullism in Fourteenth-Century France,* 118–19, 155.

43. This edict prohibited the teaching of Llull's works in Paris and included opposition to his supposed rationalism. This condemnation goes hand in hand with that of the Dominican inquisitor-general of Aragon, Nicholas Eimerich, of 1376, and his list of one hundred errors in Llull's works. See Miquel Batllori, "Entorn del lullisme a França," in *A través de la història i la cultura* (Montserrat: Publicacions de l'Abadia de Montserrat, 1979), 244–45, and Alois Madre, *Die theologische Polemik gegen Raimundus Lullus* (Münster: Aschendorff, 1973).

44. See Norman Daniel, *Islam and the West: The Making of an Image,* rev. ed. (Oxford: Oxford University Press, 1993; originally published by the University Press of Edinburgh, 1960).

Mechthild von Magdeburg

Gender and the "Unlearned Tongue"

SARA S. POOR

This essay interrogates the relationship between gender and the use of the vernacular in the medieval German religious writings of Mechthild von Magdeburg (1210–82). Scholars of German vernacular religious literature began early in the twentieth century to postulate a close, perhaps even causal, relationship between women, reading, and the beginnings of vernacular literacy.[1] This line of thinking has often led to the assumption that vernacular writing was generally intended for a female audience, especially when written down by women and in a religious context. Correspondingly, early historians of mysticism understood the emergence of vernacular mystical texts as a direct consequence of the requirement made of the mendicant orders in the thirteenth century to care for the unlearned semireligious women in their midst. This requirement resulted in what was regarded as a transposition of scholastic thought into German.[2] More recently, however, in an effort to legitimize vernacular mystical literature as *distinct* from scholastic writings, scholarly focus has turned to the relationship between the emergence of a new kind of mysticism in the thirteenth century and the emergence of the vernacular as the language best suited for its expression.[3] Women figured in this historical moment both as innovators (e.g., Mechthild and Hadewijch) and as audience (Dominican nuns, tertiaries, and beguines). Nevertheless, as Susanne Bürkle notes, even these attempts rest on the premise that the presence both of semireligious women needing guidance and of their writings (*Frauenmystik*) brings about the transition from Latin to the vernacular in mystical writing.[4] The problematic association of vernacular religious literature with a female audience and with a gender-specific set of concerns persists.

The problem with this association is that it posits a simple dichotomy equating Latin with men and the masculine, and the vernacular with women and the feminine. In the volume of his history of mysticism devoted to *Frauenmystik,* for example, Kurt Ruh lists as the first reason for the transition to the vernacular that "the *religiosae mulieres* were in large majority without higher education and mastered only their mother tongue. They spoke German,

Dutch, English, French, Italian, and if they were to be spoken to, it had to be in these idioms."[5] It is precisely this kind of statement that tends to construct such dichotomies. However, as the case of Mechthild's book, *Das fließende Licht der Gottheit* (The Flowing Light of the Godhead),[6] demonstrates, the relationship between a vernacular text and the supposedly male-dominated, masculine-coded Latinate culture cannot be thus reduced. This is not to deny the importance of gender to a discussion of vernacularity but rather to remark on the complexity of this relationship in a specific context.

Sent by God to "all religious people, both the bad and the good," Mechthild's book claims a wide, general audience. Endowed by God with the "power and voice of all creatures," Mechthild's soul claims to represent that audience in her dealings with the divinity.[7] However, rather than have her revelations recorded in Latin, the sacred and universal language of the church, she writes them down in her native language—Middle Low German (MLG), the dialect spoken in northern Germany (from the lower Rhein to Prussia).[8] In the first part of this essay, I argue that the use of the Low German vernacular here can be said to circumvent not only the official and clerical Latin but also the language of the court, Middle High German (MHG), a language that is nevertheless (and paradoxically) invoked at the same time. The revelations and visions concerning the mystical relationship with the divine display—most prominently in the first two of the seven books that make up *The Flowing Light*—the imagery and inflections of courtly literature, most of which was composed and performed in MHG. An exploration of this unusual situation thus reveals the Latin/vernacular relation to be bound up with and inflected by other linguistic, literary, religious, and political tensions: specifically, those between High and Low German, divine and courtly love, lay and cloistered forms of religious life, court and town, center and frontier or margin.[9]

In light of the text's ambitious mission, it is perhaps ironic to note that the MLG original has not survived to the present day. What has survived stems from two translations, to which I turn in the second part of the essay. The Dominicans of Halle, a city to the south of Magdeburg, made a Latin translation that was completed sometime before 1298. Some fifty years later, Heinrich von Nördlingen commissioned a translation into MHG that was completed in 1345. A cursory glance at these two branches of transmission might initially suggest a simple correspondence between female audiences and the vernacular: for example, the Latin translator made significant changes to both the order and content of Mechthild's work, changes that could be read as a masculinization of the writings for a male clerical audience. Conversely, complete copies of the MHG version were sent to communities of beguines and nuns: a fact that suggests that writing by women, especially when transmitted in the vernacular, was indeed thought most appropriate for other women. However, such a conclusion would overlook the questions about authorship, tradition, and the function of books in mendicant culture that are also raised by this transmission and that contribute to its shape.

In other words, while it may be true to some extent, it is not *enough* to say that the vernacular was considered more appropriate for women hearers and readers or for the expression and understanding of female religious experience. There is more to the story than this association. Indeed, as my analysis demonstrates, the transmission of Mechthild's text reveals that her writings could be mined for a variety of different audiences: other women mystic writers, the laity in general, and mendicant preachers. Looking more carefully at these books, their function, and the audiences they address helps us to move beyond the gendered Latin/vernacular divide. What emerges, I argue, is evidence of different degrees of ambivalence toward female authorship. This ambivalence is more prominent when the manuscript in question is more engaged with the Dominicans' and Mechthild's larger (universal, that is, didactic and salvific) mission. The transmission history thus does not attest to a simple gender dichotomy. Rather, it bears witness to a historically specific process of gendering, in which the categories of women and the universal begin to clash, as their coincidence comes to represent an ideological contradiction that must either be explained or removed.

Choosing the Vernacular

To recognize that the vernacular composition of *The Flowing Light* was significant in the late medieval context, we need only look at the introductory comments to the surviving German and Latin versions. The German version, best represented in the Einsiedeln manuscript (E), contains a Latin foreword, about a paragraph in length, followed by a kind of subject index describing what theological topics the book covers, which in turn is followed by a German translation of the initial Latin paragraph. In the foreword, the scribe declares explicitly that the writings came from God to a beguine sister in German.[10] The prologue to the Latin version, best represented by the Basel manuscript (Rb), also takes the time to mention that the revelations were "written in a primitive tongue" and that they contain "certain marvelous and previously unknown mysteries" (FL 33). For both redactions, then, it was important for readers to know that the book was originally composed in German.

We may well wonder why this is the case. The first and most obvious reason is that it was an unusual occurrence. Indeed, although Mechthild was not the first German woman associated with visionary writings, she was the first to write a book of mystical prose in German that was not a translation or adaptation of a Latin source.[11] By the 1340s, when Heinrich von Nördlingen had the Low German translated into Alemannic (a High German dialect), the writing of devotional texts in German by the "semireligious" (e.g., beguines like Mechthild) as well as by nuns had become a more common practice.[12] Yet virtually all theological writings from the twelfth century and before were in Latin, including visionary writings. Mechthild's predecessors—the Benedictine nuns Hildegard von Bingen (1098–1179) and Elisabeth von Schönau (d. 1164/5)—both published their revelations in Latin. The vernacular composition of *The Flowing Light* a century later thus marks a break with the custom of recording visionary texts in the universal and sacred language of the church.

Based on the information provided in several autobiographical chapters in Mechthild's book and in the prologue to the Latin translation, scholars have concluded that around the age of twenty Mechthild ran away from a home in a courtly setting to the city of Magdeburg, where she became a beguine.[13] She began writing in 1250, entered the convent of Helfta near Eisleben around 1270, and lived there until her death in 1282.[14] That Mechthild von Hackeborn (1241/42–99) and Gertrude the Great (1256–1301/2), Mechthild von Magdeburg's younger contemporaries at Helfta, wrote in Latin suggests that the recording of visionary material in Latin continued as a convention even as the use of the vernacular was increasing.[15] That Mechthild von Hackeborn and Gertrude were cloistered from a young age suggests that another factor in play here was the education and acculturation received in Benedictine and Cistercian convents at this time, in contrast to that received by semireligious, like Mechthild von Magdeburg, supervised by mendicant friars. Although Anne Clark correctly notes that Elisabeth's and Hildegard's visionary works mark a transition in visionary writing, pointing forward to women visionaries like Mechthild of the thirteenth and fourteenth centuries,[16] Mechthild can be distinguished from her predecessors in that she was not a member of a recognized order, or cloistered, when she began writing. She did not have Hildegard's fluency in Latin or her position of authority as founder and abbess of a convent, to say nothing of her official permission from the pope to write, garnered with the help of Bernard of Clairvaux. Nor did Mechthild have a situation like Elisabeth's, in which a brother in an adjoining monastery "managed" her visions for dissemination in Latin. These distinctions might lead us to tie Mechthild's use of the vernacular exclusively to her uncloistered lay status. This is certainly part of the story, but not of all of it.

Mechthild was not the only woman in northern Europe who wrote a mystical text in the vernacular in the thirteenth century. A few words on these contemporaries will demonstrate how difficult it is to attribute the use of the vernacular or Latin to any one sociohistorical "condition." Beatrice of Nazareth (c. 1200–1268) lived as a nun at three different convents in the vicinity of Liège, after receiving instruction in the liberal arts from beguines in Leau (Zoutleeuw).[17] As a Cistercian nun, Beatrice would presumably have been taught that Latin was the appropriate language for sacred writings, but her *vita* reports that she kept a secret written record of her revelations in the vernacular (Middle Dutch)—all, except for one treatise, now lost. Beatrice's decision to write in Dutch, in spite of her access to convent education, suggests that the choice of the vernacular for visionary writings need not have been *solely* contingent upon the person's status as lay or cloistered, beguine or nun.

Another contemporary of Mechthild's, Hadewijch of Antwerp (fl. 1240s), seems to have been a beguine. Hadewijch's letters, visions, and poetry are all written in Middle Dutch.[18] Although we know nothing of her early life and education, it is clear from her frequent allusions to theologians and to the Vulgate that she could read Latin fluently. And yet she, too, chose the vernacular. In her case, the most significant factor might indeed have been an audience of fellow beguines. Nevertheless, the fact that Letter 12 was addressed to the abbot of a local male monastery reminds us that her audience was not always uniform.

Agnes Blannbekin (c. 1244–1315), a beguine from Vienna, is also worth mentioning briefly. The daughter of a farmer, who at the age of ten formed the desire to become a beguine, Agnes dictated her life and revelations to her Franciscan confessor, who wrote them down in Latin.[19] Chapter 127 in the revelations, about her perusal of a book of hours, suggests that Agnes could read. It is unclear, however, whether she could write. In this case, then, we have a beguine, like Mechthild, dictating to a Latinate scribe, as did Elisabeth the Benedictine nun. Neither status as a beguine nor a lack of education precludes a text's being produced in Latin.

Agnes's example notwithstanding, the thirteenth and fourteenth centuries are characterized by an increased use of the vernacular for devotional writings, and not merely by women. Meister Eckhart (c. 1260–1328) and his younger contemporaries Johannes Tauler (1300–1368) and Heinrich Seuse (1295–1366) all wrote German as well as Latin treatises and sermons. These are only the best-known figures.[20] To delve into the works of each of these men would reach beyond the scope of this essay, but I wish to mention a few relevant points. While the evidence strongly suggests that Mechthild, Hadewijch, and Beatrice all composed and wrote down their texts in their mother tongues, even if some of those originals are now lost, much of Eckhart's vernacular writing stems from notes taken by people listening to his sermons.[21] Several of these sermons attracted the scrutiny and condemnation of the inquisition.[22] Most likely because of Eckhart's difficulties, Heinrich Seuse decided to organize an authoritative version of his vernacular writings, to protect himself from accusations that might arise from falsely copied material.[23] Interestingly, however, his *vita,* which he places first in the *Exemplar* collection, is based largely on the notes of one of the women in his spiritual care.[24]

It should be clear from this brief discussion that the relationship of Latin to the vernacular, and the reasons for choosing one over the other, vary from situation to situation. What, then, specifically, lay behind Mechthild's decision to write in the vernacular?

At the end of an early vision in her book, Mechthild abruptly breaks off her narrative to claim, "Nu gebristet mir túsches; des latines kan ich nit" (Now my German fails me; I do not know Latin) (II, 3:48; FL 72). While scholars generally accept this statement as sincere, it is doubtful that Mechthild knew no Latin at all. Indeed, most German noblewomen at this time (unlike men) were taught the rudiments of Latin for reading purposes.[25] Knowledge of Latin began with the Psalter, which young girls were encouraged to memorize before they reached marriageable age, in case they were chosen to enter a convent. As Marie-Luise Ehrenschwendtner's recent research on German Dominican nuns has shown, women who found themselves pursuing a religious life were generally able to recite some prayers and parts of the liturgy in addition to the Psalter, but only a few could understand or write Latin. These late-thirteenth- and fourteenth-century women had access to Latin education but were not required to learn it and, with the exception of the nuns at Unterlinden, preferred to write in the vernacular.[26]

If we accept the assumption that Mechthild was brought up in a courtly setting, in a family of lower nobility, as well as the statement in her book that she ran away to Magdeburg as a young adult, then whatever education she did receive she received while at court. Unfortunately, there is no evidence for precisely which court this might have been, or for her having received additional education from the Dominicans. Still, it seems likely that, like the nuns described by Ehrenschwendtner, Mechthild knew some Latin, but not enough to write it. The evidence of her contemporaries at Helfta as well as that of Beatrice and Agnes suggests that Mechthild's lack of Latin did *not* constrain her to write in her native language. On the other hand, the environment of the convent at an earlier age might have afforded her not only the means to write her book, or have it written, in Latin, but also, depending on the cloister she was in, the impetus to do so. From this perspective, we can view Mechthild's choice of the vernacular as rooted in her choice of a particular form of religious life. Considering the increasing number of paths for religious devotion at this time, we must consider the possibility that Mechthild could also have chosen to enter a convent at a younger age.

Although women's decisions were by law made for them by their nearest male relatives and, after they were married, by their husbands, many devout women found ways to exercise their choice not to marry but to enter a particular form of religious life. Ida of Nivelles (1197/99–1231) was nine years old when she fled from her home to a community of beguines in order to escape an arranged marriage. She entered a Cistercian convent seven years later.[27] Yolande of Vianden defied her parents' wish for her to marry, insisting on entering a local, more recently founded Dominican convent. Relenting in part, her parents suggested a more established Cistercian convent with which their family had connections. But Yolande held her ground and got her way.[28] Beatrice also is said to have expressed an ardent wish to enter an order, to which her father agreed when she was only ten.[29] Like Ida, Mechthild, too, chose to flee friends and family in order to live in the city as a beguine under the care of her only friend there, her Dominican confessor. Like Yolande, Mechthild chose a less established form of religious life. Unlike Ida, Mechthild did not enter a convent until she was sixty years old.

Indeed, a dialogue in the text itself indicates a critical stance toward traditional cloistered monastic life (II, 23). In this dialogue, Lady Minne criticizes the foolish soul who describes herself as living "in einem heligen orden, ich vaste, wachen, ich bin ane hovbtsúnde, ich bin gnuog gebunden" (in a holy order, I fast, perform vigils, I am without cardinal sins, I am well bound) (II, 23:8–9). Lady Minne finds fault with the way of life described here: "Du bist me bekúmbert mit dinem huntlichen lichamen denne mit Jhesu, dinem suessen herren" (you are more concerned with your doglike body than with Jesus, your sweet Lord) (II, 23:14–16). As Susanne Köbele points out, the problem with the ascetic monastic life here is that in its efforts to suppress or defeat the body, it places too much emphasis on the body and thereby prevents transcendence or transfiguration of the bodily in the experience of union. Köbele adds that this statement should not be taken as a wholesale critique: rather, Mechthild is against the stagnation (*ruowe*) and self-satisfaction (*boese gewonheit*) that is sometimes the result of the ordered life.[30] Nevertheless, Mechthild may have chosen life as a beguine because she believed that the conventual life did not promote the kind of devotion she was interested in.

Thus, when Mechthild obeyed her confessor's and God's commands to write down her revelations, she did not ask for an amanuensis, as Elisabeth or Agnes did, nor did she hide her vernacular writings until on her deathbed, as

Beatrice did. Having by this time (1250) had twenty years of interaction with the Dominicans, she allied herself with her confessor's order and its mission to preach and teach in the world, to reform erring Christians: a mission for which the vernacular proved to be an essential tool.

In exploring Mechthild's interpretation of the Dominican's reformist mission, it is necessary to turn our attention now to the situation of German in the Magdeburg area. On the western banks of the Elbe and established as an archbishopric by Otto I in 968, Magdeburg was one of several important launching points for the so-called *Ostkolonisation* of the Slavic regions east of the river, which took place between the twelfth and fourteenth centuries.[31] By the time Mechthild began to write, the mendicant orders were doing their part in the colonizing campaign; by 1250, both Franciscans and Dominicans were well established in Magdeburg and had founded numerous houses in settlements to the north and east.[32] Because part of the Dominican mission was, through preaching and teaching, to correct the unlearned laity's errors in worship, the friars necessarily turned to the vernacular in order to reach their public.[33] In German-speaking regions at this time, however, the situation was complicated by the fact that the different dialects stood in some tension with one another, reflecting differences not only of locality but also of social position, lifestyle, and culture. By around 1200, for example, MHG was the "standard" language for courtly lyric, or *Minnesang,* as well as for courtly epic and romance.[34] Even poets whose native dialects were Low or Middle (central) German used the vocabulary, style, and forms of High German from the southern dialects (Swabian, Alemannic, Frankish, and Bavarian). Since most courtly poets relied on royal or noble patronage and because the most important courts tended to be in the south, the language of these courts became a sort of literary lingua franca.[35]

While a culture of written MHG poetry and narrative developed mainly at the courts of the regional aristocracy, a parallel vernacular movement took place in the context of the towns. Not only did mendicant friars preach in local dialects, thirteenth-century Magdeburg and surrounding town centers began to record their city laws, peace treaties, and chronicles in MLG.[36] Indeed, the colonization of the east, the development of towns, and growing trade between them (as they formed the Hanseatic League) account for a widespread use of MLG as a written language by the mid–fourteenth century.[37]

Mechthild's book marks a convergence of these regional developments. As a beguine and not a nun, she lived within the city walls of Magdeburg and was supervised by local Dominicans. She could not write in Latin, and charted a new course in not dictating to a Latinate scribe. Searching for an appropriate vocabulary to express the inexpressible, she invoked the secular language of courtly love to describe her mystical relationship and visions. Being on the southern edge of the MLG-speaking region, and having grown up in a courtly setting, Mechthild was clearly familiar enough with courtly literature to allude to it, but perhaps not enough to write directly in MHG verse. Even if here she had no choice, though, her decision to invoke the courtly milieu of the south in the language of her urban northern milieu is still significant.

The operative distinction for Mechthild was thus not between a universal (and masculine) Latin and a local (and feminine) vernacular. For her, as for the Dominicans, the MLG vernacular allowed her to bypass the secular clergy and facilitated a more direct access to members of what at the time was an expanding linguistic community. Invoking the language of the court (most pronouncedly in book I) while using the language of the city extended this audience to the elite for whom courtly poetry and MHG was a model, even as she suggested the need for this speech community's reform. In book IV, for example, Mechthild writes of a woman who renounced the world to become a beguine and yet "still wanted to serve at court."[38] Mechthild prays for her fellow beguine, fearing that she will be made the devil's companion in the afterlife. Why? Not only because the lady loves to excess her own importance at court but also because she pays too much attention to "unnütze hovzuht," idle courtly manners. This disapproval of courtliness comes as something of a surprise after statements from earlier chapters like "He [Christ] greets her [the soul] in courtly language [hovesprache] that one does not hear in this kitchen."[39] Clearly, there is a difference between God's use of hovesprache to express his love for the humble soul of Mechthild and the beguine sister's use of it to express her sense of worldly importance and fealty to her princely superiors. But this situation also suggests something more strategic: Mechthild places the experience of mystical union in the context of a court and uses language that bears the inflections of that context. And yet Low German is *not* the standard *hovesprache*, at least *not exactly*. In the same way that Mechthild's displacement of courtliness onto heaven removes the court from the world, so her use of Low German ultimately dissociates courtly language from the worldly dangers faced by her fellow beguine. The effect of this linguistic situation is consistent with the text's larger mission of universal instruction and outreach.

Mechthild's instruction extends beyond the court, however. In a section bearing the heading, "How Bad Priests Shall Be Humiliated," Mechthild addresses the priesthood as follows: "Woe, Crown of Holy Christianity, how greatly you have been sullied. The jewels have dropped from you, for you are undermining and violating the holy Christian faith."[40] We learn precisely who is sullying Christianity in the next paragraph: "Woe, Crown of the holy priest-hood, how utterly have you disappeared. You have nothing left but your trap-pings; that is, ecclesiastical authority with which you war against God and his chosen intimates. For this God shall humiliate you before you know it."[41] This striking and unmitigated indictment of the pope comes after many other cri-tiques of and instructions for the clergy. Not all priests are bad, however. And while these chapters suggest an aim to reform all priests and save all Chris-tianity, others focus on the praise of preachers known to Mechthild through her connections with the Dominicans in Magdeburg.[42] These range from encouragement of a certain Dietrich whose humility makes him reluctant to accept the position of dean in Magdeburg (VI, 2 and 3) to petitions for the souls of Dominican friars she knew (e.g., III, 17). In all of these cases, the particular (local) case is intended to instruct a broader audience. The fate of sinful souls in purgatory provides lessons for general behavior; similarly, the prayers for local individuals simultaneously carry a message for all, and they do so in the language of the hometown.

Underlying this strategy is a theological principle about the power of col-lective faith stated openly in book VI. Responding to criticism that the cele-brant of the Mass in one of her visions was John the Baptist, a layman and not a priest, Mechthild writes: "That John the Baptist spoke God's word—such a thing can neither pope nor bishop nor priest ever bring to pass except through our intangible Christian faith alone. Was this a layman? Prove me wrong, you blind ones! Your lies and your hate shall never be forgiven you without pain!"[43] While the formulation is somewhat obscure, the implication is clear: the ordination of any person, be he John the Baptist or the pope, is made valid and effective exclusively through the power of Christian faith as a whole, which, though a collective of humans, is more than human, or beyond human understanding. The source of such supernatural wonders as speaking God's word lies not in the church institutional hierarchy but rather in the church as empowered by the faith of its members. The language of Mechthild's text addresses these members directly and thereby activates their power. More-over, it openly resists the notion that Latin and those who write it have an exclusive claim on addressing "all creatures" and preaching their salvation.

The right to make this claim, as Nicole Bériou puts it, was "one of the questions of the moment" in the thirteenth century.[44] While the Dominican mission explicitly advocated preaching to prevent heresy, the preaching rights of Dominicans themselves were contested by the secular clergy, who did not always welcome Dominicans into their parishes.[45] Theologians argued over what constituted ordination (one had to be sent out officially to preach by an agent of the pope) as well as what constituted preaching (teaching Christian doctrine in public). As Alcuin Blamires has pointed out, during the thirteenth century the legends of female saints like Mary Magdalene and Catherine of Alexandria also became part of the religious mainstream through Jacobus de Voragine's *Golden Legend*.[46] The popularity of these figures and the approbation with which their apostolic activities were met presented theologians with a contradiction: how could they reconcile the obviously praiseworthy preaching and public discourse of these women with the Pauline and canon prohibition against women's teaching?[47] With recourse to the examples of Mary and Catherine, Eustace of Arras, a Franciscan, suggested in answer to this dilemma that a woman could speak authoritatively if she were gifted with prophecy and if she herself followed an exemplary and pure lifestyle.[48]

We can never know how much of this debate Mechthild may have been aware of, but it is possible all the same to read her text and her choice, or even the effects of her choice, of the vernacular as inflected by these issues. Mechthild's text clearly shows that the figures of Mary and Catherine were positive models for the authority and legitimacy of women to transmit the divine revelations made possible by the "special gift"—an intimate relationship with God.[49] Her repeated claims that the book came from God and not "us menschlichen sinnen" (from human thought) (IV, 2:134) can also be understood in terms of this debate. Her association with other virgins grants her the aura of purity, and her denial of direct authorship points to the prophetic gift as the cause of the writings. Perhaps in this context, then, her confessor's command to write, recorded in chapter 2 of book IV, can be seen as more than a generic convention.[50] As a schooled Dominican, the confessor would have been aware of the strong clerical disapproval of women's teaching in public and of female speech, a consideration that would suggest a more strategic reason for the famous *Schreibbefehl* (command to write). It seems to me, in light of this context, that the choice to put Mechthild's teachings in writing that was vernacular and literary enabled both her and her confessors to avoid the charge that she was preaching or teaching in a transgressive (i.e., public) way.

Taking all of this evidence together, it seems clear that the choice of the vernacular in any given region must be understood in light of contemporary geopolitical and literary factors. In Mechthild's case, her claim not to know Latin means less than her choice to live as a beguine in a city where she had few connections, less than her alliance with the Dominicans, whose mission it was to teach the laity primarily through vernacular preaching. As a woman, Mechthild was not permitted to preach, but she could write, and her book's mission to reform "all creatures" clearly found a sympathetic ear among her confessors, for they encouraged her authorial endeavor. The choice of the vernacular in this context thus embodies a challenge to a particular faction of the secular clergy and a particular style of pastoral care, a challenge made by Mechthild *and* her Dominican advisors.

While this tension between the new orders and the papal authorities proved to be politically divisive within the larger ecclesiastical organization, it was theoretically a product of Christian doctrine itself. As several scholars have recently argued, the challenge just described is also a literal enactment of a central Christian belief—that is, kenosis, the doctrine that God chooses the humble, lowdown, and weak as his instruments, as he did by assuming human form in his incarnation.[51] We see this doctrine laid out in a dialogue in which God reminds Mechthild that "the course of my Holy Spirit flows by nature down hill. [. . .] It is a great honor for me [. . .] and it very much strengthens Holy Christianity that the unlearned mouth, aided by my Holy Spirit, teaches the learned tongue."[52] As both Susanne Köbele and Nicholas Watson note, this passage suggests a direct link between kenosis and the use of vernacular language.[53] By writing down her revelations, rules, and instructions in MLG, Mechthild enacts God's assertion: she, the unlearned mouth, teaches scholars in a tongue twice removed from learning's mountaintop (the Latin clergy and courtiers) and at the same time spreads the message she bears out onto the "valley floor" of this northern realm.

Female Authorship and the Universal

It is precisely *The Flowing Light*'s ambition that makes an examination of the text's manuscript transmission so intriguing. Initially, the transmission history seems to return us to the simple gendered Latin/vernacular dichotomy that turns out *not* to have dictated Mechthild's use of MLG: the Latin translation seems to be intended for men, the MHG version for women. However, a closer examination reveals that the gendering of another category, that of the universal, is at work here. The transmission history tells the story of how the attribution of female authorship becomes problematic in relation to the universal mission advocated in Mechthild's text.

As noted above, this universal mission is complicated by expressions of anxiety about the human authorship of such a project. In particular, the authorial or writing voice expresses concern about her lacking the kind of education that would legitimize a book about the teachings of God. "If I were a *learned religious man*," she writes in book II, addressing God, "and if you had performed this unique great miracle using him, you would receive everlasting honor for it."[54] In book III, she comments on a vision: "I saw there things never heard before, my confessors tell me, for *I am unlearned in Scripture.*"[55] Writing in book IV about the first time she revealed her revelations to her confessor, she records the advice she received: "Then he gave me a command that often makes me ashamed . . . that is, he commanded me, a frail woman, to write this book out of God's heart and mouth. And so this book has come lovingly from God and does not have its origins *in human thought.*"[56]

When we turn to the material changes made to the book, this concern about an *unlearned* authorship can be read as well founded. For while the Dominicans obviously agreed with Mechthild's mission to reach out to the universal church in the vernacular, their Latin translation was not merely an attempt to reach audiences whose vernaculars were other than German. Rather, their translation, known as the *Lux divinitatis,* reconfigured the text for a learned male audience that sought even further to downplay the human, in this case female, agency in the writings.[57] In effect, the translator tries to have it both ways—on the one hand, to transmit Mechthild's writings to a wider audience, thereby granting them a degree of legitimacy as bearers of a universal truth; on the other, to accede to the misogynist assumption that women cannot occupy positions of spiritual authority.

It is now commonplace in Mechthild scholarship to judge as significant the changes the translator made, reordering the book according to subject matter, rephrasing the erotic imagery, and softening outright critiques of the clergy.[58] Susanne Köbele suggests that the Latin translation was meant to return Mechthild's work into the "hermetic exclusivity of Latin" and that, in so doing, it robs her text of "what is innovative in its thought and language."[59] For example, in one of Mechthild's early dialogues involving the soul, the senses, and a youthful Christ (I, 44), the youth says to the soul: "You shall have your way with the Son of the Virgin."[60] The corresponding Latin is "Delectaberis enim ad votum super virginis filio" (You will be delighted as promised concerning the Son of the Virgin).[61] A similar line in book II, where the soul states she will "do with him whatever I want," is simply omitted in the *Revelationes.*[62] Neumann notes that the rest of the dialogue in book I is abbreviated and made more general in the Latin version, probably "to avoid giving offense."[63] And indeed, in the translator's prologue, readers are instructed that they "must read in a pious spirit. [. . .] In this way the reader will find nothing scandalous or *offensive* in it, and the writing itself will not be subjected to any perverse claim of falsehood."[64]

Why, we might ask, would Mechthild's admittedly fiery love be perceived as scandalous or offensive, especially since it repeatedly invokes the fiery language of the Song of Songs, promoted and disseminated in the sermons of Bernard of Clairvaux?[65] The answer seems to be that the author of this love is female: a fact that the translator takes pains to explain and qualify. Anticipating the objections of educated male clerics presented with an instructional text by an uneducated beguine woman, the writer of the Latin prologue invokes the biblical tradition of holy women prophets:[66]

> Quite often, in fact, almighty God has chosen what is weak in the world to confound what is stronger for its good. . . . He, who in the time of the law of Moses mercifully saw fit to perform similar works, now reveals his mysteries to the fragile sex. Because the people of Israel believed Deborah's prophecy, they won freedom from oppression and victory over their enemies. Also, a king, a religious man, was found worthy to gain solace and mercy through the prayer and advice of the prophetess Huldah. So, too, shall all who write or read this book, if they approach it with pious intent, attain an increase in solace and spiritual grace, as the Lord promises them in the book itself.[67]

While both male and female prophets are vessels of the divine, only prophetic women figure here. This should not be surprising when we recall that thirteenth-century clergymen were concerned about unauthorized preaching in general, but especially by women. In the same way that theologians praised the examples of Mary Magdalene and Saint Catherine, the translator here seeks to remind contemporary readers that the prophetic authorship of a "fragile" female has biblical precedent. If that is not enough to alleviate the suspicions of potential readers, the translator adapts Mechthild's own denials, stating that the book's true author is "the Father, the Son, and the Holy Spirit."[68] In this way, the translator legitimizes the authenticity (as God's words) of what Mechthild writes, while at the same time effacing her particular role or agency in writing it.

The Flowing Light itself shows a keen awareness not only of the problem of female authorship but also of the kind of textual labors evident in the Latin translation: in book II, for example, Mechthild asks God handsomely to reward God's scribes ("sine schribere," II, 26:34) who will copy the book after her. Despite anxiety about her role as its author, Mechthild expects the book to be copied and read by others whose versions she cannot control. But the book also records harsh words meant for people who have misunderstood her writings and criticized her for them.[69] It seems quite plausible, then, that Mechthild chose the *barbara lingua,* as it is called in the Latin prologue, not only because of her unique mission but also because she anticipated precisely the kind of tampering that took place in the scriptorium at Halle.

The MLG version that Mechthild wrote herself was not immune to similar tampering. Indeed, while the Latin transmission attests to the impulse to qualify, if not shroud, female authorship for the benefit of schooled, predominantly male readers, the transmission of the MHG translation shows that despite Mechthild's efforts to speak beyond gender and social position in her book, its promoters understood the vernacular version in its complete form as most appropriate for women like her. This conclusion might indicate that acknowledgment of female authorship could be allowed when the text was confined to a female audience. And yet, when the writings were transmitted in excerpted form, the problem of female authorship reasserted itself: when her book was mined for material aimed at a male audience preaching to a general one, Mechthild's authorship was unacknowledged or qualified. The categorization of vernacular devotional books as women's texts thus breaks down. Instead, we see in both branches of the transmission the tendency to perceive female authorship and a universal message as an unnatural pair.

Despite the fact that more and more courts in the fourteenth century kept their books of land grants and laws in German, and that the German of the eastern central areas would become the standard administrative language by the time of Luther, Mechthild's Low German text had to be translated into High German in order for it to be understood by the religious nuns and beguines in southern Germany and Switzerland around 1345. As indicated in a letter, accompanying *The Flowing Light,* to Margaretha Ebner and her sisters in the convent of Maria Medingen, Heinrich von Nördlingen thought the text quite extraordinary generally, but particularly appropriate for women's religious contemplative practices. He comments on the beauty of the language, the prayers to be said before reading it, how to read it, and finally what to do if readers have trouble understanding it.[70] The manuscript containing the complete version (late fourteenth century) further documents the role of the book in the pastoral care of religious women. This manuscript, still kept in the library of the Benedictine monastery in Einsiedeln, Switzerland, belonged to Margaretha of the Golden Ring, who bequeathed it to a group of recluse beguines living in the mountains near Zurich. According to the instructions written onto the first leaf of the manuscript by this Margaretha's confessor, the book was to serve all of the houses in the forest: each house was to keep the book for a month and then pass it on to the next house, a practice of exchange that was to be continued indefinitely, for the book "sol us dem walde niemer kommen" (should never come out of the forest). Margaretha's confessor thought no doubt to ensure that this one copy of the book would serve sisters in a number of houses. Perhaps he lacked the resources to have copies made for each house. But it seems significant all the same that the audience to which the book was directed consisted of confined groups of female readers in an isolated space.

Despite his aesthetic appreciation of *The Flowing Light,* Heinrich's letters, like the Latin translator's prologue, reveal a concept of female authorship that values the text (as divine) over its writer. To be sure, in sending the book, Heinrich means to encourage the writing of other women in his care. Earlier in the same letter, for example, Heinrich thanks Margaretha for the text (*geschrift*) she had recently sent him, advising her not to stop writing as long as God continues to give her His gift.[71] Mechthild's book is thus also meant to inspire Margaretha in her own authorial undertakings. Similarly, at the end of this same letter, Heinrich indicates that the nuns should read the book only three times instead of the nine times recommended in the prologue, for he wants to send it on to the nearby convent of Engelthal,[72] where Margaretha's contemporary Christine Ebner (1277–1356), whom Heinrich also counseled, was recording her mystical revelations.[73] Yet, while the letters clearly reflect Heinrich's support of writing women, they also reflect his relative indifference to the actual authorship of Mechthild's book. Although he gives the title of the book, he makes no mention of Mechthild's name.

This ambivalence or indifference should be understood strategically. Women's public teaching, we remember, was allowable in some quarters if granted by the grace of God's prophetic gift. Heinrich thus appropriately adopts the framing device provided by the prologue, which reiterates Mechthild's own claims, stating "that God himself is in it and has revealed himself in this book."[74] As mentioned above, the author of the prologue felt the need to remark on the vernacular in which the text was composed. But he also supplied some other information about the writer that would legitimize her publicly aimed speech, namely that she "was a holy virgin both in body and in spirit," just as Eustace of Arras suggests.[75] Finally, even though the "holy virgin's" name does not merit attention, female authorship must be explained, and not only because it breaks taboo or canon law. Gender here functions similarly to the vernacular, for like the vernacular the blessing of a female with divine inspiration mimics the kenosis of the incarnation—God's choice to become human as and live among the poor and humble. It is in light of these parameters that we must understand Heinrich's comments on Mechthild's book. He is conforming to convention in using it to teach and instruct other women as well as to encourage them to be divine vessels. And in the process he defies the opinions of authorities such as Humbert of Romans or some time later Jean Gerson, who would see the circulation of a female-authored theological text as unacceptable.

While the ownership and provenance of the Einsiedeln manuscript and the comments by Heinrich suggest that the vernacular version transmitted whole was strategically aimed at a female audience, the manuscripts containing excerpts had other functions and were directed to different audiences.[76] For example, a fourteenth-century manuscript from Würzburg (W) collects significant chunks of Mechthild's writings in between a series of outlines for sermons in Latin. None of the chapters in which Mechthild writes about herself are included. Nor are any of her comments on the Dominicans.[77] Rather, the compiler includes material that can be associated with particular biblical citations or used as exempla for sermons. The potential use is indicated in a Latin heading before each section.[78] W thus provides us with an intriguing insight into the relationship between the language of clerical instruction and the vernacular audience the mendicant orders were trying to reach. It also represents another way in which Mechthild's mission to teach the laity was carried out. Clearly meant to be an aid to preachers, the book addresses at least two groups—the preachers and those to whom they preached, making the gendered Latin/vernacular distinction no longer applicable. Both languages are present here, and the audience is clerical and lay. Significantly, Mechthild's authorship here is not merely effaced, but absent. The mission to reach out to all, learned and unlearned, requires that the female authorship of the text be made invisible.

A fifteenth-century codex containing excerpts from all seven parts of Mechthild's book complicates this picture. Naming Mechthild as the author, it rearranges excerpts from her book, flanking them with sermons and other didactic tracts. When read together, these texts present us with another type of handbook for pastoral care. The Colmar manuscript (C)[79] seems to have been put together with a specific agenda in mind. The texts assembled are aimed at teaching Dominican friars how to contemplate sacred objects and doctrines, such as the Eucharist and purgatory. Of the eighty-two chapters included from *The Flowing Light,* twenty-two deal with the fate of souls in purgatory, at the hands of devils, and in hell. Thirty relate to *Gottesminne* (divine love), describing the *einunge* (union) that is presented in other parts of the manuscript as the goal of monastic practice. Ten relate to the Dominican order or its role in the days before the Last Judgment; six treat suffering; and fourteen treat miscellaneous subjects. The topics that interest the scribe the most, though, are those relating to contemplative goals and practices and the terrible purgatorial consequences of not following these practices.

These chapters, unlike the other tracts, none of which is attributed to an author, are announced in the manuscript with some fanfare: "All of the chapters that follow are written from the seven books of Saint Mechthild and are called the Shining Light of the Godhead."[80] In the margins, the scribe also keeps track of the book and chapter numbers from his source. Such respect for the source is unique in the German transmission and raises further questions about the value of female authorship in this fifteenth-century context. The belief that Mechthild is a saint must be one reason for the central place the scribe gives her writings in the manuscript. Sanctity makes her authorship legitimate and removes the ambivalence evident in Heinrich of Nördlingen's letters. Mechthild's writings as the centerpiece of the manuscript are balanced on either side by more traditional figures. Bernard is the dominant authority in the tracts preceding Mechthild's, and two popular male saints' lives conclude the manuscript, those of Saints Christopher and Alexis. Both tell of men who gradually come to serve God in imitation of the apostles and Christ: that is, men who adopt the commandments of the New Testament and renounce the world, as is recommended in the manuscript's opening tract.[81]

In the context of the codex as a whole, then, the writings of Mechthild become part of a larger didactic message to an audience of Dominican friars whose mission outside the monastery walls has made them more susceptible to the sins of the world. The scribe appears to be attempting to legitimize this enterprise, the instruction of potentially erring friars, by reference to a series of contemplative saints. In contrast to W, then, C is a vernacular codex aimed at an audience of friars who need help, not with their sermons or outreach, but with their inner lives. Rather than make Mechthild's authorship invisible, the compiler of this book presents it as a product of sanctity within a textual context that honors the monastic virtues and the teachings of saints in general.

Clearly these two manuscripts can tell us a great deal about the vernacular theology of the time periods in which they were compiled and used, and raise significant questions about the assumed connection between the vernacular and a female audience. When Mechthild's text is used according to its mission to preach and teach to "all religious persons," the references to her particularity, the parts of her text that refer to and thematize her authorship, are jettisoned. Even in manuscript C, in which Mechthild's authority as a saint is acknowledged, the emphasis in the excerpts is shifted away from her as subject matter, for the selections convey an instructional message to the friars. When her text is transmitted in German as a whole, however, when her authorial presence is more persistent in the text, the manuscripts are aimed at enclosed female audiences.

To conclude, Mechthild's attempts to recast the languages of poetry and theology in a language with domestic accents, to make the "unlearned tongue" speak of the divine and to all, fall short of her goals, but in intriguing ways. One wonders if she would still have asked God to praise the scribes who "wrote and read" her book after her, had she seen how they did so. One also thinks of the interesting choice of the "unlearned tongue" and its paradoxically "local" universality in light of the fact that no Low German version has survived. Both the Latin and High German versions reach as far as Switzerland and then literally get lost in the mountains. Perhaps she should have supervised a Latin version after all: her sister at Helfta, Mechthild von Hackeborn, authored a Latin text that crossed the channel and was translated into Middle English, even if this version was then attributed to a male author.[82]

The complex transmission of Mechthild von Magdeburg's text allows us to see not so much the feminizing of the vernacular as the workings of the process by which women's claims to the universal begin to produce ideological contradictions with which we still grapple today. Our close attention to this process uncovers the additional paradox that it involves writers of all kinds (Mechthild *and* her editors) who actually *want* to see *The Flowing Light* accomplish its universal mission. Their efforts to negotiate the contradictions inherent in the female authorship of potentially sacred texts are clearly implicated in the fostering of those contradictions. When Mechthild's authorship is qualified in those manuscripts aimed at male or lay audiences, and when it is confined to the "private" female sphere in the manuscript that transmits her writings whole, we see the ways in which her message managed to get through. Yet we also see the ideological legacy of its strategies: the belief that the only time it is right for a woman writer to lay claim to a universal readership is when no one knows she is there.

NOTES

A longer version of this essay appears in *Journal of Medieval and Early Modern Studies* 31.2 (2001): 213–50. I am grateful to the editors for permission to republish here. Thanks are due Nicholas Watson, Fiona Somerset, Harvey Hames, Ursula Peters, Ann Marie Rasmussen, Eckehard Simon, Claire Waters, Werner Williams, and members of the Penn Humanities Forum seminar for their comments on various drafts.

1. Herbert Grundmann, "Die Frauen und die Literatur im Mittelalter: Ein Beitrag zur Frage nach der Entstehung des Schrifttums in der Volkssprache," *Archiv für Kulturgeschichte* 26 (1936): 129–61.

2. See, e.g., the remarks of Heinrich Denifle cited in Susanne Bürkle, *Literatur im Kloster: Historische Funktion und rhetorische Legitimation frauenmystischer Texte des 14. Jahrhunderts* (Tübingen: Francke, 1999), 57–58.

3. See esp. several works by Kurt Ruh: "Vorbemerkung zu einer neuen Geschichte der abendländischen Mystik im Mittelalter" [1982], in *Kleine Schriften, Bd. II: Scholastik und Mystik im Spätmittelalter,* ed. Volker Mertens (Berlin and New York: De Gruyter, 1984), 337–63; *Meister Eckhart: Theologe, Prediger, Mystiker* [1985], 2d ed. (Munich: Beck, 1989); and *Geschichte der abendländischen*

Mystik, 3 vols. (Munich: Beck, 1990–96). See also Susanne Köbele, *Bilder der unbegriffenen Wahrheit: Zur Struktur mystischer Rede im Spannungsfeld von Latein und Volkssprache* (Tübingen: Francke, 1993).

4. Bürkle, *Literatur im Kloster,* 66. Bürkle draws particular attention to the problems inherent in the assumption that the sermons of Eckhart and Tauler were composed for an exclusively female audience.

5. Ruh, *Geschichte der abendländischen Mystik,* 2:19.

6. Mechthild von Magdeburg, *Das fließende Licht der Gottheit: Nach der Einsiedler Handschrift in kritischem Vergleich mit der gesamten Überlieferung,* ed. Hans Neumann, prepared for printing by Gisela Vollmann Profe, vol. 1: Text (München: Artemis, 1990), vol. 2: Untersuchungen (Tübingen: Niemeyer, 1993). The best English translation to date is Mechthild of Magdeburg, *The Flowing Light of the Godhead,* trans. Frank Tobin, Classics of Western Spirituality (New York: Paulist Press, 1998). Here, citations to Mechthild's book indicate book, chapter, and lines, referring to Neumann's edition. Unless otherwise noted, translations are Frank Tobin's and are cited with the abbreviation FL and page number.

7. "allen geistlichen lúten beidiu boesen und guoten" (prologue 3–4; FL 39); "mit der maht und mit der stimme aller creaturen" (VI, 7:26; FL 234).

8. "Middle" refers to the time period beginning in 1050 and ending with Luther; "Low" refers to northern Germany, in contrast with "High," which refers to the southern, more mountainous regions. This terminology should not be confused with categorizations of modern German: "High German" today means standard German, as opposed to regional dialects.

9. "Frontier" is a relative term in this context. Magdeburg lies on the banks of the Elbe. To the east and north across the river was a border region heavily contested by Slavs and Germans as far back as the eighth century. For the role of colonization in the historical linguistic developments for this area, see Karl Bischoff, "Siedlungsbewegung und Sprachentwicklung im ostniederdeutschen Raum," in *Sprachgeschichte: Ein Handbuch zur Geschichte der deutschen Sprache und ihrer Erforschung,* ed. Werner Besch, Oskar Reichmann, and Stefan Sonderegger (Berlin: De Gruyter, 1985), 1268–74.

10. The German translates the Latin phrase "cuidam beguine" as "einer swester," a generic form of address.

11. See Köbele, *Bilder der unbegriffenen Wahrheit,* 33–34.

12. Bürkle, *Literatur im Kloster,* 1–2; Marie-Luise Ehrenschwendtner, *"Puellae litteratae:* The Use of the Vernacular in the Dominican Convents of Southern Germany," in *Medieval Women in Their Communities,* ed. Diane Watt (Cardiff: University of Wales Press, 1997), 49–71.

13. IV, 2:18–21; FL 140. For a summary of the scholarship, see Frank Tobin, *Mechthild von Magdeburg: A Medieval Mystic in Modern Eyes* (Columbia, S.C.: Camden House, 1995).

14. For Helfta, see Mary Jeremy Finnegan, *The Women of Helfta* (Athens: University of Georgia Press, 1991).

15. For their writings, see Louis Paquelin, ed., *Revelationes Gertrudianae ac Mechthildianae,* 2 vols. (Poitiers and Paris: Oudin, 1875–77).

16. Elizabeth Clark, *Elisabeth of Schönau: A Twelfth-Century Visionary* (Philadelphia: University of Pennsylvania Press, 1992), 78–80.

17. Roger De Ganck, ed. and trans., *The Life of Beatrice of Nazareth, 1200–1268,* Cistercian Fathers 50 (Kalamazoo, Mich.: Cistercian Publications, 1991), xiii–xvi and chaps. 19, 20, and 21.

18. Hadewijch, *The Complete Works of Hadewijch,* trans. Columba Hart, Classics of Western Spirituality (New York: Paulist Press, 1980), and the Middle Dutch editions by Jozef S. J. Van Mierlo: *Hadewijch: Visioenen,* 2 vols. (Louvain: Vlaamsch Boekenhalle, 1924–25); *Hadewijch: Strophische Gedichten,* 2 vols. (Antwerp: Standaard, 1942); *Hadewijch: Brieven,* 2 vols. (Antwerp: Standaard, 1947); *Hadewijch: Mengelgedichten* (Antwerp: Standaard, 1952).

19. Peter Dinzelbacher and Renate Vogeler, eds., *Leben und Offenbarungen der Wiener Begine Agnes Blannbekin* (d. 1315) (Göppingen: Kümmerle, 1994).

20. Others include the Franciscan preachers David of Augsburg (1200–1272) and Berthold of Regensburg (fl. 1240–72), and the chaplain of the Dominican convent of Engelthal, Friedrich Sunder (1254–1328).

21. For Eckhart's works, see *Meister Eckhart: Die deutschen und lateinischen Werke* (Stuttgart and Berlin: Kohlhammer, 1936–). The German works are edited by Josef Quint, the Latin by Josef Koch. For English translations and introductions, see *Meister Eckhart: The Essential Sermons, Commentaries, Treatises, and Defense,* trans. Edmund Colledge and Bernard McGinn, Classics of Western Spirituality (New York: Paulist Press, 1981), and *Meister Eckhart: Teacher and Preacher,* trans. Bernard McGinn, with Frank Tobin and Elvira Borgstadt, Classics of Western Spirituality (New York: Paulist Press, 1986).

22. Robert E. Lerner, "New Evidence for the Condemnation of Meister Eckhart," *Speculum* 72 (1997): 347–66.

23. Heinrich Seuse, *Deutsche Schriften,* ed. Karl Bihlmeyer (Stuttgart: Minerva, 1907). Henry Suso, *The Exemplar, with Two German Sermons,* trans. Frank Tobin, Classics of Western Spirituality (New York: Paulist Press, 1989).

24. Frank Tobin, "Henry Suso and Elsbeth Stagel: Was the *Vita* a Cooperative Effort?" in *Gendered Voices: Medieval Saints and Their Interpreters,* ed. Catherine M. Mooney (Philadelphia: University of Pennsylvania Press, 1999), 118–35.

25. See Joachim Bumke, *Geschichte der deutschen Literatur im hohen Mittelalter* (Munich: Deutscher Taschenbuch Verlag, 1990), 38, whose assertions are qualified in D. H. Green, "Orality and Reading: The State of Research in Medieval Studies," *Speculum* 65 (1990): 267–80, at 275. See also Green's *Medieval Listening and Reading* (Cambridge: Cambridge University Press, 1994), esp. chap. 6.

26. Ehrenschwendtner, *"Puellae litteratae,"* 54–56.

27. De Ganck, *Beatrice,* xv n. 11.

28. For Yolande's story, see the introduction to Ann Marie Rasmussen, *Mothers and Daughters in Medieval German Literature* (Syracuse: Syracuse University Press, 1997), 3–4; Johannes Meier, ed., *Bruder Hermann: Leben der Gräfin Iolande von Vianden* (Breslau: W. Koebner, 1889); and *Brother Herrmann's Life of the Countess Yolanda of Vianden,* trans. Richard H. Lawson (Columbia, S.C.: Camden House, 1995).

29. De Ganck, *Beatrice,* xiv.

30. Köbele, *Bilder der unbegriffenen Wahrheit,* 83.

31. Robert Peters, "Soziokulturelle Voraussetzungen und Sprachraum des Mittelniederdeutschen," in *Sprachgeschichte,* ed. Besch et al. (see note 9 above), 1211. See also Karl Bischoff, *Mittelalterliche Überlieferung und Sprach- und Siedlungsgeschichte im Ostniederdeutschen* (Wiesbaden: Akademie der Wissenschaften und der Literatur, 1966).

32. John Freed, *The Friars in German Society in the Thirteenth Century* (Cambridge, Mass.: Medieval Academy of America, 1977), 56.

33. See Claire Waters's essay in this volume.

34. The term "standard" should be understood loosely here, since the manuscript witnesses to courtly literature display regional dialect variations.

35. Willy Sanders, *Sachsensprache, Hansesprache, Plattdeutsch* (see Further Reading), 124. Two well-known examples in the medieval German tradition are Eilhart von Oberge and Heinrich von Veldeke, both from Low German areas, whose literary works are preserved in MHG. In addition, a contemporary of Mechthild's, Brun of Schönebeck, a Magdeburg patrician, composed a MHG verse paraphrase of the Song of Songs in 1275/76.

36. For examples, see Agathe Lasch, *Aus alten niederdeutschen Stadtbüchern: Ein mittelniederdeutsches Lesebuch,* 2d ed., ed. Dieter Möhn and Robert Peters (Neumünster: Karl Wachholtz Verlag, 1987), and Gustav Korlén, *Die mittelniederdeutschen Texte des 13. Jahrhunderts* (Lund: Gleerup, 1945).

37. Agathe Lasch, *Mittelniederdeutsche Grammatik,* 2d ed. (Halle: Niemeyer, 1974), 8. See also Peters, "Soziokulturelle Voraussetzungen," 1214; Sanders, *Sachsensprache, Hansesprache, Plattdeutsch,* chap. 6, 126–71; and Horst Wernicke, "Literarische Rezeptionsbedingungen im Hanseraum aus historischer Sicht," in *Die deutsche Literatur des Mittelalters im europäischen Kontext,* ed. Rolf Bräuer (Göppingen: Kümmerle, 1995), 135–47.

38. "wolte dennoch zu hove dienen" (IV, 17:3; FL 159).

39. "So gruesset er si mit der hovesprache, die man in dirre kuchin nút vernimet" (I, 2:9–10; FL 40).

40. "Owe crone der heligen cristanheit, wie sere bistu geselwet! Din edelsteine sint dir entvallen, wan du krenkest und schendest den heligen cristanen gelovben" (VI, 21:3–5; FL 249).

41. "Owe crone der heligen pfafheit, wie bistu verswunden! Joch hastu nicht mere denne das umbeval din selbes, das ist pfaeffeliche gewalt, da mitte vihtestu uf got und sine userwelten vrúnde. Harumbe wil dich got nidern, e du icht wissest" (VI, 21:10–13; FL 250).

42. For a concise discussion of Mechthild's critiques of the church in the context of conflicts between secular clergy and mendicants, see Elizabeth A. Andersen, "Mechthild von Magdeburg, der Dominikanerorden und der Weltklerus," in *Spannungen und Konflikte menschlichen Zusammenlebens in der deutschen Literatur des Mittelalters: Bristoler Kolloquium 1993,* ed. Kurt Gärtner, Ingrid Kasten, and Frank Shaw (Tübingen: Niemeyer, 1996), 264–72.

43. My translation: "Das Johannes Baptista gottes wort sprach, alsus verre mag es niemer babest noch bischof noch priester vollebringen denne alleine mit únsrem unsinnelichem cristanem gelovben. Was dis ein leie? Berihtent mich, ir blinden; úwer luginen und úwer has wirt úch niemer vergeben ane pine!" (VI, 36:19–23).

44. Nicole Bériou, "The Right of Women to Give Religious Instruction in the Thirteenth Century," in *Women Preachers and Prophets Through Two Millennia of Christianity,* ed. Beverly Mayne Kienzle and Pamela J. Walker (Berkeley and Los Angeles: University of California Press, 1998), 134–45, at 137. See also Alcuin Blamires, "Women and Preaching in Medieval Orthodoxy, Heresy, and Saints' Lives," *Viator* 26 (1995): 135–52.

45. See Rolf Köhn, "Monastisches Bildungsideal und weltgeistliches Wissenschaftsdenken: Zur Vorgeschichte des Mendikantenstreites an der Universität Paris," in *Die Auseinandersetzungen an der Pariser Universität im XIII. Jahrhundert,* ed. Albert Zimmermann (Berlin: De Gruyter, 1976), 1–37. Also David L. d'Avray, *The Preaching of the Friars: Sermons Diffused from Paris Before 1300* (Oxford: Clarendon, 1985), and Alistair J. Minnis, "Chaucer's Pardoner and the 'Office of Preacher,'" in *Intellectuals and Writers in Fourteenth-Century Europe,* ed. Piero Boitani and Anna Torti (Cambridge: D. S. Brewer, 1986), 88–119, esp. 89–100.

46. Blamires, "Women and Preaching," 142.

47. Because the biblical prohibition specifies that teaching is forbidden to women, debates concerning women's preaching usually use the more inclusive term *docere.* Ibid., 139.

48. Ibid., 142; Bériou, "Right of Women," 138–39.

49. See esp. II, 4, in which Catherine and Cecilia are among a group of virgins in the choir of a church where the protagonist of the vision, "the poor maid" (*die arme dirne*) receives communion in a vision. The women's function is to help the maid (Mechthild) accept her legitimacy and worthiness to be among them.

50. This is the thrust of Ursula Peters's argument in *Religiöse Erfahrung als literarisches Faktum: Zur Vorgeschichte und Genese frauenmystischer Texte des 13. und 14. Jahrhunderts* (Tübingen: Niemeyer, 1988), 118. Commenting on the same passage from Mechthild, she writes: "the confessor is here nothing more than a role or figure that hence does not allow us to draw cultural-historical conclusions about the command to write, in the sense of a literary collaboration between Mechthild and her spiritual guide."

51. See Nicholas Watson, "Conceptions of the Word" (see Further Reading, page 257). For a similar claim in the German context, see Köbele, *Bilder der unbegriffenen Wahrheit,* 32–51.

52. "die vluot mines heligen geistes vlússet von nature ze tal. . . . Das ist mir vor inen ein gros ere und sterket die heligen cristanheit an in vil sere, das der ungelerte munt die gelerte zungen von minem heligen geiste leret" (II, 26:29–33; FL 97).

53. Köbele, *Bilder der unbegriffenen Wahrheit,* 35–36; Watson, "Conceptions of the Word," 123.

54. My emphasis: "Were ich ein *geleret geistlich man,* und hettistu dis einig grosse wunder an im getan, somoehtistu sin ewige ere enpfahen" (II, 26:18–19; FL 97).

55. My emphasis: "Ich han da inne ungehoertú ding gesehen, als mine bihter sagent, wan *ich der schrift ungeleret bin*" (III, 1:36–37; FL 102—translation modified).

56. My emphasis: "Do hies er mich das, des ich mich dikke weinende schemme . . . das was, das er eim snoeden wibe hies us gottes herzen und munt dis buoch schriben. Alsust ist dis buoch minnenklich von gotte har komen und ist *us menschlichen sinnen nit genommen*" (IV, 2:130–34; FL 144).

57. The Latin translation is preserved in two manuscripts designated in Neumann's edition Rb (Basel, Universitätsbibliothek, Cod. B IX 11, mid-C14) and Ra (Basel, Universitätsbibliothek, Cod A VIII 6, early C15). There is also a translation of the Latin back into MHG, designated Rw (Zentralbibliothek, Luzern, 1517). In 1877, the Latin version was collected with the writings of Gertrude and Mechthild von Hackeborn in Louis Paquelin's edition, *Revelationes Gertrudianae ac Mechthildianae.*

58. See Tobin, *Mechthild von Magdeburg,* 4; Odo Egres, "Mechthild von Magdeburg: *The Flowing Light of God,*" in *Cistercians in the Late Middle Ages,* ed. Rozanne Elder, Studies in Medieval Cistercian History 6 (Kalamazoo, Mich.: Cistercian Publications, 1981), 29–31; and Margetts, "Latein und Volkssprache," 125. Compare my study of the legacy of the translation in the early modern, nineteenth-, and twentieth-century reception of Mechtild: Sara S. Poor, "Historicizing Canonicity: Tradition and the Invisible Talent of Mechthild von Magdeburg," *Women in German Yearbook* 15 (2000): 49–72, at 54.

59. Köbele, *Bilder der unbegriffenen Wahrheit,* 38.

60. "ir súllent mit der megde sun úwern willen han" (I, 44:38–39; FL 60).

61. My translation. The apparatus in Neumann's edition lists all the variants from the manuscript tradition, including those that appear in the Latin versions Rb and Ra. See Mechthild von Magdeburg, *Das fließende Licht,* 1:29.

62. My translation: "tuon mit im, swas ich wil" (II, 22:19); see Köbele, *Bilder der unbegriffenen Wahrheit,* 78 n. 185.

63. Mechthild von Magdeburg, *Das fließende Licht,* 2:24. For more examples of the changes made in the Latin version, see Egres, "Mechthild von Magdeburg," 29–31.

64. My emphasis: "et religiose intelligenda, et secundum morem aliarum sanctarum scripturarum, sane et fideliter; sic nullum in ea lector scandalum habebit vel *offendiculum,* ipsaque scriptura nullam calumniam perfidiae sustinebit." Prologue to the *Lux Divinitatis,* in *Revelationes,* ed. Paquelin, 436. The English translation here is Frank Tobin's. See FL 32.

65. For the transmission of Bernard's sermons in German, see Werner Höver, *Theologia Mystica in altbairischer Übertragung: Bernhard von Clairvaux, Bonaventura, Hugo von Balma, Jean Gerson, Bernhard von Waging und andere: Studien zum Übersetzungswerk eines Tegernseer Anonymus aus der Mitte des 15. Jahrhunderts* (Munich: Beck, 1971), 5–51.

66. See Tobin, *Mechthild von Magdeburg: A Medieval Mystic in Modern Eyes,* 11–12. My comments take Tobin's observation a step further.

67. "Elegit namque persaepe infirma mundi omnipotens Deus ut fortiora salubriter erubescant . . . sexui fragili sua revelans mysteria, qui tempore legis mosaicae dignatus est similia misericorditer operari. Et quia populus Israel Debborae vaticinio credidit, liberationem ab oppressione et de hostibus victoriam est adeptus. Rex quoque cultor Dei, per orationem et consilium Oldae prophetissae, consolationem et misericordiam meruit invenire. Sic etiam omnes qui hunc librum scripturi vel lecturi sunt, si tamen pia intentione intenderint, incrementum consolationis et gratiae spiritus, sicut in ipso promissum est a Domino, consequentur." *Revelationes,* 436; English translation: FL 31–32.

68. Ibid.

69. For example VI, 36, quoted above.

70. "wan es mir das lustigistz tützsch ist und das innerlichst rürend minenschosz, das ich in tütz-scher sprach ie gelas . . . sitlichen und nit ze vil und wolchiü wort ir nit verstandint, die zeichend und schribentz mir, so betützsch ichs euch, wan es ward uns gar in fremdem tützsch gelichen, das wir wol zwai jar flisz und arbeit hetint, ee wirs ain wenig in unser tützsch brachtint." Philipp Strauch, *Margaretha Ebner und Heinrich von Nördlingen: Ein Beitrag zur Geschichte der deutschen Mystik* [1882] (Amsterdam: P. Schippers, 1966), 246–47.

71. Ibid., 243–44.

72. Ibid., 247.

73. Gertrud Jaron Lewis, *By Women, For Women, About Women: The Sister-Books of Fourteenth-Century Germany*, Studies and Texts 125 (Toronto: Pontifical Instute of Mediaeval Studies, 1996), 19.

74. "das got in im selber ist und in diszem buch bewiszt hat." Strauch, *Margaretha Ebner und Heinrich von Nördlingen*, 246.

75. My translation: "dis buoch [wart] geoffent in túsche von gotte einer swester, was ein helig maget beide an lip und an geiste" (foreword, 34–35).

76. There are eleven listed in Neumann's edition. I have found evidence of four others. See my "Gender und Autorität in der Konstruktion einer schriftlichen Tradition," in *Autorität der/in Sprache, Literatur, neuen Medien: Vorträge des Bonner Germanistentags 1997*, ed. Jürgen Fohrmann, Ingrid Kasten, and Eva Neuland (Bielefeld: Aisthesis Verlag, 1999), 532–52. The two manuscripts I discuss in the following pages are distinguished by their large and, in one case, attributed selections from Mechthild's book.

77. W. Schleussner, *Mechthild von Magdeburg: Das fließende Licht der Gottheit nach einer neu gefundenen Handschrift* (Mainz: Matthias Grünewald Verlag, 1929), iv.

78. Paul-Gerhard Völker, "Neues zur Überlieferung des 'Fliessenden Lichts der Gottheit,'" *ZfdA* 96 (1967): 28–69, at 59.

79. Colmar, Bibliothèque de la Ville, MS 2137.

80. "alle dise noch geschribenen kapitel sint geschriben vs den vii buecheren sant mehtilden und heissent das vs lühtende lieht der gotheit." MS C, fol. 78r.

81. The title of the first tract in the manuscript is "Dis sind die gebot der nuwen E" (These are the commandments of the new Law).

82. Barbara Kline, "Editing Women's Visions: Some Thoughts on the Transmission of Female Mystics' Texts," *Magistra* 2 (1996): 3–23, at 9.

PART II: 1300–1500
Vernacular Textualities

The five essays that make up Part II of this book cover more varied ground than the essays in Part I, but all focus in some way on vernacular textualities or communities. The vernacular is just as evangelical in the fourteenth and fifteenth centuries as in the thirteenth, as several writers discussed here testify: Nicole Oresme and Richard Ullerston, writing around 1400, are as concerned with disseminating knowledge as Giles of Rome a century earlier. But if efforts to make learning widely available were on the whole ever more ambitious during this period, they were also more controversial, sometimes to the point of censorship, as with Arundel's *Constitutions*. Partly for this reason, though more because the very success of written vernaculars led to greater diversification and specialization, many of the texts analyzed here have a more specific sense of agenda and audience than those discussed in Part I.

Some, such as the philosophical poems written in the tradition of the *Roman de la rose,* thus find cause for anxiety in that same accessibility of vernacular writing in which Mechthild von Magdeburg rejoices, and seek to exclude whole classes of readers (in this case, women). Others, like the *ricordanze* kept by Florentine merchants, are to be seen only by close family or business associates. Others still, like the book of poetry Froissart had copied in the dialect of Picardy for Richard II, contain delicate messages for one reader alone. Public poetry in a "common tongue" will always have a strongly local inflection, and (except in a very few outstanding cases) local circulation: Europe's first artisan poet, Antonio Pucci, combines popular and elite forms in a manner that speaks, not to the world, but to the city of Florence.

The first two essays, by Gretchen Angelo and Charles Briggs, offer very different pictures of (mostly) Parisian clerical attitudes toward vernacularization (or, in some cases, vulgarization), from Jean de Meun and Giles of Rome in the late thirteenth century to Eustace Deschamps and Nicole Oresme at the end of the fourteenth. Angelo's philosophical poets write their speculative works in a French that wants to be read, she suggests, only by intellectual men. Keeping women at bay by deliberately offending them (as Jean's section of the *Roman de la rose* offended Christine de Pizan) is a carefully articulated misogyny. This is designed to define the reader as part of a homosocial community that recognizes the text's authority and is rewarded for doing so by being invited to applaud its own cleverness. Vernacular misogyny asks for (and, in the *Querelle de la rose,* gets) bitter controversy, from at least the late fourteenth century on, in both France and England: a fact that suggests it must be doing hard cultural work for those it includes, as well as excludes. By the time of Deschamps, the alliance between lay and clerical intellectual men was well formed, although gallantry put pressure on misogyny for both. But what is the purpose of this alliance for an earlier clerical writer, like Jean? Why, since the vernacular remains partly the domain of women and of Jean's female personifications, choose it at all? Despite the fine studies by Serge Lusignan and Alastair Minnis (see Further Reading, page 257), the early institutionalization of French still seems almost too natural, too culturally inevitable, to analyze. Angelo's essay thus offers valuable evidence of contrivance, uncertainty, and strain.

Briggs's prose vulgarizers and translators, on the other hand, produce accessible digests of learning in Latin, French, and English, always with an eye to a local audience but also in the understanding that knowledge per se is a general good. Although some of them still think of Latin as different in kind from any vernacular, most have become aware that Latin was not always the language of truth but is one in a chain going back to Greek, Hebrew, and beyond: *translatio studii* is the sign under which these writers work. Indeed, the Latin they learn as aspiring scholastics could almost be a different language from the Latin of Cicero or Ovid, or from the vulgarized Latin of their own digests, handbooks, and encyclopedias. *Latin* for these clerics is almost as heterogeneous a concept as *vernacular.* For those whose mother tongue is French, indeed, the two may not even be quite separable. Translation and vulgarization are thus both motivated by a similar practical concern to assist readerships that span clerisy and laity, with none of the mechanisms of exclusion employed by Angelo's poets. (Though how great is the gulf, in reality? Is the gender-blindness of these writers inclusive of women readers, or does it simply assume their absence?) As in Waters's account of thirteenth-century preachers, whose concern for the laity arises partly out of a sense of community, these utilitarian writers feel little of the elitism or absolute difference from the world often associated with medieval clerics.

Whether they write in French or Latin, the groups of clerics discussed by Angelo and Briggs think about authority, audience, and language on a grand scale appropriate both to their ambition and (for the Parisians) to the cultural centrality of northern France. The next two essays, by Will Robins and Andrew Taylor, swerve sharply toward more local and private forms of vernacular writing. For Robins, mid-fourteenth-century Florence is not the city of Dante's *illustre volgare* or of Boccaccian internationalism, but rather of competing municipal textualities, distinguished from one another by function and opportunity. Merchant textuality fashions itself in private account books, which trace a merchant's assumptions of risk or obligation in a medley of economic, religious, and autobiographical modes whose sum is the merchant's personal and professional integrity. Even though the account book is shown only to close business associates, the vernacular, here, is the language of moral and economic transparency. (One feels the implied presence of the books of good and evil deeds said to be kept by the soul's guardian angel or demon, to be opened at the time of Judgment.) Artisan textuality, embattled as it was, moves outward into public space, laying claim to status in this heavily documentary culture as part of a wider claim to political enfranchisement. Thus living in a community run by bureaucrats, not aristocrats, the artisan poet Pucci fashions his identity neither in private books nor (like Usk or Hoccleve) through royal patronage, but by writing performance poetry that bridges oral and textual modes. Chirping like a tormented cricket (his image), Pucci's poetic gestures announce both his exclusion from power and his availability and skill. For the artisans, vernacular textuality signifies not transparency but opportunity.

Taylor's essay brings us back to the topic of French linguistic standardization (an implied presence in both Angelo's and Briggs's essays), although from an unusual angle. Where the artisan Pucci is necessarily assertive, the aristocratic Froissart, offering his costly book to a highly cultivated king in a gesture of goodwill whose cruder agendas must never be mentioned, is required to be infinitely nuanced. We naturally think of Froissart as French, Richard II as English. But for Froissart neither term is quite right: not, at least, when one is seeking patronage from a king technically at war with France. Picardish is very like Parisian French but sounds different and, by the late fourteenth century, was already thought provincial by comparison with the language of Machaut and Christine de Pizan. By having his poems copied in *franchois,* not *françois,* Froissart appeals to Richard less through the eye than the ear, in a Gallic tongue that he elsewhere implies should not really be called *French* at all. By ignoring the cultural dominance of Parisian French, he thus implicitly makes it, not the mighty inheritor of the mantle of Latin it is for Angelo's poetical clerics, but the mere dialect of an enemy polity. All the same, for all the subtle intimacy of the gesture (which Taylor reads as a reference to Froissart's old connection to Richard's grandmother, Philippa de Hainault, wife of Edward III), the form of this repudiation of *françois* admits much. Froissart's testimony to the cultural authority of Parisian French is in some ways, indeed, the stronger here for being so indirect.

In the final essay in Part II, Fiona Somerset's discussion of Ullerston's *Determinacio* (a defense of Bible translation) and Arundel's *Constitutions* (a piece of legislation that includes an attack on such translation), we seem at first to be moving back, not only to the clerisy, but into the realm of the evangelical, in which the vernacular can straightforwardly symbolize universality of access. Ullerston's theorizing of Bible translation (delivered in Oxford in 1401) encompasses the whole history of humanity from Babel on; the relation of knowledge to goodness; and many other large issues besides. A grand current *récit* about Arundel's censorship legislation of 1407–9 gives it an impressive role in fashioning a century-long epoch of stifled religious expression. However, Somerset aims to redirect our attention away from the universal rhetoric associated with these texts, to the specific community in which they had most force, the university of Oxford. For her, the *Determinacio* is, in part, a defense of the academic freedom that allows it to be written, even at a moment of cultural crisis. The *Constitutions,* on the other hand, is most importantly an attempt (not necessarily successful) to limit that freedom in the interests of theological stability and centralization, one that may not have had any causal influence on vernacular theology at all. As so often, the relation between gestures of enfranchisement or censorship and actual practice is more indirect than it seems. In Somerset's analysis, the textual community of the academy is Ullerston's and Arundel's real target.

The fourteenth and fifteenth centuries thus admit of finer and finer distinctions, both in vernacular praxis and in modern scholarly analysis thereof. If Llull's great synthetic attempt to preach the gospel to all the world can be taken as an exemplary symbol of its cultural moment, the situation a century later might best be summed up by Froissart's deft politicization of the difference between *ch* and *ç*. Admittedly, yoking these two figures together quickly summons a sense of the futility of resting much weight on the explanatory power of any large teleological narrative. Perhaps we should, rather, be comparing Llull with Ullerston, or Froissart with Orm. The vigor, variety, and social and cultural range of vernacular textualities in the last century before printing tells not one story but many.

Creating a Masculine Vernacular

The Strategy of Misogyny in Late Medieval French Texts

GRETCHEN V. ANGELO

Christine de Pizan begins her *Cité des dames* in despair at the misogyny present in the writings of "so many famous men—such solemn scholars, possessed of such deep and great understanding, so clear-sighted in all things."[1] The antifeminism common in both classical and Christian writing is indeed manifest to any reader, medieval or modern, and Christine was not alone among her contemporaries in observing it.[2] Far from sharing her dismay, however, other writers profited from the association between authority and misogyny. I argue in this essay that misogyny was an important tool used by some French authors to present themselves, too, as "solemn scholars." Misogyny served as a hallmark of *translatio studii,* allowing male authors to place themselves in an illustrious line of scholarship. It simultaneously weakened the association of vernacular literature with the feminine by creating a masculine textual community and a masculine vernacular.

In their study of antimarriage literature, Katharina Wilson and Elizabeth Makowski distinguish three types of what they term "misogamy": ascetic, philosophical, and general.[3] The latter two terms are equally useful in classifying the misogynous content of vernacular literature. "General" misogyny appears commonly in comic French works, such as the nouvelles, the farces, and the fabliaux. Here, women are castigated for a variety of faults, but although the most usual victims of the women's transgressions are their husbands, the authors display little sense of male solidarity. The male members of the audience, reveling in *Schadenfreude,* are meant to laugh at the hapless male dupe as much as at the culpable woman.

A number of late medieval French vernacular works, on the other hand, display a "philosophical" misogyny that specifically views women as antithetical to a scholar's pursuit. Women here can be harmful, but are more often merely irrelevant. Male and female spheres of endeavor are clearly separate, and the written word falls within the province of men. The use of this type of misogyny implicitly defines every male reader as a scholar and consequently reorients the text toward a male audience.

The common motif of these works is a differentiation of language by gender. Female speech is unreliable and the object of misogynous criticism or sarcasm, while the presence of a male scribal figure, who records, evaluates, and controls women's speech, demonstrates the preeminence of a written male language. Author and audience are aligned with that male voice, creating a masculine textual community that excludes women. This community nevertheless remains hierarchical: the author demonstrates his mastery through his selection and interpretation of his materials. Just as the clerkly narrators establish their superiority by judging the contributions of the other characters, so the author who guides his readers' interpretation underlines both his work and his own authority by stressing the text's complexity and need for glossing. Simultaneously author and commentator, he leads his audience to trust in his authority.

As Serge Lusignan explains, the first wholesale attempt to produce a body of serious texts in French was directed by the nobility.[4] Translations of classical texts, histories, medical treatises, and other intellectual works were commissioned by an elite who did not have clerical mastery of Latin but nevertheless wished to possess the libraries of educated men. In this corpus, the authority of the original texts made them viable candidates for translation. When a text was composed directly in French, however, this inherited authority disappeared. Indeed, the traditional association of the "mother tongue"[5] with a female audience and content made vernacular authority difficult to establish.

The strategy of misogyny attempted to counter this difficulty. Although these works at first glance belong to typically "feminine" genres (an allegorical quest for love, a debate on love and marriage, a compendium of female wisdom), they eventually reveal their concern with weightier matters. The distinction between female speech and male writing is thus invoked as an authorizing device, with profound consequences for textual reception. This distinction allows the traditional separation between Latin, the written language of learning, and French, the spoken language of the people, to be re-created within French itself: written French becomes the province of the male author and audience, while spoken French, the realm of women, is admitted into the text only by that author. Reading in the vernacular, far from being the province of women, is not merely extended to men but metaphorically restricted to them. Ironically, it is the very accessibility of these texts to women readers that motivates their exclusion; the author asserts the right to define his own implied audience. The crucial gesture is the orientation of the text toward a male audience: the rhetorical signal that the text is worthy of men's considered attention.[6] Similarly, both the misogynous content and the

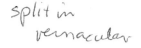

subversion of women's voices serve to distance the works from a female readership.

This technique was used profitably in a variety of works.[7] However, this essay focuses on three related texts that demonstrate its development from the late thirteenth to the beginning of the fifteenth century: Jean de Meun's portion of the *Roman de la Rose;* Eustache Deschamps's *Miroir de Mariage;* and Christine de Pizan's contributions to the debate on the *Rose.*

The dilemma of how to reorient a traditionally feminine genre toward a masculine readership was innovatively addressed and resolved by Jean de Meun in his continuation of Guillaume de Lorris's *Roman de la Rose.* His solution relied upon an abundance of a recognizably erudite misogynistic content, a misogyny that symbolically creates a pact between male author and reader, while excluding women from active or passive participation. In his text and those that copied his strategy, misogyny functions both intertextually and intratextually. First, citation of philosophic misogyny signals a mastery of the Latin *auctores* and confers a degree of inherited authority on the vernacular author by inserting his work into a line of authoritative texts. Next, the depictions of characters within the text effectively separate male and female language and replace the long-standing dichotomy between Latin and vernacular with a new dichotomy that opposes a learned, written, and masculine vernacular to a popular, oral, and feminine one.

In Jean's *Rose,* misogyny occupies a central position through its most explicit formulation, the citation of Theophrastus (8531 ff.). In a work filled with invocations of authority, the Theophrastus fragment still manages to attract the reader's attention, thanks to both its length and its *emboîtement,* analyzed by Daniel Poirion.[8] Jean de Meun places the misogynous Theophrastus segment, a text preserved only through its citation in Jerome's *Against Jovinian,* in the middle of Jaloux's speech, itself interpolated within the discourse of Ami. The location of this citation in the mouth of an unscholarly and untrustworthy character might lead the reader to discount the value of what he says, were it not for the unchallenged legitimacy of its source.[9] In addition to demonstrating Jean's erudition, this citation cements the sense of masculine community presented throughout the text. Even a man as untutored as Jaloux, it implies, can share the wisdom of the ancients. The ambiguous context of this fragment, however, again underlines the role of the author, who alone can tell us to accept or discount the words of each character.

The author is yet more important in the *Rose*'s original material. Jean complements his citation of ancient authority with his own textual misogyny, primarily through disjunctions between male and female use of language. The

Rose contains three pairings of a female speaker and a male writer: Raison and Amant, La Vieille and Bel Accueil, and Nature and Genius. All three female figures here were familiar from earlier works, and their portraits reproduce the ambiguity of the Theophrastus citation.

Virtually the first act of Jean de Meun upon assuming Guillaume de Lorris's project is to engineer the return of Raison. Her transformation inversely mirrors that of the text. As Raison descends into the courtly universe, the *Rose* gains scope and grandeur, moving beyond that female-oriented world. When Raison becomes a lady, and, later, Nature a woman, their voices lose a measure of authority, and it is the male author who must assume the responsibility for properly interpreting those voices.

In Guillaume de Lorris's portion of the *Rose*, Raison's nobility proceeds from her allegorical nature and origin: she is made by God "a sa semblance et a s'image" (in his likeness and in his image) (2975).[10] Unlike other women made from man, Raison is complete in her own right. She need not obey, but can remonstrate freely with Amant. It is true that even in Guillaume's text, Amant refuses to listen to her: "vos poriez bien gaster / en oiseuse vostre françois" (you could waste your French in idleness) (3072–73). But this refusal merely underscores the traditional opposition between Love and Reason and does not diminish her authority in the least. In fact, the contrast distinguishes Raison from other women; she alone is neither interested in nor subject to Love.

Jean's Raison, while still imposing, is diminished by her obvious femininity. Poirion describes the "surprenante coquetterie" of Jean's Raison,[11] who points out her own beauty and presents herself as the more attractive physical, as well as intellectual, choice (5765–70). Whereas Guillaume's Raison is described in terms redolent of balance and perfection (2962–72), Jean's is "Reson la bele, l'avenant" (beautiful, attractive Raison) (4196). Raison is now first and foremost a "cortaise pucelle" (courtly maiden) (6901). The celebrated discussion of her use of the word *coilles* (testicles) (5507), emphasized by Jean's deferral of it twice (5665, 6898), centers above all on this word's propriety in the mouth of a "courtly" lady. Raison's ultimate exit from the text is due, in large part, to the rules that govern what women can say.

Just as misogyny's exclusion of female readers is merely symbolic (women could still read a text, no matter how misogynous), so is the *Rose*'s rejection of Raison.[12] In their debate, Raison surpasses Amant in both style and substance. Raison chides him for his lack of scholarly acumen: "tu n'as pas bien pour moi mater / cerchié les livres anciens; / tu n'iés pas bons logiciens" (you have not, to overcome me, examined old books; you are not a good logician) (5724–26).[13] It is she who cites authority after authority in defense of her speech, to which he is deliberately deaf. While he can recite it by heart (4336), he is proud to have learned nothing from it: "De ce me vant, / je n'en sai pas plus que devant" (I flatter myself that I know no more than before) (4331–32).

Nevertheless, Amant *is* the writer of the book. The *Rose* recounts Amant's scholarly as well as his sentimental education; the poem leads him inexorably toward the moment when he will take up his stylus and write, as both Amour and Genius have commanded (10519–20, 19531–35). We are repeatedly reminded of Amant's status as writer, especially at the midpoint of the book. Here, Amant is both the *Rose*'s authors at once: Guillaume, who requires help in his present quest, and Jean, who will provide it (10496–624). It is Jean's book, produced by his reading of Amant's, that will become the *Rose*. "Car tant en lira proprement / que tretuit cil qui ont a vivre / devroient apeler ce livre / le Miroër aus Amoreus" (He will read so fittingly that all those alive should call his book *The Mirror for Lovers*) (10618–21).[14]

Not coincidentally, it is at this most explicit link between Amant and the author(s) that Raison is mentioned once more. Readers of the *Rose* will learn much from it if they only believe Jean, rather than Raison: "ja mes cil qui les orront / des douz mauz d'amer ne morront, / por qu'il le croient seulement" (those who hear these words will never die from the sweet pains of love, provided that they believe only him) (10614–17). If we should believe Jean rather than Raison, it is only because he, as male author, edits and controls each character's speech. This, indeed, is emphasized in the remarkable explanation of the poem's dual authorship, where we are reminded that Jean's duty will be to record "totes les autres paroles, / quex qu'els soient, sages ou foles" (all the other speeches, whatever they may be, wise or foolish) (10567–68).

This identification of male character with male author is repeated in the second female-male pairing, that of La Vieille and Bel Accueil. Unlike Amant, Bel Accueil does not write; he serves as a masculine conduit between narrator and readers. La Vieille's speech to Bel Accueil is notable because it is the only time that the latter is separated from the Rose. Before and after his imprisonment in the tower, he functions as the liaison between Amant and the Rose and is one facet of the woman the Rose represents. Yet the emphasis on his male gender in the scene with La Vieille ensures the continued presence of the male voice in the text.[15] Ostensibly, La Vieille is instructing the young girl in her care, but this "all-girl talk" is appropriated by the male text through the good graces of Bel Accueil. Instead of teaching a docile female pupil, La Vieille preaches to a highly critical male. Their relationship parallels that of Raison to Amant; La Vieille's speech presents yet another doctrine detrimental to the quest of the Lover.

Far from muting Bel Accueil's gender to blur his difference from the female beloved, the passage emphasizes his masculinity. La Vieille repeatedly calls him "son" or "young man" (12525, 12728, etc.), and further connects her male interlocutor to other men. La Vieille points out that her advice is necessary: "car perilleusement s'i baigne / jennes hon qui n'a qui l'ensaigne" (for a young man who has no one to teach him goes there to bathe at his peril) (12727–28). Even if Bel Accueil's gender explained the insistence upon *his* status as "young man," this unnecessary generalization of La Vieille's advice to apply to *all* young men designates them as the true *destinataires* of her speech. Her lesson will profit the male audience, who receive warning of the grasping avarice of those they are courting and a moral justification for the deceitful approach recommended by Ami.

The text's final juxtaposition, of Nature and Genius, concretizes the valorization of male writing over female speech. Behind the seeming harmony between this woman and her priest lies a strict differentiation between their fields of endeavor. We encounter Nature in the midst of physical labor, while Genius is introduced as he writes in his book. Genius, a clerical figure, possesses literary as well as ecclesiastical authority. His apparent submission to Nature veils his true power: as scribe and priest, he can choose both what part of her message to record and what part to transmit via his sermon. "Lors escrit cil, et cele dite" (Then he wrote it at her dictation) (19375), we are told—but how faithful is his transcription? When he reads to the assembled forces of Nature's army "la diffinitive santance" (19474), it quickly becomes clear that this is not entirely Nature's work, despite his claim to speak by her authority (19475). Both writer and reader, he omits, for example, her discussion of vices, instead referring curious readers back to the *Rose* (19849–54), and allegorizes the text's own earlier description of the Garden of Pleasure (20237 ff.). The circularity of this gesture again reminds readers of the link between the male characters within the text and the male author of that text.

Moreover, Genius's misogynous remarks induce the reader to value his words more than those of Nature. Despite the convergence of Nature's complaint and Amant's quest, her confessor shows little patience for her reasoning; sharply rebuking her, ordering her to "lessiez ester vostre pleur" (cease your weeping) (16281), he contrasts his objective, intellectual view with her female fussing. Undermining his original comment that her unhappiness must have serious grounds, he reflects: "Mes, san faille, il est voirs que fame / Legierement d'ire s'anflame" (But it is also true, without fail, that a woman is easily inflamed with wrath) (16293–94). Then he launches into a 380-line denunciation of "diverse and muable" woman (16298), particularly of her language, implicitly associating Nature with such a female (despite his specific exemption of her at 16671–73). Finally, we see that Genius's dismissal of the gravity of Nature's concern is justified; for while she mopes about her forge, Amant has been avidly pursuing his love, a staunch adversary of those about whom Nature complains so loudly.

Throughout the *Rose,* then, female characters speak vainly, their message either antithetical or superfluous to the purposes of their male interlocutors. Thematically, female speech is marginalized, and it can be understood properly only once the male voice of authority contextualizes it. The strategy of misogyny thus accomplishes a somewhat paradoxical double triumph: reinventing the vernacular as masculine, it simultaneously glorifies the role of the author. Although, on one level, the text congratulates its self-selected male readers on their acumen, granting its male audience the same perspicacity as the male author, on another, by establishing the authority of the latter, it renders his interpretative voice indispensable for his readers.

Interesting as Jean's use of linguistic misogyny may be, however, one might wonder whether this strategy was recognized or duplicated in later texts. Given the layers of contradiction within the *Rose,* perhaps the devalorization of women's speech, like the heroic final assault on the maiden's castle, must be read on multiple levels. In his study on the reception of the *Rose,* Pierre- Yves Badel demonstrates, first, that the *Rose,* preserved in nearly three hundred manuscripts, was not merely popular but universally acknowledged as a masterpiece; second, that particularly in the fourteenth century its main use was as a source of misogynous material.[16] Jean's dual reputation as both authority and misogynist, taken in concert with the way in which certain texts deliberately echo his strategy, thus does suggest that at least some readers found his creation of a masculine vernacular acceptable.

Two exemplars directly related to the *Rose,* Eustache Deschamps's *Miroir de Mariage* and the *Querelle de la Rose,* echo this technique in the later Middle Ages. Sylvia Huot has described the *Miroir de Mariage* as a "response to and recasting of the *Roman de la Rose,*"[17] and certainly the two works have much in common. A fourteenth-century debate on marriage and celibacy, the *Miroir* opposes Folie, who presents her pro-marriage arguments orally, and Reper-toire de Science, whose justification of celibacy is submitted in writing to the protagonist, Franc Vouloir. The female speaker's message is overwritten by the male writer, whose 7282-line letter occupies almost two-thirds of the text. Although its nominal purpose is to answer Franc Vouloir's doubts about matrimony, we must note that its composer is labeled a repertory of *science* in general, not merely of marriage. The author of the letter demonstrates scholarly procedure as well as knowledge: to respond to Franc Vouloir's inquiry, he "cerche touz ses livres" (searches all his books) (chapter XIV title). Although not announced as the adaptation it is (of Hugo de Folieto's *De nuptiis*), the letter marks Deschamps, as well as Repertoire, as erudite, and thus encourages the reader to treat the entire text respectfully. This inclination is fortified by the textual procedures Deschamps uses to strengthen his own authorial voice as he, like Jean de Meun, gradually rejects the female voice in the work.

Unlike the highborn Raison and Nature, Folie seems to declare, by her very name, the vanity of her arguments. Interestingly, however, her central importance is concealed until late in the poem. Franc Vouloir writes that the initial invitation to marry is presented him by four "faintis / qui cuident estre moult soubtis" (false friends who believe themselves very subtle) (79–80). Desir, Folie, Servitute, and Faintise, named only in the *title* of the second chapter, seem to speak in unison ("Ce me dient . . . M'ont admonnesté mariage" [They said to me . . . they advised me to marry] [84, 86]). Only at the end of their initial speech do we learn that one has been speaking for all: "Je parle en nous, c'est pour tous quatre / Aux trois a pleu pour eulx esbatre / . . . / Que ce fait au long te diroye" (I say "we," speaking for all four; the other three preferred that I tell you all) (463–66). There is little to indicate which of the four is speaking, and although three of the four are feminine, all references to them in the first part of the text are communal and use the masculine plural—"faintis" (79), "beaux seigneurs" (474), "enhorteurs de mariage" (proponents of marriage), and "docteurs" (8427–28). Instead of the typical portrait of an allegorical lady, we have an impression of hoary scholars; Franc Vouloir comments that "samble bien a vostre fait/ Que les livres avez veus/ Et estudiez et sceus" (it seems from your appearance that you have read and studied and learned from books) (488–90).

It is not until after Repertoire's letter that Folie explicitly moves to the forefront to respond and becomes the clear guiding force behind the pro-marriage party. Naturally, having absorbed the largely misogynous content of the letter, the reader is unlikely to treat with respect any feminine speaker, much less one named Folie. All four of Franc Vouloir's *enhorteurs* respond to the letter individually, but Folie speaks first, last, and over five times as much as any of her companions, and it is she who is ultimately dismissed by Franc Vouloir. Whereas earlier Folie was identified only in the rubrics, she is now named repeatedly within the text, with numerous asides on her name as well as her feminine nature. No characterization is ever given of her female comrades Servitute and Faintise, but Folie proudly presents herself, not as a relatively sexless allegorical figure, but as a married woman who, like the Wife of Bath, takes umbrage at the misogynous tradition represented by Repertoire and his text. To reject Folie, clearly, is to embrace the authority offered by Repertoire and to align oneself with the male side of the argument shared by narrator, protagonist, and audience. Repudiating the pretensions of female speech, Franc Vouloir silences her, in a statement that unexpectedly echoes her supposed male ally, Désir: "Folie, bien vous pouez taire, / Car vostre conseil ne vault rien" (Folly, you may as well be silent, for your advice is worthless) (11038–39, see 9892).

Deschamps's text, far more straightforward and less ambiguous than the *Rose,* makes much clearer the link between the figurative silencing of women and the serious nature of the text. In the *Miroir,* the late revelation of Folie's true nature and the dismissal of her feminine argument coincide with a sudden expansion of the work. Just as the scholar must avoid marriage in order to safeguard his masculine language and thought, the text gains free rein to move into more serious areas of debate once it liberates itself from the female voice. No longer simply a character foolishly promoting marriage, Folie assumes an extratextual role, excoriated by the narrator for problems ranging from the defeat of Roland to unfavorable treaties with the English and revolts in Paris before the unfinished text abruptly halts. Similarly, Franc Vouloir metamorphoses from an innocent bachelor into the personification of liberty in general: it is he who was *subjugué* by Folie (chapter XCIV title) in the numerous battles discussed.

Recent criticism has recognized the lofty aspirations of Deschamps's voluminous yet incomplete text. Monique Engel sees "la volonté . . . d'écrire une sorte de somme" or "histoire universelle," and Michelle Stoneburner sees the marriage debate as a metaphor for political union and the poem as a commentary on contemporary political and social questions.[18]

While I agree that the poem manifests a desire for greater things, I argue that the misogynous element, far from being merely a metaphor, is crucial to the establishment of the textual voice of authority. The creation of a male vernacular through misogyny is a key factor in the new importance accorded to the vernacular author.[19] Howard Bloch has argued that "the discourse of misogyny is always to some extent avowedly derivative; it is a citational mode whose rhetorical thrust displaces its own source away from anything that might be construed as personal or confessional,"[20] but the literary quarrels of the fifteenth century prove the opposite. By founding their authority on invented as well as inherited misogyny, the vernacular authors intimately link their persona to that misogyny. A. J. Minnis has said that "if, at the end of the Middle Ages, *auctores* became more like men, men became more like *auctores.*"[21] The author becomes an individual personality, and his perceived beliefs become a basis for criticism or praise. It is noteworthy that the two important literary quarrels of fifteenth-century France, on the *Rose* and the *Belle dame sans merci,* both link authority to misogyny and language. The quarrels show the extent to which misogyny had indeed become an accepted feature of vernacular works and, further, how it had contributed to a new conception of the author.

The debate on the *Rose* is interesting, first, because its dual emphasis on questions of proper language and on the authority of Jean de Meun illustrates the link between these two themes; second, because the tenor of the *querelle* itself reproduces the male/female divide established by the vernacular misogynous works.

Christine de Pizan's main objections to the *Rose* center on the vulgarity of the work and its attacks on women. In both cases, the question of female participation in the textual universe is paramount. For Christine, Jean's use of language fails on two accounts. Of minor relevance here is her contention that, in the final analysis, no cleverness of expression can outweigh the banality of Jean's material. Sex is nothing new, and there is no need to write such an elaborately disguised description of it. Far more significant is the other side of her argument: that Jean's brutal mention of *choses deshonnetes* is inappropriate for a genteel audience. Like Amant, Christine takes exception to the use of uncourtly words in a courtly setting. The gender roles are reversed: in the *Rose,* Amant accuses Reason of unladylike behavior; here, Christine accuses Jean of ungentlemanly conduct.

Christine's reaction to the *Rose,* accompanied by her praise of conventional female exemplars (typified by Griselda) in the *Cité des dames* and the *Trésor,* has led some modern readers to disown her as a feminist role model. Given her admiration of traditional feminine virtues, one might think that Christine's outraged reaction is real, not merely rhetorical: "Et dont que fait a louer lecture qui n'osera estre leue ne parlee en propre forme a la table des roynes, des princesses et des vaillans preudefemmes—a qui convendroit couvrir la face de honte rougie?" (And so what is there to praise in a book that one would not dare read or speak of properly at the table of queens, princesses, or other worthy ladies, who would be obliged to cover their faces in shame?)[22]

And yet, in light of Christine's larger body of work, I find it hard to believe that she did not sense the larger danger. Christine's emphasis on decorum may be her means of reversing Jean de Meun's argument to her own advantage. Rejecting the utility of a text that is inhospitable to women is a gesture precisely opposite to Jean's. He attempts to construct a textual universe where woman's voice is inappropriate and the right to speak belongs only to men. Christine, insisting on the female right to *hear,* as audience, implicitly asserts as well their capacity to *judge.* Christine's apparently prudish response may in fact be a rhetorical gesture as pointed as Jean's. She explicitly counters his removal of his *Rose* from a courtly context and insists that *only* a mixed audience can determine a work's true merit. As is clear in Christine's introduction to the *Cité des dames,* this woman author was keenly aware of how misogyny could create barriers to female participation in the scholarly milieu. Her insistence on language equally accessible to women and men seeks to ensure that vernacular literature retain its promise and that gestures of exclusion not render null its linguistic accessibility.

The language of the debate itself, however, shows that the split between male and female vernaculars already runs deep. Christine herself, like the authoritative figures in the *Rose,* sees her voice challenged by her male readers solely on account of its femininity. Her attempt at reframing the argument within a courtly context fails, and Christine, in order to project a more authoritative voice, must abandon the acceptably humble female demeanor she initially adopts toward her male correspondents.

For despite her description of the *débat,* in her letter to Guillaume de Tygnonville, as typically courtly, "gracieux et non haineux" (gracious and not hateful), the *querelle* in fact, like the *Rose* itself, substitutes a scholarly for a courtly milieu. The terms Christine at first uses in her version of the modesty topos, "femmenine ignorance" (feminine ignorance) (7), "femme ignorant d'entendement et de sentement legier" (woman lacking understanding and of slight intelligence), "femmenine foiblece" (feminine weakness) (12), follow a conservative pattern, emphasizing her femininity to excuse her linguistic, logical, and intellectual faults. Gontier Col's response, however, establishes that, for him, these are no mere tropes: "l'erreur manifeste, folie ou demence a toy venue par presompcion ou oultrecuidance et comme femme passionnee en ceste matiere—ne te desplaise se je dis voir" (the manifest error, madness, or insanity caused by your presumption or arrogance and [the fact that you speak] as an impassioned woman in this matter—do not be displeased if I speak the truth) (23). In her response, therefore, Christine abandons any pejorative connotations for the word *femme* and uses it only to object to Col's characterization of her: "tes deuziemes lettres plus injurieuses repprouchant mon femmenin sexe (lequel tu dis passionné comme par nature et meu de folie et presompcion)" (your second insulting letter reproaching my feminine sex [which you call impassioned by nature and moved by madness and presumption]) (25); "la petitesse de ma faculté (laquelle tu me reproches de dire 'comme femme,' etc.)" (the smallness of my understanding [as when you reproach me for speaking "like a woman," etc.]) (25). Instead, she proclaims herself proud to compare herself to "tres grant foison vaillans femmes" (a great number of worthy women) (25), and now speaks of her "veritable oppinion justement meue" (true opinion rightfully inspired) (24) rather than of her "petit engin" (small understanding) (12).

In her subsequent exchanges with Pierre Col, Christine blames any deficiencies in her style on "le deffault et l'ignorance" (error and lack of knowledge) (116), as a male author might, excluding any reference to her
femininity. Col, however, firmly returns her to courtly ground: insincerely
praising her as a woman "de grant engin" and "de hault entendement" (of
great intelligence, of superior understanding) (109, 153), he shows his true
opinion of her temerity. As a woman, she has no right to criticize a man:

> O tres fole oultrecuidance! O parole trop tost yssue et sans avis de
> bouche de fame, qui comdampne home de si hault entendement, de
> si fervant estude, qui a si grant labeur et meure deliberacion a fait si
> tres noble livre comme celluy de la *Rose,* qui passe aussy tous autres
> qui onques fussent en langage ou il escript son livre.

> [O mad arrogance! O words pronounced too quickly and without
> counsel by the mouth of a woman, who condemns a man of such
> great understanding, of such fervent study, who with such great labor
> and mature deliberation wrought such a noble work as the *Rose,*
> which surpasses all others that ever were written in the language in
> which he wrote his book!] (102)

Col's language shows that Jean's model has been integrated into literary consciousness; the simplest way to deny Christine authority is to stigmatize her
use of French as oral, feminine, and incompetent, in stark contrast to Jean's
written mastery of it.

Rita Copeland has noted that "the vernacular appropriation of a certain
cultural privilege is not necessarily a dismantling of that privilege: in many
respects it is only a transfer (literally a 'translation') of cultural authority from
one sphere to another."[23] Defending the *Roman de la Rose,* Pierre Col argues
that unlike Ovid's *Art of Love,* which women cannot understand,[24] Jean de
Meun teaches young women how to defend their castle, not merely men how
to conquer it (105). The undeniable accessibility of vernacular texts to female
readers necessitated the invention of new ways to block their access. The use
of misogyny was one of these: symbolically and perhaps in reality, it excluded
women from the audience for scholarly vernacular texts.

As male constructs of an author denigrated or rejected female speech, the
literary vernacular formerly stigmatized as female underwent a schism, displacing female vernacular to the oral and constructing a new written male
vernacular. The authority established through misogyny not only allowed a
male author to compose serious works in the vernacular; it helped to valorize

the role of the author as interpreter of his text. The authorial responsibility evidenced in the fifteenth-century *querelles* demonstrates the importance of this concept by the late Middle Ages: the male voice of authority must reveal the univocal message of the text, even if that message is directed only at a select few who can truly understand it.

NOTES

1. Christine de Pizan, *The Book of the City of Ladies,* trans. Earl Jeffrey Richards (New York: Persea Books, 1982), 4.

2. Useful texts on medieval misogyny include R. Howard Bloch, *Medieval Misogyny and the Invention of Western Romantic Love* (Chicago: University of Chicago Press, 1991); Katherine M. Rogers, *The Troublesome Helpmate: A History of Misogyny in Literature* (Seattle: University of Washington Press, 1966); and Robert Pratt, "Jankyn's Book of Wikked Wyves: Medieval Antimatrimonial Propaganda in the Universities," *Annuale Mediaevale* 3 (1962): 5–27.

3. Katharina Wilson and Elizabeth Makowski, *Wykked Wyves and the Woes of Marriage: Misogamous Literature from Juvenal to Chaucer* (Albany: State University of New York Press, 1990), 3–6.

4. Serge Lusignan, *Parler vulgairement* (see Further Reading, page 257), 129–50.

5. While the expression "mother tongue," used as early as the eleventh century, is not always associated with the feminine, some medieval commentators do describe it as the language learned from one's mother. See ibid., 41, 67, and 106, and Glenda McLeod, *Virtue and Venom: Catalogs of Women from Antiquity to the Renaissance* (Ann Arbor: University of Michigan Press, 1991), 62 and 74.

6. See Wogan-Browne et al., *The Idea of the Vernacular* (see Further Reading), 110–16, for a discussion of the types of audience and their importance in vernacular texts.

7. See Gretchen V. Angelo, "Author and Authority in the *Evangiles des Quenouilles,*" *Fifteenth-Century Studies* 26 (2001): 21–41, and idem, "A Most Uncourtly Lady: The Testimony of the *Belle Dame sans Mercy,*" *Exemplaria* 15:1 (spring 2003): 133–57.

8. Daniel Poirion, *Le Roman de la Rose* (Paris: Hatier, 1973), 125.

9. The trustworthy nature of the speaker of the *Against Jovinian* was a novelty. See McLeod, *Virtue and Venom,* 46.

10. Guillaume de Lorris and Jean de Meun, *Le Roman de la Rose,* ed. Felix Lecoy (Paris: Champion, 1965–70). Translations are from Charles Dahlberg, trans., *The Romance of the Rose* (Princeton: Princeton University Press, 1971).

11. Poirion, *Le Roman de la Rose,* 116.

12. The scope of this paper does not allow me to analyze adequately the irony and contradictions of the *Rose,* and in particular the thorny issue of Raison. It should be understood that my discussion of Raison is limited here to her role within this topos of linguistic misogyny. For a discussion of Raison's role in the poem as a whole, see John Fleming, *Reason and the Lover* (Princeton: Princeton University Press, 1984).

13. See also 6270, 6747, 6777, 7132, etc.

14. See also 2050, 2058, 10367.

15. Michel Zink offers an alternate interpretation in "Bel Accueil le Travesti," *Littérature* 47 (1982): 31–40.

16. Pierre-Yves Badel, *Le Roman de la Rose au XIVᵉ siècle: Étude de la réception de l'oeuvre* (Geneva: Droz, 1980), 135 and 142.

17. Sylvia Huot, "The *Miroir de Mariage:* Deschamps Responds to the *Roman de la Rose,*" in Debo-

rah Sinnreich-Levi, ed., *Eustache Deschamps: French Courtier-Poet* (New York: AMS, 1998), 131–44, at 131.

18. Monique Engel, "Le *Miroir de Mariage* d'Eustache Deschamps: Sources et tradition," in Franco Simone, ed., *Seconda miscellanea di studi e ricerche sul quattrocento francese* (Chambéry: Centre d'Études Franco-Italien, 1981), 145–67, at 154 and 155.

Michelle Stoneburner, "*Le Miroir de Mariage:* Misunderstood Misogyny," in Sinnreich-Levi, *Eustache Deschamps,* 145–62.

19. For the changing role of the author, see Burt Kimmelman, *The Poetics of Authorship in the Later Middle Ages: The Emergence of the Modern Literary Persona* (New York: Peter Lang, 1996); Jesse Gellrich, *The Idea of the Book in the Middle Ages: Language Theory, Mythology, and Fiction* (Ithaca: Cornell University Press, 1985); Alastair J. Minnis, *Medieval Theory of Authorship* (see Further Reading); and John Miles Foley, "The Implications of Oral Tradition," in *Oral Tradition in the Middle Ages,* ed. W. F. H. Nicolaisen (Binghamton, N.Y.: Medieval and Renaissance Texts and Studies, 1995), 31–57.

20. Bloch, *Medieval Misogyny,* 47.

21. Minnis, *Medieval Theory of Authorship,* 216.

22. Eric Hicks, ed., *Le débat sur le Roman de la Rose* (see Further Reading), 20.

23. Rita Copeland, *Rhetoric, Hermeneutics, and Translation* (see Further Reading), 224–25.

24. Col ignores the fact that Roman women would have been able to read Latin.

Teaching Philosophy at School and Court

Vulgarization and Translation

CHARLES F. BRIGGS

Recent studies of Latin-to-vernacular translation during the central and late Middle Ages have shown that this activity was often implicated, whether in a contestative or supportive way, in a complex of relationships between cultures—clerical and lay, oral and literate, official and popular, masculine and feminine.[1]

Useful and insightful as much of this work is, however, it tends to neglect the utilitarian pedagogical concerns that motivated many of the translators. In this essay, I intend to take seriously the stated intentions of translators like Nicole Oresme and John Trevisa, who argued for the utility of their translations as a means to educate their intended lay audiences. I will show that their own experience as students and masters in medieval schools, whether universities or monastic and mendicant *studia,* not only had convinced them of the practical value of the lore contained in the works they translated, but also suggested to them that vernacular translation was a natural continuation of a process well under way in the classroom, this being the vulgarization of an extensive and varied literature loaded with complex and difficult-to-comprehend philosophical concepts. To begin, I will discuss the academic preparation of many of the translators and consider how their intellectual formation influenced their views of translation and motivated their translating activities. I will also address the study and translation, during the later Middle Ages, of moral philosophy, which was the branch of the school curriculum deemed by Latinate *literati* and readers of the vernacular alike as the most useful for a lay audience.

Before proceeding, it will be helpful to define some terms. Here the term "vulgarization" is used in the narrow sense of an *intralingual* abridging, expanding, or simplifying of technical or abstruse matter, in order to make it easier to understand and thus more widely known. In contrast, "vernacularization" I define as an *interlingual* transference of matter from the language of learning to that of the mother tongue. Also, I tend to use the generalized terms "school" or *studium* to refer to any institution of clerical education, whether that be a university (Lat. *studium generale*) or a monastic or mendicant school (Lat. *schola* or *studium*).

First, it must be stressed that all scholars of the later Middle Ages were both *laici* and *illiterati* when they began their studies. Most spent their formative years in a largely lay milieu, and throughout their lives most would continue to have significant interaction with layfolk. Also, when aspiring clerks began their study of Latin, they did so in relation to their mother tongue; and during the course of their studies they developed a diglossia (or, in the case of the English before about 1350, triglossia) in which Latin and the vernacular constantly supported one another, even if Latin was seen to be the senior partner in that relationship.[2] They were, in fact, so wholly immersed in a bilingual environment that Latin became for them what amounted to a second native tongue. Claude Buridant has even argued that for Romance speakers educated in this way, Latin-to-vernacular translation was not really translation at all in the way we think of it, but rather a "transposition intralinguale" from a language of culture to a language of diffusion.[3]

For twelfth-century scholars steeped in the Roman classics, this "nativized" Latin would likely have included plenty of classical vocabulary, usages, and syntactic forms.[4] But changes in the curriculum occasioned by the translations into Latin of a prodigious number of Greek and Arabic scientific and philosophical works substantially altered the Latin-language learning environment of students in the later-thirteenth- and fourteenth-century *studia*. From the point of view of a classical purist, the Latin of these translations was graceless and pedestrian at best, and barbarous at worst.[5] To begin with, the style of Aristotle's philosophico-scientific works, and of the texts of Muslim scholars who commented upon them, was hardly Ciceronian. In the case of translations from the Arabic, moreover, many of the translators were dependent upon bilingual intermediaries who introduced elements of their own vernacular discourse into the target language. And finally, these texts, whether being translated from Arabic or Greek, presented their translators with a plethora of lexical and conceptual problems for which they had to create a terminology of loanwords, neologisms, and circumlocutions.[6]

The point here is that scholars in the later medieval schools were very aware of the difference between their own Latin discourse and the far more alien Latin of the classical Roman *auctores*.[7] This is apparent from the glosses and glossaries used in connection with the teaching of *grammatica,* to which several scholars have devoted attention of late.[8] These glosses, moreover, suggest how students must have struggled in order to achieve an elementary, much less a firm, command of the classical idiom. If this was the situation prior to the influx of Greco-Arabic philosophical and scientific texts, students'

[handwritten marginalia: debate about "contingent" status of Latin]

control of the classical form of discourse would have been further eroded when the Latin of the texts they focused upon after their initial training in *grammatica* was itself neither classical nor classicizing. Some of the vernacular translators admit to as much in the prefaces of their translations. Jacques Bauchant, in his French rendering of Seneca's *De remediis fortuitorum,* says that despite the brevity of the work, it was nevertheless difficult to translate, owing to its "laborious and strange" style. Pierre Bersuire, translator of Livy, remarked he was hampered by "constructions si suspensives, si tranchees et si brieves," while Simon de Hesdin complained of Valerius Maximus's "brieve et estrange maniere de parler, la difficulte du latin et le merveilleux stille du livre."[9]

The new Latin translations of Aristotle and the Arabs had another effect on the consciousness of medieval scholars. It made clear to them the historically contingent situation of Latin itself—a notion expressed in the topos of the *translatio studii,* or transfer of knowledge. While up until this time scholars of Western Christendom had tended, albeit naïvely, to take for granted the generalized originary status of Latin—as the language of the Vulgate Bible, the Fathers, the liturgy, and the *auctores*—the new translations forced them to recognize that much learning had originated in languages other than Latin, and that the Romans themselves had had to translate *revelatio* and *scientia* out of Greek and Hebrew and into their own mother tongue. Thus Roger Bacon proposed (in vain, as it turned out) that scholars should learn the source languages of texts, whatever those might be, rather than rely on Latin translations of them.[10] This is not to say that these scholars all readily embraced the secondary and contingent status of Latin. Witness Giles of Rome's comment in his *De regimine principum:* "Philosophers, seeing that no vulgar idiom was complete and perfect enough for them to be able to express the nature of things, the affairs of men, the courses of the stars, and other matters they wished to dispute upon, decided to fashion for themselves a sort of idiom appropriate for these ends, which is called Latin, or the literal idiom, which they would make so broad [*latum*] and copious that through it they could sufficiently express everything they thought of."[11] Still, it seems unlikely that many of Giles's contemporaries uncritically accepted this absurd account of Latin's origins. One early-fourteenth-century reader, for example, corrected Giles's apparent etymologizing of Latin from *latum:* "Rather, Latin derives its name, as it so happens, from the kingdom of the Latins, which takes *its* name from King Latinus, the son of Faunus, as Augustine says in book XXVIII [*recte* XVIII] of the *City of God;* for if Latin was so called because of its breadth [*latum*], it would follow that Greek would be called Latin, on account of its greater breadth and abundance."[12] Moreover, even Giles, in saying that children should learn Latin as they do their mother tongue, by speaking it from infancy, seems to concede that Latin's contemporary privileged status was more accidental than natural.[13]

In France, the inherently equivalent status of Latin and the vernacular was most clearly expressed by Nicole Oresme. In the preface to his translation of the *Nicomachean Ethics,* he argues that there was a time when Greek was to the Latin of the Romans as Latin is now to French, and that just as the Romans had transferred the corpus of Greek learning to their mother tongue, that is, Latin, so too is it now appropriate to carry over the learning of antiquity, now expressed in Latin, into French.[14] In an insular context, John Trevisa, writing just a few years after Oresme, expresses the same idea, when in his *Dialogue Between a Lord and a Clerk upon Translation,* he makes it quite clear that he believes English is as worthy a vehicle for the accurate transmission of information, whether sacred or profane, as any other language, including Latin, which he repeatedly refers to as a secondary, rather than an originary, language: "Aristoteles bokes and oþere bokes also of logyk and of philosofy were translated out of Gru into Latyn. Also, atte prayng of Kyng Charles, Iohn Scot translatede Seint Denys hys bokes out of Gru ynto Latyn. Also holy wryt was translated out of Hebrew ynto Gru and out of Gru into Latyn and þanne out of Latyn ynto Frensch. Þan what ha Englysch trespased at hyt myȝt noȝt be translated into Englysch?"[15]

It could be argued that the views of Oresme and Trevisa were unusual and do not, in fact, reflect the common attitude of clerks toward translation. After all, the clerk of Trevisa's *Dialogue* defends the unique and privileged status of Latin as the language of learning and Scripture. Yet I think that Trevisa's clerk is more of a foil than we have tended to suppose, and that most clerics would have agreed with Trevisa's lord that the clerk's arguments against vernacular translation deserved "to be plonged yn a plod and leyd in pouther of lewednes and of shame," unless they had been made "onlych in murthe and in game."[16] First, by the late fourteenth century, only a clerk who was, to use Trevisa's words, "blere-yȝed" and "al blynd of wyt" could be ignorant of the historically contingent status of Latin. Moreover, the Latin clerks spoke and read was associated in their minds with the practical demands and goals of the classroom: (1) to understand, transmit, and remember the *dicta, rationes,* and *sententiae* of a discrete, though by no means small, body of authoritative texts; and (2) to learn a set of discursive practices that together could be used in one's profession, be that as a preacher, pastor, lawyer, physician, bureaucrat, or courtier. This Latin was clear, straightforward, and precise, but rarely was it elegant. Its purpose was to transfer meaning, and that meaning and the discursive forms in which it was conveyed were not *necessarily* language-specific. They were, however, *contingently* so, thanks in large part to the preponderantly Latin corpus of sacred, profane, and didactic texts that formed the substrate of medieval education, the already well-established writing practices of Latin, including a relatively stable orthography and sophisticated system of abbreviations, and the international character of the universities and the religious orders.[17] In short, it was easier and more practical for young scholars to learn the Latin idiom of the schools than for the schools to discard it in favor of the vernaculars.[18]

Still, the content and form of learned discourse were by no means easy to master. Moreover, the influx of Greco-Arabic works only added to the difficulty, since there were a lot of them, and much of what they contained was damnably hard to construe. Not only was there the basic problem of cultural alienation from the worlds in which these texts were written, there were also fundamental lexical difficulties arising from the Latin translators' sometimes clumsy and excessively literal, or even inaccurate, renderings of the Greek and Arabic. This was certainly the case with the Latin versions of Aristotle's moral philosophy, whose central texts, the *Nicomachean Ethics* and *Politics,* circulated from the middle of the thirteenth century in the Greek-to-Latin translations of Robert Grosseteste and William of Moerbeke.[19] Yet late-thirteenth-century scholars soon realized that the great practical utility of these texts, especially in the fields of pastoral care and political advice, made their study worthwhile. By the early years of the fourteenth century the Dominicans had formally incorporated a series of lectures on moral philosophy (meaning mostly the *Ethics* and Aquinas's treatments thereof) into their theology curriculum.[20] Shortly thereafter Oxford and Paris adopted the *Ethics, Politics,* and pseudo-Aristotelian *Economics* as set texts for their arts courses.[21] Nevertheless, for the insufficiently erudite, dangers lurked in the moral lore of the prince of the pagan philosophers. Thus the necessity of literal commentaries, like those of Aquinas and Peter of Auvergne, which not only clarified difficult passages and concepts but also guarded professors and students alike from a host of erroneous suppositions and heterodox conclusions.[22]

To assist them in their teaching, arts masters and theologians devised a variety of derivative ancillary texts, including question summaries, *florilegia, notabilia,* examination *compendia,* and alphabetical indexes. In these one gets a better sense of how moral philosophy was taught in the *studia.* What one finds in these texts is a boiled-down, simplified, schematized moral philosophy, designed not so much to grapple with the subtleties of Aristotle's thought as to provide students with the basics of his teaching and with those elements therein that were most useful for pastoral ends. What remains might be called a vulgate moral philosophy, whose decidedly extramural goal was to help preachers exhort the faithful and confessors instruct penitents.[23] The preface

to the incunable version of the Aristotelian *florilegium* the *Parvi flores,* a work
originally compiled around 1300 by the Franciscan Johannes de Fonte and
widely diffused in manuscripts, explains that although it is destined primarily
for those studying the arts curriculum, it is also most useful for preachers
looking to ornament the thematic introductions of their *sermones ad populo.*[24]
Preachers also turned to the alphabetical collection of moral philosophy
extracts compiled in the mid-fourteenth century by Johannes Bernier de Fayt,
abbot of Saint-Bavo, Ghent.[25] Johannes introduces his collection by commenting upon an episode in 1 Chronicles 20, when King David crowns himself
with the diadem of the Ammonite idol Milcom. He encourages preachers to
follow David's example and to adapt profane subjects, in this case the teachings of the pagan philosopher Aristotle, for the sacred purpose of ornamenting
Christian sermons. To keep his readers from the pitfalls of error, moreover, he
has thoughtfully added citations to several commentaries, including those of
Grosseteste, Albertus Magnus, Aquinas, Walter Burley, Peter of Auvergne,
and Bartholomew of Bruges.[26]

In the case of moral philosophy, then, we find a body of learned texts that
were vulgarized for the purpose of classroom instruction and for use in the
care of souls, which would in turn have entailed some vernacularization, in
spoken form, of Aristotelian ideas and arguments. While, admittedly, vernacularization in this form would have been limited, the point remains that the
pedagogical impetus for the vulgarization of the Aristotelian *originalia* was
not that far removed from, and was in some ways directly related to, the pastoral goals of instructing the laity.

This relationship is much more apparent in the case of Mirrors for Princes.
Written by learned clerics (usually mendicants) for the instruction of rulers,
these books of advice were loaded with ethical precepts and, from the latter
half of the thirteenth century, were frequently influenced by the moral philosophy of Aristotle.[27] The most popular, as well as thoroughly academic and
Aristotelian of these, was the *De regimine principum,* written circa 1280 by the
Augustinian friar Giles of Rome and dedicated to the heir to the French
throne, Philip the Fair. *De regimine's* popularity is evinced by its survival in
some 350 copies, in both Latin and nine vernaculars. Its academic nature is
apparent from its more than five hundred citations of Aristotle's *Ethics, Politics,* and *Rhetoric,* as well as its narrative, which is patterned on the disciplined,
methodical discourse of the classroom lecture.[28] In many ways, the textual
history of the *De regimine* exemplifies the close relationship between vulgarization and vernacularization. On the one hand, *De regimine* aims to transpose the
form and content of academic discourse to a lay milieu, for while *De regimine* is

ostensibly aimed at a lay audience, it is also very much a scholars' book. On the other hand, Giles compiled what amounts to a simplified and Christianized version of Aristotle's moral philosophy, a version that was destined to become one of the chief textual aids for the study of moral philosophy at the universities and mendicant *studia*.[29] Indeed, it seems likely that its demonstrated classroom utility is what especially recommended it for use by a lay audience. More often than not, after all, it was clerks who commissioned or prepared Latin copies or vernacular translations of *De regimine* for lay readers.[30]

Here, then, is a text that made the lore of Aristotle more apparent and useful for scholars, while at the same time rendering the learning of the schools more accessible to a lay audience. Even so, some scholars felt the need to modify Giles's Mirror itself, in order to make it even more useful for teaching. For example, in the early fourteenth century the Italian Dominican Bartolomeo da San Concordio both abridged *De regimine* and added an extensive gloss drawn from Scripture and several patristic, classical, and scholastic authorities. Bartolomeo, who was renowned for his abilities as both a teacher and a preacher, almost certainly prepared this glossed *De regimine* abridgment, entitled *Compendium moralis philosophiae,* as a classroom text for friars studying moral philosophy in the Dominicans' *studia particularis theologiae*.[31] His decision to use *De regimine* as his base text, rather than the Aristotelian *originalia* from which it is derived, was likely due to its more user-friendly, and perhaps safer, contents and organization. Moreover, because Bartolomeo's primary goal was the pastoral training of preachers and confessors, he included the extensive gloss in order to supply additional exempla and give more in the way of Christian guidance.

Not long after Bartolomeo prepared his *Compendium,* the Franciscan Juan Garcìa de Castrojeriz compiled a vast glossed abridgement of *De regimine* in Castilian for the instruction of the infante Pedro "the Cruel."[32] Friar Juan explains that he took his cue for modifying his base text from Giles himself. Giles, Juan says, tells us that the goal of political science is not only to instill knowledge but also to inculcate good habits and behavior; in order to achieve these ends one should proceed not by subtle demonstrations but rather through the use of such rhetorical devices as concrete examples, figures, and likenesses. Yet because those very devices are in short supply in Giles's text, Juan has decided to excise many of Giles's own subtle demonstrations, while at the same time fleshing out the remainder with numerous precepts and examples drawn from Holy Scripture and the Fathers, as well as from a battery of classical and medieval authorities.[33] Friar Juan, of course, is writing for a rather different audience than Bartolomeo, and thus uses the vernacular instead of Latin. Yet his strategies and, at least in part, his motivations are similar: to abbreviate and augment an academic text so as to initiate his audience in moral philosophy.

This same motivation is found in a glossed French translation of 1330, made for a citizen of Orleans named Guillaume de Beles Voies. At the time of this translation's preparation, there had already been a perfectly adequate, nonglossed French translation in circulation in the north of France for nearly half a century. Why the translator, who identifies himself only by his first name, Guillaume, and who may have been a Dominican friar, decided to prepare an independent translation is unclear. He does, however, explain why he has provided an extensive gloss, which in some places runs to the length of a commentary.[34] The first passage of explanation appears in a gloss on Giles's quotation of Aristotle's assertion in book 1 of the *Posterior Analytics* that all instruction should proceed from preexisting knowledge:

> For example, if by means of my translation I should teach you what is contained in this book, which at your request I am translating from Latin into French, then the preexisting knowledge on my part is that I ought to have full understanding of the meaning that is contained in this book and that I should make the French in which the Latin is transmitted. On your part the preexisting knowledge is that you should have understanding of the French language, since otherwise my translation does you no good.[35]

Guillaume's concern for translating "full understanding" and "meaning" shows that he believed, like most medieval prose translators, that a good translation often needs to do more than simply give a word-for-word translation. Sometimes, in order fully to transfer the meaning of the source text to a less erudite audience, the translator must expand on his source with material drawn from his reserve of knowledge. Where the subjects of the university arts curriculum are briefly described in the second part of book 2 of *De regimine*, the translator interjects:

> For those who are sufficiently learned in Latin can find these sciences distinguished, divided, and discussed in an orderly fashion in books that are in Latin. Since, however, those who do not know Latin so perfectly could find just a small part of these sciences in Romance, I, Guillaume, who have undertaken to translate this book . . . have in mind to abridge some of the aforesaid sciences in the vernacular

according as I think it profitable for him for whom I have undertaken this task.[36]

And, in fact, that is just what Guillaume does, with copious discussions taken from Aristotle's works on logic, physics, metaphysics, and psychology, as well as from some of Aquinas's commentaries and the *Summa theologica*. In these glosses he repeatedly betrays his desire to habituate his lay audience to clerical discourse through his use of phrases like "a parler clergeaument," "si comme les clers appelent," "les paroles sont mises clergiaus senz," or "len dit clergeaument."[37] And because a substantial part of clerical learning involved setting the pagan philosophers into the canon of Christian teachings, Guillaume sprinkles a liberal dose of scriptural and patristic authorities throughout his glosses as well.[38]

In Giles's original and in these three modified versions of *De regimine*, one in Latin and the other two in the vernacular, one hears, I think, echoes of the classroom. And though the intended audiences differ, the pedagogical motivations of the writers are much the same. In every case there is a concern to make useful yet difficult and potentially confusing material accessible to an audience of tyros, be they clerical or lay. Giles himself argues that members of the ruling classes need training in the *trivium*, music, and, of course, moral philosophy. And even if they do not learn their Latin, which, by the way, he really thinks they should, they must nevertheless learn moral philosophy "vulgariter et grosse," even if that means having a clerk expound the doctrine of *De regimine* to them in the vernacular as they dine.[39] This is not to say that all laypeople should have equal access to learned texts, since commoners, being ignorant for the most part of the arts and sciences, should be content with following the example of their rulers.[40] Yet, Giles also implies that clerks trained in the arts and sciences but ignorant of theology should not consider themselves to be qualified to discuss Christian doctrine, nor should civil lawyers think themselves capable of discussing moral philosophy.[41] Instead of singling out the vernacular and the laity for discrimination, then, Giles categorizes people, and what they are qualified to discuss, according to the level and kind of education they have received. In this, Giles (as well as his translators, perhaps) seems to be thinking very much along the lines of Richard Ullerston, in the Oxford Translation Debate (discussed elsewhere in this volume by Fiona Somerset).

About a century after Giles composed the *De regimine* for Philip the Fair, another Parisian scholar, Nicole Oresme, set out to translate the entire corpus of Aristotle's moral philosophy from Latin into French for his royal patron, the Valois Charles V. In the prologue to his translation of the *Ethics*, Oresme, like Giles, stresses the utility of moral philosophy for rulers, their counselors, and others, for, he says, after the Catholic faith, it is the "doctrine la meilleur, la plus digne et la plus profitable," for the prince and for the realm.[42] However, unlike Giles, who wrote a vulgarized moral philosophy but kept it in the Latin tongue, Oresme keeps his source texts intact while vernacularizing them. Moreover, acting every inch the professor, Oresme adds extensive glosses, commentaries, glossaries, and indexes, as well as memorable schematic illustrations.[43]

Clerics believed in the value of their education and were, for the most part, eager to impart their learning to anyone (and for these translators "anyone" seems to have meant "any man") who could both benefit from it and, in turn, benefit them. They had knowledge to give, but they also had knowledge for sale, and increasingly their market was to be found in the courts and households of the upper echelons of the laity.[44] But these clerical translators knew from their own experience in the schools, pulpit, and confessional that simply to translate the prescribed texts of the curriculum would have been counterproductive. Far better to make available the more digestible and palatable derivative and encyclopedic works upon which they themselves had cut their teeth and continued to rely or, if one were to translate *originalia,* to provide them with the kinds of apparatus that they had found so useful in their own study and teaching. Were the motivations of these translators either transgressive or contestative with regard to "official" clerical culture? I should hardly think so (though by all means the translators were not averse to criticizing the works they translated). Were they overly concerned about controlling lay access to knowledge? Certainly not, if by the laity one means the common people. They translated only for their original intended audience; whither their translations went from there was no longer their concern. On the other hand, they certainly did want to control their intended audiences' access to the works they translated; otherwise, why not just give them copies of the untranslated, undoctored texts? This would have been ridiculous, of course, because, for the translators, education was all about mediation. Seen from this point of view, their desire for control was just as much a desire to guide the less instructed toward more perfect knowledge.

NOTES

1. Recent contributions to the subject of translation in later medieval England are Anne Hudson, "Lollardy: The English Heresy?" (see Further Reading); idem, "Wyclif and the English Language" (see Further Reading); Rita Copeland, *Rhetoric, Hermeneutics, and Translation* (see Further Reading); Nicholas Watson, "Censorship and Cultural Change" (see Further Reading, page 257);

Fiona Somerset, *Clerical Discourse and Lay Audience* (see Further Reading, page 257); Steven Justice, *Writing and Rebellion* (see Further Reading), 70–73. For translation in France, see Serge Lusignan, *Parler vulgairement* (see Further Reading); idem, "La topique de la *translatio studii* et les traductions françaises de textes savants au XIVe siècle," in *Traduction et traducteurs au Moyen Âge,* ed. G. Contamine (Paris: Éditions du CNRS, 1989), 303–15; Jacqueline Cerquiglini-Toulet, *The Color of Melancholy: The Uses of Books in the Fourteenth Century,* trans. L. G. Cochrane (Baltimore: Johns Hopkins University Press, 1997), esp. chap. 2; Jacques Monfrin, "Les traducteurs et leur public en France au Moyen Âge," *Journal des savants* (1964): 5–20.

2. Lusignan, *Parler vulgairement,* 9–10; Tony Hunt, *Teaching and Learning Latin in Thirteenth-Century England,* vol. 1 (Cambridge: D. S. Brewer, 1991), 434.

3. Claude Buridant, "*Translatio medievalis:* Théorie et pratique de la traduction médiévale," in *Travaux de linguistique et de littérature XXI* (Strasbourg: Librarie C. Klincksieck, 1983), 119.

4. Joseph Goering, *William de Montibus (c. 1140–1213): The Schools and the Literature of Pastoral Care* (Toronto: Pontifical Institute of Mediaeval Studies, 1992), 68.

5. F. Edward Cranz, "The Publishing History of the Aristotle Commentaries of Thomas Aquinas," *Traditio* 34 (1978): 160–61.

6. See the following entries in F. A. C. Mantello and A. G. Rigg, eds., *Medieval Latin: An Introduction and Bibliographical Guide* (Washington, D.C.: Catholic University of America Press, 1996): Stephen F. Brown, "Theology and Philosophy," 267–87; Bernice M. Kaczynski, "Medieval Translations: Latin and Greek," 718–22; Deborah L. Black, "Medieval Translations: Latin and Arabic," 723–27.

7. See the comments of Siegfried Wenzel in *Macaronic Sermons: Bilingualism and Preaching in Late-Medieval England* (Ann Arbor: University of Michigan Press, 1994), 105–29.

8. Hunt, *Teaching and Learning Latin,* vols. 1–3; Suzanne Reynolds, *Medieval Reading: Grammar, Rhetoric, and the Classical Text* (Cambridge: Cambridge University Press, 1996); Gernòt Wieland, "Interpreting the Interpretation: The Polysemy of the Latin Gloss," *Journal of Medieval Latin* 8 (1998): 59–71; A. E. Wright, "Readers and Wolves: Late-Medieval Commentaries on 'De Lupo et Capite,'" *Journal of Medieval Latin* 8 (1998): 72–79.

9. Monfrin, "Les traducteurs," 18–19; Lusignan, *Parler vulgairement,* 143–47; Peter Dembowski, "Learned Latin Treatises in French" (see Further Reading), 264–65.

10. Lusignan, *Parler vulgairement,* 62–67.

11. *De reg. princ.,* bk. 2, pt. 2, chap. 7 (citations are taken from the Rome edition of 1556, with some modifications and corrections derived from better readings found in the manuscripts).

12. Paris, Bibliothèque nationale de France, MS lat. 6466, fol. 14v (Bartolomeo da San Concordio, *Compendium moralis philosophiae*).

13. "Quare si hoc idioma est completum et alia idiomata non possumus recte et distincte loqui, nisi ab infantia assuescamus ad illa, ex parte eloquentiae, videlicet ut recte et distincte loquamur idioma latinum, si volumus literas discere, debemus ab ipsa infantia literis insudare": *De reg. princ.,* bk. 2, pt. 2, chap. 7. On this, see Lusignan, *Parler vulgairement,* 44.

14. "Or est il ainsi que pour le temps de lors, grec estoit en resgart de latin quant as Romains si comme est maintenant latin en regard de françois, quant a nous. Et estoient pour le temps les estudians introduiz en grec et a Romme et ailleurs, et les sciences communelment bailliees en grec; et en ce pays le langage commun et maternel, c'estoit latin. Donques puis je bien encore conclurre que la consideracion et le propos de nostre bon roy Charles est a recommander, qui fait les bons livres et excellens translater en françois": Maistre Nicole Oresme, trans., *Le livre de éthiques d'Aristote,* ed. Albert Douglas Menut (New York: G. E. Stechert & Co., 1940), 101.

15. Ronald Waldron, "Trevisa's Original Prefaces on Translation: A Critical Edition," in *Medieval English Studies Presented to George Kane,* ed. E. D. Kennedy, Ronald Waldron, and J. S. Wittig (Wolfeboro, N.H.: D. S. Brewer, 1988), 292.

16. Ibid., 291.

17. On the Latinate written culture of the schools, see, for example, M. B. Parkes, "Tachygraphy in the Middle Ages: Writing Techniques Employed for 'Reportationes' of Lectures and Sermons," in *Scribes, Scripts, and Readers: Studies in the Communication, Presentation, and Dissemination of Medieval Texts* (London: Hambledon Press, 1991), 19–33.

18. Not only were there the major divisions between "national" languages, but even the dialects within a single language could be mutually incomprehensible: Bernard Guenée, *States and Rulers in Later Medieval Europe,* trans. J. Vale (Oxford: Blackwell, 1985), 53–54.

19. Bernard G. Dod, "Aristoteles Latinus," in *The Cambridge History of Later Medieval Philosophy,* ed. N. Kretzmann, A. Kenny, and J. Pinborg (Cambridge: Cambridge University Press, 1982), 45–79.

20. M. Michèle Mulchahey, *"First the Bow Is Bent in Study . . .": Dominican Education Before 1350* (Toronto: Pontifical Institute of Mediaeval Studies, 1998), 273–74, 335–36.

21. William J. Courtenay, *Schools and Scholars in Fourteenth-Century England* (Princeton: Princeton University Press, 1987), 32, 56–77; Gordon Leff, *Paris and Oxford Universities in the Thirteenth and Fourteenth Centuries: An Institutional and Intellectual History* (New York: John Wiley & Sons, 1968), 146.

22. Christoph Flüeler, *Rezeption und Interpretation der aristotelischen "Politica" im späten Mittelalter,* 2 vols. (Amsterdam and Philadelphia: B. R. Grüner, 1992); René Antoine Gauthier and Jean Yves Jolif, *L'Éthique à Nicomaque: Introduction, traduction et commentaire,* 2d ed., vol. 1, pt. 1 (Louvain: Publications Universitaires; Paris Béatrice Nauwelaerts, 1970), 111–46; Martin Grabmann, *Methoden und Hilfsmittel des Aristotelesstudiums im Mittelalter* (Munich: Verlag der Bayerischen Akademie der Wissenschaften, 1939).

23. Mulchahey, *"First the Bow Is Bent in Study,"* 273–74; Jean-Philippe Genet, "La théorie politique en Angleterre au XIVe siècle: Sa diffusion, son public," in *Das Publikum politischer Theorie im 14. Jahrhundert,* ed. J. Miethke (Munich: R. Oldenbourg Verlag, 1992), 272; Jeremy I. Catto, "Theology After Wycliffism," in *The History of the University of Oxford,* vol. 2, ed. J. I. Catto and R. Evans (Oxford: Clarendon, 1992), 263–80. In addition to using the moral philosophy of Aristotle, preachers also turned to *florilegia* and alphabetized collections of Roman moral philosophy: Mary A. Rouse and Richard H. Rouse, *Authentic Witnesses: Approaches to Medieval Texts and Manuscripts* (Notre Dame, Ind.: University of Notre Dame Press, 1991), 248.

24. Jacqueline Hamesse, ed., *Les "Auctoritates Aristotelis": Un florilège médiéval: Étude historique et édition critique* (Louvain: Publications Universitaires; Paris: Béatrice Nauwelaerts, 1974), 111–14; idem, "Les manuscrits des *Parvi flores:* Une nouvelle liste de témoins," *Scriptorium* 48 (1994): 299–332.

25. Twelve manuscripts survive: Charles H. Lohr, "Medieval Latin Aristotle Commentaries," *Traditio* 26 (1970): 156–57.

26. Grabmann, *Methoden und Hilfsmittel,* 139–49.

27. Jean-Philippe Genet, ed., *Four English Political Tracts of the Later Middle Ages,* Camden Fourth Series 18 (London: Offices of the Royal Historical Society, University College London, 1977), ix–xix.

28. Charles F. Briggs, *Giles of Rome's "De Regimine Principum": Reading and Writing Politics at Court and University, c. 1275–c. 1525* (Cambridge: Cambridge University Press, 1999), 9–19.

29. Ibid., 91–145.

30. Ibid., 15–17, 53–73.

31. Cesare Segre, "Bartolomeo da San Concordio," in *Dizionario biografico degli italiani,* vol. 6 (Rome: Istituto della Enciclopedia Italiana, 1964), 768–70. The entry incorrectly identifies the *Compendium moralis philosophiae* as an abridgment of the *De regno* of Thomas Aquinas.

32. On this text, see also Charles F. Briggs, "Learned Commentaries for the Laity: Translators' Glosses on Giles of Rome's *De Regimine Principum,"* in *Reading and the Book in the Middle Ages,* ed. S. J. Ridyard (Sewanee: University of the South Press, 2001), 65–77.

33. *Glosa castellana al "Regimiento de príncipes" de Egidio Romano,* vol. 1, ed. Juan Beneyto Perez (Madrid: Instituto de Estudios Politicos, 1947), 15–16. Cf. *De reg. princ.,* bk. 1, pt. 1, chap. 2.

34. Paris, Bibliothèque de l'Arsenal, MS 2690, fol. 111v. For more on this translation and gloss, see Briggs, "Learned Commentaries," 71–75; Outi Merisalo, "Guillaume, ou comment traduire Gilles de Rome en 1330," in *Les traducteurs au travail: Leurs manuscrits et leurs méthodes,* ed. Jacqueline Hamesse (Turnhout: Brepols, 2002), 275–83.

35. MS Arsenal 2690, fols. 6r–v.

36. Ibid., fol. 111v.

37. Ibid., fols. 7v, 8r, 10r, 19r, 19v, 24v, 32r.

38. These include Ecclesiastes, the Gospels of Matthew and John, Paul's letters to Timothy and the Hebrews, Augustine, Jerome, Isidore of Seville, John of Damascus, and Pseudo-Dionysius.

39. "Vel etiam ad mensam legeretur liber De regimine principum ut ipsi principantes instruerentur qualiter principari deberent et alii docerentur quomodo est principibus obediendum": *De reg. princ.,* bk. 2, pt. 3, chap. 20.

40. "Nam licet intitulatus sit hic liber De eruditione principum, totus tamen populus erudiendus est in hac arte. Quamvis enim non quilibet possit esse rex vel princeps, quilibet tamen summopere studere debet, ut talis sit, quod dignus sit regere et principari; quod esse non potest, nisi sciantur, et observentur, quae in hoc opere sunt dicenda. Totus ergo populus auditor quodammodo est huius artis; sed pauci sunt vigentes acumine intellectus": *De reg. princ.,* bk. 1, pt. 1, chap. 1.

41. "Sic legistae, quia ea de quibus est politica, dicunt narrative et sine ratione appellari possunt idiotae politici. Ex hoc autem patere potest quod magis honorandi sunt scientes politicam et morales scientias, quam scientes leges et iura. Nam quanto scientes et dantes causam honorabiliores sunt loquentibus et non reddentibus causam dicti, tanto tales honorabiliores sunt illis. Ex hoc autem apparere potest, qui scientes magis sint honorandi. Nam primo honorandi sunt divini et scientes theologiam. . . . Post theologos vero magis honorandi metaphysici, quia . . . inter scientias humanitus inventas metaphysica primatum tenet. Post hos quidem honorari debent naturales philosophi. . . . Sic ergo scientes gradatim sunt honorandi": *De reg. princ.,* bk. 2, pt. 2, chap. 8. Regarding religious texts designed for lay consumption, see Geneviève Hasenohr, "Religious Reading Amongst the Laity in France in the Fifteenth Century," in *Heresy and Literacy, 1000–1530,* ed. P. Biller and A. Hudson (Cambridge: Cambridge University Press, 1994), 205–21.

42. Oresme, *Livre de éthiques,* 97–98.

43. Claire Richter Sherman, *Imaging Aristotle: Verbal and Visual Representation in Fourteenth-Century France* (Berkeley and Los Angeles: University of California Press, 1995), 23–33.

44. Richard Firth Green, *Poets and Princepleasers: Literature and the English Court in the Late Middle Ages* (Toronto: University of Toronto Press, 1980), 3–12, 133–67.

Vernacular Textualities in Fourteenth-Century Florence

WILLIAM ROBINS

In 1355, the Commune of Florence agreed that the autonomous commercial court, the Mercanzia, should hear all cases before its tribunal not in Latin but in the vernacular, "especially so that those things which have been done or contracted in good faith in the vernacular shall not be drawn into malicious prosecutions through the subtlety of the law and through the method of legal judgments."[1] According to this institutionalization of the vernacular, Latin does not convey authority so much as it increases the risks a merchant must face. Consequently, given that the economic history of capitalism is largely a history of the reduction of risk, Latin is banished in the merchant courts.[2]

This is the new regime of the vernacular, bringing with it an impetus toward increased literacy and increased documentation. The symbolic and class distinctions that previously might have been served by a perceived differential of authority between Latin and the vernacular are now displaced to a different realm: it is the use of texts themselves, whether vernacular or Latin, that matters. Who gets to define themselves as users of texts? Who gets to control the institutions that create, copy, interpret, and enforce written texts? The tribunal of the Mercanzia was not a legal court so much as a place for the auditing and copying of the account books of merchants who stood as creditors or debtors to each other; by overseeing the enforcement of claims, the Mercanzia ensured that the international merchants could collect from the lesser artisans and tradesmen, thus ensuring the solvency of the larger banking and trading firms at the expense of the lesser guildsmen. The tribunal institutionalized a notion of textuality as part of a process for decreasing one's exposure to risk. It also served to draw a distinction in Florentine society between those who could and those who could not control the institutions that created and interpreted and enforced textual records.

The political clashes that surrounded the "democratization" of the Florentine commune throughout the Trecento patently demonstrate that the crucial class division was that which separated the elite international bankers and merchants from the rank and file of the guilds.[3] This fault line is what differentiated two emerging paradigms for the use of vernacular texts in Trecento Florence, paradigms that are to be seen not simply as manifestations of class ideologies but, more complexly, as techniques of social communication capable of generating wide-reaching responses to the world. These are two modes of textuality, meaning by "textuality" what Anne Middleton envisages when she encourages medieval literary history to focus on "the formal factors and cognitive processes that make human beings, individually and in groups, intervene in their societies by defining themselves as makers, users, and possessors of texts, to examine how such formal concerns generate conflict rather than merely serve as a displacement for conflicts supposedly produced elsewhere, in material interests."[4]

In this essay I offer an exploratory sketch of the cultural logic of two modes of deploying written texts, distinguishing between them in formal terms while leaving room for actual instances of more complex dialectical interpenetration. I consider, first, a manner of textuality that derived from strategies of risk absorption and that was associated above all with the realm of mercantile activity; second, a textuality based on an ambition for enfranchisement, linked especially to the concerns of the lesser guildsmen. Other, more traditional models of writing—those derived from French poetic codices or from Latin legal, religious, diplomatic, and scholastic activities—were also being innovatively adapted to new needs, but the two kinds of textuality I am examining here differ from these others in having derived their characteristic logics not from ecclesiastical or aristocratic discourses but from the aspirations of the third estate.

Mercantesca Textuality

Medieval guilds had offered some shelter for the operations of merchant capital, and in most European nations (including England, whose situation I examine toward the end of this essay) guilds provided the only institutional support for activities carried out according to a *lex mercatoria*. Such activities nevertheless still fell squarely under the jurisdiction of civil and ecclesiastical authorities, with their traditions of property law, which was concerned with the possession of movable or immovable goods and with Latin notarial deeds as the preferred documents of record. By contrast, in the nascent forms of Italian commerce—with their emphases on credit, insurance, and negotiable instruments—possessions mattered above all insofar as their value could be monetarized, as their ownership could be distributed among many parties, and as their shares could be transferred to other parties and their agents. In tracing lines of credit and debt, and in tracing the fulfillment, transfer, or division of individual transactions over time, the notarial deed was only of limited use. Far more revealing, to merchants and to auditing authorities, were actual account books. The autonomy of the commercial sector of the Italian economy was predicated upon this change in documentary strategies. This autonomy was institutionalized in the new merchant tribunals founded in Italian cities in the decades around 1300. In Florence, this autonomy was fully guaranteed after 1328, when the Mercanzia gained the privilege of approving or rejecting all nominations for the city's highest governmental post.

The room for maneuver claimed by mercantile interests demonstrates the degree to which a newly powerful notion of *risk* had emerged out of the traditional anxieties about *danger*, to employ a distinction compellingly argued by Niklas Luhmann: "The distinction presupposes . . . that uncertainty exists in relation to future loss. There are then two possibilities. The potential loss is either regarded as a consequence of the decision, that is to say, it is attributed to the decision. We then speak of risk—to be more exact, of the risk of decision. Or the possible loss is considered to have been caused externally, that is to say, it is attributed to the environment. In this case we speak of danger."[5] When traders in an economy of property transactions strive to increase profits by estimating costs and advantages, the failure of an enterprise is above all ascribed to the unpredictability of external factors: human wickedness, natural calamity, the wheel of fortune, providence (i.e., *danger*, for which a more appropriate medieval term might be the Old French *aventure*). Prevention entails setting up buffers against those external forces, through shrewd bargaining, document hoarding, or religious apotropaiea. By contrast, when economic obligations are understood as divisible, distributable, and transferable, potential losses are attributed to the very process of exploiting opportunity. Danger begins to be reconstrued as risk, an inherent dimension of making transactions within a commercial system.

Despite the danger (or risk?) of overdrawing this distinction, it offers a powerful vocabulary for accounting for the particularity of commercial behavior within the Italian economy, as well as for the particularity of the fourteenth-century Italian commercial economy with respect to that of other European nations, and it is a distinction whose application here is supported by the history of the term "risk" itself, which enters the European lexicon through its adoption into the Italian vernacular, *rischio,* in the Duecento and Trecento.[6] The notion of risk emerged from the sphere of maritime insurance, where the danger of any single voyage could be distributed among many parties, each with diversified investments. The concept of a divisible and negotiable exposure to danger was subsequently useful for bypassing antiusury laws, since interest could be reconceived as compensation for taking on the risk of an enterprise rather than as excessive profiteering. Danger issues from a force that either manifests itself or does not; but risk becomes something that can be bought and sold. Exposure to loss arose now from the particular bundle of negotiable instruments and lines of credit and debt one was saddled with, involving the merchant in continual calculations, although according to a calculus in which the future was still a wildly unpredictable variable.

If the contingency of the future was now located in the decisions a merchant made, the material embodiment of that contingency appeared in the written instruments that actualized the merchant's transactions. Mercantile textuality stemmed from this intimate, almost incarnational, association of risks with texts and of risk absorption with textual management. The autonomy of the mercantile system had as its corollary the development of its own characteristic technologies of writing, technologies that originated in the habits of keeping accounts but that were eventually adapted to incorporate legal, literary, religious, and other concerns as well. From the account book derived the notebook in "register format" increasingly adopted in fourteenth-century book production: "These were always paper codices of small or medium format, lacking lining or any real ornamentation beyond simple pen designs, written in cursive (first in chancery minuscule, later and steadily more frequently in mercantile minuscule scripts), and containing an astonishing variety of poetic and prose texts, including devotional, technical, and documentary texts, which were juxtaposed apparently without specific criteria."[7] These account books and notebooks operated as elements of a network of related files, linked by the mode of extracting select items of information from one book for recopying or for summary indication in some other book; the integrity of a written text was overruled by the flexibility of extracting and recombining any number of discrete items in order to meet new interests or obligations. The apparently haphazard arrangement of material typical of merchant books is in fact a consequence of *ad hoc* rationalization, as was demanded by centrifugal lines of obligation that might lead one's concerns into unexpected debts, partnerships, or engagements. The growing independence of these techniques of book production is demonstrated by the development of the new cursive script known to paleographers as *mercantesca;* this was the script taught in merchant schools and used characteristically in merchant writing, and it is immediately distinguishable from the hands practiced by notaries, scribes, clerics, or, later, humanists.

Beyond financial calculations, other spheres of daily life were brought within the purview of *mercantesca* textuality (borrowing the adjective from the paleographers and applying it more widely) through the writing of *ricordanze*, or *libri di famiglia*. Transactions relevant to a family's own possessions might be extracted from company accounts and gathered into a new notebook; notices of wedding dowries or of children's legal independence might be added as well, perhaps followed by other kinds of information: historical events that shaped economic fortunes, personal contexts in which transactions took place, notice of important governmental posts, and so forth. Items in these memoirs were multifarious, connected by their relevance to the family's financial and social coherence and punctuated by references to the records from which these notices were drawn.

The determining features of the "I" of the merchant-writer pivoted upon his sense of responsibility to the outcomes of his own risky transactions (literally holding himself "to account"). Just as the person who made a promise and the person who made a promissory note must now be one and the same, so too must the one responsible for the contents of a book and the one who wrote it (there was no place for scribes or notaries or amanuenses) be one and the same. And just as the merchant was defined by the risks he took on, so too was his accountability associated with the management of those risks as they played themselves out over time, leading to new debts or credits or entanglements. Goro Dati, in his *Libro segreto,* depicts himself in such a pose of self-accountability, both as the merchant who has grappled with the uncertainty of the future by rearranging credits and debts and as a man retrospectively recording his past by transposing his financial records into a new venture, that of autobiography:

> Le ragioni della bottega e della compagnia ultima sono scritti adietro, a carta 8.
>
> E per le cose traverse da Barzalona e il piato che seguitò qui, e i sospetti nati per le imprese di Simone, e la invidia e le male lingue di molti, mancandoci il credito fu nicistà raccogliersi e ritrarsi per pagare ognuno, e accattare danari da amici e operare con ogni ingegno, con danni e interessi e spesa, per non fallire e per non avere vergogna. E posto che 'l mio compagno arebe voluto, per schifare danni e interessi, io diliberai più tosto volere rimanere disfatto dell'avere che dell'onore. E con gran fatica sostenni tanto che pagammo ogni gente, e solamente rimasi ad avere a fare co' miei compagni. Laudato e benedetto ne sia messer Domenedio.

> [The accounts of the shop and of the last company are written above, on page 8.

And because of the adverse affairs at Barcelona, and the suit that followed here, and the suspicions generated by the dealings of Simone, and the envy and slander of many persons, because we had no credit we were forced to secure ourselves and to shut down in order to pay everyone, and to borrow money from friends and to conduct our affairs with much scheming in order not to go bankrupt and in order to avoid shame. Although my partner, scorning all losses and interest payments, would have preferred to go bankrupt, I decided that I would rather ruin my wealth than my honor. And with great energy I persisted so much that we paid everyone, and I had now to deal only with my partners. Praised and blessed be our Lord God.][8]

Dati's *Libro segreto* is "secret" not because it was personally private but because it existed for a very small, almost conspiratorial circle of relatives and partners. After all, the information in account books and *ricordanze* was understood to confer strategic advantages within the aggressive system of mercantile exchange. Books were not meant for public view unless a merchant chose to adhere to a different kind of textual logic altogether.

A characteristic semiotic code of author, message, and audience was thus set in motion: books, existing as part of a system of risk absorption, were a main forum where the continual diligence of the merchant was made explicit to the confidential self-interest of select partners and relatives. The audience for a merchant's *ricordanze* was almost always limited to his immediate family, not only because the family provided the main network of financial and social support but also because the family was the medium through which wealth and power could be construed under a temporal aspect. As Martines describes it: "Neither wealth alone, nor civic eminence alone, normally sufficed to attain high social rank. The two, wealth and office, had to be combined; and being combined across a long enough period of time, they produced an entirely new factor—a family tradition."[9] Insofar as this temporal notion of the family projected itself backward, merchant interest in family genealogies (such as began to appear in the late Trecento) tended to mimic aristocratic forms; but insofar as it was projected into the future, it existed as a counterpart to, and indeed even become part of, that preoccupation with the future underlying the economy of risk. In making transactions and keeping accounts, any present advantage was always only provisional, its true significance deferred for a later time. The near future—the province not only of his own old age but of his children's patrimony—thoroughly determined the attention a merchant bestowed upon his books.

In the social advice to be found in Giovanni Morelli's *Ricordi,* both the content of the recommendations he gives and the very fact that he sets such advice into written form for the future use of his children and heirs demonstrate the extent to which the future was what mattered when one took up the pen:

> Fa pure che ne' tuoi libri sia iscritto ciò che tu fai distesamente, e non perdonare mai alla penna e datti bene a intendere nel libro; e di questo seguiterà che tu guadagnerai sanza troppo pericolo. Tu ti ritrarrai presto, e non per riottoli, dove sarebbe lo 'nganno; tu non arai a temere d'avere a fare ristituzione o ch'ella sia domandata a' tuoi figliuoli, e viverai libero, sentendoti fermo e sodo nel valsente tuo e sanza pensiero.

> [And make sure that all you do is written down extensively in your books, and never spare your pen, and dedicate yourself to knowing what is in the book; and from this it will follow that you will profit without too much peril; you will withdraw yourself quickly whenever there is deceit, without recourse to litigation; you won't have to worry about having to make some restitution or about any restitution being demanded from your children; and you will live at ease, feeling secure and solid in your net worth and without anxiety.][10]

The cache of family records was for the Florentine merchant what the purity of a bloodline was for an aristocrat: an organizing principle of a family's identity. Familial records were guarded in shrinelike chests in the most secure rooms in the house; their loss was seen as a family calamity.

Mercantesca textuality thus became heavily laden with values of family honor, as is evident in the way Luca di Totto da Panzano spoke of his motivation for writing at least one entry into his *Ricordi:*

> Questa è una memoria la quale d'altre scritture i' oe ridotta in questo libro per vera e perpetuale memoria, e perch'io voglio essere, come debbo, interamente obbligato, io e miei figliuoli e rede e discendenti; ciò sia chi ae le carte, come a chi ae promesse o scritta, voglio che ciascuna promessa sia carta o scritta, e che sieno tutti sodisfatti interamente; perocché mi prestaro i sottoscritti fiorini in Lucca, quando i' era nella pregione al Sasso, e tuttodì guasto e molestato della persona e collato, arrandellato la testa.

> [This is a record that I have transferred from other papers into this book as a true and permanent record, for I wish, as I ought, to fully
>
> and because

acknowledge this obligation, I and my sons and heirs and descendants. To whomever holds the documents, and to whomever has the promissory notes or written instruments, I wish that every promise, whether in a document or a written instrument, should be entirely fulfilled. For in Lucca they loaned me the florins written below, when I was in the prison of Il Sasso, when every day I was beaten and bodily persecuted and tortured and cudgeled on my head.][11]

Here, Luca di Totto da Panzano's rescue from bodily danger did not solidify a bond of personal loyalty to those who made his rescue possible, but rather a bond of fidelity to the financial obligation thus incurred, an obligation that in itself was transferrable: the person who held the negotiable instrument would not necessarily be the same person who lent the original sum. Inclusion of this record in his memoirs indicates that fulfilling this obligation was a matter of personal and family honor, yet those values of honor were construable according to the logic of mercantile transactions.

These quotations from merchant memoirs are informed by the values of religion, family identity, and personal honor respectively. Recourse to such values can be explained in terms of the limits to the functional efficiency of the medieval commercial system. In fourteenth-century Italy, a bookkeeping apparatus emerged to support an economy of risk, but not until the eighteenth and nineteenth centuries would a science of statistics emerge to provide a calculus of probabilities to further tame the uncertainty of the future.[12] Because functional efficiency alone could not be trusted to regulate the absorption of risk, the logic of risk-taking aligned itself with traditional terminologies of social value. This concomitant exposition of accountancy and norms of merit is precisely what enabled a *mercantesca* textuality to develop out of financial records and into those of personal and social concerns. But it also meant that risk absorption was construed as part of a social program with clearly defined premises: that Florence's prosperity depended upon large movements of capital in the domain of international trade and banking; that the flourishing of international trade required keeping local costs low and predictable; that the communal government existed to guarantee these two economic ideals; and that the model of communal deliberation ought to be one of consensus reached by the elite. This program could only be achieved by shaping the apparatus of taxation, judicial review, physical coercion, and bureaucratic archiving so as to favor the interests of the elite; and this stacking of the deck could be guaranteed only by controlling electoral procedures. Accordingly, the Mercanzia and the Parte Guelfa, which were privileged to approve all candidates for office, became strongholds from which the oligarchy exerted political pressure.

With commercial and bureaucratic procedures thus weighted, the riskiness of commercial ventures brought with it a secondary risk (which for the lesser guildsmen should be thought of as a danger): would the very system of commercial exchange be manipulated by others to one's own disadvantage? The value-laden limitations of the mercantile system effectively restricted the spread of *mercantesca* textuality, which flourished where two conditions were satisfied. First, the scope of one's involvement in commercial bookkeeping had to be extensive enough to govern one's self-representation and to permit taking the established parameters of risk absorption for granted. Second, ideals of economic internationalism and consensus-based governance had to enjoy sufficient acceptance that familial and personal concerns could be viewed as coterminous with the mercantile system itself (so allowing textual subjects to move from accounts to other concerns). These conditions did not hold for more than a small number of Florentines.

The Textuality of Enfranchisement

On the eve of the 1378 revolt of the *ciompi,* the priors of Florence detained one of the conspirators, who was asked what the insurgent woolworkers wanted:

> Disse che le scardassieri, pettinatori, vergheggiatori, tintori, conciatori, cardaiuoli, pettinagnoli, lavatori, e altri che sono sottoposti all'arte della lana, non vi vogliono più essere sottoposti; e vogliono in tutto, che l'uficiale non sia più, nè avere a fare più nulla con lui; imperochè sono molto male trattati, sì dallo ufiziale, che per ogni piccola cosa ci martoria, e sì da maestri lanaioli, che gli pagano molto male, e, del lavorìo che si viene dodici, ne danno otto. Il perchè questi cotali dicono, che vogliono consoli per loro, e non vogliono avere a fare, nè con lanaiuoli, nè co' loro ufiziale. E anche dicono, che vogliono avere parte nel reggimento della città. E vogliono, che ogni ruberia e arsione fatta, non se ne possa conoscere per nessun tempo.

> [He said that the wool carders, combers, strippers, dyers, dryers, carders, polishers, workers, and others who are subordinates [*sottoposti*] to the Wool Guild want to be its subordinates no longer. In all, they want the guild official to exist for them no longer, and to have nothing more to do with him, considering that they are treated very

badly, both by the official who tortures them over every little affair, and also by the master wool merchants who pay them very badly, since for a piece of work worth twelve they pay eight. That is why these men say they want their own guild consuls, and want nothing to do either with the wool merchants or with their official. And they also say they want to have a share in the governance of the city. And they want none of their acts of vandalism or arson ever to be held against them.][13]

To achieve steady, reasonable wages for their labor and a cessation of violent physical coercion, the *sottoposti* demanded a guild of their own and, as a consequence of that guild status, the prerogative to participate in the communal government. The woolworkers submitted a petition to this effect to the priors, and when it was rejected, they took to the streets and seized the halls of government, where they installed their own leaders as interim priors, appointed a notary, and promptly approved their own petition. They next burned the name cards kept in the electoral bags from which the names of priors would be drawn, and called for a new "scrutiny" of eligible names, among which members of their newly formed guilds were to be included.

The relative "restraint" that modern historians have noted in the woolworkers' revolt, and the retention of established legislative procedures, were consequences of a plan not to replace the given model of governance but rather to become enfranchised within it. The *ciompi*'s deployment of the techniques of petition and electoral scrutiny are instances of what Weber has called the permanent character of bureaucratic machines: "The objective indispensability of the already existing apparatus, with its peculiar 'impersonal' character, means that the machine—in contrast to feudal orders based upon personal piety—is easily made to work for anybody who knows how to gain control over it." Bureaucratic permanency makes true revolutions "technically more and more impossible, especially when the apparatus controls the modern means of communication . . . and also by virtue of its internal rationalized structure."[14] The Florentine communal bureaucracy presided over a multitude of specialized systems of textual archiving, review, and enforcement, which, because the individuals in high office were elected to very short tenures, increasingly defined the operations of governance. To become "part of the government of the city" involved not only eligibility to hold office but also familiarity with and direction over the procedures and technologies of documentation.

The enfranchisement demanded by the woolworkers in 1378 had already been demanded by members of the minor guilds in preceding decades, for the

danger vs risk

priorate had at first been reserved for members of the six major guilds alone. The ideal of corporate *libertà* had in fact first been given form by the wealthiest merchants when they wrested control of the city from the aristocratic magnates in the 1290s, and that ideal remained so central to Florentine self-definition that throughout the Trecento most political discussion revolved around issues of enfranchisement. When the woolworkers made use of this vocabulary, they were taking an established ideology to its logical next step. The brutal end to their short-lived regime marked the limit of the extension of such an ideology, and subsequently, in the Quattrocento, the ideals of a corporatist commune yielded to the consolidation of elite interests around the princely regime of the Medici.

The attitudes toward textual culture associable with the concerns of the lesser guildsmen and townsfolk are marked by ambitions for enfranchisement in those procedures and technologies that constituted the most important avenues of social communication. We are here concerned with an attitude toward texts that arises when there are no autonomous textual institutions or techniques for a group and where the aim is thus to lay claim to existing textual strategies (be they mercantile, bureaucratic, religious, etc.). We are primarily concerned with environments where the actors possess neither the material means nor the political power fully to participate in a commercial system of transferable debts and credits and where the uncertainty of the future is seen to arise rather from *danger* than from *risk* (in the sense used above). In this domain, the use of texts is meaningful to the degree that enfranchisement in documentary culture might defend against some of these dangers.

The textuality of enfranchisement can be said to be at work when certain dangers appear as consequences of a subordinate political status, when the remedy at hand for such subordination is full participation in a relatively impersonal bureaucratic apparatus, and when that participation is to be achieved through a strategy of corporatism. I use the term "corporatism" in the sense developed by John Najemy to describe the "essential principles" of guild-based republicanism: "equality among the members, the collective rule of the full membership, the delegated quality of ascending executive authority, and a theory of consent that recognized the right of either direct participation or representation for each of the constituent parts of a corporation. At the level of communal politics, these principles translated into a vision of the Florentine republic as a sovereign federation of equal and autonomous guilds."[15] The double movement of corporatism, outward toward participation in an overarching regime and inward toward the consolidation of infraguild commitments, generated an analogously two-pronged strategy for laying claim to the procedures and techniques of documentary culture. One impulse was to enjoy the protections offered by the general bureaucratic system; a complementary impulse was to textualize guild relations, or those guildlike relations among the practitioners of a distinct activity, in order to re-create those protections in the more local setting. In this mode, the writer is defined as one who has gained access to the techniques of documentary culture, yet also as one who is thoroughly dedicated to a specific shared vocation. The audience is, in a general sense, the commune as a whole, but more primarily consists of the fellow members of a specific group. Although the ambitions of the nonelite may have led them to experiment with various kinds of writing (commercial accounts, religious instruction, etc.), it was the communal bureaucracy that provided the dominant model of a relatively impersonal textual system predicated upon corporate notions of enfranchisement.

The textuality of enfranchisement is visible in spheres other than the strictly political. In vernacular literature, a striking example is the career of the fourteenth-century poet Antonio Pucci. Pucci was a lower-class entertainer retained by the city government through his appointment as a minor servant of the commune, first as bell ringer and then as town crier. In some respects, Pucci was typical of medieval entertainers: subservient to the whims of presiding lords and prized for performative improvisation to meet the demands of his listeners. But in other respects, Pucci's career was novel. At Florence, the palace servants were permanent, while the ruling priors changed every two months; Pucci's civic poetry stressed a republican ideology that curtailed the arbitrary power of individual governors; and in fact the civic poet, like other provisioners of communal symbolism, was expected to tell the elites how to behave, rather than the reverse. In other words, even though Pucci was no guildsman and thus could not hold elected office, yet he was encouraged by many aspects of his post to think of himself as much more enfranchised in the system of governance than was an entertainer at an aristocratic court.

Poetic performance, for Pucci, entailed a dynamic between the entertainer's competence on the one hand and the imposed constraints of the performative situation on the other. Competence involved the performer's facility with verbal, vocal, and gestural techniques, as well as an ability to address a specific community and raise that address to the level of spectacle. But the performer was not in control of the situations for which the performance was requested. Instead, subordination to the arbitrary power of masters and to the possibility of public scorn exposed the performer to dangers of bodily pollution, economic uncertainty, and wasted labor. Where the rebellious woolworkers envisaged an escape from subordination by laying claim to the bureaucratic protocols of corporatist government, Pucci, in a structurally analogous maneuver, envisaged an escape from the constraints of performance by laying claim to documentary culture, with its concepts of individual authority, textual fixity, and lasting record.

The direction in which Pucci's poetry changed is visible in a sonnet addressed to his patrons, the priors:

> Signor priori, i' sono una cicala
> ch'a' fanti dato son per penitenza;
> ma non so sí cantar ch'ancor licenza
> mi dien ch'a voi i' venga in su la sala.
>
> Per me parola ma' da voi non cala
> e di venir sanz'essa ho gran temenza,
> però che s'io venissi e' m'è credenza
> ch'i' sarei messo poi sotto la scala.
>
> Ond'io faccendo de le bracce croce
> vi priego che vi piaccia ch'io su vegna,
> tosto però, ché lo 'ndugiar mi nuoce.
>
> Deh fate partorir la mente pregna,
> c'ho di voglia d'udir di boce in boce
> com'è usanza de la gente degna.
>
> Quand'udirò quella voce benigna
> dicendo a' fanti, a ciò che non si crucci,
> che lascin su venire Antonio Pucci?

[My Lord Priors, I am a cricket who has been given to the page boys to make me suffer, but I still can't sing well enough for them to give me permission to appear before you up in the hall.

No summons ever comes down from you for me, and I am too wary to appear without one; for it's my belief that if I did appear, I would be tucked under the stairs.

So now, with my arms crossed in supplication, I beg you that it might please you that I should appear—but quick, because this waiting is painful.

Come now, let my pregnant mind give birth. I want to hear it face-to-face, in the manner of respectable people.

When will I ever hear that kind voice telling the page boys, so that I fret no more, that they should let Antonio Pucci ascend?][16]

Here, Pucci's public role is identified as that of a performer—eager to put his abilities into effect but excluded from control over the parameters of performance, not to mention the realization of such a performance.

[handwritten margin notes: "14th c. poet shows 'popular' poetry of lower class"; "1st lay's claim to full apparatus of written culture"]

This poem itself, of course, is an attempt to intervene in that patronage system, an intervention made possible by the poem's status as a written document, since "face-to-face" (literally, "mouth-to-mouth") engagement has been forestalled. This written poem becomes a way of asserting the name and the skill of "Antonio Pucci," even in the absence of a summons from the patrons. But even if the written poem is read by the priors and leads to invitations to perform, it will only bring about further repetitions of the constraints of performance. An escape from the dynamic of performance is effected only insofar as writing achieves different ends as well. In the first place, Pucci, by advertising his capacities as a writer, indicates another metier for earning commissions. More significant because more wide-reaching, the deployment of written technologies established networks of circulation that circumvented the hierarchical structure of patronage and even went beyond the professional cadre of civic entertainers. The circulation of Pucci's poetry among the "artisanal" poets of the next two generations indicates success in creating such a readership, especially among other writers. This sonnet has established two contexts for its own reception: it gestures deferentially to the priors, who control the pertinent parameters of oral performance; yet it also claims, and enacts, enfranchisement in other networks of support that render the poet (and his poems) less vulnerable.

The poetry of Antonio Pucci marks the moment when the "popular" poetry of lower-class poets first laid claim to the full apparatus of written culture. The increasing textualization of Pucci's poetry kept pace with the increasingly bureaucratic nature of his communal employment. The same grasp of documentary procedures that insulated his poetry from the constraints of courtly patronage enabled his rise in the civil service, especially in his final post as "Guardian of the Acts" of the Mercanzia, archivist of the burgeoning records of the communal court. Pucci, however, was at the Mercanzia, but not of the Mercanzia. The Mercanzia, which gave institutional definition to the autonomous mercantile system of exchange, marked the fault line that separated the oligarchic elite from less enfranchised Florentines. Pucci, falling on the more vulnerable side of that line, drew his social self-definition and his textual strategies not from commercial records but from civic and poetic domains.[17]

Textuality of the Affinity, Textuality of Justice

The specific circumstances of Florence, where the necessary conditions for the emergence of both a *mercantesca* textuality and a textuality of enfranchisement

England's case

were satisfied, can be elucidated by contrasting them to the situation of merchants and other commoners in a country, in this case England, in which monarchic and feudal structures held more sway. England knew an appreciable level of mercantile activity and can be said to have generated a distinct merchant class with considerable privileges in towns and cities. Nevertheless, without effective mechanisms for extending the habits of bookkeeping into other spheres of life, the English merchants did not develop a distinctive mercantile textuality, at least nothing like the autonomous *mercantesca* enterprise defined above.[18] One reason for this was the constant intervention of the royal fisc in all matters of trade, such that no tribunal for commercial law ever gained effective autonomy. The court of the wool staple in Calais was the most prominent court that kept to the *lex mercatoria,* but in order to survive, the small oligarchy that ran the staple as a monopoly had to provide the king with sufficient revenue. Whenever the king was involved, the tactics of parliamentary petitions and feudal alignments overwhelmed the logic of commercial obligations.[19] Another reason that accounting practices did not organize merchants' efforts at self-representation was the incompatibility of English common law with commercial activity. In common law, debts and credits were not transferable; negotiable instruments were not recognized; and cases of debt, limited to single issues at a time, aimed at collection rather than dispute resolution. Since the *lex mercatoria* was effectively driven out from regional fairs, cases of debt resolution were decided by private arbitration or else, as at the Guildhall of London, had to assume the documentation appropriate to common-law procedures. Even where law merchant was effective, it relied either upon the oral testimony of witnesses or upon official recognizances of debt, and only rarely upon contracts or accounts.[20] In short, commercial disputes remained textually informal or were subordinated to the king's common law. This subordination is made explicit in ordinances from fourteenth-century Bristol: "Common law . . . is the mother of the law merchant and . . . endows its daughter according to certain privileges and within certain localities."[21]

Prudent merchants had every reason to reconceive their commercial winnings in terms of property and to assemble deeds, titles, and legal rulings accordingly. Not the account book, but the muniments chest containing deeds and charters, which might be stored at home or in a nearby church or monastery and might be copied into a roll or booklet for personal reference, provided the body of texts through which a merchant secured his or her family's position. The earliest merchant's book we have, that of John Lawney from the 1430s, accumulates papers as a "calendar" to defend his claim to properties:

> Also of the tenementz in London & in Southwerke that were partey-
> nynge to Mergrete my Wyfe the terme of here lyf & aftir here dissese
> to be sold. Thanne the forseyd Jon Lawney purchasid here reversiun
> of the feffez and payde ther fore liche as ye schul see in this same
> book so that the fee symple was in me to gyf hit & selle hit. And for
> the grete love that my Wyef & y hadde to oure children, We dede
> entayle hit to oure eiris, like as ye may see aftur in this book, And
> copiid the dedis of the forseyd tenementiz of London and of Lynne in
> this book for a Kalender to all oure eyris.[22]

Merchants strove for the kind of security associated with a career of landown-
ership, professional practice, or royal service. Successful merchants prepared
their children to become something else, especially lawyers, clerks, or courtiers. Very few English families lasted more than one or two generations as
merchants.[23]

In privileging the documentary practices of other discourses—especially
legal and administrative, but also courtly or ecclesiastical—mercantile and
burgher attitudes concerning the importance of texts for one's family's security cannot be said to have differed significantly from the attitudes among the
minor gentry. In England it is the needs of these lesser landholders, the com-
mons, that lay behind the extension of vernacular textuality to members of
the third estate. Record keeping, legal knowledge, and cultural literacy were
important factors in maintaining one's place within an aristocratic "affinity"—a circle of persons united by local proximity and by semifeudal ties
("vertical" ties linking them to a magnate and "horizontal" ties among themselves), who shared administrative responsibilities and collaborated with each
other to stack the local juries required by common law, to return a lord's
retainers to Parliament, and to provide the other apparatus needed to safeguard their title to property.[24] For merchants or guildsmen or landholders or
administrators, in the context of bastard feudalism, textual competence was a
means for warding off possible *dangers,* not for managing *risk.*

These networks of protection did not, except within the limits of some
guild structures, take a "corporatist" form.[25] The government of the city of
London, for instance, was not chosen by the guilds, but was made up of aldermen who were chosen by district and who served long terms, thereby ensuring
rule by the city's elite. With the possible exception of the mayoralty of North-
ampton from 1378 to 1381 (contemporaneous, in fact, with the regime of the
woolworkers in Florence), guild members themselves tended to promote the
idea that only such an elite could be trusted to gain privileges from the king,
from the barons, and from Parliament in return for keeping order in the city.

Royal, baronial, and city administrations demanded functionaries with legal sophistication who could also cultivate avenues of patronage. Such feudal patronage, rather than an ideology of enfranchisement, dominated the strategies of writing that emerged out of the halls of the bureaucracy. While for Antonio Pucci entry into a community of writers offered the only escape from the constraints of courtly performance, for English poets like Usk and Hoccleve court patronage offered a remedy for the insecurities attendant upon being a civil servant.[26] The direction of their anxieties is reversed.

Persons without the support of an affinity were at a severe disadvantage in the effective use of texts, as can be glimpsed in the fairly typical case of the widow Alice of Louthe, who in 1391 accused the local abbot of sending a monk "to Louthe church where he and others by covin forcibly seized a red box, containing charters and muniments concerning the premises and other of Alice's lands, from Alan Forman, chaplain, who had them in his custody, and brought them to the said abbot to the disinheritance of the heirs of the said Walter and Alice," and of then imprisoning her son until he signed a bond forfeiting his claim to a disputed property.[27] Alice appealed to a royal inquest, since local authorities were clearly ready to use violence to manipulate all kinds of documentary evidence. Alice's appeal to a higher justice is emblematic of the way that the textuality of bastard feudalism took shape for the oppressed. The rebelling peasants of 1381, raging against the malfeasance of those lawyers, sheriffs, and lords who were intermediaries in the enforcement of the law, differed from Alice only in the fact that they had yet to gain access to the same processes of inquest and appeal, as well as in the collective extension of their rage. They made concerted attacks upon manorial and institutional archives, burning documents wherever they went; yet they also appealed to earlier documentary foundations, such as Domesday Books or ancient charters or the royal laws promulgated at Winchester.[28] Local lords and official representatives perverted the execution of justice, yet the rebels expected justice to be anchored by recovered originary texts, as also by the universal promises of Christian doctrine and of royal common law.

Rebellions within feudal systems frequently included the wholesale destruction of bureaucratic archives, and in this sense the actions of the English peasants are in line with the burning of documents in the revolt of the Florentines against the duke of Athens in 1343 or the rising of the Sienese populace against its oligarchic rulers in the 1370s.[29] What makes the 1378 revolt of the Florentine woolworkers so seemingly modern is their adherence to a different logic altogether, for they did not decry the current documentary structure as a corruption of some idealized, true justice, but rather they demanded full enfranchisement in the mediatory powers of that bureaucracy.

In fourteenth-century England the spread of textual culture to nonaristo-cratic and nonecclesiastical classes was dominated by an aim to gain access to traditional legal and administrative practices, in order to serve the political purposes of local communities structured around aristocratic affinities or to serve political or religious ideals of justice. Networks of patronage and politi-cal factions were just as strong in medieval Italy, but after the beginning of the fourteenth-century they did not so comprehensively dominate documen-tary strategies. In Florence, the prominence of commercial and corporatist activities made possible the emergence of two modes of textuality—*mercantesca* textuality and the textuality of enfranchisement—that differed from earlier models of vernacular literacy and from the paradigms of bastard feudalism in not being derived from ecclesiastical or aristocratic arenas but developing instead out of aspirations and practices particular to the third estate.

NOTES

Thanks to the editors of this volume, and to the participants at the conference "Vernacularity: The Politics of Language and Style," University of Western Ontario, March 4–7, 1999, for their advice and comments. All translations are my own unless noted otherwise.

1. "Ut presertim que bona fide fiunt seu vulgariter contraruntur, per iuris subtilitatem et iudici-arum ordinem in calupniam non trahantur." Archivio di Stato di Firenze, Provvissioni Registri 42, fol. 96r.

2. Antonella Astorri, *La Mercanzia a Firenze nella prima metà del trecento: Il potere dei grandi mer-canti* (Florence: Olschki, 1998); on risk, esp. 34–36.

3. John Najemy, *Corporatism and Consensus in Florentine Electoral Politics, 1280–1400* (Chapel Hill: University of North Carolina Press, 1982), esp. 11–12.

4. Anne Middleton, "Medieval Studies," in *Redrawing the Boundaries: The Transformation of English and American Literary Studies*, ed. Stephen Greenblatt and Giles Gunn (New York: Modern Language Association, 1992), 26–27.

5. Niklas Luhmann, *Risk: A Sociological Theory*, trans. Rhodes Barret (New York: De Gruyter, 1993), 21–22. Luhmann locates the rise of the concept of risk in the transition between the medieval and modern periods, by which he, focusing on Mitteleuropa, means the sixteenth century; the situa-tion of Italy is precocious in this respect. Jacques Le Goff, "Merchant's Time and Church's Time in the Middle Ages," in *Time, Work, and Culture in the Middle Ages*, trans. Arthur Goldhammer (Chi-cago: University of Chicago Press, 1988), 29–42, implies that the calculations of merchants, by establishing "an oriented and predictable time," eliminated uncertainty, while Luhmann considers such calculations rather as a displacement of the way in which uncertainty was conceived.

6. For the history of the Italian word *rischio*, see *Grande dizionario della lingua italiana*, vol. 16 (Turin: UTET, 1992), 772–73.

7. Armando Petrucci, "Reading and Writing *Volgare* in Medieval Italy," in *Writers and Readers in Medieval Italy* (see Further Reading), 187.

8. Goro Dati, *Libro segreto*, in *Mercanti scrittori: Ricordi nella Firenze tra medioevo e rinascimento*, ed. Vittore Branca (Milan: Rusconi, 1986), 552.

9. Lauro Martines, *The Social World of the Florentine Humanists, 1390–1460* (London: Routledge & Kegan Paul, 1963), 55.

10. Giovanni di Pagolo Morelli, *Ricordi,* in *Mercanti scrittori,* ed. Branca, 178–79.

11. Angelo Cicchetti and Raul Mordenti, *I libri di famiglia in Italia, 1: Filologia e storiografia letteraria* (Rome: Edizioni di Storia e Letteratura, 1985), 180.

12. The growing sophistication of actuarial sciences, and the widening of capitalistic enterprises, have made it possible for modern economists to speak of *risk* not as one way of conceiving of uncertainty but in fact as a term to be opposed to uncertainty, as formulated in Frank Hyman Knight, *Risk, Uncertainty, and Profit* (Boston: Houghton Mifflin, 1921). Only recently has attention returned to the dangers that attend the very use of risk calculations. See Mary Douglas, *Risk and Blame: Essays in Cultural Theory* (London: Routledge, 1992); Ulrich Beck, *Risk Society* (London: Sage, 1992).

13. Alamanno Acciaioli, *Cronaca,* in *Il tumulto dei ciompi: Cronache e memorie,* ed. Gino Scaramella (Bologna: Zanichelli, 1917), 21.

14. Max Weber, *From Max Weber: Essays in Sociology,* ed. and trans. H. H. Gerth and C. Wright Mills (New York: Oxford University Press, 1958), 229–30; translation slightly modified.

15. Najemy, *Corporatism and Consensus,* 9; and for his definition of the "consensus" model of republicanism favored by the aristocracy, 13.

16. Giuseppe Corsi, ed., *Rimatori del trecento* (Turin: UTET, 1969), 819–20.

17. See William Robins, "Antonio Pucci, Guardiano degli Atti della Mercanzia," *Studi e problemi di critica testuale* 61 (2000): 29–70.

18. For another claim that English merchants lacked an autonomous textual culture, see Lee Patterson, *Chaucer and the Subject of History* (Madison: University of Wisconsin Press, 1991), 324–33. Recent attempts to distinguish a particularly mercantile use of texts in England are Carol M. Meale, "*The Libelle of Englyshe Polycye* and Mercantile Literary Culture in Late-Medieval London," in *London and Europe in the Later Middle Ages,* ed. Julia Boffey and Pamela King (London: Centre for Medieval and Renaissance Studies, 1995), 181–227, and Sheila Lindenbaum, "London Texts and Literate Practice," in *The Cambridge History of Medieval English Literature,* ed. David Wallace (see Further Reading), 284–309.

19. Eileen Power, *The Wool Trade in English Medieval History* (London: Oxford University Press, 1941); David Grummitt, "The Financial Administration of Calais During the Reign of Henry IV, 1399–1413," *English Historical Review* 113 (1998): 277–99.

20. J. Milnes Holden, *The History of Negotiable Instruments in English Law* (London: Athlone, 1955); J. H. Baker, *An Introduction to English Legal History,* 3d ed. (London: Butterworths, 1990).

21. "Cum lex comunis que est mater legis mercatorie et que suam filiam ex certis privilegis et in certis locis dotavit." Quoted in E. E. Rich, ed., *The Staple Books of Bristol* (Bristol: Bristol Record Society, 1934), 38.

22. Quoted in Sylvia L. Thrupp, *The Merchant Class of Medieval London (1300–1500)* (Ann Arbor: University of Michigan Press, 1962), 123–24.

23. See ibid., 191–233.

24. Christine Carpenter, "The Beauchamp Affinity: A Study of Bastard Feudalism at Work," *English Historical Review* 95 (1980): 514–32; P. W. Fleming, "The Hautes and Their 'Circle': Culture and the English Gentry," in *England in the Fifteenth Century: Proceedings of the 1986 Harlaxton Symposium,* ed. Daniel Williams (Woodbridge, Suffolk: Boydell Press, 1987), 85–102.

25. See David Wallace, *Chaucerian Polity: Absolutist Lineages and Associational Forms in England and Italy* (Stanford: Stanford University Press, 1997), on the expression of corporatist and absolutist ideologies in Chaucer's *Canterbury Tales.*

26. Derek Pearsall, "Hoccleve's *Regement of Princes:* The Poetics of Self-Representation," *Speculum* 69 (1994): 386–410; Ethan Knapp, "Bureaucratic Identity and the Construction of the Self in Hoccleve's *Formulary* and *La Male Regle,*" *Speculum* 74 (1999): 357–76.

27. *Calendar of Inquisitions Miscellaneous (Chancery) Vol. v: 1387–1393* (London: Her Majesty's Stationery Office, 1962), 176–77.

28. See Steven Justice, *Writing and Rebellion* (see Further Reading, page 257), and Richard Firth Green, *A Crisis of Truth* (see Further Reading).

29. Samuel Cohn Jr., "Florentine Insurrections, 1342–1385, in Comparative Perspective," in *The English Rising of 1381,* ed. R. H. Hilton and T. H. Aston (Cambridge: Cambridge University Press, 1984), 143–64.

"Moult Bien Parloit et Lisoit le Franchois," or Did Richard II Read with a Picard Accent?

ANDREW TAYLOR

The history of western European vernaculars is written in the language of the victors. One such victor is Parisian French, or what Chaucer calls "Frenssh of Paris," which has long been a synecdoche for the *mission civilisatrice* and already carried overtones of cultural sophistication by the thirteenth century. Another victor is Standard English, which began to coalesce in the late fourteenth century. In at least one way, the establishment of Standard English and French echoes the reestablishment of standard medieval Latin during the Carolingian revolution of the eighth and ninth centuries: in both cases the result was to widen the gap between the written word and the vernacular.[1] This gap between text and sound widened yet further with the spread of print, whose drive to universality and free circulation has taught us to regard a book as a self-sufficient object (rather than as something that needs to be explained, sung, read aloud, or otherwise performed) and to approach a text as something that is either essentially silent or dialectically and acoustically normalized (rather than as a phonetic transcription). The result is often a remarkable indifference to the sound of early poetry.[2] In the following pages, I wish to consider the cultural politics of the *sound* of a particular vernacular, fourteenth-century Picard, in a collection of poems presented by the poet and chronicler of the Hundred Years' War, Jean Froissart, to King Richard II in 1395. Curiously, while all Froissart's editors chose this manuscript as their base text precisely because it was in his own dialect, none found his decision to employ this dialect for a presentation manuscript for the king of England worthy of comment. However clearly the text's dialect may be described as Picard, in the mind's ear the text is heard, if it is heard at all, in Standard French.

Let us begin with the story of the presentation. In 1395, the aging Jean Froissart made one last trip to England, where he had been received warmly some thirty years earlier, in the glorious days of Edward III. His principal motive, or so he claims in the account of his visit written in his *Chroniques,* was to recapture the joys of his youth, when he had served in the household of "good King Edward, of happy memory, and noble Queen Philippa, his wife," and had been treated "with all possible honor, generosity, and courtesy."[3] In preparation for his visit he secured letters of introduction from a number of aristocratic patrons and ordered a luxury presentation volume of his collected poems:

> I had ordered in preparation [or "through foresight," *par porvèance*] all the works on love and morality that I had completed, with the grace of God, during the last thirty-three years to be written, engrossed, illuminated, and collected. This greatly rekindled and inflamed my desire to go to England and see King Richard of England, son of the most noble Prince of Wales and Aquitaine, whom I had not seen since he was held above the baptismal font in the cathedral of Bordeaux.[4]

Through the chinks in the account that follows, one can detect that Froissart's reception in England was cool. He had some trouble getting presented to Richard. As Michel Zink puts it, "People let Froissart know that it was not the best moment to give the king the beautiful book he had planned for him."[5] Finally, Froissart encountered an old friend, Sir Richard Stury, who counseled patience, and after waiting several days for an audience, Froissart was finally given the opportunity to present his elegant book.

> When the king opened it, it pleased him well, and well it should, for it was illuminated, written, and historiated, and covered with crimson velvet, with ten buttons of silver and gilt, and roses of gold, in the middle, with two great gilt clasps, richly wrought. Then the king asked me what it was about; and I said, "Love." The king was pleased with this answer, and looked in it, and read in many places, for he could speak and read French very well [*moult bien parloit et lisoit le franchois*]. Then he gave it to one of his chamber knights, named Sir Richard Credon, to bear it into his secret chamber, and he received me ever more warmly and made me very welcome.[6]

The moment is well known to cultural and literary historians, who seize on it as evidence of the status of the book and the court poet, or of the level of proficiency in French in Ricardian England.[7] The standard interpretation is that, for Froissart, Richard's command of spoken French was a cultural accomplishment, one that by this point was noteworthy in an Englishman, even if he was the king. However, Froissart's meaning is subtler and more allusive.

Now, the value of the *Chroniques* as a historical source is highly questionable. The accounts are deceptively vivid and have often been read as straight reportage, but they are also highly structured literary fictions. Froissart's poetry is elaborately self-reflexive, filled with moments in which the poem depicts how it is being written into existence. As we are coming to realize, the same can be said of the *Chroniques*.[8] Even the impression that Froissart had little pull at the new court and depended on contacts from an earlier period fits the literary pattern of the last chapters of the work. While Froissart waits for the opportunity to present his book of poems to the king, he describes the negotiations for Richard's marriage to a French princess, so that we see one book, the *Chroniques,* being composed before our eyes in a space defined by the delay in presenting the other.[9] Yet the social tensions, the embarrassments of the intellectual parvenu, and the chain of patronage used to gain access to the court—all ring true. Froissart's account of the presentation, while a textual construct, presents the dissemination of poetry as a series of social exchanges. Froissart conceives of a journey, and his first step is to secure letters of introduction from a patronage network in Picardy and the Low Countries. His sponsors include Albert of Bavaria, who reigned as count of Hainault for over a century, had moved his court from Valenciennes to the Hague, and was an important patron of German and Dutch musicians and poets; his son William, one of the few continental members of the Order of the Garter; and of course Froissart's long-standing patron, Jeanne, duchess of Brabant and Luxemburg.[10] In attempting to understand the presentation of 1395, then, we must approach it both as an actual historical event and as a literary fabrication.

This was not the first time that Froissart had attempted to deliver a book to Richard. In 1381, he commissioned a copy of the *Chroniques* for the king, but it was seized by Louis d'Anjou, the duke of Orléans.[11] Although the manuscript has not been satisfactorily identified and may not survive, there is a family of late-fourteenth- and early-fifteenth-century copies that appear to be descended from it. All reproduce versions of a frontispiece divided into four panels: the first showing Froissart presenting the book to Richard; the following three showing how Isabelle, queen of England, fled from her husband, Edward II, was welcomed by her brother Charles IV, and returned with a force led by Jean of Hainault to depose her husband and place her son Edward III on the throne in 1327. In 1381, this history would have evoked Richard's claim to the throne of France at just that period when he passed from boyhood (*pueritia*) to adolescence (*adolescentia*) and might have been expected to take a more aggressive role in public affairs.[12] Froissart's lost original presentation copy thus combined authorial self-fashioning with a dangerously overt gesture of support for the English cause. The controversy surrounding this earlier abortive presentation suggests that the mission of 1395 was more politically charged than Froissart allows. Significantly, he mentions the lord of Coucy could not write directly in support, because of his allegiance to the king of France.[13]

There is one further window into the 1395 presentation; the book itself still survives, or at least so the evidence strongly suggests. It is frequently identified with Bibl. Nat. fr. 831, a luxury anthology of Froissart's poetry that omits only the enormous *Méliador* and a number of poems that might be offensive to the English on political grounds. The inscription on the recto of the opening flyleaf reads "Se livre est a Richard le gentil fauls conte de Waryewyck," showing that it belonged at one point to Richard's godson, Richard Beauchamp, earl of Warwick.[14] It is just conceivable that Froissart brought two books to England and that only the one acquired by Warwick survives, but Froissart never mentions a second copy, and this hypothesis, although advanced by none other than Kervyn de Lettenhove, seems far-fetched.[15] Most scholars are content to accept BN 831 as the famous presentation copy. And even if we were to entertain Lettenhove's hypothesis, BN 831 would have to be closely related to the king's manuscript and was definitely prepared for an influential English reader.[16]

BN 831 is, then, a manuscript that Froissart personally commissioned at significant expense as part of his continued self-promotion and in circumstances that were politically charged. It is surely significant that Froissart had what was arguably his single most prestigious presentation volume copied not in standard Northern French (Francien) but in his own Picard. For some, this may not seem that shocking. The differences between literary Picard and literary Francien are relatively minor and certainly do not prevent anyone who can read Francien from reading Froissart's works. The *Chroniques*, after all, were copied in Picard more often than not, and it is a Picard manuscript that serves as the basis for the standard complete edition, that of Kervyn de Lettenhove. The differences between the two dialects are certainly not nearly as marked as those between Chaucer and the Gawain Poet. Literary Picard was, in the words of Théodore Gossen, "a composite and hybrid language that we must not identify with the spoken language of the time," and it borrowed heavily from Francien.[17]

Compare two versions of the opening lines of "Le paradis amoureus" as they appear in BN 831 and its sister manuscript BN 830, a very similar volume that was copied in Francien a year earlier, probably in the same atelier. Many of the lines are almost identical.[18]

Je sui de moi en grant mervelle	Je sui de moi en grant merveille
Coument tant vifs, car moult je velle,	Comment je vifs quant tant je veille
Et on ne poroit en vellant	Et on ne poroit en veillant
Trouver de moi plus travellant,	Trouver de moi plus traveillant
Car bien sachiés que par vellier	Car bien saciés que par veillier
Me viennent souvent travellier	Me viennent souvent travillier
Pensees et merancolies	Pensees et merancolies
Qui me sont ens ou coer liies.	Qui me sont ens au coer liies.
BN 831	BN 830

There are scribal variations (as in line two), but only one word shows a vivid dialectical difference, the Picardian *sachiés* on line 5 as opposed to the Francien *saciés*. At first glance the difference does not seem that significant. But the very fact that Froissart had scribes "translate" his writings into Francien and employed them to prepare manuscripts such as BN 830 for his French patrons shows that the difference mattered to some.[19] Apparently, Froissart either did not think the difference would matter to an Englishman, and so gave all his attention to the book's bejewelled cover and decorated pages, or for some reason felt that for this especially important commission Picard would be preferable.

The dialectical differences would become a lot more charged if we could actually hear or mentally intone the sounds. One need only consider the extreme anxieties associated with various forms of Canadian French to realize the impact of apparently minor phonological differences. For years a recurring slur in predominantly monolingual English Canada was that the French of Canadian Francophones was not "real French." Insofar as Anglophones learned French, they usually attempted to acquire a Parisian accent. The distinctive "rolled" *r* and the strong nasalization of many Canadian Francophones were stigmatized as uneducated and provincial, the mark of "un peuple inculte et bègue" (an uncultivated and stammering people), to use the bitter terms of Michèlle Lalonde's famous satirical poem "Speak White."[20] Accent was politically coded. The intellectualism and aristocratic disdain of Prime Minister Pierre Trudeau was reflected in his mastery of both French and English, which he spoke in accents devoid of regional associations. In contrast, the current prime minster, Jean Chrétien, has employed the voice of the *p'tit gars,* or Québécois bumpkin, as a populist gesture, one that gains votes in English Canada but is reviled in Quebec. More recently, some Anglo-Canadian politicians have begun to abandon schoolroom Parisian French for what we might call Radio Canada French, mastering an accent neither of the *p'tit gars* nor of someone pretending to be from France, but of an educated Canadian. The Canadian *r* is becoming the mark of an accent that can be elected. Its use marks a significant cultural shift, yet only a modern phonetic transcription would distinguish this Canadian *r* from the trilled *r* of France. However obscure these differences may seem to an outsider, to members of a particular linguistic community they are deeply felt.

Picardy, home to the language chosen by Froissart for his book and spoken in wealthy cloth-manufacturing towns such as Lille and Amiens, "corresponded to no geographical or political area; it was a region set apart by its dialect and ethnicity."[21] The distinctive Picardian accent was often belittled. One of the best-known pieces of evidence for the stigmatization of Picard comes in a late-twelfth-century lyric by Conon de Béthune, who expresses self-consciousness about the provincialism of his speech (he speaks "words from Artois" and not from Ponthoise, to the northwest of Paris) and says that the French at the royal court have mocked his language, thus silencing him.[22] Similarly, Bartholomeus Anglicus, the thirteenth-century English Franciscan, described Picard as the "idiomatis magis grossi [sic] aliarum Gallie nationum" (the crudest of all the dialects of the Gallic peoples).[23] Such attitudes tend to provoke a reaction.

The stigmatization of Picard or of other dialects could only have occurred to the extent to which Parisian French was becoming a national standard. By the fifteenth century, as Anthony Lodge has shown, non-Parisian dialects were beginning to be assimilated, and "the dominant group began to see their language as a symbol of a new national identity."[24] But the rise of Parisian French can be traced back much further. In the 1290s the bilingual Flemish court poet Adenet le Roi, in his romance *Berte as grans piés,* described the desire among aristocrats to surround themselves with those who spoke Parisian French in teaching their sons and daughters.[25] This attitude must have been greatly strengthened by the increased use of French in the royal chancellery during the fourteenth century, a practice that was clearly intended to reinforce royal authority.[26] "Frenssh of Paris" was recognized on the continent as a unifying political force and a source of cultural prestige. For that very reason it was a threat to neighboring dialects. Froissart, for his part, was demonstratively not French. He notes in his *Chroniques* that an English knight, Sir William de Lisle, courteously welcomed him, "seeing that [he] was a foreigner and from the marches of France (for they [the English] consider as French all people who use the Gallic language, whatever country they may be from)."[27]

As the two short samples from "Le paradis amoureus" suggest, the differences between literary Picard and literary Francien are not, at first glance, overwhelming. As with continental and Canadian French, the differences are largely phonological. One of the most striking lies in the treatment of Latin / k/ followed by a vowel. In Francien /k/ before /a/ palatalizes to /ch/, whereas in Picard it does not. So Latin *cantus* becomes Picard *cans* but Francien *chanz*, and Late Latin *franka* becomes Picard *france* but Francien *franche*. On the other hand, in Picard Latin /k/ before *e, i,* or a central vowel is often palatalized, giving Picardian forms such as *merchi* or *canchon*. To Francien speakers, accustomed to stigmatizing Picard as a crude provincial dialect, the Picardian use of the palatal fricative /ch/ must have sounded as intrusive as the Cockney *h* did to Henry Higgins. Where Francien BN 830 has *chacier, chambre, chanter, chançon,* and *franchise,* BN 831 has *cachier, cambre, canter, cançon,* and *francise.* Even to a modern ear, the difference is striking. We might wonder whether these unpalatalized consonants sounded to Francien ears the way Yorkshire English sounded to at least one Southerner, the Cornishman John Trevisa, who sneered at it because it was "so scharp, slyttyng, and unschape, þat we Souþeron men may þat longage unneþe undurstonde" (so sharp, slitting, and shapeless that we Southerners can scarcely understand that language).[28]

Of course, establishing the connotations of lost sounds is a highly speculative venture, but there is, at the very least, a strong indication that Froissart was proud of his Picardian identity and conscious of it as a minority identity, recognizing (and apparently resenting) that, as far as the English were concerned, he was just French. He would have been equally irritated by a contemporary like John Barton, who, in his *Donait françois,* assured his English readers that he would teach them the "droit language du Paris et de pais la d'entour, la quelle language en Engliterre on appelle 'doulce France'" (the true speech of Paris and the surrounding area, which in England we call "sweet French").[29] In 1395 Froissart registered his protest. He placed in King Richard's hands a manuscript copied in Picard. The king read aloud, read not *françois* (with its fronted fricative) but *franchois,* the palatalized sound of Picard. And this moment is carefully recorded in the *Chroniques,* which Froissart was composing during the visit itself, in Picard, the language in which the manuscript was also most often copied. For those attuned to the sounds of the dialect, the crucial line "car moult bien parloit et lisoit le franchois" might even be understood, for the king read and spoke Picardian well.

The choice of Picard cannot have been merely a matter of personal satisfaction for Froissart, however. The details of presentation volumes, from the choice of texts and illuminations to the page layout and binding, were carefully selected to appeal to the targeted patron. Why then did Froissart feel that Picard, while inappropriate for his French patrons, was appropriate for the king of England? Let us tentatively consider two almost antithetical explanations. One way of defining Picard would be as the language of the cloth-trading urban bourgeoisie of one corner of the Low Countries. Gossen, for example, specifically associates the establishment of Picard as a legal and literary language with the moment when "the Picardian bourgeoisie became cognisant of its own worth and importance."[30] This language was not unknown in England. Commercial traffic with the Low Countries had increased from 1279 on, when Ponthieu became a royal possession. One result is that a significant number of fourteenth-century French texts copied by English scribes are in Picard or have Picardianisms.[31] Froissart's decision to work in Picard might, therefore, be seen as a reflection of commercial ties and as a decision to appropriate local business French, just as Chaucer had appropriated what was in a sense business English, a language stabilized through legal and chancellery practice. In this case, it would seem natural if Froissart's valorization of Picard, like Chaucer's valorization of English, was defiant and hedged around by insecurities. David Wallace has recently speculated that, for Chaucer, Flemish, the language of an area of vigorous capitalist expansion and bourgeois insurgency, could function as a symbol of English, that "funny-sounding mother tongue that would command little respect in Florence, Avignon, Paris, or even, as yet, parts of Westminster."[32] The Flemish nobles themselves regarded French as the language of prestige, speaking it with enough determination to evoke mockery in the Middle Dutch *Reinaert* (a version of the Roman de Renard), where the ridiculous little dog Courtois speaks French on all occasions.[33] These attitudes toward Flemish might well have extended to the language of Picardy. Froissart's decision to use the vernacular would become, in this reading, an act of plucky resistance against cultural hegemony, an act that allied him with the progressive spirit of the rising local bourgeoisie.

It seems out of keeping with Froissart's sustained aristocratic tone, however, to have employed a dialect because of its bourgeois associations. There is nothing in his works to suggest sympathy for the bourgeoisie, no sign, as there is on occasion with Chaucer, that he thought more vibrant cultural activity might be found outside the court, no interest in the rougher forms of colloquial speech. Although he based his *Chroniques* on interviews with a diverse collection of English and continental knights, Froissart makes no effort to reproduce their dialectical peculiarities. Ironically, the king that Froissart was so anxious to impress appears to have had a strong taste for poetry and even conversation in another nonmetropolitan dialect, that of Cheshire, the power base from which he had drawn a large personal bodyguard only the year before Froissart's visit.[34] But Froissart gives no indication he was even aware of this interest. There is no clear evidence that Froissart consciously imitated or drew inspiration from English practice; indeed, he never mentions English poetry in any of his writings.[35] Tempting as it may be to draw parallels between Froissart's use of the vernacular and that of contemporary English poets, his values were fundamentally different.

It is far more likely that Froissart valued Picard for its aristocratic associations. In particular, Froissart's use of Picard might have had an immediate political point, that of stressing his connection to his earlier patron Philippa of Hainault, wife of Edward III and grandmother of Richard II. Whatever form of French Philippa herself spoke (and it might well have been Francien), she had spent part of her childhood in the palace in Froissart's hometown of Valenciennes, and she had other Hainaulters at her court. Picard was the language of her county. In 1395 Froissart had a special reason for evoking this connection. When he sought an audience, he may, as Zink suggests, have made two claims on Richard: that he had seen his birth and that he had been under the patronage of his grandmother at the time.[36] Froissart entered into the service of Philippa in 1361 and was with her, the Black Prince, and Joan, princess of Wales, in Bordeaux in 1367 when Richard was born. More was at stake here than one might suspect. By the end of his reign Richard's feeble military performance had led some to question his paternity, since he hardly seemed a fitting son of the Black Prince. Some had gone so far as to insinuate that "Richard of Bordeaux," a term that had come to have derisive overtones, was the son "of French cleric or canon" whom the princess of Wales had met in Bordeaux.[37] Froissart's presence in Bordeaux at the time would make him a credible witness who could confirm that the allegations of Richard's illegitimacy were a recent invention; his presence might even be taken as a witnessing to the legitimacy of the royal succession. At a period when England's military prowess and the virility and legitimacy of its monarch were in doubt, the evocation of manly Edward and good Queen Philippa would have been a powerful reassurance. Perhaps it is significant that in his initial account of his reasons for undertaking the journey, Froissart specifically refers to Richard as the son of the Black Prince, "fils . . . au noble et puissant prince du Galles et d'Aquitaine."

For Froissart, Philippa belonged to an older and happier time, happier for him personally, for chivalry in general, and for the realm of England, and her language was that best suited for an English king who wished to read of love. If to Richard's ear Picard had an old-fashioned sound, recalling the days of his grandmother, this would be in keeping with the nostalgic tone of the entire voyage as described in the *Chroniques*. It would also be in keeping with the visual appearance of the manuscript, which is copied in "a conservative hand that is reminiscent of the middle of the fourteenth century rather than the end."[38] At the same time, the use of Picard might also be taken as a symbolic rebuke to the Paris-based Valois dynasty and its assertion of royal power over a widening body of French-speaking lands. Froissart's cultural nationalism and his political sympathies for England would have reenforced each other. The sound of the manuscript, read in a language that recalled past glories, would have echoed its visual impact, in its distinctly old-fashioned hand.

Did Richard hear the dialectical difference inscribed in the book, let alone its connotations? It is hard to tell. Certainly contemporary illuminators expected their readers to be attuned to the symbolism of relatively minor *visual* cues. Parisian and Flemish ateliers, for example, while they remained faithful to the text of the *Chroniques,* manipulated the illuminations in accordance with their own political sympathies. In one pro-French manuscript of the fifteenth century the debris of battle includes an English banner; in another, Edward III is placed beside the executioner as the burghers of Calais plea for mercy, and stumbles as he lands in France; and a pro-English manuscript takes care to include the *fleur de lis* in the canopy held above Edward III at his coronation, a visual reminder of his claim to the French throne.[39] But was the patron's eye as acute as the artist hoped, or the patron's ear as acute as the patron's eye?

Richard's ear might have been acute enough. It is likely, as Nigel Saul suggests, that French was Richard's first language; he left France at the age of four, but his two nurses came from Aquitaine, and his father wrote to his mother in French.[40] (Beyond that, we enter a hermeneutic circle: the single most commonly cited piece of evidence for Richard's grasp of French is Froissart's account of the 1395 presentation.) If Richard appreciated the finer points of Froissart's choice of language, however, he would have been one of the few who did. By this point even the English aristocracy was beginning to use French as a language learned in school, and many of the upper gentry were not well schooled.[41] Whenever he finds an English knight who can speak French, Froissart rejoices.

Nor would it be out of keeping with the entire episode if Froissart's subtle linguistic tribute passed largely unnoticed. The last chapters of the *Chroniques* are increasingly bleak. By 1395 Froissart's life, his great historical project, Richard's reign, and ultimately the entire chivalric enterprise were losing their vigor. Froissart's trip was not a triumph but a sad echo of his reception in southern France by the count of Foix, who had him read to the entire court from his *Méliador* for the space of a full month. Richard was only a few years from the fatal moment when his greyhound would desert him to fawn on

Henry Bolingbroke, earl of Derby, thereafter acknowledged as duke of Lancaster.[42] Yet this very sense of decline and isolation of both king and poet is one that Froissart himself has carefully shaped. The dominant theme of the episode is time's passage. The journey itself is one Froissart takes to recapture his youth. While he lays great stress on the legitimacy of Bolingbroke, as if "to ensure by every means possible the effective succession of the *true* sons of Edward III, as well as the unfailing transmission to posterity of the ancient values of chivalry," his sympathies lie with the king who had shown him such favor.[43] In his *Chroniques* Froissart acknowledges Henry as the new king, but it is a book of poetry on love that he chooses to present to Richard, as if offering an escape from the harsh dictates of politics and history.[44] King and poet come together in the twilight of their lives, turning for solace to the poetry of their youth. And their union takes place in the vernacular. Froissart places the words of his youthful compositions into the king's mouth, and orders them written so that if the king does sound them and lets the manuscript guide him, he will be speaking Froissart's native tongue, speaking not *françois* but *franchois*.

NOTES

1. Roger Wright, *Late Latin and Early Romance* (see Further Reading), argues that prior to this standardization, Latin was pronounced according to vernacular norms. His position is qualified but generally reendorsed in the essays collected in *Latin and the Romance Languages in the Early Middle Ages,* ed. Roger Wright (London: Routledge, 1991).

2. This indifference is far more pronounced in Old French studies than in those in Old or Middle English. Compare the wealth of recordings discussed by Betsy Bowden in *Chaucer Aloud: The Varieties of Textual Interpretation* (Philadelphia: University of Pennsylvania Press, 1987) to the limited number of recordings of works such as *The Song of Roland.*

3. Kervyn de Lettenhove, ed., *Oeuvres de Froissart,* 28 tomes in 29 vols. (Brussels: Académie Royale de Belgique, 1867–77), 15:140. For this, as for other French passages, I have supplied translations.

4. Ibid., 15:141–42. The passage is discussed by Kristen M. Figg, "The Narrative of Selection in Jean Froissart's Collected Poems: Omissions and Additions in BN MSS fr. 830 and 831," *Journal of the Early Book Society* 5 (2002): 37–55.

5. Michel Zink, *Froissart et le temps* (Paris: Presses Universitaires de France, 1998), 21.

6. *Oeuvres,* 15:167.

7. See, for example, Roger Chartier, *Forms and Meanings: Texts, Performances, and Audiences from Codex to Computer* (Philadelphia: University of Philadelphia Press, 1995), 39.

8. Peter F. Ainsworth, *Jean Froissart and the Fabric of History: Truth, Myth, and Fiction in the Chroniques* (Oxford: Clarendon, 1990).

9. Zink, *Froisart et le temps,* 22.

10. On Froissart's patrons in the Low Countries, see W. Prevenier, "Court and City Culture in the Low Countries from 1100 to 1530," and Frits van Oostrom, "Middle Dutch Literature at Court (with Special Reference to the Court of Holland-Bavaria)," both in *Medieval Dutch Literature in Its*

European Context, ed. Erik Kooper (Cambridge: Cambridge University Press, 1994), 11–29, 30–45; and N. Wilkins, "A Pattern of Patronage: Machaut, Froissart and the Houses of Luxembourg and Bohemia in the Fourteenth Century," *French Studies* 37 (1983): 257–84.

11. *Oeuvres,* tome I, pt. 1: 286–87, and tome I, pt. 2: 81–82, and Lawrence Harf-Lancner, "Image and Propaganda: The Illustration of Book 1 of Froissart's *Chroniques,*" in *Froissart Across the Genres,* ed. Donald Maddox and Sara Sturm-Maddox (Gainesville: University Presses of Florida, 1998), 221–50.

12. Nigel Saul, *Richard II* (New Haven: Yale University Press, 1997), 108.

13. *Oeuvres,* 15:141.

14. Figg, "Narrative of Selection," n. 9, suggests that *fauls* may be a variation of *faulfeu* ("fated" or "destined"), indicating that the book was given to Richard Beauchamp before 1401, when he actually became earl.

15. *Oeuvres,* 1:390–91.

16. For a description of the manuscript, see Jean Froissart, *L'espinette amoureuse,* ed. Anthime Fourrier (Paris: Klincksieck, 1963), 7–10. On those poems whose exclusion suggests it might have been prepared for an English readership, see also Peter Dembowski, ed., *Le paradis d'amour/L'orloge amoureus* (Geneva: Droz, 1986), 3–4, 6–12.

17. Charles Théodore Gossen, *Grammaire de l'ancien picard* (Paris: Klincksieck, 1970), 44.

18. The lyrics in BN 830 have been edited by Auguste Scheler, *Oeuvres-poésies,* 2 vols. (Brussels: V. Devaux, 1870–72). All other editions I am aware of use BN 831 as their base text. The manuscripts are often described as "matching," but this overstates the similarity. They are copied by separate hands, although the hands resemble each other quite closely. The layouts of the ruled grids and the decorations are similar, but the two manuscripts are not wholly alike. According to their inscriptions, 830 was copied in 1393, 831 in 1394.

19. On Froissart's copyists, see Alberto Varvaro, "Il libro I delle *Chroniques* de Jean Froissart: Per una filologia integrata dei testi e delle immagini," *Medioevo romanzo* 19 (1994): 3–36, and Jean Porcher, *The Rohan Book of Hours* (London: Faber & Faber, 1960), 8–9. A full investigation of the copying of the *Chroniques* is under way by the Froissart Project at the University of Liverpool under the directorship of Peter Ainsworth.

20. Laurent Mailhot and Pierre Nepveu, eds., *La poésie québécoise* (Montreal: TYPO, 1996), 389.

21. William W. Kibler, *An Introduction to Old French* (New York: Modern Language Association of America, 1984), 251.

22. Axel Wallensköld, ed., *Chansons de Conon de Béthune* (Helsingfors: Imprimerie Centrale de Helsingfors, 1891), 223.

23. Cited in Gossen, *Grammaire,* 27.

24. R. Anthony Lodge, *French: From Dialect to Standard* (see Further Reading), 131.

25. Adenet le Roi, *Berte as grans piés,* ed. Albert Henry (Geneva: Droz, 1982), lines 149–55.

26. Lodge, *French: From Dialect to Standard,* 122–24. This development is being studied by a team directed by Serge Lusignan, which has undertaken an examination of royal charters. Lusignan has pinpointed a major shift in 1330, when the royal chancellery largely abandoned Latin. See his "Langue française et société du XIIIe au IVe siècle" (see Further Reading).

27. *Oeuvres,* 15:144.

28. Quoted by Barbara M. H. Strang, *A History of English* (London: Methuen, 1970), 160.

29. Quoted in E. Stengel, "Die ältesten Anleitungsschriften zur Erlernung der französischen Sprache," *Zeitschrift für neufranzösische Sprache und Literatur* 1 (1879): 1–40, at 25; cited in Jacqueline Cerquiglini-Toulet, *La couleur de la mélancolie: La fréquentation des livres au XIVe siècle, 1300–1415* (Paris: Hatier, 1993), 22.

30. Gossen, *Grammaire,* 44.

31. Andres Max Kristol has noted that the *Manière de parler* of 1396, a French phrase book for

English readers, retains the Latin unpalatalized /k/ in the Picardian manner. "Le début du rayonnement Parisien et l'unité du français au Moyen Âge: Le témoignage des manuels d'enseignement du français écrits en Angleterre entre le XIIIe et le début du XVe siècle," *Revue de linguistique romane* 53 (1989): 335–67, esp. 363–66.

32. David Wallace, "In Flaundres," *Studies in the Age of Chaucer* 19 (1997): 63–91, at 85.

33. Prevenier, "Court and City Culture in the Low Countries," 18 n. 10.

34. John Bowers, "*Pearl* and Its Royal Setting: Ricardian Poetry Revisted," *Studies in the Age of Chaucer* 17 (1995): 111–55. Froissart's ally Sir Richard Credon was in fact the Cheshireman Sir Richard Cradock; see 121 n. 43.

35. In "Froissart's *Dit Dou Bleu Chevalier* as a Source for Chaucer's *Book of the Duchess,*" *Medium Aevum* 61 (1992): 59–74, Susan Crane argues persuasively against Froissart's having drawn on Chaucer.

36. Zink, *Froissart et le temps,* 13.

37. *Oeuvres,* 16:200; see Zink, *Froissart et le temps,* 101, and Ainsworth, *Jean Froissart and the Fabric of History,* 213.

38. Figg, "Narrative of Selection," 40.

39. Harf-Lancner, "Image and Propaganda," n. 15.

40. Saul, *Richard II,* 13.

41. Mary-Jo Arn notes that Charles d'Orléans's experiences in captivity in the 1430s suggest that "French was not commonly spoken by anyone in the household of the earl of Suffolk"; *Fortunes Stabilnes: Charles of Orleans's English Book of Love* (Binghamton, N.Y.: State University of New York at Binghamton, 1994), 31. On the gradual loss of French at a lower social level, see William Rothwell, "À quelle époque a-t-on cessé de parler français en Angleterre," in *Mélanges offerts à Charles Camproux* (Montpellier: C.E.O., 1978).

42. *Oeuvres,* 16:187–88. The passage is discussed by Ainsworth, *Jean Froissart and the Fabric of History,* 214–15.

43. Ainsworth, *Jean Froissart and the Fabric of History,* 214.

44. On the significance of Froissart's selection of a collection of poetry rather than history for Richard, see Ainsworth, "Configuring Transience: Patterns of Transmission and Transmissibility in the *Chroniques* (1395–1995)," in *Froissart Across the Genres,* 15–39, and Zink, *Froissart et le temps,* 129.

Professionalizing Translation at the Turn of the Fifteenth Century

Ullerston's *Determinacio,* Arundel's *Constitutiones*

FIONA SOMERSET

Censorship is never quite as perfect or as invisible as when each agent has nothing to say apart from what he is objectively authorized to say: in this case he does not even have to be his own censor because he is, in a way, censored once and for all, through the forms of perception and expression that he has internalized and which impose their form on all his expressions.

Among the most effective and best concealed censorships are all those which consist in excluding certain agents from communication by excluding them from the groups which speak or the places which allow one to speak with authority. In order to explain what may or may not be said in a group, one has to take into account not only the symbolic relations of power which become established within it and which deprive certain individuals (e.g. women) of the possibility of speaking or which oblige them to conquer that right through force, but also the laws of group formation themselves (e.g. the logic of conscious or unconscious exclusion) which function like a prior censorship.

—Pierre Bourdieu

Bourdieu's remarks on how authoritative groups make statements unsayable or exclude those who might say them will probably ring true for many who work in corporate environments of whatever kind.[1] But censorship is of course never as perfect as the invisible censorship described in the epigraph's first paragraph—or, at any rate, never consistently so. Forms of perception and expression internalized through processes of education or training may "impose form" to the extent that they determine what counts as well-expressed statement, what genres or forms of expression count as authoritative, and what their standards of excellence are—even what kinds of statements can be made in certain contexts without in the process performing one's own self-exclusion. But of course even the unsayable is nonetheless often said, however covertly. And while some modes of dissent if expressed openly may exclude their speaker from "orthodox" membership in a group or profession because they are seen as departing from the group's sanctioned forms of expression and venturing into heterodoxy, others are unorthodox in ways that

a given profession may tolerate, or even encourage. Bourdieu's own unorthodox analyses of the politics of the academic profession have not precisely been
discouraged by the profession itself, for example.

This description of exclusionary censorship may especially remind Middle
English scholars of current work on the politics of late medieval vernacular
translation, which would suggest that not only were speakers, readers, and
writers competent merely in the English vernacular excluded from the kinds
of communication accessible to those (mostly university-educated clerics) who
were highly competent in Latin, but at the end of the fourteenth and beginning of the fifteenth century the clerical establishment was increasingly anxious to preserve these prerogatives by restricting translation into the
vernacular and imposing an increasingly rigid orthodoxy on its own members'
views about the possible benefits of translation.[2] Yet I think that reflecting
upon Bourdieu's remarks can also help us to reconsider the details of this
account. For Richard Ullerston, my first example, has much more than "nothing to say" in what has been called the Oxford Translation Debate of around
1401. Scholars have found it rather difficult to explain how Ullerston could—
without, apparently, being censured in any way—strongly defend vernacular
translation of the Bible at a time when advocacy of this cause was linked in
the official mind with the Wycliffite heresy, in the same year that the penalty
of execution by burning was brought to England to combat this heresy, and
a mere six years before Arundel's *Constitutions* stringently limiting any such
biblical translation were formulated.[3] But rather than puzzle at Ullerston's
failure to censor himself, perhaps we could use Bourdieu's remarks to consider
him from another angle. Ullerston's position within his authoritative group is
quite similar to Bourdieu's. And he seems to share Bourdieu's finely tuned
awareness of how groups establish their own orthodoxies, as well as his ability
to manipulate his own group's conventions and speech genres and forms of
expression in such a way as to use sanctioned modes of academic dissent to
his own advantage.

Reconsidering Ullerston's success will also provide a new perspective on my
second example, Thomas Arundel, whose *Constitutions* are often cited by scholars as the culmination of increasing constraints on vernacular translation in
England. Arundel's provisions to limit vernacular translation and preaching
have been seen as opposed to theories of vernacular access such as Ullerston's:
Arundel thinks the laity should know nothing beyond the minimum necessary
for salvation, whereas Ullerston wants vernacular translation to make every
kind of knowledge accessible to all. But a careful reading of the *Constitutions*
as a whole reveals that Arundel is far less interested in controlling lay access
to clerical knowledge than in seeking better control *within* his authoritative

group. Even where he might seem to be concerned with lay access, Arundel's focus is on attempting to produce the conditions—well-patrolled internal hierarchies, narrowed bounds of orthodox opinion, sanctions on employment—that would make possible the sort of perfect censorship of the clergy that Bourdieu describes. This new assessment of Arundel's aspirations will also prompt a reconsideration of his legislation's effects.

We should begin by revisiting some current academic orthodoxies about late medieval English attitudes toward the vernacular and Ullerston's place among them. Interest in the politics of late medieval translation arose first among scholars of Wycliffism, the first heresy indigenous to England, and has since spread to other scholars who have seen its implications for their own areas of study.[4] The received narrative about Wycliffism's use of the vernacular and its wider effects goes something like this. Wycliffite ideas were apparently disseminated by means of vernacular preaching and texts, starting as early as the late 1370s, when Wyclif and some early supporters were, it seems, preaching in English, and continuing well into the fifteenth century through the preaching, writing, and translations of later Wycliffites despite efforts at repression in 1382 (the Blackfriars Council, where ten propositions of Wyclif were condemned as heretical), 1388 (when mandates from the king required various authorities to search out writings in Latin and English by Wyclif, Aston, Purvey, and Hereford), 1401 (*De Heretico Comburendo,* which forbade any unauthorized preaching, book writing and/or ownership, or teaching, and provided for those who relapsed into heresy to be burned), and 1409 (Arundel's *Constitutions,* which among other provisions imposed strict controls on all writings containing biblical translation since Wyclif's time). Not only was Wycliffism perceived as the "English heresy" because its adherents used English rather than Latin to promulgate their views, but the use of English was in itself linked to heresy: increasingly, any use of English to provide information previously confined to Latin, and any ownership of books in English, could become suspect.[5] After the 1409 *Constitutions'* "draconian . . . censorship . . . going far beyond its ostensible aim of destroying the Lollard heresy and effectively attempting to curtail all sorts of theological thinking and writing in the vernacular that did not belong within the pragmatic bounds set by earlier legislation," Nicholas Watson has suggested, "the commonest and most influential response . . . among writers and their scribes was silent compliance."[6] The vernacular had become so closely linked to heresy that most writers stopped using it to say anything theologically interesting, let alone defended its use, lest they be suspected.

Against the backdrop of that narrative, scholars have had some trouble explaining why Richard Ullerston defended vernacular translation in the debates over biblical translation at Oxford around 1401, at just about the same time that *De Heretico Comburendo* was enacted and that William Sawtry (prematurely, just before enactment of the legislation) became the first heretic burned in England, on charges of Lollardy. Admittedly Ullerston's *Tractatus de translatione Sacrae Scripturae in uulgare* was written six years before 1407, when the *Constitutions* were drafted in Oxford; but scholars' efforts to convince one another that these six years made a crucial difference, when the reaction against Wycliffites' use of English goes back to the 1370s, have met with only limited success.[7] Ullerston's stance would be easy to understand if he had Wycliffite sympathies or affiliations. But there is no hint that he did. Even though the bulk of his arguments in favor of Latin translation were later incorporated into a vernacular Lollard tract on the subject, there is no record that Ullerston himself was ever suspected of Wycliffism.[8] A fellow of Queen's College at Oxford, he was resident in the college from 1391 to 1402, then again in 1403–4 and 1407–8. Apart from his treatise on translation, he wrote three scriptural commentaries (dated to 1410, before 1415, and 1415), a sermon on the canonization of Saint Osmund, delivered at Salisbury cathedral in 1416, and a number of polemical works, dated from 1401 up to 1413 or so. These show an interest in reform but suggest active participation in issues of ecclesiastical governance rather than any sort of heterodoxy.[9] If the scholarly assessment of the prevailing views on vernacular translation and of the extent to which they enforced a rigid orthodoxy of expression is correct, then Ullerston's defense of translation seems to pose a problem: Why are his views not unsayable? Why did they not result in his exclusion?

Examining Ullerston's translation treatise in detail will help us in reconsidering this question. As is conventional in a determination of this kind, Ullerston presents both sides of the argument, staging a debate between two doctors over the question "Utrum sicut Jeronimo licuit ab hebreo et greco in latinum transferre sacrum canonem ita liceat ipsum in alias lingwas minus principales et famosas transferre" (Whether, just as it was permissible for Jerome to translate Scripture from Hebrew and Greek into Latin, it can be translated into other less important and famous languages).[10] No less than thirty arguments for and against are considered. Ullerston includes the conventional submission to the approval of Holy Church: "teneo partem questionis affirmatiuam tamquam michi probabilem, nichil temere asserendo; nec aliter intendo in hac materia seu quauis alia quam sancta mater ecclesia katholica et Romana sentire" (I hold the affirmative side, for it seems to me probably right, but I do not assert anything with temerity, nor do I intend anything in this matter or any other otherwise than Holy Mother Church does) (fol. 197v, col. i). Yet despite this semblance of evenhandedness and willing submission, Ullerston's interests are clear: he devotes eight times as much space to arguments in favor of translation as to arguments against. Nor does Ullerston rely merely on long-windedness to make his point: his arguments on the affirmative side give a more searching and thoughtful discussion of the possibilities of writing in English than do those of any of his near contemporaries, Wycliffite or not, that I have encountered.

For example, in contrast to Thomas Palmer's compendium determination against translation, and specifically against Lollards, of four or five years later—Palmer and Ullerston are not disputing with one another directly, yet clearly they are participating in a common debate over whether faithful translation into English is possible—Ullerston gives detailed arguments in defense of the capacity of English to express anything that Latin can.[11] Palmer's technical arguments for the limitations of English appear in the section of his debate that appears to interest him most. They are the second of the *aliae veritates* (other truths) that he appends to his first complete determination, and his six-point exposition is the most sustained and detailed discussion of a given point that he gives anywhere in his treatise.[12] For Palmer, English is a barbarous language, whose speakers sound like pigs grunting: even to write it down, the Latin alphabet must be supplemented with extra letters. What is more, English lacks vocabulary required for translation from Latin. And it has no grammatical regularity: the lack of specific inflections for each case, of the sort found in Latin, leads to falsehood and ambiguity in translation. If it is impossible to preserve grammar point for point in a translation even from languages with grammar, as, for example, when translating from Greek into Latin, all the more is faithful word-for-word, or even sentence-for-sentence, translation into English impossible.

Ullerston in reply goes further than simply defending the grammar of English: he goes on the attack, warmly dismissing all academic bias against the grammar, logic, and rhetorical eloquence of English.[13] His defense is two-pronged. On the one hand he claims that English is a fully adequate vehicle not only for grammar but for the expression of any of the seven liberal arts—concentrating on the hardest case, logic. On the other he insists that Sacred Scripture contains no such complexities in any case. Even if the *populus simpliciter rusticanus* (untaught populace) cannot, without *magnam asuefaccionem* (lots of specialized training), readily understand translated logic, because of all the anglicized Latin it would include, nonetheless the laity are fully capable of understanding what is needful from translated Scripture. Indeed they already do so when it is retailed to them in the form of vernacular sermons.

What *do* the laity need to know, though? Should their knowledge be carefully limited? What effects would new knowledge have upon them? Ullerston flies in the face of the common clerical bias against the laity's acquiring knowledge, lest clerical prerogative be somehow disendowed and the office of priesthood usurped, since the clergy would no longer be the only possessors of "clergie."[14] Instead, Ullerston doggedly insists that the laity will always benefit from more knowledge and that the effects will not be disruptive.[15] One should never avoid accomplishing something good because something bad might accidentally result, he argues: that would be like not planting a tree in case someone might hang himself from it, or not building a window in case someone might throw himself out of it. Bishops can ensure that priestly prerogative is preserved; but in any case reading Scripture is sure to *prevent* the laity's usurping clerical prerogative rather than the reverse. For Scripture "in infinite places" recommends that each should remain in his own social status, accomplishing his calling, in humility rather than presumption, "ex quibus laici essent disuasi ad vsurpandum officium sacerdotum, sed nullatenus prouocati" (and by these passages laypeople would be dissuaded from, not provoked into, usurping the office of priesthood) (fol. 202v, col. ii).

Ullerston's defense of lay capacities is even more strikingly unorthodox in the rhetorical flourishes of the appeal to his readers' judgment that (as is conventional) he engages in before laying out the affirmative side of the debate.[16] Here he overturns, and turns on its formulators, the usual characterization of uneducated layfolk and their vernacular speech. Ullerston counterposes the "solid man" whose judgment accords with reason and conscience to the *rudibus,* the "lewed," as he would probably say in Middle English, who like pigs or dogs or birds are moved by the grunt or bark or call of one to clamor tirelessly, "indefesse," in mindless imitation. But Ullerston's target here is not the laity, and not vernacular speech, the *vox populi* so often insultingly likened to animal noises, as David Aers analyzes with reference especially to the Peasants' Revolt and as depicted in Palmer's determination.[17] Instead, Ullerston is speaking of his colleagues: anyone "moved by the world" who in his efforts to please "satrapes" (despotic rulers) and seek out benefices speaks in such a way as to enhance his institutional position. Rather than keep vernacular speech and its speakers out of the discussion through the sort of exclusionary censorship Bourdieu criticizes, Ullerston mockingly turns this mode of dismissal upon self-serving academic factionalists—and in particular upon *their* censure of the vernacular and its speakers.

Ullerston's impulse toward education is thus as far-reaching in its intended benefits as is that of Trevisa's Lord in his *Dialogue.* Goaded by the Clerk's repeated misunderstanding of his plans for facilitating lay education through translation, the lord in the *Dialogue* proposes that under the broadest definition of "need" as whatever is beneficial, *everyone* needs to read Higden's *Polych-*

ronicon.[18] But although the Lord does not refer to it explicitly here, Trevisa, like many Wycliffite writers, shares—or pretends to—the common clerical belief that lay education will lead to the destabilization of the church hierarchy and a loss of clerical prerogatives.[19] Rather than fear this possibility, Trevisa and Wycliffites hope for it: they advocate the disendowment of much of the church's wealth and count that possibility as a benefit to be accrued from the dissemination of "clergie." Ullerston would not agree on either count, it seems. His *Defensorium Dotacionis Ecclesie,* or *Defense of Church Endowments,* was written in the same year as the *Tractatus.* And in the *Tractatus* itself, as we have seen, he refutes the notion that lay education would entail any depreciation of clerical status whatever. As Bourdieu might say, concurring with Ullerston, education is in itself the imposition of form, an indoctrination into the group and its attitudes that preemptively quells dissent and imposes its own perfect self-censorship.

This statement returns us to where we began, and to the need for some rethinking. If the clerical establishment was as opposed to vernacular translation as has often been supposed, then the problem—to put it in Bourdieu's and Ullerston's own terms—is how, given Ullerston's own clerical indoctrination, his position at the university, and the received views on lay education dominant within that setting, he could make the argument he made. Trevisa's equally strong advocacy of scriptural translation in the *Dialogue* was clearly produced when the Bible was not yet such a hard case, in 1387 at the latest, in fact.[20] Trevisa assumed that the Scriptures were in a way the *easier* example of a clearly beneficial sort of translation, as perhaps it was still just possible to do; and in any case, although Trevisa too was not a Wycliffite, he shared the Wycliffite convictions on disendowing church property, whereas Ullerston did not. Ullerston was apparently not subject to the sort of self-censorship that we might expect the strength of current opinion to impose. Yet at the same time he was not, nor at the time was he taken to be, voluntarily ruling himself out of the group by defying its norms while still sharing its assumptions. If scholars' chronology of steadily increasing repression, and their assumptions about what could and could not safely be said at the time, are accurate, then Ullerston's cynicism—or is it optimism?—about the effects of education seems to leave no room for his own dissent. Some sort of readjustment is required.

What needs adjusting is not Ullerston, though, but our sense of the context in which he was writing—both before and after Arundel's *Constitutions.* Ullerston's views on the usefulness and even necessity of educating the laity, and on the role of the vernacular within such education, belong to a competing orthodoxy (or at the very least sanctioned unorthodoxy) that had support within university circles from at least the early thirteenth century up until Arundel's *Constitutions* attempted to curtail debate on lay education and beyond. The reforming tenor from which Wyclif's ideas emerged, whose supporters would include a line of bishops who advocated vernacular education while criticizing clerical corruption, such as Grosseteste, Pecham, Thoresby, and Fitzralph,[21] would have been respectable even among those who might have rejected Wyclif's own extremity and intemperance of expression. The clerical establishment was not as unified an entity as it may often be made to appear.

Arundel's *Constitutions* make clear that his assessment of the possibilities of lay vernacular education is very different from that of such reformers. But limiting these possibilities is far from his main target. For Arundel, controlling access to clerical learning by restricting vernacular translation is just one dimension of an overall concern with attaining greater control over every aspect of the clergy's education and professional activities, for example by stipulating the subject matter and methods of teaching in both elementary schools and universities, mandating monthly examinations for heresy of every student in every Oxford college, regulating the authorization and content of all parish preaching and celebration of Mass in his province, strictly limiting the dissemination of books containing writing by Wyclif and his associates or even scriptural translation in any form, and providing the sanction, against university members in particular, of a three-year ineligibility for any benefice in the province.[22] Even where the *Constitutions* refer to Pecham's syllabus (the truths necessary for salvation that Pecham had included in his 1281 *Ignorantia Sacerdotum* as the syllabus all priests must teach), Arundel is not interested in limiting lay knowledge to its contents, as Watson claims.[23] Instead, at this point he is concerned with shoring up clerical hierarchy and placing it more firmly under his supervision. Some preachers will be permitted to discuss matters beyond the syllabus, others not: the article aims strictly to regulate who may be permitted to teach beyond the syllabus, where, and under what authorization.[24] Although Arundel's distrust of lay learning seems clearly implicit, he never refers to any potential impact that his rulings might have on the laity, but only to the "reforms" he hopes to effect among the clergy.

Rather than contribute to scholarly discussion of the benefits of lay education in the vernacular, then, Arundel would really prefer to end it. He writes legislation rather than disputation, and article 8 of the *Constitutions'* provisos, aimed specifically at the freedoms permitted by disputational convention, reveals his opinion of the genre: scholars will no longer be allowed to frame conclusions or propositions that even *sound* opposed to Catholic faith or good morals, whether prefaced with a protestation or not, whether the scholars are in the schools or not, disputing or communicating, asserting the content or merely proposing it, and even if their statements can be defended through ingenious argument.[25] But we should not be too quick to assume that Arundel succeeded. While, as Anne Hudson has pointed out, there is evidence to suggest that the *Constitutions* were not *merely* a pious (or impious) hope, they were nonetheless much less than a fully implemented system of draconian censorship.[26] The *Constitutions* had effects, certainly; but nothing like the effects they claim to intend or that have been attributed to them. The long-standing opposition of the university's self-governing colleges to undue outside interference in the conduct of their affairs would have strengthened the sympathies of a number of their members with Wyclif's ideas or with the broader reformist tradition with which these ideas had been allied. That the Oxford colleges remained difficult to control is clear from ongoing efforts to do so.[27]

The *Constitutions'* effects beyond the university, on vernacular readers and writers, also need reconsideration and greater differentiation. While ownership of books could and did become corroborative evidence in accusations against lower-class laypersons in the fifteenth century, legislation aimed at seeking out heretical books was of course not new in 1409. And even among these audiences the *Constitutions* did not have the effect of confining teaching to the contents of Pecham's syllabus, any more than they had the intention. Rather, many later prosecutions in which book ownership was implicated were far more zealous, accusing lay villagers of owning (or even just being familiar with) material *within* the syllabus.[28] Book ownership remained merely a consideration in the investigation of suspected heretics, which might proceed with greater or lesser fervor, depending on the zeal of the local bishop rather than the grounds for systematic searches. Moreover, even though the *Constitutions* forbade ownership of Wyclif's and Wycliffite books as well as any translations of Scripture in whatever form from Wyclif's time onward, it seems that these provisions were not used against members of the gentry and nobility. As far as we can tell from the paucity of prosecution records, from records of book ownership, and from manuscripts still extant, higher-status laity continued with impunity to own books of the prohibited kinds. Although Watson repeatedly concedes this point in his article, its implications for his argument would seem worthy of further exploration. If one of the most important markets for adventurous vernacular writing was largely unaffected by the *Constitutions,* would the legislation really have seemed dangerous enough to writers that it would have scared them away?

The notion that any writers would have been scared into "silent compliance" seems partly based on the comments of one group of writers upon whom the *Constitutions* certainly did have a demonstrable impact: those who refer to them directly, either in order to protest against them or in order to advertise their compliance. But while such comments are undeniably worthy of attention, they are not of course a reliable guide to how even these writers themselves felt affected. Like Ullerston's grunting pigs, the compliant are self-promoting: Nicholas Love's theatrical orthodoxy in his *Mirror,* for example, is plainly opportunistic. Those who complain about restrictions on preaching and writing, on the other hand, such as the author of the *Lanterne of Liȝt,* are less concerned with those restrictions' effectiveness than with the opportunity to cast themselves as successors to the early martyrs and display their willingness to die for their beliefs if necessary. Such responses, by their very nature, do not reveal to us the views of writers who may have reacted otherwise, somewhere between or beyond these extremes. And the difficulty of inferring these intermediary, unvoiced reactions is compounded by the danger of circular argument. If we proceed on the assumption that works written after the *Constitutions* would have censored themselves from saying certain things or would not have said them without mentioning their authorization or protesting their lack of it, we are in peril of dating and classifying works to suit the polarized view of possibilities for vernacular expression that we already have.

This reassessment of the relationship between censorship and use or advocacy of the vernacular in late medieval England suggests that that relationship, while close, is not as simple as it may appear. The choice between using or advocating the vernacular and keeping silent is not necessarily a choice whether to exclude oneself from discussion or to submit to a prior self-censorship: if we assume that it is, we limit our analysis. For scholars interested in analyzing similar relationships between a debased, common vernacular and an educated language used by a dominant authoritative group, this example can suggest that discussions of that vernacular within the dominant group are often more inward looking than they may at first appear: they may have much more to do with how education confers power within the group than with any of those left outside.

NOTES

1. Pierre Bourdieu, "Censorship and the Imposition of Form," in *Language and Symbolic Power* (Cambridge, Mass.: Harvard University Press, 1994), 138.

2. For details, see below. My *Clerical Discourse and Lay Audience* (see Further Reading) would largely agree with this account, and this essay presents in part a rethinking of some of my own ideas, though in my notes I will mostly attempt to open new conversations with other scholars. This essay began as a joint paper at the "Vernacularity" conference with Andrew Cole: for conversations and

mutual readings, I thank him, Claire Fanger, Shannon McSheffrey (see note 28 below), and Nicholas Watson.

3. For more on these difficulties, see below, esp. note 6. The *Constitutions* were produced in convocation in Oxford in 1407 and issued and publicized more broadly in 1409: see Anne Hudson, "Lollardy: The English Heresy?" (1985) (see Further Reading, page 257), 146 n. 22.

4. See esp. ibid.; idem, "Wyclif and the English Language" (see Further Reading); Margaret Aston, "Lollardy and Literacy," in *Lollards and Reformers: Images and Literacy in Late Medieval Religion* (London: Hambledon, 1984), 193–217; idem, "Wycliffe and the Vernacular" (see Further Reading); and Nicholas Watson, "Censorship and Cultural Change" (see Further Reading).

5. This is Hudson's main argument in "Lollardy: The English Heresy?"

6. Watson, "Censorship and Cultural Change," 826 and 831.

7. Thus Anne Hudson raises the possibility that Ullerston was not the author of the *Determination* (yet only to reject it). She then suggests that Ullerston was insulated from controversy by the fact that he was writing in Latin in Oxford for other scholars, and on a topic that could still be entertained in theory. See "The Debate on Bible Translation, Oxford 1401," in *Lollards and Their Books*, 67–84, at 75–76, 80, and 83 (originally published in *EHR* 90 [1975]: 1–18). But in "Lollardy: The English Heresy?" she expresses reservations about her previous claims: "To think that the switch of views amongst the orthodox came between 1401 and 1407 is unconvincing, . . . there is evidence that this debate did not reveal the whole picture" (150). Kantik Ghosh conjectures that Ullerston's tract was perhaps written long before 1401, then revived in that year—a conjecture that would dismiss the tract's incongruity with his narrative of developing attitudes toward authority and interpretation (see chap. 3, "Vernacular Translations of the Bible and 'Authority,'" in *The Wycliffite Heresy: Authority and the Interpretation of Texts* [Cambridge: Cambridge University Press, 2002], 86–111; for the conjecture, 109–10). He admits this explanation of what he labels Ullerston's "curious myopia" (87) is unlikely, but finds the tract difficult to explain otherwise: Ullerston's vision of meaning is "almost naïve"; his "apparent unawareness of the questions he is begging is startling" (92). Was he simply unable to recognize that when the scriptures were in the vernacular, clerics would not be able to control lay interpretations and ensure proper lay use of scriptural knowledge? Or was his naïveté "deliberate" (105)? The suggestion that Ullerston was naïve cannot, I think, stand up to what we now know about Ullerston's other writings on the Bible and on polemical subjects (see note 9 below); nor does it seem to be borne out by the contents of Ullerston's determination itself (see below).

8. On the vernacular tract, see Hudson, "The Debate on Bible Translation," 67–71. For editions, see Margaret Deanesly, *The Lollard Bible and Other Medieval Biblical Versions* (Cambridge University Press, 1920), 439–67; C. F. Bühler, "A Lollard Tract: On Translating the Bible into English," *Medium Aevum* 7 (1938): 167–83.

9. Anne Hudson has traced records of Ullerston's connections with Queen's College; see "The Debate on Bible Translation," 78–80. Richard Sharpe's admirably thorough handlist of Latin writers makes it easy to assess Ullerston's known writings: in the order mentioned in the text these are his commentaries on the Creed (1410), the Psalter (before 1415), and the Song of Songs (1415); his sermon of 1416; his polemical works on the popular topics of clerical poverty and mendicancy (before 1401), translation (1401), and church endowments (1401); a disputation on a topic unknown (1402); his petitions for church reform at the Council of Constance (1408); and a work that from its title appears to be a military manual (*De officio militari,* before 1413). See Richard Sharpe, *A Handlist of the Latin Writers of Great Britain and Ireland Before 1540* (Turnhout: Brepols, 1997), 516–17. Hudson, in "The Debate on Biblical Translation", 76–77, notes similarities of style between the *Defensorium* and *Determination*.

10. I cite Ullerston's *Tractatus* from my own rough transcription of the text in Vienna, Österreichische Nationalbibliothek, Codex Vindobonensis Palatinus 4133, fols. 195–297v. The script is

extraordinarily difficult to decipher; readers are welcome to suggest corrections. All translations are my own. In the transcriptions I add modern punctuation but retain medieval spelling; subsequent references will be by folio and column number. This passage appears on fol. 195, col. i.

11. For Palmer's determination, apparently compiled from perhaps as many as six separate arguments, see Deanesly, *The Lollard Bible,* 418–37. Both Hudson ("The Debate on Bible Translation," 67–68 and 81–82) and Watson ("Censorship and Cultural Change," 842–43) have briefly discussed the tract. Here I assume that it was Palmer who made the compilation, but of course it need not have been.

12. See Deanesly, *The Lollard Bible,* 426–29. Here I summarize Palmer's key points.

13. For the arguments in this paragraph, see the whole of Ullerston's lengthy response to argument 9, fol. 201, col. ii–fol. 202, col. i. At the top of fol. 202, col. i, Ullerston points out that untaught people would be unable to read difficult translated material full of neologisms.

14. See note 2 above.

15. For the following, see the responses to arguments 13 and 14, fol. 202v.

16. See fol. 199, col. ii.

17. David Aers, "*Vox Populi* and the Literature of 1381" (see Further Reading).

18. For Trevisa's *Dialogue,* see Ronald Waldron, ed., "Trevisa's Original Prefaces on Translation: A Critical Edition," in *Medieval English Studies Presented to George Kane,* ed. E. D. Kennedy, Ronald Waldron, and J. S. Wittig (Woodbridge, Suffolk: D. S. Brewer, 1988), 285–99; see esp. 291, lines 70–81.

19. Trevisa's political sympathies are especially clear in his translations of the pseudo-Ockham *Dialogus inter militem et clericem* and of Richard Fitzralph's *Defensio curatorum:* for a discussion, see Somerset, *Clerical Discourse and Lay Audience,* 78–100.

20. The *Dialogus* was included as a preface to Trevisa's translation of Ranulph Higden's *Polychronicon,* dated to 1387 by its colophon. See Waldron, "Trevisa's Original Prefaces," 285–88, for further details.

21. In fact, Ullerston mentions the words or actions of all four of these bishops in the course of his determination. Grosseteste and Fitzralph each seem to have got themselves into terrible trouble in the course of their reforming efforts, but to have avoided any excommunication or removal from office. Pecham and Thoresby, who concentrated on reforming their own underlings, had fewer difficulties. Wyclif seems to have regarded both Grosseteste and Fitzralph as models for his own activities; Arundel may have viewed himself as a second Pecham.

22. The *Constitutions* are printed in David Wilkins, ed., *Concilia magnae Britanniae et Hiberniae,* 3 vols. (Oxford, Clarendon, 1964), 3:314–19. In order, I describe here the content of articles 5, 8, and 9; 11; 1, 2, 3, 4, and 10; 6 and 7; 12. Article 13 allows suspects to be tried even if they do not present themselves at summons; defendants could no longer escape prosecution by evading trial.

23. Watson, "Censorship and Cultural Change," 827–28.

24. "Sacerdotes vero parochiales, sive vicarii temporales . . . in forma supradicta non missi, in ecclesiis illis, in quibus officia hujusmodi gerunt, illa sola simpliciter pradicent, una cum precibus consuetis, quae in constitutione provinciali a bonae memoriae Johanne, praedecessore nostro . . . quae incipit, 'Ignorantia sacerdotum,' continentur expresse" (But parish priests or temporal vicars . . . who have not been sent according to the form previously described should preach in their own churches only the doctrine [together with the customary prayers] expressly contained in the provincial constitution of our esteemed predecessor John . . . which begins, "The ignorance of priests"). From article 1, in Wilkins, *Concilia magnae Britanniae et Hiberniae,* 3:315, col. ii. The earlier part of the article had described procedures for authorizing other sorts of preaching: this is the default case.

25. "inhibemus, ne quis, vel qui, cujuscunque gradus, status, aut conditionis existat, conclusiones aut propositiones in fide catholica seu bonis moribus adverse sonantes . . . in scholis, aut extra, disputando aut communicando, protestatione praemissa vel non praemissa, asserat vel proponat, etiamsi

quadam verborum aut terminorum curiositate defendi possint." Wilkins, *Concilia magnae Britanniae et Hiberniae,* 3:317, col. ii.

26. Hudson, "Wyclif and the English Language," 94. For the censorship claim, see Watson, "Censorship and Cultural Change," 826 and 831.

27. For an overview, see Anne Hudson, "Wycliffism in Oxford, 1381–1411," in Kenny, *Wyclif in his Times,* 67–84. For a more general survey of the early years of the movement in which Oxford plays a prominent role, see Anne Hudson, *The Premature Reformation: Wycliffite Texts and Lollard History* (Oxford: Clarendon, 1988), 69–119.

28. For a handful of examples, see Hudson, "Lollardy: The English Heresy?" 161–62. In "Heresy, Orthodoxy, and English Vernacular Religion, 1480–1525" (forthcoming), an important new study of late-fifteenth- and early-sixteenth-century book ownership and religious practice among Lollards, Shannon McSheffrey has investigated why it was that in later years suspicion could be aroused by ownership of vernacular versions of even the most basic prayers.

PART III: 1500–2000

Making the Mother Tongues

The four essays in this final group deal with the formation and elevation of
national or ethnic languages and literatures in the half millennium after 1500.
The choice of any specific topic in this vast field has an inevitable arbitrariness
to it. However, each of the language situations discussed here, like that of
English in the later medieval period, is in some sense marginal to western
European vernacular politics, offering a perspective on this politics from a
position geographically or symbolically near or beyond Europe's edge. Each
essay, that is, reflects on western European culture (or a specific polity, such
as France or England) as a colonizing entity from which the language or literature in question must distinguish itself, using the tools provided by the colo-
nizer as a vital resource. Focused on four different cultural moments at which
the "medieval" has played a central, if not always acknowledged, role, the
essays also implicitly reflect on crucial stages in the development of Europe's
historical self-understanding.

During much of the last two centuries, when the story of medieval vernaculars was told as that of a triumphal rise from the language of a "people" to
that of a "nation" (independent, secularized, and with its own literary canon),
these last four essays might have been expected to tell the story of the emergence of national "mother tongues" as a defining characteristic of modernity
(see the Preface). This narrative remains a postmodern temptation, even in
seminal work such as Benedict Anderson's *Imagined Communities*. Yet it is fundamental to the argument of this book that none of the themes it pursues is
specific to any one period. The "evangelical" vernacular is not only a thirteenth-century phenomenon, despite the emphasis of Part I (as is clear from
essays by Briggs, Somerset, and Fairey). The formation of a plurality of vernacular textual "communities" is not only a fourteenth- and fifteenth-century

phenomenon, despite the emphasis of Part II (as is clear from essays by Hames, Poor, Fairey, and Bhatia). Just so, the vernacular as a national mother tongue is already in evidence before the end of the Middle Ages. For example, the "nation-building" functions of Middle English and Anglo-Norman have been extensively researched (e.g., by Thorlac Turville-Petre). French's sense of itself as the language of nation is implicit in the distinction Froissart makes (according to Taylor's essay) between "French," a mother tongue, and "Gallic," a regional tongue of which French and Picard are local manifestations. And by the mid–fifteenth century, "Scots" is at work separating itself from its dialectal cousins spoken in the north of England and announcing itself a "language" (see Wogan-Browne et al., *Idea of the Vernacular*).

This is not, of course, to claim that the story of the European vernaculars told in this book involves no change, or that the story of that change has no shape. Rather, it is to reemphasize that the story needs to be written using resources beyond those provided by the narratives of the Renaissance, Enlightenment, or Romantic periods: narratives that strongly influence our assumptions and thus the way we come at the historical evidence. As these essays make clear, modern ways of thinking about language often ground themselves in or differentiate themselves from a fantasy of the medieval past. The medieval thus functions as a site of difference for language reformers from the sixteenth century down to the present. Historical connections and causes of difference between medieval and postmedieval linguistic politics that deserve attention are occluded in the process.

In the first two essays in this group, Jeroen Jansen's discussion of early modern Dutch attempts at language reform and Jack Fairey's account of the making of standard Serbian and Romanian in the Austro-Hungarian Empire, versions of the medieval and ancient past justify or provide leverage for a variety of positions on the present and future of the vernacular language in question. Indeed, despite the gulf of time, space, and terminology that separates them, there are striking similarities between the preoccupations of Fairey's Romantic language reformers and Jansen's humanists, both of whom use the "medieval" as one of a number of possible pasts to which they wish to return or from aspects of which (in the case of Fairey's secularists) they want to escape. There are also intriguing similarities (and, potentially, historical connections) between the language politics discussed in both essays and many aspects of medieval language politics.

Jansen traces sixteenth- and seventeenth-century attempts to create a standard written Dutch in the face not only of a complex dialect and language situation but also of a long struggle for independence from the Habsburgs. Language reformers striving to make a Dutch accessible and impressive enough to be fit for use in, say, an authorized version of the Bible could not draw on the courtly linguistic registers that lent dignity to other European vernaculars, since Dutch "courts" worked largely in French and both that language and the courts were perceived as agents of colonial power. Universities, on the other hand, used Latin for most purposes into the nineteenth century. Humanistic reformers thus fought a lonely (and not very successful) battle for an "authentically Dutch" form of Dutch, by which they meant a Dutch "purified" of foreign, especially French, linguistic influence. French, in most European contexts a language of high culture as early as the twelfth century, was here recast as "barbarous."

Many aspects of this situation have parallels with later developments, and few are new to the sixteenth century. For example, Dante's efforts to imagine an *illustre volgare* similarly aim at dignifying the vernacular and reflect the need to compete with classical literature and prestigious vernacular traditions. Although Dante's agenda is universalist, it was easy for nineteenth-century *Dantisti,* anxious to see the poet as a father of Italian unification, to cast his attempt to choose the best from every Italian dialect in a nationalist light.

Yet, in Jansen's account, Dutch language reform publicly bases itself, not on actual medieval precedents, but on a fantasy about the medieval as the period when an "authentic Dutch," unpolluted by French vocabulary, was still spoken: as though, until 1415 or 1500, the Dutch language "naturally" retained a primal separateness from its powerful linguistic neighbor. Not only is this claim certainly untrue; the ideal the reformers project onto the past—an ideal of purity, which in some sense is a harbinger of Romantic language theory—is the very element in play here hardest to find in medieval language theory. The idea of linguistic "purity" is derived, rather, from humanist grammatical and editorial theory, and its drive to purge the classics and language of error and barbarism. Dutch language reformers vernacularize and make local humanism's Europe-wide program of cultural reform (with what debt, one wonders, to Erasmus of Rotterdam?). In so doing, they organize their program around the grammarian's metaphor of cleansing, rather than the rhetorician's metaphor of enrichment. If their attempt to free the Netherlands from French taint is partly a Protestant's return to Eden, it is also a humanist's return to Athens.

Nationalism, standardization, linguistic purity, Eden, Babel, and Athens: all these symbols and concepts are afloat in the sea of nationalisms developing in the last century and a half of the Austro-Hungarian Empire. Fairey's thoughtful analytic survey follows the very different trajectories of the languages that are constructed around two of these nationalisms, Serbian and Romanian. Serbian, the language of a prosperous minority, is formed slowly, and after much controversy, into a standard language with a coherent ideology. Powerful groups advocate adherence to a Serbian literary tradition with roots in Church Slavonic and high culture; others, influenced by German Romantic philologists like Jakob Grimm, demand the building of a new, folk language around a version of the spoken vernacular. Two competing pasts, one ecclesiastical and literary, one tribal and oral, serve to imagine two different futures. The first movement assumes an integral relation between a nation and its faith, high culture and social or ecclesiastical hierarchy. The second movement assumes a mystical identity between a spoken language and the "genius" of a people, takes no note of religion, and is theoretically democratic. Long held under suspicion, especially by ecclesiasts, the conclusions of this second movement are finally accepted, and the idea of Serbian as a secular Slavic vernacular is born.

Meanwhile Romanian, the language of a less advantaged people, evolves a sense of separateness from its Slavic neighbors by stressing its status as a Romance language, derived from Latin. The rediscovery of this relationship after centuries in which it seemed uninteresting has a transforming effect on Romanian culture. Dismissing the work of early intellectuals, who consider Church Slavonic and Greek as classical models, Latinizers and francophilic "Bonjourists" denounce the use of Slavic vocabulary and Cyrillic orthography, forge cultural ties with France, and initially produce a standard written Romanian distant from speech. Less culturally secure than the Serbians, Romanian intellectuals only near the end of the nineteenth century apply the precepts of Romantic language theory, evolving a vernacular standard Romanian "of the people" and comprehensible to the people.

Both these linguistic situations—in which a plethora of dialects, several high-status vernaculars (French, German, Russian), and not one but three classical languages (Greek, Latin, Church Slavonic) are in play—are of exemplary complexity, urged on by the lurking presence of a newly powerful Magyar culture, whose imperialist ambitions give cause for alarm. In sorting through these complexities, the intellectual battles fought about the future are as strongly grounded in competing versions of the past as we saw medieval language debates to be grounded in the myth of Babel or the topos of *translatio* (see the Introduction). The past is continuously cited to justify or prevent social change, sometimes in diametrically opposing ways. Medievalists will again recognize analogies from the thirteenth to the fifteenth centuries: especially the trilingual situation of Anglo-Norman England, where linguistic reform comes from many sources—ecclesiastics and aristocrats, intellectuals like Ullerston and priests like Orm (see the essays by Worley and Somerset). Most striking, though, is the sidelight offered on research into the past during the century when the modern disciplines of literary history and philology were forging institutional and intellectual structures that are still with us.

Jansen and Fairey's essays are primarily concerned with linguistic, rather than literary, history, offering glimpses of postmedieval societies in which relations between church and state, intellectuals and the unlettered, the present and the mythical past, and different conceptions of the vernacular are as multifaceted as they are in twelfth-century England or thirteenth-century Germany. The other two papers in this group, Nandi Bhatia's analysis of the uses to which Shakespeare was put in colonial India and Larry Scanlon's study of Langston Hughes, are focused, rather, on the role of literature as a force in establishing national or ethnic languages. In both cases, literary texts or topoi from European literary history are bearers of energies that can be used to reinforce or to critique British and/or white cultural hegemony. The medieval and early modern English past provides structures for colonization, for postcolonial formations of national or ethnic identities, and on occasion for forms of political and cultural dissent.

Bhatia's essay gives a complex picture of how Shakespeare, a poet central to British pedagogical strategy in India, becomes an *auctoritas* to whom the British, Hindi nationalist intellectuals, and Urdu thinkers and writers all appeal. As in other cultural domains, the humanistic British cultivation of Indian languages and education through Shakespeare—taken to be a "civilizing" force in his own right, through translation, but also used as a symbol of a literary perfection that Indian writers should not hope to attain—is, in a sense, too successful. A century after William Jones names the fourth-century Sanskrit poet Kalidasa the "Indian Shakespeare" (in 1789), this cognomen is being used by Hindi intellectuals to assert the superiority of their own carefully Sanskritized literary language to Urdu. Attempts to link Hindi literature with Shakespeare help to drive a wedge between the initially very similar Hindi and Urdu vernaculars: a process the British help instigate through their association of Hindi with Sanskrit and Hinduism, Urdu with Persian and Islam. Slowly (as Bhatia reads the journal articles, scholarly books, and adaptations of Shakespeare that emerge in the decades before and after 1900), Hindi intellectuals come to regard the association between Shakespeare and Kalidasa as a symbol of Hindi equality with English. (Urdu here remains a backdrop, a language and culture Hindi defines itself against.) Common themes and motifs are found between the two writers and used to assert a common Aryan heritage. Shakespeare becomes Hindu; Hindi, Shakespearian. As Hindu nationalism gains anti-British momentum, it thus partly detaches Shakespeare from his association with British rule, even if he remains linked to the prestige of English (partly because this language increasingly represents international, not specifically British, culture.) In this way, Hindu nationalism appropriates an important organ of British imperialism.

Bhatia comments briefly on Urdu versions of Shakespeare but notes that further work is needed on this topic, earlier scholarship having largely reinforced Hindi and anti-Urdu ideological positions. British reactions to the Hindu assimilation of Shakespeare are also of relevance here, for in some respects colonial British concepts of India's "infinite variety" and of Shakespeare run parallel. Indeed, the Indianization of Shakespeare is an outstanding example of the power and ambiguity of the myth of *translatio studii:* a myth that sets up unresolvable tensions between West and East, present and past, displacement and imitation (see the Introduction). In this imperial context, however, *translatio* runs not westward but "back" to the east, where Shakespeare (in mythic terms, inevitably) "turns out" to have been anticipated by a forebear, Kalidasa. To pursue this thought to the conclusion that Shakespeare himself "is" Hindu is to use *translatio* against the very occidentalizing ideologies it was designed, from Roman times, to serve. India becomes a nation defined around a Hindu cultural agenda by constructing itself as a figure of Europe's past. This idea, that India in some sense *is* Europe's middle age, Kalidasa India's Shakespeare (anterior, hence superior or at least legitimately separate), is the more powerful because of the ways it resonates in British as well as Hindu intellectual terms. The link Jones "found" in terming Kalidasa the "Indian Shakespeare" has uses that he could not have anticipated and generates arguments he could not have refuted.

Like the first essay in this volume, by Meg Worley, Larry Scanlon's essay begins with a separate discussion of the theme of vernacularity and history. That Langston Hughes becomes, early in his career, the "laureate of the Negro race"—a phrase that consciously yokes the medieval world of Petrarch and Chaucer with modern America—suggests that the needs of the African-American urban literati are met by deployment of a fantasy Middle Ages in rather the way different pasts serve different presents throughout this last group of essays. Although the cultural configurations differ, especially in the values they ascribe to past and present, "laureate of the Negro race" constructs a "golden" African-American literary future as "Indian Shakespeare" constructs a golden Sanskrit past. Indeed, where "Indian Shakespeare" begins as a colonial rhetorical gesture and is slow to adapt to the interests of Hindu nationalism, "laureate of the Negro race" originates close to Hughes himself and quickly acquires wide currency. Versions of the phrase are still widely known through modern literary anthologies.

Yet whereas the earlier essays in this group evoke situations in which there is no necessary connection between the imagined past of a "pure" Dutch, a "folk" Serbian, or a strictly "Aryan" Hindi and the actual history of these languages and literatures, Scanlon argues that the phrase "laureate of the Negro race" involves more than projection. In his analysis, "laureate," far from being quaintly archaic, names a living cultural institution with a continuous history vital enough to act as a conduit between a medieval past and a modern, African-American present. Through this conduit comes, not only the idea of the poet whose quality and cultural centrality makes him worthy of the wreath of *fama,* but laureation's association with political and literary competition, with the struggle between learned and popular, and with notions of community—in short, with the medieval idea of the vernacular. The stage is thus set, in Scanlon's essay, for a rich theoretical discussion of the strange parallels between Middle English studies and African-American studies, in their deep (but apparently unrelated) current engagement with their vernaculars, and for a rich critical discussion of Hughes's creation and celebration of a poetic mother tongue in his late poem *ASK YOUR MAMA.* As a laureate, Hughes is here also a "medieval" poet (in the same sense in which Chaucer might be described as a modern one), and his use of a mixture of styles, modes, influences, and vocabularies indeed resembles Middle English aureation as closely as it resembles other works in the modernist canon. This vernacular poetry has nothing to do with linguistic purity. It is authority-seeking (related intertextually to high canonical poetry) but equally authority-defying (setting that poetry alongside fragments of the people's "common speech" at its most improvisational). Above all, it is Parnassian: inspired, not rationally ordered. As such, Hughes's literary vernacular is yet another translation of the idea of revelatory "Adamic" language discussed in the Introduction: a vernacular that is as clearly constructed as the hybrid prayers of the *Ars notoria* but that still presents itself as given or found, as well as made. Scanlon's claim that the long diachronic story he tells reveals real cultural continuities— medieval traditions that yet have the power to inflect contemporary culture—is this book's most direct expression of hope that medieval studies can engage with the postmedieval in deeper ways than merely by exposing the ideological agendas of the myriad of European medievalisms.

Purity and the Language of the Court in the Late-Sixteenth- and Seventeenth-Century Netherlands

JEROEN JANSEN

In the period between 1150 and 1500, several dialects were spoken and written in the present Dutch-speaking region: what we know today as the Netherlands and about half of Belgium, including the towns of Antwerp, Bruges, and Ghent.[1] All of these earlier dialects, like modern Dutch and English, have Germanic roots. However, there were also many loanwords imported into these dialects from Old and Middle French, via cross-border contacts and through trading centers and aristocratic culture. French influence on the dialects of Middle Dutch dates from as early as the twelfth century. But since Latin was the language of the church and the university, many loanwords were also taken from Latin, and (as is also true with English) it is not always clear whether Middle Dutch words were borrowed from Latin or French.

In the sixteenth century, the status of these loanwords came under discussion. For many reasons, including increasing national consciousness, the Dutch language came to be considered fully equal to other languages, including Latin. During this period, both humanist scholars and vernacular authors began to argue that the Dutch vernacular had been neglected and needed to be "purified" (purged of non-Germanic elements),[2] as well as promoted more widely and made more sophisticated (urged toward more formal and learned registers). All these changes resulted, over several centuries, in a huge production of Dutch dictionaries, grammars, spelling prescriptions, and the like. More and more, the vernacular took the place of Latin in institutional and scholarly fields. This process was only completed toward the end of the nineteenth century, when the scientific language became Dutch instead of Latin.

Once purists became self-conscious about the status of the language, they began to advance objections to the French and Latin words in current use among speakers and writers of Dutch. These objections were concerned especially with the official language, used in court circles and by rhetoricians.[3] It is important to note that almost all of these purists were against Romance loanwords, not Germanic ones.

By the late sixteenth century, the various dialects in use in the Low Countries no longer had equal cultural authority; rather, their value depended on the economic and political power of the provinces. For instance, when Antwerp fell into the hands of the Spaniards in 1585, the town was divided into north and south. Its occupation until around 1630 resulted in a massive emigration, especially to the province of Holland, mostly for religious and political reasons: in 1622, for example, 62 percent of the population of Leyden consisted of immigrants. The economic emphasis moved from the south to the north, and Amsterdam took over from Antwerp as the principal trading city. Not surprisingly, the language spoken in the province of Holland, the language that was to become standard Dutch, was influenced by Flemish and Romance elements.

As early as the fifteenth century, some authors, aware of writing in a specific regional dialect and wishing to address an audience across dialect boundaries, made an attempt to write in a literary standard, but this practice did not produce a unitary language. In the late sixteenth century, due to increasing contacts between several provinces of the Dutch Republic, as well as to increasing national unity, need arose for a "supraregional" means of communication. Its development started in the north. Although written dialects continued to flourish in the Netherlands into the seventeenth century, dialect differences were increasingly standardized in writings for a general audience, especially translation of the Bible. In view of the origins of the many immigrants to the province of Holland, it is understandable that so many southern (Brabantish and Flemish) elements were included in the standard language. This standard form of written Dutch, which developed in the towns of the province of Holland, spread little by little to the larger population.

While the spoken language continued to be characterized by great diversity, the lack of uniformity in the written language became a major concern. The main authority for standard Dutch in the first half of the seventeenth century was the authorized version of the Bible (1637), while the work and the ideas of Dutch writers such as Pieter Hooft (1581–1647) and Joost van den Vondel (1587–1679) were considered illustrations of the proper use of standard language. About twenty years after the publication of the authorized Bible, every reformed pulpit and all reformed families in the Dutch Republic were in possession of the new translation.[4] In preaching in churches, reading in the home, and education using Bible passages in schools, this authorized version had a vital function.[5]

The translators of the 1637 Bible had to negotiate between different dialects in their efforts to produce a literary standard that would be generally acceptable. By choosing translators and revisors out of different provinces, some from the Northern Netherlands, others from the south, they tried to create a general language, avoiding characteristics belonging to one dialect area. Whether this resulted in a decrease of loanword usage cannot be determined. It depends, for example, on the kinds of usage in question (official, familiar, and so on) and on the differences between the written and the spoken language.

At the court in Brussels, as at the courts of the stadholders in various provinces of the Dutch Republic, French was the official language. It was also the international trading language. Further, French became the spoken and written colloquial language among a small elite in the Netherlands, whose usages were sometimes imitated by other groups. However, French words and expressions were mangled in assimilation; seventeenth-century publications repeatedly ridicule the phenomenon. Despite all attempts to the contrary, French loanwords infiltrated the Dutch language more and more during the seventeenth and eighteenth centuries. As a consequence, the criticism of French loanwords was not silenced, but continued during the eighteenth and even through the nineteenth century.

Such were the main linguistic features of Dutch in its development over several centuries. I now focus on a small but significant feature of the pursuit of linguistic "purity" as an aspect of national consciousness: negative attitudes toward the language of the court in the late sixteenth and seventeenth centuries. Courtly language was considered to exert a barbarizing Romance influence on the vernacular. I note several distinctive features of the Dutch courtly situation and consider the effects they had on attitudes toward court language in the seventeenth-century Low Countries. Finally, I describe how this influenced the pursuit of a "pure" vernacular.

It may seem surprising that, in comparison with other western European countries, the influence of courtly treatises was never very substantial in the Netherlands of the sixteenth century and first half of the seventeenth. Treatises like Castiglione's *Il cortegiano* (1528) and Della Casa's *Galatheo* were not available in translation, and Stephano Guazzo's *La civil conversatione* (1574) was published in translation only in 1603.[6] Neither the background of this phenomenon nor its consequences has been studied in detail.

We may start from the hypothesis that the absence of Dutch translations of Italian and French courtly-conduct treatises did not imply lack of acquaintance with these treatises among governors of the Dutch Republic. For in the courtly milieu of the Netherlands, the language of politicians and of the administration was French. And in that language *Galatheo, Il cortegiano,* and *La civil conversatione* were available in plenty as early as the 1590s.

Indeed, although Dutch dialects had predominated as the language of administration in the various provinces since the Middle Ages, French was the

[handwritten annotations in top margin: "War vs. Spanish helped more French unpopular (Catholic?)."]

language most often used by the States General and in correspondence with other dynasties.[7] The agelong influence of French on the vernacular helped make the language of the court increasingly unpopular, as Dutch nationalism came into its own during the Eighty Years' War against Spanish rule (1568–1648). Moreover, this war had the effect of abolishing administrative relations with the French-speaking provinces, eliminating any administrative need to use French. By contrast with the stimulating effect most European courts had on literary and intellectual activities, court influence in the Northern Netherlands was out of step with popular and intellectual culture during the sixteenth and seventeenth centuries. During a period when language constructors and purists were striving for a vernacular that would represent the highest common factor of the dialects written in the Low Countries, without a surplus of French loanwords, the court had, essentially, nothing to contribute.

In the Low Countries, then, as in all other Calvinistic courts,[8] the language of the court was French.[9] The court was in Brussels, while the monarch Charles V, and after 1555 his son Philip II, lived in remote Spain, reigning by way of ambassadors, governors, and stadholders.[10] The language used at the courts of the stadholders, if we may call them "courts," was therefore French. Due to the bourgeois character of the province of Holland and the fading influence of the nobility, no centralized courtly culture (and this is central to my argument) developed in the Northern Netherlands during the second half of the sixteenth century, as it did in Elizabethan England or in the France of Henry IV. Political and religious commotion, too, may have retarded the realization of a prosperous center. Merchants increasingly formed the center of society, and it was they who combined prosperity with power, raising the province to a new grandeur. The government of the republic was constituted by the citizenry of the cities: a few governing families provided burgomasters, aldermen, and council members. Even in the first decades of the sixteenth century, the province of Holland, by far the most densely populated and prosperous of the seventeen provinces, counted half of its population in the cities. The administrative system was structured accordingly. In the Netherlands an upper civil servant would have been defined as a statesman and politician with defined tasks as advisor, governor, or magistrate. Could a constitution and mentality of this kind have influenced the translation of courtly treatises that were so popular in model countries like Italy and France? From a literary point of view, as compilations of anecdotes with a didactic character, these treatises were still valuable. Due to their application as books of conduct, however, the treatises were considered inapt for the common people. The social and intellectual elite could help itself to the original, untranslated texts.

A characteristic feature in the criticism of courtly language in the Renaissance Netherlands is the confrontation between, on the one hand, "humanistic" ideals of language construction, stylistic purity, perspicuity, and, on the other hand, social practice. The sixteenth-century need for a grammar of the Dutch vernacular, as well as a dialectic and a rhetoric, also in the vernacular, was satisfied in the trivium (1584–87) of the Amsterdam chamber of rhetoric, *In Liefd' Bloeyend'* (In love we flourish). The 1584 grammar, entitled *Twespraack vande Nederduytsche Letterkunst,* contains a refrain entirely dedicated to the destructive influence of loanwords upon the Dutch language. In these verses, the reader is showered with barbarisms, particularly French loanwords. The refrain argues that Romanizing tendencies have penetrated church, trade, and administrative jargon, the juridical machine, even the chambers of rhetoric themselves. Even names of dishes are borrowed from French. Such pursuit of purity was not particular to Dutch. In other countries, too, especially France, warnings against Italian, Latin, and Greek barbarisms were rife. But only in the Dutch provinces was courtly language automatically associated with French and Latin barbarisms, rather than held up as exemplary of pure language. Especially in Dutch-language grammars, which circulated mainly outside the sixteenth- and seventeenth-century school circuit, one comes across the view that courtly language negatively affected the purity of language. In the preface to the *Nederduytsche Helicon* (1610), for example, bookseller Passchier van Westbusch argues that in this treatise "all foreign words" (*alle geleende uytheemsche woorden*), which originated from the "pretty, ostentatious courts of Lords" (*d'oogh-cierlijcke Heeren pronck-hoven*), not "simple, life-giving farmers' cottages" (*de slechte Lijf-herghs boeren wand-hutten*), were avoided.[11]

The best-known advocate for a "pure" vernacular was Dirck Coornhert (1522–90), a Dutch author, theologian, and moral philosopher, who wished to banish all words of Latin and French origin. In the preface to the *Twespraack,* in which the central theme is the glorification of the mother tongue, Coornhert states: "The fact that the Dutch language of our ancestors was so wise and rich may be seen in their writings. All scum of foreign languages is alien to them. That purity was clouded once foreign gentlemen and foreign-speaking governors with their train imported a bastard language."[12] This statement invites the question of how far back in time we must go to encounter writings in a clear, "old" Dutch language, the writings "of our ancestors." Joost van den Vondel, the famous seventeenth-century tragedian, advises the future poet to master "the particular expressions in Dutch charter books" (*de eige manieren van spreecken of Neerlantsche hantvestboecken*).[13] Presumably he is referring especially to charters from the period before French influences

*gap bet.
theory & prac-
tice*

appeared in the vernacular, but an exact date is missing here. If we want to date this phenomenon, we meet with a discrepancy between more or less contemporary reflections and social practice. If we take literally statements on the barbarizing influence of the court on language, the Romanizing of the Dutch language must have taken place at the beginning of the sixteenth century. When we look at social practice and try to give a historical explanation for the phenomenon, however, we find traces of Latinization more than a century earlier, around 1400. How is this difference to be explained?

The literary sources are not very exact in this respect. Maybe Romance influences were not noticed until the growing self-assuredness and nationalism of language constructors brought them to light—at which point historical exactitude seemed less important than halting the influx of barbarisms. According to Dirck Coornhert, in his preface to Cicero's *Officia* translation of 1561, this "contamination" (*besmetting*) started "forty years earlier" (*veertich iaren herwaerts*), so circa 1520.[14] In other treatises of this period, authors roughly speak of "some years ago" (*enige jaren geleden*). Such a treatise is *Het tresoor der Duytsscher talen* (The treasure of Dutch language), the purist dictionary of Antwerp lawyer Jan vande Werve, which remained popular into the eighteenth century. In 1553 he dates the phenomenon to "some years ago" (*over luttele Jaren*).[15] The *Twe-spraack* by the Amsterdam chamber of rhetoric *D'Eglentier,* the first published Dutch grammar, states that "our language has been mixed up so much with foreign words in only a few years time that it would be almost unusual for the common people to speak only Dutch" (onze spraack in korte Jaren herwerts [. . .] zó zeer met uytheemsche wóórden vermengt is, dattet schier onder t'vólck een onghewoonte zou zyn enkel Duits te spreken).[16]

But official sources indicate that the barbarizing tendency must have started much earlier, at least in the fifteenth century. In 1433 the provinces of Holland and Zeeland fell into the hands of the Burgundian monarch Philip the Good. The other provinces received a common administration only under Charles V, in the first half of the sixteenth century. Despite its assertion that the starting point of barbarization was "some few years ago," the *Twe-spraack* also suggests, perhaps contradictorily, that foreign linguistic influence has been a factor "since we and the Walloon cities were under one common sovereign and court" (sedert dat wy met de Walsche steden onder een ghemeen Vorst ende hóf zyn gheweest).[17] This implies that the start of French-language influence was 1419, the first year of government of Philip the Good, who was sovereign of both Burgundies, as well as count of Flanders. So far back the memory of the sixteenth-century literators did not reach. I presume that they may have let the starting period of French (and Latin) influence coincide with the first printed reactions to this phenomenon. I also assume that indications such as "some years ago" (*in korte Jaren herwerts*) relate to more recent history, that is, the period under Charles V and Philip II.[18] When Coornhert refers to "foreign gentlemen and foreign-speaking governors with their train" (vreemde Heren ende vreemdtongighe landvooghden met der zelver ghezinde), he may mean the regents and governors of the period in which the Dutch provinces were ruled by Margaret of Savoy (1507).[19]

The humanist pursuit of "pure" language, which already occupied such a prominent position in classical rhetoric, acquired new currency in the struggle to develop the Dutch language into an adequate medium of communication. That struggle, and aversion to the lawful sovereign, were so strong that courtly language did not acquire the status and authority in the Northern Netherlands that it obtained in surrounding countries. Instead, it became a focal point of suspicion. The republic could not refer to the authority of a monarchy. In the *Twe-spraack,* all hopes for the establishment of a pure Dutch language were thus based, not on courtly idioms, but on the scholars from the only university in the Northern Netherlands, Leyden. The author hopes that "we Dutchmen may someday taste scholarship in our own language, which we must now labor for in unknown languages"; "God will perhaps produce a monarch (as he has done in France with Francis I and in Italy with various princes) with the intent of furthering Dutch scholarship."[20]

One wonders if it may be characteristic of the Dutch situation in this period that the dialectic of the Amsterdam chamber trivium was dedicated, not to any sovereign, prince, or stadholder, but to the burgomasters of Leyden and its university, that stronghold of the Neo-Latinists.[21] The humanist academy of Leyden was asked in vain to use the vernacular, since the idea behind this trivium was that popular education was necessary to overcome antagonisms and further the commonwealth.

The dedication of the *Twe-spraack* states that the French king had instructed Petrus Ramus to write the French equivalent of this trivium. This statement may only be understood in the light of a certain jealousy with respect to a flourishing courtly culture that derived prestige from its own use of the vernacular.

Given a prestigious French courtly culture versus a completely French-speaking Dutch court, with its seat at Brussels and with the stadholders from the Northern Netherlands making use of French only for official purposes, how could the battle for the vernacular be waged otherwise than with the arms of an unremitting protest against the courtly language?

The court may have had its seat at Brussels, and the stadholders may have literally been substitute monarchs. Nonetheless, during the 1630s and 1640s the idea of a real courtly milieu developed in the Northern Netherlands. The moderate stadholder Frederik Hendrik, who lived in The Hague, tried systematically to enlarge his power, status, and residence. Authors like Pieter Hooft and Hugo Grotius could therefore publicly declare themselves advocates of a monarchical form of government.

The idea of a "real" court at The Hague developed not only in the mind of the stadholder but also in that of Constantijn Huygens (1596–1687) and Hooft. Hooft even discerned something approximating a "courtly style." Huygens, who was not only a famous Dutch poet but the secretary of Frederik Hendrik, played an important role as an intermediary between the stadholder and poets who wished to dedicate their work to him. This happened, for example, in 1634, when Huygens showed the stadholder an important book in manuscript on Dutch history by Hooft. Hooft, a poet and prose writer who held a minor diplomatic and military post in the province of Holland, testified, both in this document and elsewhere, to being a fanatic purist, a constructor of language, one who recorded the most daring purisms.

Even though, in Hooft's view, the Dutch and French languages were different worlds that could not and must not be interwoven, his letters directed to whichever administrative authority were interlarded with French jargon.[22] In his position as a bailiff, he availed himself of juridical jargon. As a literary man, as a writer of letters to his humanist friends, he scrupulously avoided every word of French origin. In the *Nederlandsche Historien,* a Dutch history written according to the model of Tacitus's *Histories,* Hooft experimented widely with neologisms and purisms. When Hooft learned that, without his knowledge, Huygens had lent manuscripts of this work to stadholder Frederik Hendrik to read and judge, he expressed the fear that he might have overdone the purisms, all the more because the court was accustomed to another kind of language: "Although they were solid enough of body and limbs, nevertheless they are not fit for the court, and miserably hideous, due to the heresy of preferring strange words to un-Dutch ones."[23]

Shortly afterward, Hooft sent to a friend a letter in which he mentioned his reflections on writing pure Dutch instead of courtly barbarisms. In the meantime he had been informed that the stadholder had indeed condemned the purisms in his prose, including many neologisms. Hooft admits in this letter: "The punctiliousness of my conscience in this matter displeases me a little, and I have sometimes considered whether it would not be better to let up by speaking courtly Dutch. But if I start doing that, I do not see where the decline of language will end. Maybe it would be more useful to write in pure Latin, even though the deeds of a race with one language cannot, I think, be expressed properly in another language."[24] To be less scrupulous in working toward linguistic purity, rather than "courtly Dutch," was not a serious option for Hooft. That this would mean the decline (*verloop*) of the vernacular[25] had already been expressed in the *Twe-spraack*. Hooft's contacts with the court often took place with Huygens as an intermediary, and it was to him Hooft sent the draft of his dedication, as he wrote in a letter of November 7, 1641: "to be rearranged and decorated by Your Honor, after the manner of the court."[26]

Hooft left to Huygens not only the correction but also embellishment according to the taste of the court. Obviously the bailiff was not familiar with that taste, and who other than this "courtier," as Huygens called himself, could he entrust with the final editorship? Hooft showed himself characteristically modest, but in this special case he was not only uncertain about courtly *decorum* but also anxious about whether his maneuver between his own purism and the written style of the court was acceptable in the eyes of the stadholder. Sending Huygens the draft of the letter of dedication, Hooft states that it is "to be improved, cut, drawn out, or tightened up, indeed, also greatly changed, as Your Honor thinks fit. . . . For the rest I understand as little of the courtly style as most inexperienced people. And thus it is necessary to strut in borrowed feathers."[27] Judging by the reaction from The Hague, Hooft's text was not in fact much altered: the verdict of the stadholder concerning Hooft's prose contains mainly criticism of the pervasive purisms. Of course, Hooft wanted more readers for his history book than the prince. But one wonders whether formulation of the linguistic situation in this way, writing it down in a letter of dedication to a prince, may not indeed bespeak a mentality characteristic of the Dutch courtly situation.

In any case, one must conclude that both the bourgeois character of the Netherlands and the absence of an influential court culture affected the appreciation of the vernacular and reduced the propagation of something like a courtly style. As I have stated, the absence of a prestigious courtly milieu caused all hopes for the establishment of a pure Dutch language to be based initially, at the end of the sixteenth century, on scholars from the Leyden University. In the opinion of authors like Huygens, they failed. Leyden University remained a Latinist bulwark. Due to the increasing role of barbarisms in the seventeenth-century vernacular, language reformers did not point only at the language of the court but also at the pedantry of scholars. This might have had something to do with a wider European rift in literary criticism. On the one hand, scholars adhered to a more theoretical use of language, and on the other hand, administrative practice called for a more practically minded usage. As I have shown, neither humanist scholars nor civil practice could make any use of the authority of the court and its language where it concerned the struggle for a pure language in the seventeenth-century Netherlands.

NOTES

1. This opening is based on L. van den Branden, *Het streven naar verheerlijking* (see Further Reading); Marijke van der Wal (in cooperation with Cor van Bree), *Geschiedenis van het Nederlands* (see Further Reading), 179–231; idem, *De moedertaal centraal* (see Further Reading, page 257), 23–41.

2. See J. C. Scaliger, *Poetices libri septem* (Lyon: Antonium Vincentium, 1561), lib. 4, cap. 1 (p. 180): "Purum cui nihil admissum alieni" (Pure is that which is not mixed with any foreign elements).

3. A recent study on rhetoricians is Jelle Koopmans et al., eds., *Rhetoric—Rhétoriqueurs—Rederijkers* (Amsterdam: Koninklijke Nederlandse Akademie van Wetenschappen, 1995).

4. Henk Duits, "17 September 1637: De nieuwe bijbelvertaling wordt aangeboden aan de Staten-Generaal: Bijbel en literatuur," in *Nederlandse literatuur, een geschiedenis,* ed. Maria A. Schenkeveld-van der Dussen (Groningen: Martinus Nijhoff, 1993), 226.

5. Van der Wal, *De moedertaal centraal,* 35.

6. During the second half of the seventeenth century, a Dutch translation of *Il cortegiano* appeared; a translation of *Galatheo* only appeared in the eighteenth century.

7. A recent view of this subject is given by Marijke J. van der Wal, "De opstand en de taal: Nationaal bewustzijn en het gebruik van het Nederlands in het politieke krachtenveld," *De zeventiende eeuw* 10.1 (1994): 110–17; see also idem, *De moedertaal centraal,* 37.

8. Klaus Conermann, "Der Stil des Hofmanns: Zur Genese sprachlicher und literarischer Formen aus der höfisch-politischen Verhaltenskunst," in *Europäische Hofkultur im 16. und 17. Jahrhundert: Vorträge und Referate Wolfenbüttel, 1979,* ed. August Buck et al., 3 vols. (Hamburg: Hauswedell, 1981), 1:45–56; also Hugh Trevor-Roper, "The Culture of the Baroque Courts," in ibid., 1:11–23. Most Calvinist courts (Sedan, Zweibrücken, Hanau Heidelberg, Geneva) were on the edge of the French empire.

9. Stadholder Frederik Hendrik must have spoken and heard more French than Dutch. His father (William the Silent) had chosen French for his official justification of the revolt against the Spanish.

10. H. A. E. van Gelder, *Vijf eeuwgetijden* (Amsterdam, 1948), 11 ff.; *Twe-spraack vande Nederduitsche letterkunst (1584),* ed. G. R. W. Dibbets (Assen and Maastricht: Van Gorcum, 1985), 512–13.

11. *Den Nederduytschen Helicon . . .* (Haarlem, 1610), "Toe-egheningh Brief," 3–4.

12. Dirck Volckertszoon Coornhert, "Voorreden: Allen kunstlievenden Lezers, wenscht lust tót, vlyt in, ende recht ghebruyck van alle ghoede kunsten," in *Twe-spraack,* fols. A6r–v: "Dat nu onzer voorouderen Nederlandsche tale zó verstandigh ende ryck is gheweest, zietmen in hare schriften ghants vreemd zynde van alle schuim der vreemder talen: de welcke namaals door vreemde Heren ende vreemdtongighe landvooghden met der zelver ghezinde, begraven is gheweest met invoeringhe eens bastaards tale."

13. Joost van Vondel, "Aenleidinge ter Nederduitsche dichtkunste," in *Poëzy* (Amsterdam, 1650).

14. Cicero, *Officia Ciceronis,* trans. D. V. Coornhert (Haarlem: Ian van Zuren, 1561), *6v: "Dit heeft onse nederlantsche sprake binnen veertich iaren herwaerts alsoo verkeert ende gheraetbraeckt: dat sy meer gemeenschappe heeft metten Latijnen ende Franchoysen, dan metten hoochduytschen, daer sy wt ghesproten is: dies sy oock vanden slechten borgheren ende huysluyden, die Latijn noch Walsch en connen, nauwelijcx half verstaen en werdt." This option is shared by van den Branden (*Het streven naar verheerlijking,* 13 ff.).

15. J. vande Werve, *Het tresoor der Duytsscher talen* (1552–53), reprinted in 1559, 1568, and 1577

under the title *Den schat der Duytsscher talen* (I used the edition Antwerpen, 1577, fol. A2r). In this lexicon vande Werve put pure Dutch terms next to the loanwords common on the juridical circuit.

16. See Dibbets, *Twe-spraack*, 98, §§ 10–12 and § 16, and 327–28, 512–13.

17. Ibid., 6.

18. See Ibid., 70, § 2–4.

19. The court at Brussels was a meeting place for *grands seigneurs* (courtly nobility), the lower nobility, and representatives of the upper civil servants. Van Gelder, *Vijf eeuwgetijden,* 24–25.

20. Dibbets, *Twe-spraack,* 11–12: "Ghód zal moghelyck enigh Vórst daar toe verwecken (als hij in Vranckrijck an Franciscum ende in Italyen an verscheyden Prinsen ghedaan heeft) die de Nederlandse gheleerdheid vorderen zal."

21. The first university in the Northern Netherlands was Leyden, dating from 1575. Latin Humanism became a significant cultural factor in Leyden after the founding of this university. Famous humanists, like Justus Lipsius, Josephus Justus Scaliger, Daniel Heinsius, and Gerardus Johannes Vossius, were professors at this university. The lectures were given in Latin up to the end of the nineteenth century.

22. See L. Peeters, "Zeventiende-eeuwse taalcultuur: P. C. Hoofts proza," in *Taalopbouw als renaissance-ideaal: Studies over taalopvattingen en taalpraktijk in de zestiende en zeventiende eeuw* (Amsterdam, 1989), 91–118, at 111 (originally published in *Gramma* 11 [1987]: 15–42).

23. Pieter Corneliszoon Hooft, *De briefwisseling,* ed. Hendrik Willem van Tricht, 3 vols. (Culemborg: Tjeenk Willink/Noorduijn, 1976–79), 2:492 (letter by Hooft to Constantijn Huygens): "Al waeren zij ook flux genoegh van lijf en leden, zoo en zijnze doch echter niet afgerecht op zijn hoofsch, ende schendigh afzichtigh om de ketterije van liever wurghende woorden te gebrujken, dan Ondujtsche in te rujmen."

24. Ibid., 2:534 (letter by Hooft to Jacob Wijtz): "De vieze naeuwheit van gewisse in dezen mishaeght mij zelven eenighszins, ende hebbe somtijds in beraedt gestaen, oft niet beter waer den schoot te vieren, met spreken van hoofsch Duitsch. Maer, zoo men die deure open zet, ik en zie niet waer 't eindighen wil met het verloop der taele; ende 't zoude misschien nutter zijn in zujver Latijn te schrijven: in 't welk nochtans het bedrijf eens geslaghts van andre tonge, mijns bedunkens, niet even eighentlijk uyt te drukken waer."

25. See the letter of June 30, 1634 to Huygens (ibid., 2:536–37).

26. Ibid., 3:390.

27. Ibid., 3:393 (letter by Hooft to Huygens).

The Politics of ABCs

"Language Wars" and Literary Vernacularization Among the Serbs and Romanians of Austria-Hungary, 1780–1870

JACK FAIREY

> To write ABC in Romanian is to make Romanian politics.
>
> —Gheorghe Bariţiu, 1812–93

The early nineteenth century was a time of "national awakening" for most ethnolinguistic groups in the Habsburg Empire.[1] The revival of many forgotten and stateless peoples' nationalist aspirations in Austria-Hungary and throughout eastern Europe moved one observer, the Romanian critic Titu Maiorescu, to predict that the nineteenth century would be called "the century of the nationalities."[2] He warned, however, that not every group would succeed in being recognized as a "nationality." The key to achieving such desired recognition would be the development of a national language and literature. After all, he stated elsewhere, "language and nationality are . . . words that are almost identical."[3]

In saying this, Maiorescu was merely repeating what had been a truism since the late 1700s, when Johann Gottfried Herder had declared it an absurdity (*Unding*) to imagine that a nation (*Volk*) could exist without its own distinctive language.[4] This was, however, a troubling paradigm for the peoples in Austria-Hungary who did not yet have standardized literary languages at the beginning of the nineteenth century.[5] Anxious for admittance into the European family of nations, these peoples invested tremendous energies in creating the "national languages" they imagined they ought to possess. The resulting selection, elaboration, and codification of literary languages were thus directed by a desire to build not merely literatures but nations.

The proposed linguistic changes stirred fierce public debates within the affected communities in what were referred to at the time as "language wars."[6] This essay looks at two of these "language wars" that took place among Serbs and Romanians in Austria-Hungary between 1770 and 1870,[7] and focuses in particular on the symbolic or representational function of liter-

[handwritten note in top margin: Romanians mostly peasants + diven franchised]

ary languages in these debates—that is, the use of the form and structure of a language to communicate specific ideas, values, and group self-images.

Serbs and Romanians in Austria-Hungary at the End of the Eighteenth Century

Although Serbs and Romanians were minorities within Austria-Hungary,[8] the two peoples constituted sizable populations in the empire's southern and eastern borderlands. Serbs lived mostly in Croatia-Slavonia, the Banat of Temesvár, and Dalmatia; Romanians in Transylvania, the Banat of Temesvár, and Bukovina.[9] Ethnographically, Serbs and Romanians straddled both sides of the Austrian-Ottoman border, with the majority of Romanians living on the far side of the Carpathian mountains, in Moldavia and Wallachia, while most Serbs lived south of the Sava and Danube rivers in Serbia and Bosnia.

Since the Habsburg dynasty, most of Austria-Hungary's subjects had been Roman Catholics; Serbs and Romanians were conspicuous for belonging to Eastern Christian churches. Most belonged to the Eastern Orthodox Church and followed the Serbian metropolitan bishop of Sremski Karlovci (Karlowitz/ Karlóca), while a smaller number of Romanians—and even fewer Serbs— belonged to the Greek Catholic sees of Blaj (Blasendorf/Balázsfalva, Transylvania) and Križevci (Kreutz/Körös, Croatia).[10]

Aside from their common faith and geographical proximity, however, the two peoples had little in common. The Romanians (often referred to as Vlachs/Olàchs) were an almost entirely peasant people, laboring on the lands of their Magyar, Székely, and Saxon lords. Lacking wealthy patrons and educational facilities, Romanian culture and language had suffered centuries of neglect and contempt. Romanians were also deprived of political representation, even though they formed the majority of the population in Transylvania. Membership in the Transylvanian diet was restricted to representatives of the three official "nations" of the region (Magyar, Széklers, and Saxons) and the four "established" churches (Roman Catholicism, Calvinism, Lutheranism, and Unitarianism).

Serbs, on the other hand, had done much better under the Habsburgs. In return for their military services to the dynasty, Serbian refugees from the Ottoman Empire had been permitted to settle in southern Hungary and were granted a limited form of cultural and administrative autonomy in the 1690s. Just as the Magyar and Saxon lords were recognized by the crown as political *nationes* in Transylvania, Serbs were granted special status along the Military

[handwritten margin notes: only in late 18th c. was there search for literary lay. among Serbs + Romanians]

Frontier (*krajina*) as freemen of the "Illyrian nation."[11] Serbs thus stood largely outside the jurisdiction of local Magyar and Croatian authorities for many years, and dealt directly with the imperial court through their *caput nationis*, the Orthodox metropolitan of Sremski Karlovci. Under such conditions, the Serbs prospered and developed a small middle class of career officers, lawyers, and merchants.

Church Languages, Josephine Reforms, and the Posing of the "Language Question"

[handwritten margin note: diglossia]

One of the most important consequences of their common religious culture was that Orthodox Serbs and Romanians traditionally shared a common ecclesiastical language and literary tradition, using the Church Slavonic language and the Cyrillic alphabet invented by Saints Cyril and Methodius.[12] Like many cultures, Serbs and Romanians were diglossic societies, using a "high," religiously sanctioned language and script for formal written compositions, and "low" languages and dialects for speaking on quotidian affairs. Church Slavonic had traditionally served as the "high" literary language of Serbs and Romanians. It was also in some ways a "national language" that distinguished Serbs and Romanians from their non-Orthodox neighbors while connecting them to their own history and culture. In ordinary conversation, on the other hand, Serbs and Romanians used local vernaculars,[13] German, Magyar, or a mixture of all three.

Already by the 1770s, however, Church Slavonic had declined outside of strictly ecclesiastical circles. Among Serbs, secular works were increasingly being written in what was known as Slaveno-Serbian (*Slaveno-Srpski*), a blanket term that described not so much a single language as the general practice of writing in different vernacular dialects with heavy infusions of Church Slavonic and literary Russian (believed to be very close to Church Slavonic).[14] Among Romanians, Church Slavonic was replaced even earlier in secular writings and in the liturgy by a form of Romanian known as the "church language" (*limbă bisericii*), Italic in structure but strongly influenced by Church Slavonic in lexicon and use of the Cyrillic script.[15] These changes, however, did not amount to abandonment of the diglossic model, which continued to dominate Serbian and Romanian literature into the early 1800s. Only after the reforms of Emperor Joseph II (r. 1780–90) did Serbs and Romanians begin to search in earnest for their own polyvalent literary languages.

Arguably the most important of these Josephine reforms for the minorities

[handwritten margin note: hybridity]

of Hungary was the *Ratio Educationis Publicae* of 1777, which set up a state-run system of public schools for the kingdom.[16] Overturning the previous system of educating children in Latin, German, or Church Slavonic, Joseph II stipulated in the *Ratio* that primary schooling would be carried out in the native (*vernaculus*) languages of Hungary.[17] The decree blithely ignored the absence of any consensus on what exactly the native "Serbian" and "Romanian" languages were. Communities were simply directed to begin preparing "vernacular" textbooks and class materials.

Using their old literary languages for the first time to write on the sciences, mathematics, agronomy, and stock raising, Serbian and Romanian writers quickly discovered that neither Church Slavonic nor ecclesiastical Romanian was adequate to the task. Not surprisingly, the texts they finally submitted for printing were composed in a veritable Babel of dialects, church scripts, and spellings. It became clear that without universally accepted prescriptive grammars, dictionaries, or guiding principles, written Serbian and Romanian had become highly idiosyncratic, with authors drawing from the language of the church and local vernaculars at their own discretion.[18]

Besides these practical difficulties, the old literary languages had also become politically unsatisfactory. In 1784, Joseph II tried to speed the centralization of his empire by briefly replacing Latin with German as the sole language of administration and higher education in Hungary. The resulting conflicts between Vienna and the Hungarian diet provoked a dramatic flowering of Magyar language, culture, and patriotism, which was to continue into the early 1800s. As Magyar nationalism became ever more assertive, something of a "domino effect" could be observed among the non-Magyar peoples of Hungary, who were forced to choose between assimilation into Magyar society and the development of their own nationalist movements.

Like most of these peoples, Serbs and Romanians found that their traditional means for asserting political and cultural independence were unequal to the new circumstances. In practical terms, Church Slavonic and ecclesiastical Romanian could not compete with powerful, polyvalent languages like German and a renascent Magyar. Church Slavonic and ecclesiastical Romanian had shown themselves ill suited to a modern educational system, and Romanian, in particular, lacked sufficient *dignitas* for its users to resist the siren song of other cultures.

More important, the confessional identities these ecclesiastical languages embodied were unequal to the challenge of secular nationalism. Whereas in the past being Orthodox or Greek Catholic had been a sufficient marker of non-Magyar identity, in the nineteenth century Magyar nationalists readily

NB plural options for fortnightly languages [handwritten marginalia]

accepted Eastern Christians as Hungarians so long as they used Magyar in the public sphere and were loyal to the Kingdom of Hungary.[19]

Under these circumstances, Serbs and Romanians who rejected Magyarization were forced to reassess their cultural resources. Given a choice of remodeling their literary languages on archaic languages, foreign languages, or local vernaculars, Serbian and Romanian writers reacted in very different ways.

The War for the Serbian Language and Orthography

Serbs were divided into two opposing camps over how best to construct their new literary standard: linguistic conservatives, who remained close to the Slaveno-Serbian literary tradition, and vernacularizers, who rejected that tradition and tried to build anew on the foundations of the spoken vernacular.

Vernacularizers

The idea of modeling the Serbian literary language after ordinary speech had first been introduced during the reign of Joseph II by such enthusiastic Serbian promoters of the Enlightenment as Dositej Obradović (1739–1811) and the dramatist Emanuel Janković (1758–92). These writers continued to use the old Slavonic orthography and drew liberally on the Church Slavonic language, but they simplified their style to reach a wider audience. This vernacularized Slaveno-Serbian was distasteful to many, but it was found less offensive than later reforms because of its modest ideological content. *as in Chinese* [handwritten marginalia]

A new perspective on the value of the vernacular was introduced into the Serbian literary debates by the Slovene scholar Jernej Kopitar (1780–1844).[20] Besides being imperial censor for Slavic books, Kopitar was an active member of literary circles in Vienna and Ljubljana, and co-edited the *Wiener Allgemeine Literaturzeitung*. Inspired by contacts with the German literary world and the works of the linguist Johann C. Adelung, Kopitar had been active in standardizing the Slovenian vernacular. Encouraged by his successes there, Kopitar believed that Serbian was ripe for a similar process. Unable as an outsider and a Catholic to take a direct hand in affairs, Kopitar encouraged one of his Serb protégés, the young writer Vuk Karadžić (1787–1864), to throw open the parameters of the Serbian language debate.[21]

Having been introduced to Romantic ideas by Kopitar and by correspondence with Jakob Grimm and Goethe, Vuk was encouraged to see the vernacular not as a "vulgar" tongue but as the most precious expression of the genius of each nation.[22] Vuk and Kopitar hence argued that Serbian grammar could not be constructed in an *a priori* and inorganic fashion. Literary standards were to be abstracted meticulously from samples of the "living language" such as folk songs, oral tales, and aphorisms. To become truly authentic, they argued, Serbian speech had to be freed from all artifice, restored, as it were, to a state of nature. For the Hungarian Serbs to make any cultural progress, a clear distinction had to be drawn between the "living," national language of the Serbian people and the "dead," supranational Slavonic tongue.

In his *Serbian Grammar* of 1814, and still more clearly in his 1818 *Serbian Dictionary*, Vuk set the guidelines for future Serbian linguistic development, rejecting any amalgamation of Church Slavonic and literary Serbian beyond that which existed in everyday speech. In an 1816 announcement in *Novine Srbske* inviting subscriptions to his forthcoming Serbian *Rječnik* (Dictionary), Vuk wrote: "What kind of dictionary do we need? The correct answer is: we need most of all a dictionary of the national Serbian language [*narodnoga Serbskog ezyka*], which will contain only those words the Serbian people use—that we may see in entirely our own words the whole field of our language; that we may see who we are. . . . The Serbian dictionary must, now for the first time, present to the Serbs their own language, their holiest nationality, as it exists in itself."[23] In place of Slaveno-Serbian, Vuk promoted a standardized version of the što-kavian dialect of southern Hercegovina, claiming it to be the easiest, purest, and most pleasing Serbian.[24] Vuk also advocated a thoroughgoing reform of the Cyrillic alphabet and the adoption of a purely phonetic orthography. The intention of these orthographic reforms was to ensure that written Serbian be closely tied to the spoken standard and widely accessible. To insist on the archaic script and Slavonic orthography was, for Vuk, to subordinate the national language to an ecclesiastical and elitist system of values. "Better we should leave such letters to the priests and monks," he wrote, "who all wish to possess distinctions from the rest of the people."[25]

Conservatives

Not unexpectedly, Vuk's reforms were met with hostility from the Serbian cultural establishment, led by Metropolitan Stefan Stratimirović (1757–1836) and the literary patron Sava Tekelija (1761–1842). The church hierarchy was scandalized by Vuk's orthographic reforms and his revised alphabet, as well as by his plans to publish a translation of the New Testament into the što-kavian vernacular. Metropolitan Stratimirović banned further publication of Vuk's writings within Hungary and, in effect, forced the writer to move to Vienna. In 1832, the newly independent Principality of Serbia followed the metropolitan's example and imposed a total ban on books printed in Vuk's orthography. This ban stood for almost thirty years, during which Vuk carried on a running debate with the leading lights of the Serbian literary world.

The first Serbian literary society, the Matica Srbska (founded in 1826), came out strongly against Vuk's language and orthography.[26] The public also reacted poorly to Vuk's vernacular and did not subscribe to his publications. As an unkind reader wrote to Vuk: "Many believe that if you'd spent the time which you have devoted to writing in keeping pigs or . . . sheep, you would have done better."[27]

To most members of the small Serbian middle class and intelligentsia Vuk's reformed language seemed vulgar, and they assumed non-Serbs would also find it so. Considering the efforts of Serbs to establish the dignity of their culture vis-à-vis German and Magyar, Vuk's reforms seemed counterproductive. Responding to Vuk's criticisms of his latest novel, the well-known writer Milovan Vidaković (1780–1841) countered by asking why educated Germans did not write as their swineherds and goatherds spoke? Sava Tekelija, one of Vuk's most prominent opponents, put the matter just as bluntly: "Would it not be better and more commendable for us to return to our proper Slavonic language, which is the true Serbian language. . . . If we do not write in Slaveno-Serbian, then in which dialect will we write? In Hercegovinian? In Croatian? Dalmatian? Sremian? . . . All these are regional, provincial, uneducated. . . . The French and other peoples all have their provincial dialects, but a cultivated language is different."[28] For Tekelija and others, it was the duty of the learned to correct the uneducated, not to confirm them in their errors.[29] In a pointed jab at Vuk's studies of South Slavic folklore, Tekelija noted in the margins of his own copy of Vuk's *Pismenica* that "most people study so as to know better . . . but he [Vuk] studies, wanting to become foolish."[30]

Conservatives such as Tekelija believed instead that their literary language should spring from the best of Serbian history, religion, and traditional culture, evoking the glories of the Orthodox Church and the medieval Serbian Empire. It was believed that a judicious mixture of the local Vojvodina dialect, Church Slavonic, and literary Russian would result in a language that was urbane, dignified, and easy to use. The modern tendency to dismiss this conservative linguistic program as self-interested, elitist, and antediluvian underestimates its appeal for ordinary Serbs and for the many talented writers who believed that this was how Western literary languages had been created.

Beyond practical disagreements over Vuk's reforms, conservatives questioned his motives. In the eyes of most Orthodox, and certainly in the eyes of the church, to move Serbian language and writing away from Slavonic texts was to risk betraying the faith contained in those texts. The very shapes of the traditional Cyrillic letters conveyed to readers a suffused assurance of a text's authenticity, of its organic connection with the universal community of the Orthodox faithful and the hallowed past. To compromise was to risk undermining the entire interwoven structure of church, language, and history.

For most clergy and pious laymen, the logical conclusion was that by promoting Latinization of the Cyrillic script and the radical vernacularization of Slaveno-Serbian, Vuk served as an agent of Roman Catholicism and denationalization. Vuk's marriage to an Austrian Catholic and friendship with the ardently Catholic Kopitar were seen as proof of his collusion in an Austrian plot to undermine Serbian confessional identity.

Nor was it lost on members of the clergy that Vuk and his supporters, by defining the vernacular, rather than the Orthodox faith, as the true bearer of Serbianness, were subtly altering the very definition of the Serbian nation itself. To a "Vukist," those who spoke the što-kavian dialect, from Slovenia to Albania, were Serbs whether they were Catholic, Muslim, or Orthodox. Only those who spoke the kaj-kavian dialect were held to be true Croats. Acceptance of such a paradigm implied a radical reorientation of Serbian culture and identity that few were prepared for in the early 1800s.

Conversely, when the tide of public opinion did finally turn in favor of Vuk's linguistic reforms in the 1840s, it was because his ideas about Serbian language and identity found a readier audience. Before the 1840s, the circle of Serbian readers and writers had been small and closely tied to the traditional order of their society, consisting mostly of clergymen or merchants educated in church-run schools. In the 1830s, Serbian students began to go abroad, and they returned from France, Germany, and England much better disposed toward Vuk's teachings. Even those who remained were exposed to new ideas during the years before the Hungarian revolution of 1848. As this new generation of Western-educated youth began to form such influential nationalist organizations as the Serbian Literary Society (Društvo Srpske Slovesnosti), the United Serbian Youth (Ujedinjena Omladina Srpska), and the Liberal and Progressive parties in Serbia, they carried Vuk's linguistic reforms with them into the mainstream of Serbian society.[31]

Political conditions in Hungary during the 1840s were also more congenial to the Illyrian/Yugoslav ideology that Vuk's teachings fostered. As Magyar chauvinism came to pose a greater threat to the survival of Serbian and Croatian culture, Serbs and Croats turned to each other for mutual support. Linguistic conservatives such as Tekelija hesitantly approved of South Slav unification, but only on their terms. Their insistence that Croatians should adopt the Orthodox Slaveno-Serbian literary language alienated those younger activists impatient to build bridges to their Catholic peers.[32] Locating

Romanians'
Standardizing

national identity, as Vuk did, in the shared Serbo-Croatian vernacular and folk culture held out greater promise. The convergence of Vukian linguistic reforms and Illyrianism (later Yugoslavism) was made official in March of 1850, when, with Đura Daničić (1825–82) and five prominent Croatian writers, Vuk declared the Serbs and Croats a single people, bound together by their use of the standardized što-kavian vernacular.[33]

The Romanian "War of the Languages"

Romanian disagreements over language planning involved greater consensus. Even so, one can distinguish at least five different approaches to the standardization of literary Romanian: (1) traditionalist, (2) Latinist, (3) "Bonjourist," (4) populist, and (5) Magyarone.

Traditionalists and Ecclesiastical Romanian

Romanians possessed a sounder basis for agreement between the different schools in that virtually all Romanians looked to the language of the church (*limbă bisericii*) to provide the foundations for their literary language. Possessing a sizable literature, ecclesiastical Romanian was understood by all Romanians, whether in Austria-Hungary, Moldavia, or Wallachia.[34] Despite these virtues, the weaknesses of ecclesiastical Romanian were also apparent: it enjoyed negligible cultural status among non-Romanians; its syntax differed from the spoken language; and its vocabulary was seriously deficient in many areas.[35]

Early attempts to develop ecclesiastical Romanian by Orthodox Transylvanians such as Dimitrie Eustatievici (c. 1730–96), T. I. Corbea (1670–1725), and Ioan Piuariu-Molnar (1749–1815) aimed to make it resemble classical languages: Church Slavonic, Greek, Latin. This was in keeping with these Transylvanians' image of Romanians as an Eastern people, linked to the Byzantine and Slavic worlds. As long as they preserved traditional elements such as the Cyrillic script and Church Slavonic loanwords, these early Romanian philologists found favor with the Serbian church hierarchy in Sremski Karlovci.

Latinism

A different perspective emerged in Greek Catholic circles, in particular among a group of seminarians known as the Transylvanian School (Şcoală Arde-

leana).[36] While studying in Rome and Vienna in the 1770s, Samuil Micu/
Klein (1745–1806), Gheorghe Şincai (1754–1816), and Petru Maior (c.
1756–1821) each rediscovered the origins of their people in the second-cen-
tury Roman colony of Dacia. Before this, many Romanians knew about their
Italic ancestry but attached little significance to it. The members of the Şcoală
Ardeleana, however, proceeded from this central fact to reinterpret all of
Romanian history and culture.

The members of the school realized that if the humble Vlach was indeed
the direct heir to the glories of Rome, then he had a right to the respect of his
German and Magyar oppressors, since these latter peoples revered Latin so
highly and had built an entire state ideology around "the Holy Roman
Empire." Embracing their new national self-image, members of the school
insisted that Romanians were of unmixed Italian descent, their Roman ancestors having obliterated the autochthonous Dacians. Some, such as Petru
Maior, even argued that Romanian and Italian had been dialectical variations
of the same language until Dante, Boccaccio, and Petrarch caused Italian to
vary more significantly.[37] Romanian was not simply one Romance language
among many, they concluded, but perhaps the most purely Latinate modern
language.

Latinity (*Latinitate*) thus became the defining essence of Romanianness, and
anything not Latin became, by extension, a foreign and undesirable accretion.
purging
Latinist intellectuals accordingly began to purge their language of "foreign"
lexical elements, whether of Church Slavonic, Magyar, or Greek origin, and
to replace the offending words with pedigreed Latin substitutes.[38] The many
lexical deficiencies of literary Romanian were similarly made good by heavy
borrowings from the "Latin mother."[39]

Not content with changing the content of written Romanian, Latinizers
showed an inordinate concern with its "barbaric Eastern" appearance.[40] They
reviled the Cyrillic alphabet and recommended that it be replaced by the Latin
alphabet, those "ancient letters of the Romanians."[41] To complete the face-
lift, Micu and Şincai devised an etymological orthography that more clearly
displayed the Latin origins of Romanian.[42]

The central principles of the Şcoala Ardeleana were quickly accepted by
most educated Romanians, but their specific reforms were not always so well
received. While many Romanian Orthodox clergymen supported Latinization,
the Serbian-dominated hierarchy in Hungary resolutely opposed it. Fearing
that use of the Latin script would spread Greek Catholicism among his Romanian flock, Metropolitan Stratimirović placed a ban on it and dismissed anyone caught teaching it in Orthodox Romanian schools.[43] Even the notion that

186

*attempt to
show Latin
origins*

arguments for hybrid "civil" script

Romanians were descendants of Roman colonists was attacked by prominent Serbian intellectuals and clergymen such as Tekelija.[44]

The Greek Catholic hierarchy was similarly slow to embrace the more radical linguistic reforms of its seminarians, fearing these would alienate Orthodox Romanians and divide the community. Use of the Latin alphabet was particularly controversial, and many intellectuals such as Gheorghe Barițiu argued instead for the creation of a modified "civil script," which would combine Cyrillic and Latin letters.[45]

Despite these hurdles, Latinization made great strides during the 1820s and 1830s as cultural and political leadership of the Romanian community passed from the hands of conservative church leaders to the rising class of teachers, lawyers, and civil servants.[46] A new generation of scholars, led by Timoteiu Cipariu (1805–87), Aron Pumnul (1818–66), and Simion Barnuțiu (1808–64), rose to carry on the reforms of the Transylvanian School, while the first Romanian newspapers in Austria-Hungary, such as Gheorghe Barițiu's *Gazeta de Transilvania,* helped disseminate their ideas. By the 1840s most Transylvanian publications showed the hallmarks of Latinism—the Latin alphabet, an etymological orthography, extensive borrowings from Latin—and Latinism had spread across the Carpathians into Wallachia and Moldavia.

Bonjourism

In the Danubian principalities, the linguistic ideas of the Transylvanian School took on a different complexion. Wallachian and Moldavian writers such as Ion Heliade Rădulescu (1802–72) and Gheorghe Asachi (1788–1869) accepted the precepts of Latinism but interpreted them in light of their own cultural influences, especially French literature.

elite knew French

Knowledge of French had spread rapidly within the Romanian upper classes in the late 1700s, following the arrival in Bucharest of French aristocratic refugees from the Revolution. A veritable flood of translations were made from French and Italian into Romanian during the 1820s and 1830s, providing important models and inspiration for Romanian writers. By 1847, French was held in such esteem that it was nearly made the exclusive language of higher education in both principalities,[47] and it even became fashionable among educated Wallachians to affect a sort of Franco-Romanian *patois.*

While most Romanian writers ridiculed the more extreme forms of "Bonjourism" (*Bonjurism*), many agreed that literary Romanian had more to gain from its living sisters (French and Italian) than from its dead Latin mother. In the 1830s Wallachian writers such as Ion Heliade Rădulescu increasingly

[handwritten marginalia: "gap between Latinists + populists"]

[handwritten marginalia: "fantasy of descent from lingua rustica"]

experimented with French and Italian orthographies while borrowing words *en masse* from French and Italian. This trend had little influence in Austria-Hungary, where critics such as Ioan Maiorescu (1811–64) accused Wallachian authors of having created a grotesque and superficial culture through their imitation of mediocre French literature. It was this French influence, however, that helped pave the way for the fourth linguistic trend—linguistic populism (*poporanism*).

Linguistic Populism

As we have seen, vernacularized literary languages held little attraction for Romanian intellectuals at the end of the 1700s. They were seeking to create a "high" literary language of their own, not rediscover the peasant dialects that their enemies claimed were all Romanians could produce. Although many Latinizers were happy to claim that their language was descended from the *lingua rustica* of the Latin colonists, the literary standards they promoted were far removed from the modern Romanian vernacular and were difficult for most ordinary Romanians to read. Not only did the Latin script remain alien to most Romanians well into the 1860s, but the host of neologisms generated by the tiny educated elite enjoyed no currency among the general populace.[48]

In the 1840s, a new group of Romanian intellectuals coalesced around the journal *Dacia Literara,* sharply critical of what they saw as the excesses of both the Bonjourists of the principalities and the Latinists of Transylvania. These writers, sometimes referred to as the Anti-Bonjourists, or Messianists—led by Mihail Kogălniceanu (1817–91), Alexandru Russo (1819–59), Nicolae Bălcescu (1819–52), and Vasile Alecsandri (1819/21–90)—were concerned that the common people were becoming alienated and that Romanian literary culture was diverging into separate Transylvanian, Wallachian, and Moldavian streams. In their estimation, not only was Transylvanian Latinism pedantic, it was also harmful to national unity and reflected an undesirable political ideology.[49]

The revolutions of 1848 further highlighted the differences between Latinists and populists. Although prominent Latinists participated in the Romanian resistance to the Magyar government of Lajos Kossuth, in doing so they helped defeat political liberalism in Austria-Hungary and demonstrated loyalty to the house of Austria. The Paşoptişti (the generation of 1848) intellectuals of the principalities, on the other hand, were political revolutionaries, educated abroad and well versed in the writings of French liberals and Romantics such as Victor Hugo, Jules Michelet, and Alphonse de Lamartine.

1848 Liberals

THE POLITICS OF ABCS

liberals
Search for roots
in <u>medieval</u> *texts*

Returning to the Danubian principalities, these writers divided their energies between fighting for a "nationalized" Romanian literature and actively conspiring against the political order.[50]

In politics, they hoped to build a united national Romanian state founded on Western democratic and egalitarian ideals, what Michelet described as a Mazzinian "Italy of the Orient."[51] Since these writers clearly believed that their literature and language ought to reflect their political ideals, it is not surprising that they should declare themselves out of sympathy with Latinism. The Transylvanian linguistic school was conceived and shaped by an express need to advance Romanian interests within the framework of the Austro-Hungarian Empire. Outside its Habsburg milieu, Latinist representations of the nation often appeared quirky, semifeudal, and outmoded.

These populist writers also differed from Latinists in refusing to make Roman Dacia the sole basis of national identity.[52] Where earlier scholars relied on classical histories and philology for their construction of Latinism, the Romantics of the late 1840s mined medieval chronicles and folklore to uncover an image of Romania as a single nation, the child of both Dacians *and* Romans, which had striven courageously through the centuries to preserve its love for liberty.[53] Since this idealized, republican "Romania" had no basis in a common historical, religious, or state tradition, it had to be formed around the notion that such a state existed in embryo wherever the vernacular "Romanian language" was spoken. New stress was therefore laid on the vernacular as the surest foundation for a truly national literary language.

Romanian linguistic populism was set in motion in the 1840s and 1850s, but it still lacked a figure like Vuk to write authoritatively in the language of the villages. The first proponents of the "language of the people" were dissident members of the *boier* nobility, more comfortable writing in French then peasant dialects. It was typical in this regard that the foremost composer and collector of popular Romanian poetry, Vasile Alecsandri, wrote his earliest poetry in French and even later in life often composed his prose works in French before translating them into Romanian.[54]

It was not until the 1870s and 1880s that truly vernacularized literature began to appear in print, through the encouragement of the *Junimea* (Youth) literary movement founded by Titu Maiorescu (1840–1917) and Iacob Negruzzi (1842–1932). For the first time, authors from humble backgrounds, such as Mihail Eminescu (1850–89), Ioan Creangă (1839–89), and Ion Caragiale (1852–1912), produced literary works that were based on the spoken Romanian idiom in practice as well as in theory.

In Austria-Hungary, the most notable representatives of *Junimism* and robust vernacularization were the poet Mihail Eminescu and the novelist and

vs purging — new ideal of language as words in use

editor of Transylvania's first Romanian daily (the *Tribuna*) Ioan Slavici (1848–1925). The essence of populism, Slavici told readers in an article praising Eminescu, was the realization that "words are not concocted, but spring up like blades of grass in the field; the Romanian language is not, as is said, a daughter of Latin but older than that, and Romanian is [made up of] which-ever words are used by all Romanians because they are easy to use, sound good to the ear, and have well-established meanings for them."[55] Believing "language is a creation of the people and not of language manufacturers," Slavici also preached that society in general should be directed by ordinary people.[56] In essays such as his 1893 *Race or Class? (Rase ori clase?)*, for example, he argued that the true enemies of Transylvanian Romanians were not their Magyar neighbors but all aristocrats, whether Magyar or Romanian. Slavici went so far as to say that political unification under the Romanian *boier* class would be worse for Romanians than the continuation of Habsburg rule. If ordinary Romanians were to take charge of their own destiny, he argued, they had to build a nation through the construction of a unified popular culture that transcended the boundaries set by states and social elites.

Magyarones

The last approach to the standardization of literary Romanian, which we may call the Magyarone, was less of a formal school than the others and lacked the support of any major Romanian literary figures. Instead, it consisted primarily of the Romanian writings, transcriptions, and translations of Magyar linguists, ethnographers, authors, and journalists, Protestant missionaries, and some lesser Romanian authors.[57] These writers favored Magyar culture and tended to adopt a positive attitude toward Magyar political dominance in Hungary. Their written Romanian reflected these attitudes through the use of Magyar orthography and—ironically—through an often very pure and uncomplicated use of local Romanian vernaculars.

Being indifferent to the political and cultural arguments of nationalist Romanian intellectuals, Magyarone authors had no interest in censoring their works for Slavic, Greek, or Turkish—let alone Magyar—words, and they wrote as they thought would best be understood. Domokos Kosáry, for example, has argued that of all the various Romanian periodicals published in Hungary during the late 1840s, it was the Romanian-language edition of the Magyar newspaper *Nép Barátja* that most accurately reflected contemporary Romanian speech.[58]

Although the Magyarone trend was rejected by Romanians as a further

key point

step toward denationalization, it nevertheless serves to underline yet again the primacy of symbolic and political factors in the fate of any language reform.

ASTRA

Faced with so many contending views and the grave threat posed by Magyarization, Romanian cultural leaders in Austria-Hungary recognized in the late 1850s that a compromise would have to be worked out between the different linguistic schools. The vehicle for this compromise was the creation on November 4, 1861, of a cultural society for all Romanians in Austria-Hungary: ASTRA (Asociatia Transilvana pentru Literatura Româna şi Cultura Poporului Român—The Transylvanian Association for Romanian Literature and the Culture of the Romanian People). Presided over by Metropolitan Andrei Şaguna and the moderate Latinists Gheorghe Bariţiu and Timoteiu Cipariu, ASTRA created guidelines for literary Romanian that struck a successful balance between Latinism and vernacularization in language and between etymology and phonetics in orthography.[59]

Conclusion

As diglossic systems began to break down among the Eastern Christian minorities of Austria-Hungary at the end of the eighteenth century, a variety of views surfaced regarding how best to create standardized "native" literary languages. Invariably, these conflicting literary trends were connected with larger questions of ideology and representation.

As Gale Stokes and others have argued, the spoken vernacular tended to stand in these debates for political populism, liberal democratic values, and a "changing of the guard" within the cultural elite, with philologists, folklorists, poets, and school teachers replacing clergymen as the arbiters of taste.[60] For these intellectuals "folk speech" served as a sacred language over which they could claim mastery, unlike ecclesiastical languages, over which the clergy would always have the final say. It is also true that vernacularization tended to follow the spread of literacy and the emancipation of the peasantry in Austria-Hungary after 1848.

But the dynamics of the Serbian and Romanian language wars cannot be reduced to internal questions of social change or control. From its first appearance among Serbs and Romanians, the "language question" was inextricably linked to political movements and literary trends outside their individual com-

Shaped by inc
Gined foreign
audiences

munities. The reforms of Joseph II and the rise of state languages first stimulated the search for polyvalent literary languages, while the spread of German
and Magyar nationalism pushed the minorities of the empire to reimagine
their own communities and cultures. In articulating new ideas, Serbian and
Romanian reformers used language as a powerful symbolic device to include
or exclude others from the nation and to support either a confessional or a
ethnolinguistic definition of society. Their differing programs of linguistic
reform thus ultimately reflected deeper conflicts over the idealized contours,
composition, and orientation of the nation itself.

Serbian and Romanian writers also disagreed over how to establish the
prestige and specificity of their respective languages. In attempting to create
languages capable of contesting the hegemony of Magyar and German, each
writer partly depended on what he or she thought literary languages were like
in the rest of Europe. The protagonists of the debates designed their "native"
language with specific foreign audiences in mind.

Defenders of Slaveno-Serbian and Latinism, for example, appealed to neo-
classical sensibilities abroad, while arguing at home that the official languages
of France, England, Russia, and the German states were elite languages
shaped by historical models, the speech of the courts, and the writings of aca-
demicians. More crudely, the *Bonjuriști* and some conservative Serbian writers
tried to appropriate the prestige of established literatures by borrowing words
and etymologies from French, Italian, and Russian.

Supporters of the vernacular, on the other hand, responded to the latest
cultural trends in Europe: Romanticism and the revolutionary ferment that
effected intellectuals throughout Europe in 1789–1848. Not only did foreign
Romantics support the early pioneers of vernacularization in Austria-Hungary, but the Romantic vogue for "authentic" *Volksdichtung* created an unprec-
edented international audience for literature in the Serbian and Romanian
vernaculars. It was of great importance to the outcome of the "language wars"
that vernacularizing works such as Alecsandri's *Poesii populare* (Popular poetry)
and Karadžić's *Pjesnarica* (Serbian songbook) were among the first Romanian
and Serbian works to receive critical acclaim abroad. The vernacularization of
literary Serbian and Romanian was thus indicative of the rise among both
peoples of Romanticism in literature, of liberalism in politics, and of ethnic
nationalism in society.

NOTES

1. The epigraph is cited in Victor V. Grecu, *Limbă și națiune: Unitatea limbii în periodicele românești* (Timișoara: Editură Facla, 1988), 254.

2. From Titu Maiorescu, "Despre scrierea limbei române," *Critice*, vol. 2 (Bucharest: Editură Pentru Literatura, 1967), 11.

3. Titu Maiorescu, *Opere*, vol. 2 (Bucharest: Editură Minerva, 1984), 350.

4. Johann G. Herder, *Sämtliche Werke*, vol. 1, ed. B. Suphan (Berlin: Weidmannsche, 1877), 147.

5. A standardized language has been defined by A. Issatschenko as follows: "1) it is polyvalent, that is to say it is suitable for serving all spheres of the national life; 2) it is normalized (with respect to orthography and orthoepy, grammar and lexicon); 3) it is obligatory for all members of the given national society and consequently permits of no dialectal variation; 4) it is stylistically differentiated." Cited in Robert Auty, "Literary Language and Literary Dialect in Medieval and Early Modern Slavonic Languages," *Slavonic and East European Review* 56.2 (1978): 193.

6. In Serbian, these debates are known as the *Rat za Srpski Jezik i Pravopis* (War for the Serbian Language and Orthography), after the title of an 1847 book by the same name by Djura Daničić. Similarly, Romanian writers such as Alecu Russo and Gheorghe Barițiu during the same period dubbed the literary arguments of Romanians *Razboiul limbilor* (the War of the Languages).

7. Readers interested in other "language wars" in Austria-Hungary are referred to the following. For Ukrainians in Galicia, see Paul R. Magocsi, "The Language Question as a Factor in the National Movement in Eastern Galicia," in *Nationbuilding and the Politics of Nationalism: Essays on Austrian Galicia*, ed. Andrei S. Markovits and Frank E. Sysyn, Harvard Ukrainian Research Institute Monograph Series (Cambridge, Mass.: Harvard University Press for HURI, 1981), 220–38. For the Rusyns of northern Hungary, see Paul R. Magocsi, "The Language Question Among the Subcarpathian Rusyns," in *Aspects of the Slavic Language Question*, vol. 2, ed. Riccardo Picchio and Harvey Goldblatt (New Haven: Yale Concilium on International and Area Studies, 1984), 65–86. For Croats, see Ivo Banac, "Main Trends in the Croat Language Question," in *Aspects of the Slavic Language Question*, vol. 1, ed. Riccardo Picchio and Harvey Goldblatt (New Haven: Yale Concilium on International and Area Studies, 1984), 189–260. For Slovaks, see Peter Brock, *The Slovak National Awakening: An Essay in the Intellectual History of East Central Europe* (Toronto: University of Toronto Press, 1976). For Slovenians, see Rado Lenček, *The Structure and History of the Slovene Language* (Columbus, Ohio: Slavica, 1982). For Magyars, see Lóránt Czigány, *The Oxford History of Hungarian Literature: From the Earliest Times to the Present* (Oxford: Clarendon Press, 1984).

8. See further Wayne S. Vucinich, "The Serbs in Austria-Hungary," *Austrian History Yearbook* 3, bk. 2 (1967): 3–47, and Stephen Fischer-Galați, "The Rumanians and the Habsburg Monarchy," *Austrian History Yearbook* 3, bk. 2 (1967): 430–49.

9. By 1900, there were c. 1,142,000 Serbs in Austria-Hungary and 3,033,000 Romanians. Figures are taken from Paul R. Magocsi, *Historical Atlas of East Central Europe* (Toronto: University of Toronto Press, 1993), 97–98.

10. The term "Greek Catholic" is used in this paper to denote Christians in full communion with the papacy ("Catholic") but whose rites, heritage, and canon law are Byzantine ("Greek") rather than Roman.

11. A *natio* in the Habsburg Empire should not be confused with the modern "nation." A *natio* was a community of free individuals, rather than an ethnolinguistic community. A Magyar, Croatian, or Romanian nobleman might be considered part of the "Hungarian nation"; a Magyar peasant was not.

12. The language created by these two Byzantine missionaries and their disciples was actually the oldest form of Church Slavonic: Old Church Slavonic. Similarly, the alphabet invented for their new language was not modern Cyrillic *per se*, but the Glagolitic script. Seeking to transmit the gospel message to the widest possible audience, Cyril and Methodius constructed Old Church Slavonic out of several different Slavic languages. The result was partially understandable to all Slav peoples but native to none.

13. The spoken vernaculars usually had no proper names as such to distinguish them from

Church Slavonic, and were referred to as "simple language"—*prosti jezik* in Serbian and *limba prostimei* in Romanian. See further Silvia Toscano, "Orthodox Slavdom," in *History of Linguistics*, vol. 3, ed. Giulio Lepschy (London: Addison Wesley Longman, 1998), 123–45, and references therein.

14. This approach to composition was also known as the "middle style," in reference to the literary "Theory of Styles" that was elaborated for Russian literature by Mikhail Lomonosov in his *Predislovie o pol'ze knig tserkovnykh v rossiiskom iazyke* (1757). In general terms, Lomonosov's theory proposes: the more Slavonic used, the more dignified the work; the more vernacular used, the wider the intended audience.

15. Many factors militated against the survival of full Church Slavonic literacy among Romanians: the anti-Slavonic policies of the Habsburgs, the non-Slavic character of the Romanian vernacular, and the general lack of qualified Church Slavonic teachers in Transylvania. On the decline of Church Slavonic printing among Romanians, 1635–1715, see Dennis Deletant, "Rumanian Presses and Printing in the Seventeenth Century: II," *Slavonic and East European Review* 61.4 (1983): 497–511.

16. See Philip J. Adler, "Habsburg School Reform Among the Orthodox Minorities, 1770–1780," *Slavic Review* 30.1 (1974): 23–45.

17. These were to be the languages of "Hungaros videlicet proprie dictos, Germanos, Slauos [Slovaks], Croatas, Ruthenos [Rusyns/Ukrainians], Illyrios [Serbs], Valachos [Romanians]." *Ratio Educationis Publicae totiusque rei literariae per Regnum Hungariae et Provincias eidem adnexas* (Buda: Typis Regiae Univer. Hungaricae, 1806), iii, v. Similarly, in 1775 an episcopal commission of the Catholic Church in Austria-Hungary directed that all nonliturgical Greek Catholic publications were to be printed in "Lingua vulgari Valachica et Illyrica." Cited in Péter Király, "The Role of the Buda University Press in the Development of Orthography and Literary Languages," in *The Formation of the Slavonic Literary Languages*, ed. Gerald Stone and Dean Worth (see Further Reading, page 257), 30.

18. As early as 1648, Metropolitan Simion Stefan of Transylvania noted in the preface to his translation of the New Testament that "Romanians do not speak in all lands in one way, neither in one land do they all speak in one way; for this reason it is difficult to write so that some should not understand a thing in one way and others in another way." In Ioan Bianu and Nerva Hodoş, eds., *Bibliografia românească veche, 1508–1830*, vol. 1 (Bucharest: Atelierele Socec & Co., 1903), 170.

19. Magyar literature provides examples of ethnic non-Magyars who accepted Magyar political and cultural identity. One member of the famous "Triad of Pest," the poet Mihály Vitkovics (1778–1829), was the son of a Serbian Orthodox priest and consciously used the traditions of Serbian folk poetry to enrich his Magyar writings. The poet laureate of the Hungarian Revolution, Petőfi, was similarly of Slavic origin.

20. For a review of Kopitar's life and views, see Sergio Bonazza, "Austro-Slavism as the Motive of Kopitar's Work," *Slovene Studies* 5.2 (1983): 155–64.

21. Duncan Wilson, *The Life and Times of Vuk Stefanović Karadžić, 1787–1864* (Oxford: Oxford University Press, 1970).

22. On the relations between Vuk and the German Romantics, see Jacob Grimm's foreword to Vuk's 1824 *Kleine serbische Grammatik;* also Wilfried Potthoff, ed., *Vuk Karadžić im europäischen Kontext: Beiträge des Internationalen Wissenschaftlichen Symposiums der Vuk Karadžić–Jacob Grimm–Gesellschaft am 19. und 20. November 1987, Frankfurt am Main* (Heidelberg: Carl Winter Universitätsverlag, 1990).

23. Vuk Stefanović Karadžić, *Skupljeni gramatički i polemički spisi Vuka Stef. Karadžića,* vol. 1 (Belgrade: Štamparija Kraljevine Srbije, 1894), 92–93.

24. Serbo-Croatian dialects are categorized according to whether they use što/šta, kaj, or ča to signify the interrogative "what." Što-kavian is spoken from eastern Serbia to western Croatia, kaj-kavian mostly in the northwestern region of Croatia around Zagreb, ča-kavian in Istria and parts of Dalmatia. Što-kavian dialects are further divided into e-kavian, ije-kavian and i-kavian: the Serbo-

Croatian word for "milk" is pronounced *mleko* in eastern dialects, *mlijeko* in western dialects, *mliko* in the north. Vuk promoted the ije-kavian variant of Bosnia-Hercegovina at the expense of the i-kavian spoken by many Hungarian Serbs.

25. From a letter Vuk wrote Kopitar in 1816. Vuk Stefanović Karadžić, *Pisma* (Novi Sad: Matica Srpska, 1969), 20.

26. For the history of this long-standing antagonism between the Matica Srbska and Vuk Karadžić, see, e.g., Peter Herrity, "The Role of the Matica and Similar Societies in the Development of the Slavonic Literary Languages," *Slavonic and East European Review* 51.124 (1973): 368–86.

27. Cited in Wilson, *Life and Times of Vuk*, 214.

28. Karadžić, *Skupljeni gramatički i polemički*, 3:149.

29. Bishop Stratimirović urged his flock not to follow the example of those who would "corrupt and confuse their language, but [to imitate] those who attempted to refine, adorn, and broaden their speech." Cited in Đoko Slijepčević, *Stevan Stratimirović* (Belgrade: Izdanje Knjižare Vlad. I. Rajković i Komp., 1936), 161.

30. Cited in Živan Milisavac, *Matica srpska i Vukova reforma* (Novi Sad: Matica Srpska, 1987), 175.

31. See, e.g., Gale Stokes's biography of Vladimir Jovanović: *Legitimacy Through Liberalism* (Seattle: University of Washington Press, 1975), esp. 31.

32. Tekelija himself underlined what divided Serbian conservatives from Catholic philologists such as Kopitar and Šafařik: "for them the Slavonic language is not united to a [religious] creed, whereas for us the Slavonic language is the language of faith." In Karadžić, *Skupljeni gramatički i polemički*, 3:150.

33. Kenneth E. Naylor, "Serbo-Croatian," in *The Slavic Literary Languages,* ed. Alexander Schenker and Edward Stankiewicz (see Further Reading), 79.

34. Gheorghe Barițiu testified to this attachment in an article he wrote for *Foia pentru Minte* in 1858: "We are indebted forever to our forebears for, despite their poverty and their wretched condition, they left us a common ecclesiastical language that is for all Romanians, from peasant to scholar, for Transylvanians, Moldavians, and so on." Cited in Grecu, *Limbă și națiune,* 51.

35. As Ion Heliade Rădulescu concluded in 1839, a Romanian "language of the Church" (*limbă Bisericii*) would never be an adequate substitute for a true "language of the Academy" (*limbă Academiei*). This did not mean, however, that ecclesiastical Romanian ought to be cast aside. Grecu, *Limbă și națiune,* 51–52.

36. For the role of these seminarians and of Greek Catholicism in the Romanian national awakening, see Radu R. Florescu, "The Uniate Church: Catalyst of Rumanian National Consciousness," *Slavonic and East European Review* 45 (1967): 324–42.

37. Elizabeth Close, *The Development of Modern Rumanian* (see Further Reading), 20.

38. Ironically, zealous Latinizers such as Petru Maior often ascribed Latin roots to words that were clearly of Church Slavonic or Magyar origin. George Calinescu, *Istoria literaturii române de la origini până în prezent* (Madrid, Paris, Rome, and Pelham, N.Y.: Fundația Europeana Dragan/Editură Nagard, 1980), 69.

39. The Wallachian Barbu Paris Mumuleanu assured Romanians that "we must not be ashamed to borrow [these words], nor must we have scruples, saying that they are not Romanian." Why should Romanian not borrow from "its Latin mother" rather than from "shaggy [*flocoasă*] Slavonic"? In ibid., 118.

40. Petru Maior complained that Cyrillic had concealed the Latin roots of Romanian. In his *Dialogu pentru începutul limbei română,* Maior has a character exclaim: "How many times has this happened to me, . . . that whenever I was in doubt whether a word was Latin, I have written it with Latin letters, and at once its gleaming Latin face would appear and would seem to smile at me for having freed it from slavery and from its poor Cyrillic rags." In Petru Maior, *Scrieri: Istoria besericei*

românilor, disputaţii, ortografia română, dialog, ed. Florea Fugariu (Bucharest: Editură Minerva, 1976), 316.

41. From the foreword to *Maestria ghiovasirii româneşti cu litere latineşti* [The art of reading Romanian with Latin letters], published by G. C. Roja in 1809. In ibid., 14. The Wallachian writer Ion Heliade Rădulescu well expressed the sentiments of the Transylvanian School when he wrote: "The Latin letters [*litere*] with which our ancestors wrote, are the teats through which our language can suck in the milk of the Latin mother, for literature [*literatură*] can be born only of Latin letters [*litere*], while from Slavic letters [*slove*] can come only words [*slovnire*]." Cited in John Coert Campbell, *French Influence and the Rise of Roumanian Nationalism,* Eastern Europe Collection (New York: Arno Press, 1971), 42.

42. Thus, "son" was written as *filiu* (Latin *filius*) but pronounced as *fiu,* and "good day" was written as *bona dia* but pronounced *buna ziua.* The hard *k* sound was written *qu* (e.g., *Quand*) in imitation of Latin, where modern Romanian has *c* (eg. *Când*). For further examples, see Samuil Micu and Gheorghe Şincai, *Elementa linguae daco-romanae sive valachicae* (facsimile of the 1780 edition, ed. and trans. Mircea Zdrenghea, Cluj-Napoca: Editură Dacia, 1980).

43. Đoko Slijepčević, *Istorija Srpske pravoslavne crkve,* vol. 2 (Belgrade: Beogradski Izdavačko-Grafički Zavod, 1991), 163.

44. In debates with the Romanians Damaschin Bojinca and Eftimie Murgu in 1827–30, Sava Tekelija argued that the Vlachs were primarily descended from the aboriginal Dacians, not from Roman colonists. Since the Dacians were widely considered in the nineteenth century to have been Slavic, the Romanians must themselves be Slavs, even if they had partly adopted the speech of their conquerors. Sava Tököly [Tekelija], *Erweis, dass die Walachen nicht römischer Abkunft sind, und dies nicht aus ihrer italienisch-slavischen Sprache folgt, etc.* (Ofen: Gedruck mit königl. ung. Universitäts-Schriften, 1827), 162. For the Romanian response, see Damasceno Th. Bozskinka, *Animadversio in Dissertationem Hallensem sub Titulo, etc.* (Pest: Typis Ludovici Landerer de Füskút, 1827), and E. Murgu, *Widerlegung der Abhandlung, welche unter dem Titel vorkömt, etc.* (Ofen: Gedruckt mit königl. ung. Universitäts-Schriften, 1830).

45. Grecu, *Limbă şi naţiune,* 68.

46. The decision by the diet on January 31, 1842, to make Magyar the official language of Transylvania further weakened ecclesiastical control of the national movement, drawing more of the Orthodox and Greek Catholic laity into the struggle for Romanian linguistic and cultural survival. Keith Hitchins, *The Rumanian National Movement in Transylvania, 1780–1849* (Cambridge, Mass.: Harvard University Press, 1969), 173.

47. Campbell, *French Influence and the Rise of Roumanian Nationalism,* 94–95.

48. As late as 1875, the British and Foreign Bible Society in Vienna had to print its Bibles in either Cyrillic or mixed Cyrillic/Latin script. When the society allowed a prominent Transylvanian scholar to prepare its 1859 edition of the Book of Psalms in Romanian, the result was so confusing to ordinary Romanians that footnotes had to be added, giving readers the better-known Church Slavonic equivalents for the obscure Latinized words of the text. E. D. Tappe, "Rumania and the Bible Society, 1853–1920," *Slavic and Eastern European Review* 51.123 (1973): 279, 286.

49. Writing about his experiences in 1848, Alecu Russo declared that "the Transylvanians have doomed themselves to be completely divided into two nations: one Latin, the second Romanian. Because of these [linguistic beliefs], there is not one book printed in Transylvania that can be read and understood by all Romanians." Alecu Russo, *Scrieri alese,* ed. Geo Şerban (Bucharest: Editură Albatros, 1970), 77–78.

50. In Moldavia, the writers Vasile Alecsandri, Gheorghe Sion, Alexandru Russo, Costache Negri, and Mihail Kogălniceanu were all prominent political activists who demanded an end to the Russian-imposed Organic Regulations, the sanction of civil and political liberties, agrarian reform, and the abolition of serfdom and class privileges. Most were sent into exile or were arrested in 1848. In

Wallachia, literary men such as Nicolae Bălcescu, Ion Heliade-Rădulescu, and Constantin Rosetti played key roles in the overthrow of Prince Bibescu and even took posts in the provisional government that replaced him.

51. In an open letter to Romanian youth, Jules Michelet declared: "De toutes les nations qui viennent tour à tour s'asseoir au foyer de la France, nulle plus que la vôtre ne s'est plus viv[ement] imbue de son âme, et pénétré de son esprit. . . . V[ous] êtes les Italiens de l'Orient et vous vous sentez vraiment [des] Roumains." In Marin Bucur, *Jules Michelet și revoluționarii români în documente și scrisori de epocă (1846–1874)* (Cluj-Napoca: Editură Dacia, 1982), 212.

52. Russo delighted in lampooning the pseudo-Roman pretensions of Latinists: "It would therefore be more adequate and more logical, given our love of Latinism, to abandon the Romanian language and adopt Latin . . . to exchange trousers and jackets for the toga . . . and to reclaim the former mastery of the world." Russo, *Scrieri alese*, 83–84.

53. For a classic formulation of this idea, see the inaugural lecture on Romanian history given at the Mihaileana Academy of Iași in 1843 by Mihail Kogălniceanu: "Cuvînt pentru deschiderea cursului de istorie naționala în Academia Mihaileana, rostit în 24 noiemvrie 1843," in Mihail Kogălniceanu, *Opere,* vol. 2, ed. Alexandru Zub (Bucharest: Editură Academiei Republicii Socialiste România, 1976), 389.

54. Alexandre Cioranescu, *Vasile Alecsandri,* trans. E. D. Tappe and Maria Golescu (New York: Twayne Publishers, 1973), 147. Many of Alecsandri's other works, especially his drama and prose, borrowed substantially from Victor Hugo and other French authors and playwrights.

55. Ioan Slavici, from an article entitled "Eminescu și limba Românească," which appeared in the journal *Convorbiri literare* in 1909. In Ioan Slavici, *Opere,* vol. 9, ed. C. Mohanu (Bucharest: Editură Minerva, 1978), 42.

56. Cited in Pompiliu Marcea, *Ioan Slavici* (Bucharest: Editions Meridiane, 1967), 115.

57. See, e.g., *Evangeliile la tóate Duminecsele si szerbetórile preszte tót anul etc.* (Buda: Al doilea prea kitit si asezat Tiparju Tipérit en Tipografia U Krejesty, 1799); Stefán Atzél [Ștefan Acel], *Szpre bukurie Márelui si pre vrednikului ál Boros Jenõului Domnului Atzél Stefán Inperátestilor sztepanir táinelor szfetnik etc.* (Orádeá Máre: Cu Typáriul lui Joánn Fránciscu Tichy, 1808); Joan Mihail Mökeschi, *Preátenul szau Voitoriul de bine ál Pruntsilor schi a tinerimií Romaneschti, etc.* (Sibiu: Tiperite en Tipographia Mostenilor lui M. de Hochmeister, 1837). See also L. Gáldi, "Contributions Hongroises à la découverte de la langue Roumaine," *Acta Linguistica Academiae Scientiarum Hungaricae VII* (1958): 1–39.

58. Domokos Kosáry, *The Press During the Hungarian Revolution of 1848–1849* (Boulder, Colo.: Social Science Monographs, 1986), 281.

59. Thus, for example, the Latin alphabet was officially adopted by ASTRA's Philological Commission on October 2, 1860, but the same committee later adopted the phonetic principle in orthography. Grecu, *Limbă și națiune,* 239.

60. See Gale Stokes, "Church and Class in Early Balkan Nationalism," *East European Quarterly* 13.3 (1979): 263.

"Indian Shakespeare" and the Politics of Language in Colonial India

NANDI BHATIA

The late nineteenth century in India saw the revival of ancient Sanskritic texts such as *Sakuntala* by Kalidasa, identified as the fourth-century poet belonging to the "golden age" of the Gupta period, when Sanskrit literature, arts, and culture supposedly flourished and reached their high point.[1] As scholars have pointed out, such recuperation of an ancient literary and cultural past had an intimate relationship with the contemporary historical context. In the case of colonial India, claims to a "golden" Hindu past served to "instill pride among its members in the past and to create confidence in [the subordinate group's] ability to mold its own future."[2] To this end, cultural representations of the modern Indian nation through ancient artifacts helped galvanize "a compelling sense of contemporary collective belonging" against a common enemy.[3] In the Hindi heartland, the nineteenth-century revival of India's cultural and literary heritage and the symbolic value attached to it helped shape an anticolonial consciousness in the present that was also central to the formation of a modern Hindu religious, linguistic, and national identity.[4] While the modern nation's revival of its literary-cultural past helped forge a nationalist anticolonial identity, it also paradoxically inspired extensive comparisons with Shakespeare, undertaken in literary-critical studies especially after the 1870s.[5] Of note among these, as Harish Trivedi points out, are Smarajit Dutt's commentaries on *Macbeth*, *Othello*, and *Hamlet*. With each of the books subtitled *An Oriental Study*, Dutt systematically takes up one or more celebrated passages from the plays and then demonstrates "that each of these could be matched and indeed excelled by comparable passages from Sanskrit poetry."[6]

Harish Trivedi argues that this impulse to compare Shakespeare with classical texts and writers was shaped by a patriotic response to the colonial dissemination of Shakespeare's works in India. Because Shakespeare, for some Indians, came to represent "an agent of colonial subjugation," argues Trivedi, critics such as Dutt saw it as "their patriotic duty . . . to disparage and debunk" the bard.[7] Underlying comparisons drawn between Kalidasa and Shakespeare was, thus, a nationalistic stance: to uphold the power of a Hindu

Sh, enlisted for Hindi as nat. lang.

nation that had been rendered powerless by the derisive discourses of the West.[8] With Shakespeare signifying the authority of the ruling nation, according a comparable status to one of the central texts of the Hindus became a way for the Indian literati to assert its own civilizational superiority in ancient times.

Trivedi's assessment of the critical anticolonial self-fashioning through an ostensibly oppositional response to the colonialist constructions of Shakespeare as "a supreme achievement of the [English] race, as a measure of England's general world-wide superiority, and as an emblem of that English heritage whose propagation could properly be regarded as part of the white man's civilizing burden" is indeed valid.[9] However, not all such critical agendas were directly anti-imperialist. For criticism of Shakespeare and Sanskrit texts, and translations and adaptations of his works in Hindi, also accommodated the colonialist version through laudatory responses that simultaneously valorized Shakespeare.[10] The laudatory literary-critical attention to Shakespeare in Hindi and Sanskrit, then, can be seen as being mediated by the nationalistic attempt to prop up Hindi as the national language at a time when Hindustani split into Hindi and Urdu, initiating linguistic rivalries that were to give shape to communal identities in the literary sphere. Because "Shakespeare" had been disseminated as an icon of a "superior" civilization, the Hindi literati sought to establish the legitimacy of Hindi as a superior, cultured, and complex language with a superior literary heritage by first establishing Hindi's links with Hindu classical texts and then comparing those to the works of Shakespeare. The Hindi literary and linguistic revival, thus, enlisted the project of colonial rule—a project that sought to establish its "civilizing mission" via Shakespeare—to its own project of establishing the status of Hindi as a national language.

Against the backdrop of intensifying language conflict over the Hindi and Urdu vernaculars during the late nineteenth and early twentieth centuries, this essay examines a variety of texts that positioned themselves in relation to Shakespeare: critical studies, journal articles, and drama. This examination explores the representation and construction of Hindi language and Hindu culture through the revival of ancient texts and their subsequent validation through comparisons with Shakespeare. To this end, I first provide an introduction to the institutionalization of Shakespeare in India, followed by a brief background to the Hindi-Urdu controversy. Then I focus on the strategies deployed to propagate Hindi—among them the use of Shakespeare. Finally, through a reading of Bharatendu Harishchander's Hindi translation of *The Merchant of Venice,* titled *Durlabh Bandhu,* I suggest that the Shakespearean text came to serve the interest of Hindi, perpetuating in the process a Hindu nationalism that excluded Muslims—with whom Urdu came to be identified—from its purview.

Colonial Representation of Shakespeare in India

The institutionalization of Shakespeare in India was facilitated by the education system, traveling companies from abroad, and literary-critical representations in academic and journalistic discourses. The initiation of the bard into the Indian academy coincided with the introduction into India of the discipline of English literature, which became an important part of the educational curriculum after the establishment of universities in Bombay, Madras, and Bengal in 1857. As Gauri Viswanathan has shown, the introduction of English language and literature, on the pretext of offering a liberal education to "regenerate India," actually served as an instrument of the British Empire. The "humanistic functions" traditionally associated with literature—for example, the shaping of character or the development of an aesthetic and disciplines of ethical thinking—were considered essential to sociopolitical control.[11] In India, the discipline of English was invested with "human and moral attributes," an investment that was interwoven with the "civilizing mission" of English in relation to the colonized and would function as a "conduit to western thoughts and ideas."[12] Like English literature generally, whose humanistic function was crucial to imperialist strategy, Shakespeare was defined by the same attributes of "humanism," "morality," and "wisdom" and presented as the universally transcendental text. Constituting the core of English literature courses, Shakespeare's works became central for upholding the "humanistic" ideals of British civilization and functioned as a legitimate object of study in India. Reinforced via colonial policies regarding education and civil-service exams,[13] Shakespeare's works came to signify not just English texts but also texts of colonial authority; and "Shakespeare" became a metaphor for modernity, rationalism, and wisdom. At the time of an expanding colonialism, Shakespeare became an "instrument of empire" and perpetuated what Jyotsna Singh calls "the myth of English cultural refinement and superiority—a myth that was crucial to the rulers' political interests in India."[14] However, as writers and critics educated in the new colonial curriculum undertook translations of his plays into the vernacular languages—Bengali, Urdu, Marathi, Gujarati, and Hindustani, for instance—and as local theater companies began producing Shakespeare in these languages, the reach of the bard began to extend far beyond the academy or the exclusive Western stage in India.[15]

devaluation of vernaculars

Such institutionalizations of the bard and the English language were not devoid of negative implications for the vernacular languages. In the late nineteenth century, when the British Indian Association of the North-West Provinces petitioned the viceroy for the use of the vernacular (meaning Urdu) in higher education, the government responded by saying that "while some progress had been made in enriching the vernaculars, chiefly through translation of European works, they still lacked sufficient materials to be suitable for higher education."[16] Vernaculars (Hindi-Urdu) were not considered worthy enough even "to merit inclusion in regular degree courses as subjects in their own right until 1923."[17] In 1888, for example, the registrar of Punjab University declared that the teaching of Indian sacred texts could best be accomplished through the medium of English. Nor did elite Indians consider the vernaculars any more suitable as media of instruction than did British officials, as evident in the following statement by Shiva Prashad, an eminent Indian: "English, being the language of our rulers, and having all its advantages attached to it, is . . . the means of all improvement and elevation."[18] The institutionalization and imposition of English, which has led to its inclusion among the numerous "official" languages today, thus conduced to a systematic disabling of the vernaculars.[19] Consequently, by the 1920s, government officials and some Western-educated Indian elite came to regard the vernaculars "as inferior to English as well as to the classical languages from which they derived their scripts and much more of their vocabulary. As a result, the vernaculars did not become the medium of instruction in higher education until the 1920s in most institutions."[20] English, however, was unable to wipe out the vernaculars, and literary productions in the vernaculars continued despite the efforts of the colonial authorities to censor native publications and drama through the Vernacular Press Acts of 1879 and 1910 and the Dramatic Performances Censorship Act of 1876.[21] One consequence of the imposition of English was that it brought to the fore matters regarding the development of a national literature, which, in the case of Hindi, was complicated by its rivalry with Urdu. To understand the developments affecting the status of Hindi as a national language, it is necessary to return briefly to the politics of Hindi-Urdu.

Background of the Hindi-Urdu Controversy

Scholars such as Amrit Rai and Vasudha Dalmia attribute the strengthening of the Hindi-Urdu controversy to British intervention in the early nineteenth century,[22] when John B. Gilchrist, a proponent of Oriental learning, engaged a group of writers at Fort William College (founded in Calcutta in 1800 to educate employees of the East India Company in the native languages) to write Hindustani prose channeled into two distinct styles.[23] One style was shaped by Hindi without Persian vocabulary, and the other style involved the use of Urdu that remained as close as possible to Persian.[24] According to Rai, this exacerbated the existing cleavage between Hindi and Urdu and greatly affected the formation of modern Hindi and modern Urdu.[25] Hindi, Hindavi, or Hindustani, as it was called, overlapped significantly with what is identified as Urdu. As such, Urdu (or Hindi and Hindustani) was spoken by both Muslims and Hindus and was understood largely across the subcontinent. In terms of script, it could be written in either Devanagari or Persian-Arabic. However, as Dalmia asserts, it was the British who initially introduced the notion of a national language and initiated a process that, in the case of Hindustani, "quickly led to a split and to the creation of Hindi and Urdu as the national languages of Hindus and Muslims, and to their subsequent development as two autonomous print languages."[26] This association of language and script with the cultural and religious identity of Hindus and Muslims was later picked up by nationalists and initiated debates that escalated the divisions between Hindi and Urdu.[27]

The debates that developed in the mid–nineteenth century over the status of Hindi and Urdu as the national languages of India led to intense pro-Hindi activism. While some Hindu enthusiasts argued that Hindi be given the stature of the "national" language, Muslim leaders made their case for Urdu. As Hindu and Muslim nationalists sought mass support from their respective communities via propagation of the two languages, the debate intensified. The Hindu leadership stressed the need for popularizing Hindi to serve as a link for interregional communication and to rally mass support against imperialism. Efforts to make Hindi the national language included the encouragement of vernacular education, the establishment of Hindi newspapers in Bengal, and the introduction of Hindi into law courts and schools in Bihar around 1900, after an intense agitation by literate sections of the Hindus.[28] And organizations such as the Brahmo Samaj, the Arya Samaj, and the Nagari Pracharini Sabha (Society for the Promotion of Hindi) made additional efforts. The threat of Hindi domination over Urdu also resulted in the emergence of several organizations for the propagation of Urdu. Of these, the Aligarh movement initiated by Syed Ahmed Khan in the late nineteenth century was most vocal in asserting the status of Urdu as a national language.[29] Such conscious segregation of the two languages sharpened the differences between Hindi and Urdu at the elite level even though at the popular level there were (and continue to be) numerous linguistic overlaps. Premchand, one of the *differences of script came to be id'd w/ differences of religion*

most important Hindi writers and social activists of the early twentieth century, in fact, drew attention to this complexity in several essays and addresses on the issue of national language. Urging his audience to accept Hindustani as the national language, he chastised those interested in emphasizing the demarcation between the two languages.[30] Nonetheless, differences continued to sharpen and ultimately exacerbated communal divisions as "differences of script and language came to be progressively identified with differences in religion, embedding communalism at a very deep level in the popular consciousness."[31]

A prominent approach to the promotion of Hindi in the late nineteenth and early twentieth centuries (one that has received scholarly attention) was to make claims about Hindi's antiquity by going back to its roots in Sanskrit, a language with which it also shared its script, that is, *dēvanāgarī*. Such concern with Hindi's roots in antiquity, specifically Sanskrit language and literature, came to focus on Sanskrit as a source, an origin, of the Hindu civilization, and served as a frame of reference for the development and evolution of Hindi. In effect, Hindi was shown to have constituted a historical past with roots in Sanskrit, and its importance and history could then only be understood through its connection to antiquity. Construing Hindi as a language that had become a symbolic signifier of Hindu culture, language, and civilization, this regression to the past became a tool for explaining the civilizational qualities of Hindus and their language, Hindi. To establish Hindi's lineage from Sanskrit, organizations such as the Arya Samaj and the Nagari Pracharini Sabha began promoting the *dēvanāgarī* script (of the Hindi language) and launched an aggressive campaign for a style that incorporated Sanskrit vocabulary while consciously removing Persian and Arabic words.[32]

Another important forum for addressing questions regarding the status of Hindi was the periodical, which opened, according to Dalmia, "a space for a variety of experimental modes."[33] The periodicals, in fact, did not merely create their own readership; as Dalmia asserts, it "was in the periodical literature in Hindi, which emerged as a vital cultural and political forum in Banaras and later in Allahabad in the seventies of the nineteenth century, that the collective identity of the emergent Hindu middle class, as it formed itself in the North Western Province, found the most forceful articulation."[34] Although Dalmia focuses her discussion on nineteenth-century journals, particularly those started by Bharatendu Harishchandra, it is important to note that even literary journals such as *Sarasvati,* which became one of the most influential literary magazines in Hindi during the first few decades of the twentieth century, promoted Hindi by taking an open stance in its favor. For instance, one of its editors, Mahavir Prasad Dvivedi, the chief proponent of Hindi poetry,

Orientalist Scholarship

advocated a Sanskritized style and recommended the replacement of Urdu words. His own efforts to propagate this style included invitations to poets to write verse in Hindi, which he painstakingly corrected before publishing in the journal, and encouragement to young poets to imitate his own lyrics. The publication of a Sanskritized style of Hindi verse in *Sarasvati* in the first decade of the twentieth century gave a tremendous boost to Hindi. Because of the emphasis placed on the revival of a Sanskritized Hindi, the language also acquired a highly literate character.

The return to Sanskrit, which served to establish Hindi's descent from classical languages and literature, was also motivated by Orientalist researches. As Vinay Dharvadker points out, "following Sir William Jones' discovery of the unmistakable connections between Sanskrit, Persian, Greek, and Latin, the 'roots' of ancient civilization had become inseparable from the whole theory of an antecedent 'Indo-European' civilization, the origin of all origins. . . . Sanskrit thus became central to any understanding of the Occident or the Orient." Max Müller, the German Orientalist and philologist, had reinforced such emphasis on Sanskrit and in 1859 had argued that "no one who takes an interest in the philosophy and the historical growth of human speech,—no one who desires to study the history of that branch of mankind to which we ourselves belong, and to discover in the first germs of the language, the religion, and mythology of our forefathers . . . can, for the future, dispense with some knowledge of the language and ancient literature of India."[35] The nationalist ethos in the nineteenth century and its evocation of Sanskrit and the "golden" Hindu age then grew out of the framework of Orientalist learning.

Having identified Hindi's philological roots in Sanskrit, the literati also needed a new literary aesthetic for the language. As Dalmia asserts, "by the last decade of the nineteenth century the firm conviction that Hindi as the national language could evolve only with the growth of its literature, and that this growth reflected the degree of development of the nation itself, had begun to find widespread articulation."[36] A national language also needed a national literature. As yet, the "corpus of national literature in Hindi had not been constituted." Its constitution "involved not only a revival of and search for classical literature but also a purge of what was attributed as the literature of Muslims."[37] As well, it had to be configured in contemporary terms. This was a "multidimensional project" that involved, in addition to selection and publication of texts, an identification of the various genres that constituted it. Once this was accomplished, "the history of their respective development could be written and the aesthetic criterion used to evaluate them set up afresh." According to Dalmia, from this emerged the "question of the validity

project of modernity → imperial rule Shakespeare

of the existing aesthetic categories and the need to coin new sets of categories in order to encompass and evaluate the new." One strategy for defining and validating the older genres through new aesthetic criteria was to rewrite the plots and characters of Kalidasa's and Sudraka's plays as Shakespearean, then establish the links of Hindi literature by securing some kind of ancestry for it in the Sanskrit literary canon, and finally undertake translations of Sanskrit as well as Shakespeare into Hindi. Thus, says Dalmia, "could Hindi literature . . . achieve a status lofty enough to lift the nation to higher thoughts and ideas, and to insure it to a higher social, moral, and political existence."[38]

Shakespeare, Sanskrit, and Hindi

In search for a new aesthetic for Hindi that would enrich the language through a variety of experimental modes, the Hindi literati began to claim civilizational status for their language through the translation into Hindi of Kalidasa's *Sakuntala,* which was declared the first drama in modern Hindi literature.[39] Emerging simultaneously were comparisons of Kalidasa with Shakespeare, which by the 1920s had become commonplace. Additionally, beginning with the 1870s efforts to translate Shakespeare into Sanskrit and Hindi intensified. Leading Sanskrit magazines (such as *Sahridaya*) started publishing prose versions of Shakespeare's works in the last quarter of the nineteenth century,[40] promoting ancient Hindu culture through translation into Sanskrit. Sanskritists, as Venkatarama Raghavan notes,

> [n]ot only came to hold Shakespeare as the model or high watermark of dramatic [art] . . . but even when they studied Kalidasa and other Sanskrit dramatists, they applied to their appreciation of Sanskrit dramas the conceptions and values which they had learnt in their study of Shakespearean criticism. . . . Even among the celebrated writers and thinkers such as Tagore and Aurobindo, the evaluation of Sanskrit drama or of Kalidasa in particular always brought in comparisons with Shakespeare and his plays.[41]

In the translations of "Shakespeare," which Raghavan refers to as "foreign classics," lies the project of modernity associated with imperial rule. Raghavan's own article on Shakespeare in Sanskrit reflects this sentiment in his recounting of the story of this translation of Shakespeare. He argues that "Sanskritists" of both the "modern" and the "traditional" styles started on a new phase of Sanskrit writing: "The new works that they wrote—prose, poetry, plays—all of them had a new impress. The most prominent among those who influenced the educated Sanskritists was Shakespeare, whose plays all of them studied in colleges."[42] Through Shakespeare, then, critics such as Raghavan reinstated Sanskrit as an effective participant in the project of modernity.

This project of modernity became all the more visible when critics began to call Kalidasa the "Indian Shakespeare," a peculiar label considering the nearly one thousand years by which Kalidasa preceded Shakespeare. The use of this label reflects an interesting interface of nationalist and Orientalist researches, especially since the label was first used by Orientalist scholar Sir William Jones. Impressed by the lyricism and pastoral charm and beauty of *Sakuntala,* Jones had admired the virtues of Sanskrit in this classical text and had developed deep reverence for Kalidasa. In 1789 he undertook a translation of the play, giving it the title *Sacontala or the Fatal Ring,* and called Kalidasa "the Indian Shakespeare."[43] Such translations, as Romila Thapar points out, "were partly a response to intellectual curiosity and partly an aspect of the practical function of East India Company officials in India," which involved an attempt to better understand the "high culture" of the colony, which understanding, in turn, would enable better control over it.[44] Within the institutional framework of colonialism, thus, Jones's intent in making such comparisons was to enlist Sanskrit texts to aid the imperialists' task of effective governance, not to create symmetry between the ruling and the subject races. Hence, while Jones compared Shakespeare to Kalidasa, Kalidasa's status was still deemed somewhat inferior by bodies such as the Asiatic Society, with whom Jones was connected. Even though *Sakuntala* was an exotic representation of Indian art, it was perceived by the *Asiatic Journal* of the Asiatic Society as a specimen of a somewhat "subordinate genius."[45]

On another level, Jones's reference to Shakespeare also indicates a position that the bard had come to occupy in British literature and anticipates the authority that Shakespeare came to occupy in India. Jones's suggestion spawned a number of similar comparisons between Kalidasa and Shakespeare, including those by prominent nationalists such as Sri Aurobindo and Rabindranath Tagore. However, to attribute these comparisons solely to the workings of European hegemony is simplistic; rather, in such readings lies a peculiar project that uses the symbolic authority of Shakespeare to validate the authority of the ancient Hindu text in the present. With Shakespeare signifying the best of the British nation, the representation of Kalidasa as the "Indian Shakespeare" becomes a compelling trope in the nationalist imagination. Thus, instead of shunning the label accorded to Kalidasa, the literati makes it a crucial part of its own ideological project, which seeks to carve

cultural texts   *ideal of*
womanhood

for itself a special cultural space that enables the Hindu middle class to feel empowered in the domain of colonial politics.

In the context of the escalating Hindi-Urdu rift, the symbolic value of the label "Indian Shakespeare" gets redeployed for the specific purpose of elevating Hindi to the level of "Shakespeare." To this end, between 1901 and 1915, *Sarasvati* rapidly increased its publication of Hindi articles and commentaries on Shakespeare, including biographical sketches and translations of Shakespearean plays.[46] Written in standard modern Hindi, these articles are addressed to the literate Hindu reader. The critique of Shakespeare in these articles is formulated within the framework of the Hindu linguistic, social, religious, and political landscape. The descriptions of plot and characters, and especially the discussions of Shakespeare's women, evoke Hindu ideals—the Hindu woman as virtuous wife and good mother. Additionally, the articles' frame of reference becomes the Hindi language and its virtues, in which, by implication, the nation should take pride. For example, in a *Sarasvati* advertisement for a Hindi translation of Shakespeare's works, the journal comments on the qualities of Hindi within the referential framework of Shakespeare: "Shakespeare is one such genius who not only people in Europe but men all across the world should be proud of. . . . The same world respected poet has been translated into Hindi. Hindi is an easy and engaging language and capable of being easily understood by everyone. . . . Please order [this book] soon."[47] The statement above rests on the assumption that in fact the easily understandable nature of Hindi will facilitate an appropriate understanding of what Dinadayalu Srivastava calls "the exemplar of Literature and language," namely Shakespeare.[48] Because the talents of Shakespeare are seen to represent the best of English literature and civilization, the Shakespearean text is appropriated as the means through which Hindi, the modern language of Hindus, can be upheld as a sophisticated and developed language of Hindu civilization. Through such articulations of the importance of Shakespeare and its easy accessibility in Hindi, the journal also fosters the creation of a Hindu middle-class readership. For these middle-class readers, the importance of nation and language is also emphasized through critical assessments of Shakespeare. Thus, in another *Sarasvati* article—a response to an earlier article from *Sarasvati* on Shakespeare's *Hamlet*—the later author chastises the earlier for the brevity of his treatment. Leaving, as he says, the "task of praising Shakespeare up to Shri Dixit," he adds what he feels is an important detail Dixit neglected to mention: that Shakespeare "had tremendous faith in his nation and his language."[49] And in an article titled "Shakespeare," its author, Gangaprashad, especially praises Shakespeare for being a nationalist, and his plays for exhibiting "a very good picture of nationalism."[50] Even the tribute

new reader-ship

accorded to Shakespeare in some of these articles cannot escape reference to canonical Hindi texts. For instance, Gangaprashad, in the same article, notifies his readers that "in comparison to the works of Shakespeare, poet Tulsidas' *Ramayana*'s dissemination would increase if the influence of Hindi and Hindus were more."[51] While the article primarily praises Shakespeare, such interspersed comments reveal the author's preoccupation with Hindi, which he evokes through Tulsi's *Ramayana*—a text that, by this time, had been established as part of the Hindi literary canon and identified with Hindu religion.

In elevating Hindi, critics transform Shakespeare into a Hindu and project his works as documents that uphold orthodox Hindu social norms and hierarchies. Criticism comparing Kalidasa and Shakespeare consists now in establishing links between Shakespeare and Sanskrit works through plot, characters, and language, as in the case of the comparisons drawn between *The Winter's Tale* and Kalidasa's *Sakuntala*. Even the plays are critically judged according to the aesthetic criteria of Sanskrit poetics, as in Gangaprashad's article that praises the plays of Shakespeare for possessing all the *rasas: premrasa, hasyarasa, karunarasa, virarasa,* and so forth.[52] Further, in articles such as "Portia aur Sita" (Portia and Sita), Portia is likened to Sita, the heroine from the Hindu epic the *Ramayana,* who provided the divine model for the ideal Hindu woman. This valorization of the Shakespearean heroine, according to Hindu social codes, serves the ideological function of glorifying and upholding Hindu ideas of femininity. Such comparisons are reinforced in critical works like N. A. Narasimhan's *Kalidasa and Shakespeare: A Parallel* (1921). A lecturer of English at the government college at Kumbhakonam, Narasimhan compares *Sakuntala* with *The Winter's Tale* and traces similarities between Sakuntala and Shakespeare's female protagonists. While such appropriation destabilizes imperialist authority through critiques and comparisons that claim Shakespeare as Hindu, the Hindu literati also begins to revive, secure, and consolidate a Hindu identity.[53]

Bharatendu Harishchandra's *Durlabh Bandhu*

A similar preoccupation with Hindi and Hinduness can be seen in Bharatendu Harishchandra's drama *Durlabh Bandhu* (1880),[54] a translation of Shakespeare's *Merchant of Venice.* As mentioned earlier, by the late nineteenth century periodicals, literary criticism, and drama had become important public media for the propagation of Hindi language and literature and contributed to the dissemination and consolidation of Hindi as the language of Hindus

and Hindustan in the Hindi heartland.[55] This, argues Dalmia, enjoyed particular success in Banaras through the efforts of Harishchandra—poet, publicist,
dramatist, critic, and polemicist and one of the central literary figures of the
Hindi world. Harishchandra contributed significantly to the formation of a
Hindu cultural and political identity through what Dalmia calls the "nationalization of Hindu traditions," and openly propagated the slogan "Hindi-
Hindu-Hindustan" in his periodicals, poetry, speeches, and drama. In fact,
journals such as *Balabodhini,*[56] in which Harishchandra experimented with the
dramatic genre, "pioneered the creation of language and new literature in
Hindi," inspiring other similar periodicals in Hindi.[57] In addition to writing
plays such as *Bharat Durdasha,* a political allegory, *Andher Nagari,* a play
about the tyranny of the British government, and *Nildevi,* a play about the
tales of Rajput valor, Harishchandra in 1884 wrote a lengthy treatise called
"Natak" (Theater), in which he made a plea for the establishment of a
national theater. Such a national theater in Hindi never took off, in part due
to colonial censorship of drama, but theater in general was, apart from the
press, "the one medium that could serve as an effective public forum" in the
Hindi heartland.[58] Since drama was an especially important medium for the
dissemination of Hindi, and since Shakespeare's literary and linguistic authority had by this time gained recognition, perhaps the appeal of Shakespearean
drama was heightened at a time when the pro-Hindi activists searched for
aesthetic models to recast Hindi into the modern mold and give it a national
status.[59]

Following a story line similar to that of the *Merchant of Venice, Durlabh Bandhu,* as suggested by its title (which literally translates as "dependable
friend"), focuses on the themes of character development, friendship, loyalty,
and wisdom. Moreover, one can surmise that the theme of the play would
have appealed to Harishchandra, who was a merchant-aristocrat himself. And
since he also wrote against the British government, Harishchandra's translation of Shakespeare's play can be seen as an allegory of anticolonial nationalism. Written soon after the Vernacular Press Act of 1879, the play exposes
specific colonial practices through its focus on issues pertaining to legal justice
and economic drain and to the struggle for identity and power between two
oppositional groups. In this struggle, Anant (Antonio), who loses his fortune
in a shipwreck, resembles the colonized, and Shailaksha (Shylock), a foreigner
in Vanshnagar, where Anant resides, symbolizes the foreign foe: with deceit,
cunning, and manipulative legal rhetoric, Shailaksha attempts to kill an hon-
est citizen of Vanshnagar and appropriate his wealth.

Harishchander's *Durlabh Bandhu,* however, does not simply oppose colonialism but also affirms the dominant order of Hindu society (equated here

with Indian society), especially by assigning to Anant the high-caste position of an Aryan. Anant's eventual victory over Shailaksha and the latter's expulsion from Vanshnagar seeks to forecast the ultimate victory of the Hindus. Even Vanshnagar, which literally translates as "city of high lineage," implies a space for Aryans, or high-caste Hindus (*vansha* means "of high lineage," and the term *nagar* means "place"). The court of Vanshnagar even orders Shailaksha to become an Aryan. Thus, Harishchander's play is not only an anticolonial narrative but also a narrative of an orthodox nationalism that privileges Hindu society as the norm and uses it synonymously with Indian society. By the 1880s the idea of the Hindus as an Aryan race had gained wide currency as a result of Hindu revivalism and reform movements such as the Arya Samaj. Further, ideas advanced by Orientalist scholars regarding the roots of Aryan society in an Indic past had revived the ancient era as the "Golden Aryan Age" and given Hindus an identity defined by the codes of an Aryan identity. Intellectuals and writers fighting for self-determination in the late nineteenth century found in this revival a way of wresting back their cultural historicity, which had been written off by the colonizers as "barbaric" and "uncivilized." Yet, with the sharpening of the Hindi movement in the 1860s, such an identity gave Hindi the symbolic value of Hindu and "culminated in slogans such as 'Hindi, Hindu, Hindustan' whose creators saw no room for non-Hindi speakers and non-Hindus in Hindustan."[60] Thus, the exclusionist vocabulary of Aryanization articulated through a rewriting of Shakespeare represented Harishchandra's desire for Hindu hegemony. Harishchandra even plays with the language and with its various registers and vocabulary to enrich its flavor. The author combines prose with rhyming couplets and a couple of songs in the dialogue and even formats the Indianized versions of the names of people and places according to the phonetic affinity of English with Hindi: compare Purushri and Portia, Antonio and Anant, Shylock and Shailaksha, Bassanio and Basant, and Nerrissa and Narashri. For Harishchandra, as for other proponents of Hindi who wanted to expand and enrich the language, such experimentation also expressed "the expressive capacity of the language in a variety of directions."[61]

Additionally, the play presents a Hindu woman constructed in the role of Purushri (Portia). As the representative "new woman" (an identity constructed by the nationalist patriarchy in the nineteenth century for the Hindu woman as virtuous, chaste, spiritual, educated, and intelligent—the perfect wife and mother for the modern Hindu man), Purushri provides an occasion to contrast colonial portrayals of the oppressed Indian woman. This contrast is evident as well in Purushri's name (derived from Sanskrit), which connotes vigor, energy, and beauty as opposed to passivity and submissiveness.[62] In

*ideal of female
equality*

fact, as Dalmia asserts, Harishchandra himself was quite a vital debater on the issue of women and wrote several essays on women's issues during the reformist debates of the nineteenth century. In these debates, Harishchandra, like other nationalist patriarchs, constructed a familial and social role for women that drew upon imagined ideas about women in an ancient pre-Muslim past—a past without evil practices such as female infanticide and dowry, in which the men treated women as equals and the women in return became learned and educated wives and mothers. This role "was an important constituent in the self-definition of the emergent middle class and the resuscitation of the Hindu tradition" and was to be aided by reinterpretations from Sanskrit literature and newly interpreted Pauranic models, which provided the script for the new Hindu woman.[63] Among these, Kalidasa's *Sakuntala* was to provide the ideal.[64]

In revealing these complex positions, Bharatendu's play offers an interesting paradox. On the one hand, even as it consolidates its own brand of Hinduism via Hindi, the space of the drama brings English literature, especially Shakespeare, into its fold and disseminates the authority of Shakespeare (as constructed and witnessed in British India since the nineteenth century) to the middle-class Hindu public. Translation into Hindi of a play by the most canonical playwright in English literature,[65] on the other hand, serves to raise the status of Hindi and privileges Hindu culture over that of Muslims. Harishchandra's ideological orientation reinforces his pro-Hindu position, which, in addition to fiercely advocating Hindi, assumes Muslims are potentially ruinous to Hindustan.[66]

Shakespeare and Urdu

What was the stance of the Urdu writers toward Shakespeare? While the translations are difficult to access, the summation by Mohammad Hassan in his article on Shakespeare in Urdu shows that Shakespeare was equally revered among the Urdu writers by the late nineteenth century. However, unlike some Hindi literary critics who were concerned with the language and its complexities in their assessment of Shakespearean translations, Hassan's commentary notes that the early-nineteenth-century translations were concerned mainly "with the twists and turns of the plot, and almost indifferent to the superb characterization and deep philosophic significance of Shakespeare's plays."[67] Yet, Aga Hashr (b. 1879) carefully adapted Shakespearean plays in his melodramatic poetic prose for the Cowasji Theatrical Company and later for his own theatrical company, formed in 1912, which he named the Indian

[handwritten marginalia: "recast as a class issue —"]

[handwritten marginalia: "Urdu Sh — closer to nee. of a popula..."]

Shakespeare Theatrical Company. He also, incidentally, came to be known as the "Indian Shakespeare," for his service in popularizing Urdu translations of Shakespeare drama. According to Hassan, Urdu translations/adaptations also changed the names of the plays and the locales according to local contexts. For the most part, the language remained colloquial in order to cater to the demands of the popular audiences, which included the nonliterate. Whether there was an underlying political motive to propagate the cause of Urdu is hard to discern from this little information and warrants a separate study. What is known is that by the 1920s, because of the interest of more "serious scholars" who paid careful attention to the language and focused on faithful translations, the language became more literate.[68] Literary institutions and publishing houses such as Anjuman Taraqqui-e-Urdu, which published Aziz Ahmad's translation of *Romeo and Juliet* in 1961, continued their efforts toward a more literary engagement with Shakespearean drama.[69]

Yet for all the efforts of the Urdu playwrights and writers, available accounts show that the Hindu literati frowned upon their translations. Harishchandra, for instance, found the Urdu productions by the Parsi theater "vulgar," and formed his own theater company as an alternative to those productions. Even critical studies of Shakespearean adaptations did not fully endorse the Urdu productions. In his detailed study of Shakespeare in India, R. K. Yajnik, for example, condemns an Urdu production of *The Comedy of Errors* for catering to "a less cultured audience," and says of the plot innovations in the play that they are a way to provoke "cheap laughter."[70] On the other hand, Yajnik praises a Marathi production of *A Midsummer Night's Dream* as being "remarkable" insofar as the "preface starts with a Sanskrit quotation which extols the enjoyment of pure poetry."[71] He praises most Marathi productions for their "Hindu touches," which "add to the beauty of the situations."[72] While Yajnik's comments reveal the divisions between high and low culture that crept into theater criticism, his praise of the Marathi productions, in contrast to his condemnation of the Urdu, clearly bears the traces of Hindu separatism.

Conclusion

In the struggle to elevate the status of Hindi with respect to English and its vernacular rival Urdu, literary criticism of Shakespeare, and translations and adaptations of his plays that apparently accommodated the existing valorization of Shakespeare, were not devoid of political connotation; rather, in the context of the vexed conflict of the vernaculars and the escalating aspirations of Hindi, the critical and translational enterprise acquired political dimensions that, while serving an anticolonial end, also worked out a manifestly Hindu culture of which Hindi language and literature were a composite part. Thus the essays, translations, and adaptations became a collective enterprise for the reflection and consolidation of Hindi language and literature and a Hindu sensibility. Shakespeare's texts provided the framework for a reassessment of the Hindi language, the past achievements of Hindu texts, as well as the position of the Hindu woman—all of which were inextricably linked and central to the emerging narrative of the Hindu nation. With Shakespeare as the frame of reference, the literati forged a sense of past achievement in recuperating, for example, Kalidasa as the "Indian Shakespeare." And by attaching the lineage of Hindi to this past (recuperated in the imperialist authority of Shakespeare), writers and thinkers attempted to forge a new social and political awareness of the importance of Hindi language and literature. In other words, recuperating Hindi as the national language involved the authority of an author whose introduction into the literary curriculum in India bore the ideological underpinnings of imperial authority.

Thus, the literary-critical space accorded to Shakespeare for the articulation of Hindu nationalist aspirations is somewhat of a paradox. For proponents of Hindi, the affirmation of the greatness of Hindi language through Shakespeare elevated its literary and linguistic status and gave "Hindi" a modern edge. The flip side of the paradox was that it simultaneously validated the symbolic authority of Shakespeare and affirmed India's subjection to colonial rule. As well, the translations and adaptations were to have important consequences for the critical reception of Shakespeare in India. Drawn to raise the stature of Hindi and Hindu culture, parallels with ancient Hindu texts and translations of Shakespeare's plays into Sanskrit shaped literary criticism and thought in ways that reinforced the iconic image of Shakespeare. This is reflected in a comment by J. P. Mishra, who in 1970 attributed the Indians' understanding of their "own ancient classical lore" to "the intrinsic merit of . . . [Shakespeare's] works."[73] Similarly, in 1976, Henry Wells contended that "whoever has sympathetically and intensively studied Shakespeare's plays will be in a more advantageous position to understand and enjoy the Sanskrit drama than anyone who has not."[74] And in the introduction to a 1978 study entitled *The Tragicomedies of Shakespeare, Kalidasa, and Bhavabhuti*, P. B. Acharya claims: "If I were to be asked the question, 'what books of literature have moved you most?' my immediate response would be. . . . 'The plays of Shakespeare and Kalidasa's *Sakuntala* . . . in Sanskrit.'"[75]

Such authority accorded to Shakespeare survives powerfully into the present. With the increasing global hegemony of English and its status as a language that guarantees ruling-class power in postcolonial India, Shakespeare, as a representative of "English literary classics," continues to dominate the English departments.[76] According to Harish Trivedi, an analysis of a sample syllabus for a master's degree in English, undertaken by the Curriculum Development Center under sponsorship from the University Grants Commission of India, found Shakespeare to be "the most heavily canonized of all English authors, a largely unquestioned and abiding traditional preference underlined by the comparatively small weightage given to a new and avowedly post-colonial course such as the one on Indian writing in English."[77] However, despite the continuing preference for Shakespeare and English studies in education, the bard remains a basis for incompatible nationalist claims. That criticism in postcolonial India resorted to the authority of Shakespeare to elevate the position of Hindi is evident in a statement made by critic and translator Rangeya Raghava at the height of national consciousness soon after the linguistic division of the nation in the 1950s: "A Language that does not possess translations of Shakespeare cannot be counted among the more developed languages."[78] On the other hand, the Sahitya Akademy's (Academy of Literature's) commissioning of translations of Shakespearean plays by a canonical Hindi writer, Harivansh Rai Bachchan, whose passages were written alternately in Hindi and Urdu, may be seen as a way of resolving the linguistic controversy that had continued into the 1960s and emphasizing the spirit of secularism that constituted the mainstay of Nehruvian ideology at this time.[79] The discourses of power that the empire had allocated to Shakespeare in colonial India and that "English Language Teaching" in postcolonial India continues, then, find themselves subjected to continual negotiation.

NOTES

All translations from Hindi are my own.

1. For a discussion of readings of Sakuntala in changing historical contexts, see Romila Thapar, *Sakuntala: Texts, Readings, Histories* (Delhi: Kali for Women, 1999).

2. Paul Brass, *Language, Religion, and Politics in North India* (Cambridge: Cambridge University Press, 1974), 29.

3. Gyan Prakash, "The Modern Nation's Return in the Archaic," *Critical Inquiry* 21.3 (1997): 538.

4. For a detailed and powerful reading, see Vasudha Dalmia, *The Nationalization of Hindu Traditions: Bharatendu Harishchandra and Nineteenth-Century Banaras* (Delhi: Oxford University Press, 1997).

5. In the 1870s, Shakespearean plays began to be translated and adapted into several Indian languages as well as produced for the Bengali, Urdu, Gujarati, and Marathi stage. Hindi alone, surmises Harish Trivedi, in "Shakespeare in India: Colonial Contexts," in *Colonial Transactions: English Literature in India* (Manchester: Manchester University Press, 1995), 16, saw "over seventy

full-length translations and adaptations and over one hundred further abridgements and narrative renderings of his plays."

6. Ibid., 14. Trivedi argues that this response seems to be a direct reaction to William Miller (1838–1923), an Englishman who taught Shakespeare to college students in South India and published commentaries on Shakespeare's tragedies. His books *King Lear and Indian Politics* (1900), *Macbeth and the Ruin of Souls* (1901), *Othello and the Crash of Character* (1901), and *Hamlet and the Waste of Life* (1902) are all, according to Trivedi, studies that value Shakespeare for his "realistic-psychological characterization." Further, argues Trivedi, "Miller's practical and literal-minded deployment of Shakespeare as a stern pedagogic device for colonial character-building comes through clearly in the very title of a collected edition of all his above volumes: *Shakespeare's Chart of Life* (1905)."

7. In the case of Dutt, for instance, says Trivedi, the "impulse behind this painstaking patriotic procedure was summed up in a Sanskrit couplet epigraphically cited by Dutt in one of his prefaces: 'Slavery enforced by brute force is degrading enough, Your Majesty! / But slavery of the mind is truly a hundred times more deplorable,'" Trivedi, "Shakespeare in India," 14.

8. Ibid., 18.

9. Ibid., 14.

10. As Trivedi, "Shakespeare in India," 16, himself acknowledges, attitudes toward Shakespeare were wide-ranging, varying "from eager adoption and assimilation on the one hand to what may be called literary subversion on the other, with many moderate shades represented in between." An extreme example of such laudatory criticism is in the work of Lala Sitaram (1861–1937), a civil servant with a degree from Calcutta University, who translated six plays of Shakespeare into Urdu and fourteen into Hindi. In one of his prefaces he wrote: "An attempt to publish a translation of Shakespeare, the chief glory of English literature, does not stand in need of any apology. . . . Need I then say that an English drama has value for my countrymen as throwing a flood of light on the social customs and modes of thoughts of those whom Providence, in His Infinite Goodness, has been pleased to place in authority over us?" (cited in ibid., 17–18).

11. Gauri Viswanathan, *Masks of Conquest* (see Further Reading, page 257), 3.

12. Ibid., 134.

13. For a detailed discussion of the Orientalist-versus-Anglicist debate, see ibid.

14. Jyotsna Singh, "Different Shakespeares: The Bard in Colonial/Postcolonial India," *Theatre Journal* 41 (1989): 446.

15. For a detailed account of vernacular Shakespearean performances in western India, see R. K. Yajnik, *The Indian Theatre: Its Origin and Its Later Development Under European Influence* (New York: E. P. Dutton & Co., 1934). For an account of Shakespeare in Bengali, see Prabhucharan Guha-Thakurta, *The Bengali Drama: Its Origins and Development* (London: Kegan Paul, Trench, Trubner & Co., 1930; reprint, Westport, Conn.: Greenwood Press, 1974); S. K. Bhattacharya, "Shakespeare and Bengali Theatre," *Indian Literature* 7.1 (1964): 27–40; and Sushil Mukherjee Sushil, *The Story of the Calcutta Theatres: 1753–1980* (Calcutta: K. P. Bagchi & Co., 1982). For a discussion of Shakespeare in Hindi, see Trivedi, "Shakespeare in India," and Suresh Avasthi, "Shakespeare in Hindi," *Indian Literature* 7.1 (1964): 51–62.

16. Christopher King, *One Language, Two Scripts* (see Further Reading), 92.

17. Ibid., 93.

18. Cited in ibid., 94.

19. Paul Brass (*Language, Religion, and Politics in North India*) describes India as a nation where Hindi is spoken by a large minority of the people and accepted as an official language but where English, a foreign language, is also deployed for official purposes, as are a dozen other languages that are used regionally and spoken by large numbers.

20. King, *One Language, Two Scripts*, 88.

21. For a discussion of the Press Acts, see Gerald N. Barrier, *Banned: Controversial Literature and*

Political Control in British India, 1907–1947 (Columbia: University of Missouri Press, 1974); for a discussion of the Dramatic Performances Censorship Act, see P. K. Bhattacharyya, *Shadow over Stage* (Calcutta: Barnali, 1989).

22. Amrit Rai, *A House Divided: The Origin and Development of Hindi/Hindavi* (Delhi: Oxford University Press, 1984). General consensus among scholars is that the word "Urdu" for the language dates back to 1776, in the works of the poet Mashaji (1750–1824).

23. It is simplistic to assume that the Hindi-Urdu controversy was entirely the work of the colonizers; however, the following comment by John B. Gilchrist from *The Oriental Linguist* indicates that he, anyway, certainly escalated existing divisions: "Hinduwee I have treated as the exclusive property of the Hindoos alone and have therefore constantly applied it to the old language of India, which prevailed before the moosulman invasions and in fact now constitutes among them the basis or groundwork of the Hindoostanee, a comparatively recent superstructure composed of Arabic and Persian" (cited in ibid., 2).

24. The distinction made between Hindu and Urdu can be identified in the following text from a letter that Hindi professor William Price wrote to the secretary of the college council, Captain D. Riddel: "The great difference between Hindee and Hindustanee consists in the words, those of the former being almost all in Sanskrit, and those of the latter being for the great part Persian and Arabic. . . . Another important difference is the character of Hindee, to be correctly expressed, must be written in Nagari letters; the Persian alphabet, when applied to any work in which Sanskrit predominates, forming words that are quite unintelligible" (cited in ibid., 16). See also David Lelyveld, "The Fate of Hindustani: Colonial Knowledge and the Project of a National Language," in *Orientalism and the Postcolonial Predicament: Perspectives on South Asia,* ed. Carol Breckenridge and Peter van der Veer (Philadelphia: University of Pennsylvania Press, 1993), 189–214.

25. For a detailed and powerful discussion of how Hindi came to be identified as the language of the Hindus despite existing overlaps with Urdu, see Dalmia, *Nationalization of Hindu Traditions.*

26. Ibid., 146. For an in-depth understanding of the complex linguistic situation in the nineteenth century and the ways in which Hindi came to be identified as the language of the Hindus, see chap. 4, "Hindi as the National Language of the Hindus," in ibid.

27. In postcolonial India, Hindu revivalist organizations devoted to the dissemination of Hindi and its adoption as the official national language continue to identify the Hindi-speaking heartland (concentrated in the northern states of Uttar Pradesh, Madhya Pradesh, Harayana, and Bihar) with a Hindu nation. For more information, see Brass, *Language, Religion, and Politics in North India.*

28. According to Jyotirindra Das Gupta, *Language Conflict and National Development* (see Further Reading), 83, within the Hindi area, the Nagari Pracharini Sabha, founded in Banaras in 1893, and the Hindi Sahitya Sammelan, founded in Allahabad in 1910, became the most significant organizations for propagating Hindi.

29. See ibid.; King, *One Language, Two Scripts.*

30. Premchand, *Kuch vichar* (Some thoughts) (New Delhi: Diamond Pocket Books, n.d.), consists of three essays out of eleven on the issue of Hindi. The first one is tiled "Urdu, Hindi or Hindustani" (Urdu, Hindi, and Hindustani, 105–18); the next one, titled "Rashtrabhasha, Hindi aur uski samasyaen" (National language, Hindi, and its problems, 119–40), was addressed on December 24, 1934, to the Dakshin Bharat Hindi-Prachar Sabha (South Indian Society for the Propagation of Hindi); and the last, "Quami bhasha ke vishay mein kuch vichaar: Bhasha hi rashtra ki buniyaad hai" (Some thoughts on the subject of community language: Language is the foundation of the nation, 141–60), was the text of a welcome address on October 27, 1934, for the Rashra Bhasha Sammelan (National Language Conference).

31. Sumit Sarkar, *Modern India* (Delhi: Macmillan, 1981), 85.

32. See Dalmia, *Nationalization of Hindu Traditions.*

33. Ibid., 224.

34. Ibid., 225. Hinduness, as Dalmia observes, came to be defined both against Western culture as well against Islam.

35. F. Max Müller, *A History of Ancient Sanskrit Literature So Far As It Illustrates the Primitive Religion of the Brahmans* (London: Williams & Norgate, 1859), 2–3. Cited in Vinay Dharwadker, "Orientalism and the Study of Indian Literatures," in *Orientalism and the Postcolonial Predicament: Perspectives on South Asia,* ed. Carol Breckenridge and Peter van der Veer (Philadelphia: University of Pennsylvania Press, 1993), 176.

36. Dalmia, *Nationalization of Hindu Traditions,* 222.

37. Ibid., 223.

38. Ibid., 224.

39. Ibid.

40. V[enkatarama] Raghavan, "Shakespeare in Sanskrit," *Indian Literature* 7.1 (1964): 110. According to Raghavan, one scholar translated *Cymbeline* as *Sribalacarita* in volume 21. Other adaptations of Shakespeare's works in Sanskrit included P. L. Vaidya's *Vijayini.* A number of other works appeared about the same time: Rajaraja Verma wrote a prose version of *Othello* under the Sanskritized title *Uddalkacarita. Bharativilasa,* an adaptation of *The Comedy of Errors,* appeared in 1877 from Madras. In 1933, M. Venkataramanacarya published a Sanskrit version of Charles Lamb's *Tales from Shakespeare* entitled *Shakespeare-Nataka-Kathavali.* In 1924, P. V. Ramchandra published a collection of poems called *Laghu Kavya* (Malika series no. 2), which included passages from *As You Like It* and *Hamlet.* In the same year, Pandurang Mahadev Oko of Poona, a Marathi Sanskritist, published a book of quotations of wisdom, of which twenty-seven were taken from Shakespeare. In 1925, J. V. Kulkarni of Dhulia brought out an anthology of parallel quotations, which contained passages from Shakespeare. The theme of caste distinctions in Hindu society was played out in R. Krishnamacharya's *Vasanti Karvanpana,* an adaptation of *A Midsummer Night's Dream* (1892) in which the lower-class characters speak Prakrit (the language of the commoners).

41. Raghavan, "Shakespeare in Sanskrit," 109.

42. Ibid.

43. In *Siting Translation: History, Post-Structuralism, and the Colonial Context* (Berkeley and Los Angeles: University of California Press, 1992), Tejsawini Niranjana examines William Jones's translation of *Sakuntala* (among other works) "to show how he contributes to a historicist, teleological model of civilization that, coupled with a notion of translation presupposing transparency of representation, helps construct a powerful version of the 'Hindu' that later writers of different philosophical and political persuasions incorporated into their texts in an almost seamless fashion" (13). She subsequently discusses the influence of Jones's translation of *Sakuntala* on James Mill's *History of British India,* in which the author derives evidence about Indian history and laws from the play *Sakuntala.* "History" says Niranjana, "is dismissed as fiction, but fiction—translated—is admissible as history" (25).

44. Thapar, *Sakuntala,* 198.

45. "Wilson's Hindu Theatre," *Asiatic Journal* (1835): 110.

46. See J. P. Mishra, *Shakespeare's Impact on Hindi Literature* (New Delhi: Munshi Manoharlal, 1970), for details.

47. *Sarasvati* 16.1 (March 1915).

48. *Sarasvati* 25.1, no. 3 (March 1940): 291.

49. *Sarasvati* 8.2 (February 1907).

50. *Sarasvati* 61.1 (March 1915): 189.

51. *Sarasvati* 16.1, no. 3 (March 1915): 178.

52. *Sarasvati* 16.1, no. 3 (March 1915): 180.

53. Such was the impact of these critiques that even Captain Richardson, a teacher at the prestigious Hindu College at Calcutta, proclaimed that Shakespeare must have been a Hindu because Desdemona is like "a typical Hindu wife."

54. Bharatendu Harishchandra, *Durlabh Bandhu*, in *Bharatendu Granthavali*, ed. Shivaprashad Mishra (Varanasi: Nagaripracharini Sabha, 1974).

55. See, for instance, the mythological plays of Radheyshyam Kathavachak (in the early twentieth century), who under the guise of mythological drama attacked British colonizers as well as propagated the cause of Hindi.

56. His journal *Balabodhini* (1874–78) became a public forum for literary Hindi and established his reputation as *acharya*, or master, of Hindi. For a full discussion of the journal, see Dalmia, *Nationalization of Hindu Traditions*, 135.

57. Ibid., 335.

58. Ibid., 313.

59. According to Dalmia, despite Harishchandra's contribution to, and efforts to activate, a sociopolitical drama, the momentum in the Hindi region, relative to that in others, was stalled. This could be a result, in part, of the Dramatic Performances Censorship Act passed by the British government in 1876. However, says Dalmia, the dramatic texts by Harishchandra point out "overriding concerns and tensions: the need to establish theatre as a public forum, as an arena where the heterogeneous elements which were ultimately to form the middle class, could consolidate and voice their national identity, defined against the interests of the British and their princely allies." Ibid., 313 n. 92.

60. King, *One Language, Two Scripts*, 177.

61. Dalmia, *Nationalization of Hindu Traditions*, 242.

62. For the construction of the "new woman," see Partha Chatterjee, "Nationalism, Colonialism, and Colonized Women: The Contest in India," *American Ethnologist* 16.4 (1998): 622–33.

63. Dalmia, *Nationalization of Hindu Traditions*, 315. For a discussion of the construction of the Hindu woman in the nineteenth century, see also Chatterjee, "Nationalism, Colonialism, and Colonized Women," and Uma Chakravorty, "Whatever Happened to the Vedic Dasi? Orientalism, Nationalism, and a Script for the Past," in *Recasting Women: Essays in Colonial History*, ed. Kumkum Sangari and Sudesh Vaid (Delhi: Kali for Women, 1989), 27–87.

64. For an excellent discussion of the various interpretations of Kalidasa, see Thapar, *Sakuntala*.

65. As Dalmia, *Nationalization of Hindu Traditions*, 97, asserts, English, as the national language of the British, from this time forward "was to increasingly acquire a model function."

66. For a detailed discussion, see ibid.

67. Mohammad Hassan, "Shakespeare in Urdu," *Indian Literature* 7.1 (1964): 132.

68. According to Hassan, of note is Inayatullah Dehlavi's translation of *Hamlet* entitled *Denmark ka Shahzada*.

69. The Sahitya Akademi published Majnoon Gorakhpur's translation of *King Lear* in 1963. According to Hassan, "Shakespeare in Urdu," 137, "Shakespeare . . . has remained a fountain-head of inspiration and guidance to the Urdu Stage."

70. Yajnik, *The Indian Theatre*, 130.

71. Ibid., 131.

72. Ibid., 142. In commenting on a Marathi version of *The Taming of the Shrew*, Yajnik tells his readers that "it is claimed to be such as perfect stage version that even if Shakespeare were a Hindu, he could not have improved upon it" (135).

73. Mishra, *Shakespeare's Impact on Hindi Literature*, v.

74. Henry H. Wells and Anniah Gowda, *Shakespeare Turned East: A Study in Comparison of Shakespeare's Last Plays in India* (Mysore, Karnā(taka: University of Mysore, 1976), 9.

75. P. B. Acharya, *The Tragicomedies of Shakespeare, Kalidasa, and Bhavabhuti* (New Delhi: Meherchand Lachhmandas, 1978).

76. For statistical information on the total number of students studying English Honours at Delhi University in comparison to the number of students for Hindi literature (Honours), Panjabi,

Bengali, Urdu, Arabic, and Persian, see Trivedi, "Shakespeare in India." For more information on how Shakespeare is taught in the academy in India, see also Ania Loomba, *Gender, Race, and Renaissance Drama* (Manchester: Manchester University Press, 1989).

77. Trivedi, "Shakespeare in India," 21.

78. In 1957–58 Raghava published fifteen translations of Shakespeare in Hindi.

79. Bachchan's plays were performed in Delhi and attended by the prime minister, Jawaharlal Nehru. See Bachchan's *Macbeth* and *Othello* in *Bachchan Rachnavali* (Delhi: Prabhat Offset Press, 1983).

Poets Laureate and the Language of Slaves

Petrarch, Chaucer, and Langston Hughes

LARRY SCANLON

The Vernacular: A Brief Manifesto

Despite its Latin origins, the *vernacular* is itself a vernacular category. That is, the wide, informal use of the term in humanistic scholarship makes it an example of the phenomena it describes. Of varying importance across a variety of fields—art history and the history of architecture, folklore, history, the history of science, linguistics, literary studies, and musicology—the term belongs to no one of them in particular and possesses no consistent definition. Linguistics might have the best historical claim, inasmuch as one can trace the term's application to language study at least as far back as Varro's *De lingua Latina* (47–45 B.C.). Yet, perhaps because of this antiquity, modern linguistics has shown little interest in a precise definition. Thus, John Rickford, in his magisterial survey, *African American Vernacular English,* draws his definition of the term not from previous linguistics scholarship but the *American Heritage Dictionary.*[1] Indeed, it is difficult to find a systematic account of the term in any field; nor does there seem much awareness or interest in a particular field in the term's function in others. Instead, "vernacular" seems to mark a place where disciplines allow themselves to become a bit less than systematic, less than disciplined, where they aspire to speak of what lies beyond them, the unlearned, the predisciplinary, or nondisciplinary, or antidisciplinary, and not only to speak of it but to speak for it, to get beyond their own learned boundaries and speak from it and with it. Such transcendent aspirations no doubt conflict with the ideal of scholarly detachment that motivates most modern disciplines, but scholarly detachment is itself no simple matter, and one of the most effective ways to demonstrate a discipline's boundaries is by continually retesting them.

Literary studies in English, where the notion of the vernacular has stimulated some extremely innovative and compelling work in the past two decades, provides a notable measure of such complexity. Strikingly this work has not been equally distributed across the discipline. Instead, it has been concentrated in two subfields. One of them is the discipline's most traditional, Middle English. The other is one of its newest, African-American.[2] Given the obvious dissimilarities between these two subfields, what is most surprising about this trend is the similarities underlying its emergence in both of them, particularly when one recognizes it emerged in each in almost complete isolation from its emergence in the other. The similarities are both methodological and thematic. In both cases, literary scholars drew on the authority of linguistics, a discipline literary studies has traditionally viewed as more rigorous than itself. Medievalists were returning to their field's foundational dependence on historical linguistics; African-Americanists were responding to the emergence of sociolinguistics and its most signal achievement: the identification and analysis of the Black English Vernacular, or African-American English Vernacular, as it has more latterly come to be called. In both cases, these scholars correctly understood themselves to be defending a vernacular against the hostility of a previous critical tradition. Medievalists were offering critiques of the hegemony of Robertsonian criticism, or Patristics, as it was sometimes called, which held that Augustinian theology, and therefore Latin clerical tradition, was the determinant force behind all Middle English literature. African-Americanists were confronting a deeper and more general problem: the continuing skepticism of a dominant white tradition regarding the autonomy and sophistication of African-American traditions. (I should note in passing that this skepticism has substantially collapsed, largely as a result of the work of these scholars.) Finally, in both cases, the scholarship was driven by the same underlying assumptions about the vernacular as a category: that the vernacular is autonomous and self-sufficient, and that because of such autonomy it is inherently subversive. As the estimable Russell Hope Robbins declared in 1979: "Middle English itself, by its very existence, advocated dissent . . . to break away from Latin and French and use English was a major act of rebellion . . . the vernacular destroyed the intellectual and political control of the aristocrats of church and state."[3] It is true that few, if any, subsequent scholars in either field express these assumptions quite this categorically. Nevertheless, their general currency, no matter how carefully qualified in individual instances, makes them worth a second look.

The shortcomings of these assumptions become particularly evident if one tries to reconcile their operation in one field with their operation in the other. We might well ask how the vernacular tradition that emerged in Britain at the end of the fourteenth century could be inherently subversive in its own time and also provide the historical source of hegemony against which the African-American vernacular tradition later struggled. As Alison Cornish notes, regarding one aspect of the literary emergence of European vernaculars: "although the authoritative text in late medieval and early modern translation was indeed moved from the old imperial language (Latin) into common speech, this translation was done for the sake of those in positions of secular authority."[4] On the other hand, if we dismiss late medieval vernacularization as a false dawn, as the consolidation of a hegemony against which real vernacular subversion emerges only in the nineteenth and twentieth centuries, we risk oversimplifying the language politics not only of the later Middle Ages but of the more recent period as well. If recent scholarship has made it clear that African-American literature has had a generally subversive relation to a more dominant tradition, recent scholarship has also made it clear that late medieval vernaculars could be equally subversive in specific instances. Here we might cite the wealth of recent work on the Lollard heresy or Nicholas Watson's powerful readings of advocacy for universal salvation in William Langland and Julian of Norwich.[5]

One way out of this dilemma would be to argue that the subversiveness of a given vernacular is not an inherent quality at all, but is instead entirely dependent on the historical particulars surrounding its deployment. Such a solution would mandate an exclusively synchronic approach to the problem of vernaculars, conforming to the boundaries of historical periodization— arguably the discipline's single most powerful institutional structure— encouraging medievalist and African-Americanist alike to stay on their own patch and not to concern themselves with the discipline as a whole. Indeed, there is no gainsaying the power and importance of periodization. In recent decades, it has proved of particular benefit to these two fields: in the case of African-American studies, enabling it to map and document the African-American tradition and begin to establish its integrity and importance; in the case of Middle English studies, to recover dissident and peripheral voices long ignored. Nevertheless, for all of its success, such synchronic scholarship cannot continue indefinitely without some reference to the diachronic or it will vitiate the very specificity from which it draws its explanatory power. Thus in this case we have two disparate subfields claiming similarly unique moments of vernacular liberation in two very different historical contexts.

In what follows, I make an alternate suggestion, that the real problem with current assumptions about the vernacular has to do not with the question of its subversiveness, but its putative self-sufficiency. In contrast to the current ideal, I argue that incompletion is the sign of the vernacular, an incompleteness it embraces and proclaims. Moreover, vernacular subversion depends on this incompleteness, for it is precisely the vernacular's self-proclaimed incompleteness that gives it the syncretic power to appropriate and redefine other traditions, whether dominant or not. To demonstrate this point, I focus on the notion of the poet laureate. Geoffrey Chaucer, under the influence of Petrarch, introduces this term into the language. The African-American tradition returns to it to define its own greatest poet, Langston Hughes. The persistence of this term in Anglophone literary culture from the end of the fourteenth century to the present makes it a useful shorthand for a vernacular desire for a source of poetic authority beyond itself. In tracing the trajectory of this desire from the later Middle Ages to Hughes I am interested not only in what it offers the modern poet but also in the way his poetry illuminates the entire tradition. Accordingly, the second half of the essay is devoted to an analysis of *ASK YOUR MAMA,* Hughes's "most ambitious single poem" and one of his most sustained meditations on the interdependence between poetic tradition and African-American vernacular culture.[6]

The trajectory from Chaucer to Hughes should also encourage us to reconsider the relation between literary studies and linguistics. Modern linguistics takes as its proper object "the spoken word alone."[7] As Leonard Bloomfield declared, "Writing is not language, but merely a way of recording language."[8] Obviously, this claim expresses a certain suspicion of the literary, a suspicion that investigations of the vernacular necessarily highlight. Thus, Rickford's dictionary definition reads: "the everyday {and informal] language spoken by a people as distinguished from the literary language" (brackets in original).[9] Taken literally, this definition would make a vernacular literature a contradiction in terms. Moreover, the principle from which it flows (i.e., that the spoken language is linguistic study's only proper object) banishes to an uncertain hinterland learned innovations like Chaucer's.[10] Nevertheless, for all of its scientific pretensions, this principle has itself a long literary pedigree. Its articulation in Ferdinand de Saussure, Leonard Bloomfield, and others can be traced back to ideals of natural language in Romantic and proto-Romantic thinkers like Condillac, Diderot, Herder, and the Scots rhetorician Hugh Blair.[11] The most famous expression of that ideal in English can be found in the preface to *Lyrical Ballads,* where Wordsworth declares his poetry to be selected from "the language of real men."[12]

"Poet laureate" straddles the standard divide in historical linguistics between the exterior and interior histories of the language. As a new lexical item, it belongs to the interior history. At the same time, as the innovation of the culture's leading poet, it also constitutes an authoritative exterior commentary, especially since it will inaugurate a critical tradition that increasingly associates the authority of the English vernacular with poetic achievement. Fifteenth-century praise of Chaucer typically presented him as the refiner of the native tongue, "the firste fyndere of our faire langage," in the words of

linguistic
tables spoken
words

one of his earliest disciples.[13] By the turn of the seventeenth century, the claim that through the accomplishments of its poets English had earned a place of distinction among both Latin and the other modern vernaculars had become a critical commonplace.[14] This view of linguistic reality is nearly antithetical to the synchronic, structural concerns of modern linguistics, yet no account of the history of English would be complete without it. How much more crucial might the laureateship of Langston Hughes be to a vernacular whose institutional support has been confined almost exclusively to its cultural traditions?

What is at stake here is not simply the difference between linguistic objects, the everyday and informal as against the literary, but also the difference between methods of approach, the synchronic as against the diachronic. Modern linguistics understands the spoken language it takes as its primary object in predominantly synchronic terms: as a set of structures interrelating in the undifferentiated present of Chomsky's "ideal speaker-listener."[15] As an alternative to the ideal structures of theoretical and formal linguistics, sociolinguistics offers "a systematic survey of real speech in its social context."[16] Yet this alternative is itself defined in primarily synchronic terms—no doubt necessarily so, inasmuch as one of the field's greatest achievements is its careful delimitation and analysis of speech communities through extensive tape-recorded interviews. While this synchronic methodology can certainly be supplemented by the more traditional diachronic methods of historical linguistics,[17] a conceptual problem remains. Because synchronic approaches achieve their systematicity by bracketing the diachronic, they have difficulty returning to such questions in other than the initial terms. For this reason, the diachronic can never be fully incorporated or fully escaped.

No one expresses this dilemma more memorably than Ferdinand de Saussure himself, the originator of linguistics' turn to the synchronic. On the problem of language change, he notes, "At any time, a language belongs to all its users. It is a facility unrestrictedly available throughout the whole community." This fact distinguishes it from all "other social institutions": it "is something in which everyone participates, and that is why it is constantly open to the influence of all." Yet paradoxically, this radically democratic condition produces a certain conservatism. Because everyone has a stake in it, everyone has a stake in preserving it: "It is part and parcel of the life of the whole community, and the community's natural inertia exercises a conservative influence upon it." As he goes on to explain, this "inertia" is only measurable over time:

> None the less, to say that a language is a product of social forces does not automatically explain why it comes to be constrained in the way

*object of
study*

it is. Bearing in mind that a language is always an inheritance from the past, one must add that the social forces in question act over a period of time. If stability is a characteristic of languages, it is not only because languages are anchored in the community. They are also anchored in time. The two facts are inseparable. Continuity with the past constantly restricts freedom of choice. If the Frenchman of today uses words like *homme* ("man") and *chien* ("dog"), it is because these words were used by his forefathers. Ultimately there is a connexion between these two opposing factors: the arbitrary convention which allows free choice, and the passage of time, which fixes that choice. It is because the linguistic sign is arbitrary that it knows no other law than that of tradition, and because it is founded upon tradition that it can be arbitrary.[18]

The radical, synchronic claim with which Saussure begins, "At any rate, a language belongs to all its users," is balanced against the diachronic one with which he ends, "It is because the linguistic sign is arbitrary that it knows no other law than that of tradition, and because it is founded upon tradition that it can be arbitrary." He can cast his synchronic view of language in such radical terms only by referring all questions of historical specificity to the diachronic constraint of "tradition." Beginning from this radical premise, one can differentiate speech communities only on the basis of their differing traditions. One must determine how, over time, certain users acquire more influence than others. While the most obvious way to do this is by tracking the power one community may acquire over another, one loses some of the force of the initial premise if the dynamics of tradition are ascribed solely to such extralinguistic relations. Contradictory as it may seem, if we are to grant that at any given time any language is equally available to all of its users, we are simultaneously committed to the proposition that even as a purely linguistic matter certain users become more influential than others. Clearly, such differentiation could involve groups of users, rather than individuals—an obvious example would be adolescent speech in the United States and other current Western societies. But it must also involve certain types of individuals as well, of which poets (and writers generally) would provide a leading instance. It may not ever be possible to reconcile the methodological rigors of sociolinguistics with the ostensibly archaic view that poets are refiners of the vernacular. But surely there would be much to be gained from a linguistic as well as a literary perspective in regarding them as particularly authoritative native informants.

Langston Hughes is easily the most critically neglected of all major modern American poets. His work offers an especially rich resource for reflection on

verna –
slave

African-American vernacular culture, for the relation between that vernacular and poetic tradition was one of the defining concerns of his entire career. Moreover, this fact alone makes Hughes a crucial authority on the vernacular in Anglophone culture generally—leaving aside the question of his own considerable genius. The African-American literary tradition is the first Anglophone tradition to originate in a condition of enslavement. By a weird and sobering irony, applying "vernacular" to that tradition literally returns the term to its original Latin roots. Houston A. Baker Jr. dramatizes this irony in the first epigraph to *Blues, Ideology, and Afro-American Literature: A Vernacular Theory* with a dictionary entry for vernacular. It offers two senses:

> *Of a slave:* That is born on his master's estate; home-born
> *Of arts, or features of these:* Native or peculiar to a particular country or locality[19]

As Baker will make abundantly clear, the vernacular cannot be analyzed absent its implication in relations of power. While it designates the local, what it designates in the local is precisely the point where it is disrupted by these power relations. The Roman slave was by birth or ancestry a foreign element introduced into the household and necessary to its constitution; he or she embodied a household's imbrication with Rome's imperial might. The *verna,* the Roman-born slave, embodies at once a local household's imperial power of appropriation and its continuing dependence on the foreign. The African-American vernacular, summed up for Baker in "the rhythms of Afro-American blues," provides a neat mirror image. Like the *verna,* it is indigenous but not integrated; from its engagement with the "material conditions of slavery in the United States" it emerges as "an ancestral matrix that has produced a forceful and indigenous American creativity."[20] Baker's recourse to the dictionary definition, that most traditional resource of nineteenth-century philology, demonstrates that the spirit of philology lives even in vanguardist political and poststructuralist criticism, and with it the conviction that a culture's ideological boundaries can be traced in the meanings of its words. If the African-American tradition is the first in English that can claim literally to be vernacular, associations between language and slavery have been an important, if occasional, feature of the term's long history. For example, while Varro shows no explicit interest in the word's etymological association with slavery, in his introductory discussion of inflection he twice appeals to the management of household slaves for an analogy to the linguistic generation of nouns. More immediately relevant to our purposes is a passage by Richard Mulcaster from *The First Part of the Elementarie,* his 1582 introduction to the English language. Writing at a time when the authority of the vernacular was a particular critical concern, Mulcaster was one of its most vigorous apologists: "For is it not in dede a mervellous bondage, to becom servants to one tung for learning sake, the most of our time, with losse of most time, whereas we maie have the verie same treasur in our own tung, with the gain of most time? our own bearing the joyfull title of our libertie and fredom, the Latin tung remembring us of our thraldom and bondage?"[21] Mulcaster argues somewhat later for the naturalization of foreign neologisms as appropriate to "a conquering mind." It seems clear his work participates in the protoimperialist discourse prevalent in England in the last two decades of the sixteenth century, which Jeffrey Knapp has convincingly demonstrated forms an important intellectual context for the first book of *The Faerie Queene*.[22] That makes Mulcaster's metaphors of enslavement even more striking. For they occur as part of a position that is clearly antecedent to the modern ideal of the vernacular as self-sufficient, and they reveal a certain will to dominance. Mulcaster presents the vernacular's Latin master as pure excrescence, but he can do so only because the enslavement is purely metaphorical. English is not disempowered; it already possesses the power it mistakenly ascribes to Latin; it needs only to recognize this power it already possesses. Thralldom and bondage become a matter of pure moral choice.

This analysis no doubt strikes some readers as too functionalist, if not downright cynical and unfair to Mulcaster. Nevertheless, even if I am wrong about the imperialist implications of this passage, we still have to come to terms with the excessiveness of its enslavement metaphors. Why should one who is not enslaved describe himself as if he were? What is the nature and significance of this desire to identify with the slave? The relevance of these questions is not restricted to Mulcaster, or even to the ideal of vernacular self-sufficiency he anticipates. It encompasses the issue of the vernacular in its entirety. "Vernacular" is an affirmative term, and that makes it unusual, if not unique, among words in English with etymological connections to slavery or legal disenfranchisement. To cite for contrast: "churlish," "slavish," "servile," "vile," "villain," "villainous." What appropriations, admissions, and contradictions may be hidden in the metaphorical extension of enslavement to cultural traditions that did not actually issue from enslaved or disenfranchised conditions? On the other hand, where the term has masked a dominant desire to appropriate the subaltern, to what extent has that very appropriation proved enabling to subsequent forms of subaltern resistance? One of the most striking features of the "forceful and indigenous . . . creativity" of the African-American tradition has been its appropriation and redefinition of contradictory elements of traditions hostile to it. As I shall argue, in his quasi-official laureateship Langston Hughes not only annexed to African-American poetry a structure of vernacular desire the Anglo-American tradition had treated as its own, he also redeemed that structure, revealing in it a vitality the dominant tradition had long since ceased to recognize. Baker follows his dictionary definition with another epigraph drawn from a traditional blues lyric:

> If you see me coming, better open up your door,
> If you see me coming, better open up your door,
> I ain't no stranger, I been here before.[23]

The Poet Laureate: A Brief Genealogy

Hughes's proverbial status as "Poet Laureate of the Negro Race" emerged early in his career and has endured ever since, both among scholars and the more general reading public. To cite three representative instances and one variant: Henry Louis Gates and Anthony Appiah use the term in the introduction to a recent collection of Hughes's criticism,[24] as does Arnold Rampersad, in the introduction to his definitive edition of Hughes's poetry, and *The Norton Anthology of African-American Literature*, which appeared in 1997.[25] A year earlier, the *New York Daily News*, in its roundup of activities in the New York area for Black History Month, touted the annual Langston Hughes Day celebration at Queens Library by terming him the "Poet Laureate of the Harlem Renaissance."[26]

This Latinate survival may seem at once idiosyncratic and banal: idiosyncratic because the term is by definition a singular one and because it belongs to the sphere of high culture, where such survivals are to be expected; and banal because it alludes to a minor, antiquated cultural institution. Yet Hughes and his laureateship remain very much a living part of African-American culture, especially in its contemporary poetry. Kevin Young's 1999 elegy, "Langston Hughes," tropes ironically on Hughes's laureateship, addressing him as "FAMOUS POET©." But the poem also treats Hughes's death in 1967 as a matter of continuing communal immediacy, a metonym for the long political stasis that has followed the struggles of the sixties: "Been tired here / feelin' low down / Real / tired here / since you quit town / . . . We got no more promise / We only got ain't."[27] Young's elegy draws on the blues idiom Hughes himself made famous. But it also draws on an impulse in Anglophone poetry that is fairly archaic. The lament for great poets now lost was a hallmark of the later Middle Ages. Perhaps the most famous instance is Dunbar's widely anthologized *Lament for the Makers*, with its haunting Latin refrain, *Timor mortis conturbat me* ("The fear of death confounds me").[28] These laments formed part of the "matrix" of laureation, a cluster of signifying practices that, as both Seth Lerer and Richard Helgerson have shown, constituted the center of the literary system of late medieval and early modern Britain.[29] With their insistence on personal loss, these laments had the practical effect of consolidating the poetic reputation of their subjects. Moreover, the connection they drew between lost poet and the fate of the community rendered poetic reputation a source of political unity. What should we make of Young's recursion to this trope, and indeed to the trope's surprising vitality? Could it be that the obsolescence of the laureate system has been exaggerated? A brief consideration of its trajectory from the Middle Ages to the present will show that is indeed the case.

The institution of poet laureate in English is conventionally assigned one of two starting points. There is either John Skelton's laureation at Oxford in 1488 or John Dryden's royal appointment in 1668.[30] However, it is possible to understand "poet laureate" as a term at the center of a cluster of traditions and signifying practices, of which the office is simply a leading instance. Laureation assumes that poets play a crucial role in the constitution and preservation of political community, and these traditions and practices all return in some way to that general problem. Under this broader conception, we need to take the Anglophone point of origin all the way back to Chaucer and his importation of the term into the language. Chaucer is the earliest English poet to be read continuously from his own time to the present. "Poet laureate" can thus be said to have been part of the poetic tradition in English for as long as that tradition has been continuous and self-conscious.

Its introduction occurs in the *Canterbury Tales,* in the prologue to the *Clerk's Tale.* The Clerk speaks:

> I wol you telle a tale which that I
> Lerned at Padowe of a worthy clerk,
> As preved by his wordes and his werk.
> He is now deed and nayled in his cheste;
> I prey to God so yeve his soule reste!
> Fraunceys Petrak, the lauriat poete,
> Highte this clerk, whos rethorike sweete
> Enlumyned al Ytaille of poetrie,
> As Lynyan dide of philosophie,
> Or lawe, or oother art particuler;
> But Deeth, that wol nat suffre us dwellen heer
> But as it were a twynkling of an ye,
> Hem bothe hath slayn, and alle shul we dye.[31]

vernacula
profusion dep

Here we can already see the linkage not only between poet and political community—Petrarch's poetry illuminates all of Italy—but also between laureation and death. At the moment of the term's entrance into the English language it is already secondary. Petrarch is now dead and nailed in his chest, and like Kevin Young to Langston Hughes, Chaucer comes to the laureateship Petrarch embodies already hopelessly belated. The tale that the Clerk goes on to tell is of course the Griselda story, which Chaucer also introduces to Britain and which will become, with the exception of the Arthurian cycle, the most widely retold of all medieval narratives, in Britain as well as in the rest of northern Europe. Petrarch translated the story into Latin from Boccaccio's *Decameron.* It is this Latin translation, rather than Boccaccio's Italian original, that enables the story's subsequent vernacular profusion. The story itself is noteworthy for its juxtaposition of domesticity and statecraft. Griselda is an Italian peasant girl wedded by Walter, her marquise, because of her great virtue. Early on, she demonstrates her natural nobility by her judicious exercise of Walter's duties in his absence; later Walter subjects her to a series of cruel tests, in which her children are taken from her and she is led to believe they have been murdered. Finally, impressed with the imperturbable patience she displays throughout these trials, Walter restores her children to her. Although these tests seem unavoidably premised on Walter's social superiority as both husband and lord, the Clerk, following Petrarch, recommends Griselda as an ideal not simply of wifely obedience but of patient endurance applicable to all. In the tale's envoy, Chaucer insists on the unattainability of this ideal in terms that strikingly reprise the loss of Petrarch: "Griselde is deed, and eek hire pacience, / And both atones buryed in Ytaille" (IV, 1177–78). The parallel is suggestive, given the already traditional association of the vernacular with the maternal and the domestic, and the tale's complicated translation history.

Moreover, the tale's prologue situates the notion of the laureate within a rivalry between the vernacular and the learned, and the oral and the literate. The Clerk offers his tale in response to an injunction from Harry Bailly, the emcee of the Canterbury collection, to eschew the Latinate resources of the "Heigh style" in which he was well versed, the "termes . . . colours . . . and . . . figures" of classical rhetoric he would ordinarily use in writing to "kinges." As an emissary from this learned world to the vernacular tale-telling contest of the *Canterbury Tales,* he draws on the model of Petrarch, whom he presents as another clerk whose own mastery of classical learning illuminated all of Italy with poetry. The Clerk is now about to bring some of that learning to English poetry, yet he describes the transmission of Petrarch's Latin narrative as an oral, rather than literate, process. He learned the tale not from Petrar-

on Latin

ch's text but from Petrarch personally, while in residence at Padua. This imaginary moment of personal contact invents an oral context for Petrarch's ostentatiously literate translation. In so doing, it also insists on the interdependence between the oral and the literate and the vernacular and the learned. The vernacular community of Italy seeks the prestige of Petrarch's learned, clerkly, Latinate laureateship. But without that community to illuminate, his laureateship literally has no meaning. The Clerk reaffirms Petrarch's laureateship precisely by bringing it to another vernacular community, the oral tale-telling contest of the Canterbury pilgrims, and by extension Chaucer's English-speaking readership. Yet, as I have already said, the Clerk expresses his reaffirmation as a form of loss. If, in his desire for the vernacular, the Clerk renounces his terms, his colors, and his figures, no sooner has he entered the vernacular sphere than he rearticulates his desire for the learned culture he has just left. I want to suggest that it is this contradictory double desire—the learned seeking vernacular expression, the vernacular striving for a unattainable learned prestige—that Chaucer bequeaths to the English language and to Anglophone culture with this translation of the Latin *poeta laureatus*.[32]

It is worth noting that Petrarch himself, whose own interest in the vernacular was modest, nevertheless anticipated this dynamic of incompletion and belatedness, in a different but related form. The opposition between sacred and secular provides one of the central tensions in his "Coronation Oration," the address he gave at his laureate ceremony in Rome in 1341. The address is largely an exposition of a small piece of text, a line and a half from Virgil's third *Georgic;* in this respect it resembles a sermon. In his introduction he offers a prayer to the Virgin, but he also distinguishes poetic modes (*poetico . . . more*) from theological declamation. Moreover, while he further distinguishes poetry from all other forms of human activity on the basis of its infusion of the poet's soul "with a certain internal and divinely motivated force," he draws his authority for this claim entirely from Cicero and the classical poets.[33] The line from Virgil that provides his text—"But a sweet love sweeps me up along the desert heights of Parnassus" (Sed me Parnassi deserta per ardua dulcis raptat amor; *Georg. III*, 291–92)—offers an anticipation of Christian rapture (literally, in its choice of verb), but one that is both pagan and specifically poetic.

As Petrarch continues, he links poetry not merely to the secular but to his own political community. Punning on *arduum* ("heights" and "hard task"), he suggests the "sweet love" of the Parnassian heights is also a love of the difficulties inherent in the poet's calling. The "spiritual disposition" of the successful poet "springs from three roots, of which the first is the honor of the

[handwritten margin note: poetry's relative cultural center ...]

republic, the second, the adornment of one's own glory, and the third, the spur to the efforts of others."[34] Thus, the poet's calling, at once internal and divinely produced, is also radically social. By being crowned in Rome, Petrarch hopes to restore to the city some of its lost glory, and to bring glory to the city of his own birth and all of Italy. He also hopes to inspire other Italians to follow his lead, and even his desire for personal glory he ascribes to a communal impulse. He cites the same line from the *Aeneid* to explain it that he uses to explain his desire to honor Italy: "Love of the fatherland has conquered and immense desire for praise" (Vicit amor patriae laudumque immensa cupido, *Aeneid* VI, 823).

He concludes his exposition of Virgil with the declaration that poetic genius is a gift from God, appealing for authority to the satirist Persius. Petrarch presents poetry as ultimately subordinate to theology, but also as distinct, with its own source of divine inspiration. To theology's direct divine authority it counterpoises the authority of Roman antiquity, albeit belatedly, as a lost ideal it is striving to recapture. Petrarch offers this belated authority as a source of political unity. While in this address he shows no interest in the vernacular, he nevertheless shows a profound commitment to the present and local, and he offers poetry as a discursive rival to theology, and thus, potentially, to the Latin clerical traditions that theology ultimately underwrote. Petrarch was certainly no democrat; his view of the poet as counterpart to Caesar can obviously be read as an epitome of cultural elitism. Yet for all of its elitist impulses, his view also insists on the random specificity of poetic achievement. It is reducible neither to theological authority nor to political power; the purely internal origins of Parnassian desire give it an access to the divine at least potentially beyond the reach of clerical authority, and this internally originating form of authority is as much constitutive of political community as it is subordinate to such community. Paradoxically, this random, indeterminate element in Petrarch's account is its most poetic. It is this aspect that will enable Chaucer to recast laureation as a specifically vernacular dilemma.

[handwritten margin note: More — as desire for rule?]

Chaucer's immediate successors wrote in a vernacular still less prestigious than not only Latin but also French and Italian, and for a society whose interminable dynastic struggles would make political authority precarious for nearly a century. They sought authority for themselves by seeking authority for their language, and they sought that by crowning Chaucer retrospectively with the notion he introduced. In an aside in book III of his epic *The Troy Book* (1412–20), John Lydgate proclaims of Chaucer,

> . . . he owre englishe gilt with his sawes,
> Rude and boistous first be olde dawes

That was ful fer from al perfeccioun
And but of litel reputaticoun
Til that he cam & thorug his poetrie
Gan oure tonge first to magnifie,
And adourne it with his eloquence.[35]

Lydgate moves deftly back and forth between Latinate and more properly English diction, suggesting that Chaucer came to "magnifie" and "adourne" "oure tonge" by literally making it more Latinate. Yet the terms he first chooses to describe Chaucer's language are not Latinate at all: "he owre englishe gilt with his sawes." Both "gilt" and "saw" have their roots in Old English; Chaucer's magnifying and adorning began from within the vernacular, drawing on its own resources. Despite its "litel reputaticoun," it already contained the makings of its own greatness. In part because of the efforts of Lydgate and others, Chaucer's more distant successors grew more confident of their own tradition. As a result, they began to focus the tropes of laureation less on the tradition as a whole and more on the problem of their own individual authority. Thus, Helgerson argues, by the late sixteenth century laureation had become a mode of poetic "self-fashioning."[36] But this change constituted an inflection rather than a complete break. Throughout the entire period from Chaucer to Dryden, the discourse of laureation provided a crucial vocabulary for defining the shape of poetic achievement, the transmission of poetic tradition, and the poetic constitution of political community.

Ironically, the establishment of poet laureate as a royal office in 1668 had the effect of dissipating some of laureation's symbolic power. Or perhaps it would be more accurate to say that power got driven underground. Less than a half century after Dryden's death, Alexander Pope made Colley Cibber, the current poet laureate, the hero of *The Dunciad* and became, in Helgerson's words, "the first anti-Laureate laureate."[37] Fourteen years later, Thomas Gray refused to become poet laureate, declaring "the office itself has always humbled the professor." Thus, Helgerson explains, "to be Poet Laureate had come to mean that one was decidedly *not* a laureate poet" (emphasis original).[38] Such antithetical logic only works if it assumes a laureate ideal that is purer than the instituted office and that can therefore stand in judgment of it. This ideal must return to the Petrarchan model and reaffirm it at its most random and indeterminate: the poetic disposition as irreducible to any other form of authority, yet constitutive of communal unity in that very irreducibility. In this submerged form, the logic of laureation has persisted from the eighteenth century to the present. We can find it expressed in Shelley's declaration, "Poets are the unacknowledged legislators of the world," and in James Joyce's paradigmatic modern poet Stephen Dedalus.[39] One of the early markers of Stephen's vocation is his dismissal of the laureate Tennyson as "only a rhyme-ster." Nevertheless, on the last page of *Portrait of the Artist as a Young Man,* as he prepares to leave Ireland, "the old sow that eats her farrow," he declares to his journal, "I go to encounter for the millionth time the reality of experience and to forge in the smithy of my soul the uncreated conscience of my race."[40] Even more significantly for our purposes, this antithetical version of laureation also informs the Wordsworthian claim I cited above. One of Wordsworth's purposes in writing the preface is to defend himself from the charge that in putting his poetry into "the language of real men" he has defaulted on his readers' expectations: "it will seem to many persons I have not fulfilled the terms of an engagement . . . voluntarily contracted" (244). But these expectations arise from "the gaudiness and inane phraseology of many modern writers," who "indulge in arbitrary and capricious habits of expression in order to furnish food for fickle tastes and fickle appetites of their own creation" (244, 246). These fashionable poets, like sham laureates, have created a community, but one that is entirely arbitrary and capricious. With his "selection of language really used by men," Wordsworth proposes to recover a purer, more authentic form of community, originating in "low and rustic life." He chooses the language of "rural" men "because such men hourly communicate with the best objects from which the best part of language is originally derived; and because . . . being less under the influence of social vanity they convey their feelings in simple and unelaborated expressions" (245). He caps off this evocation of rural purity with an appeal to—who else?—Chaucer. In a footnote he explains, "It is worth while here to observe that the affecting parts of Chaucer are almost always expressed in language pure and universally intelligible even to this day" (246). Expressing itself in "real language" was to become one of the twentieth century's most basic and most widespread poetic ideals, even when it presented itself as breaking with the nineteenth. Thus, Ezra Pound, who despised Wordsworth, nevertheless declares in one of his manifestos for Imagism that its first principle is "To use the language of common speech."[41] Hughes will bring the same ideal to bear on the African-American vernacular.

From this perspective, the laureation of Hughes begins to seem a good deal less quaint. In the early twenties, no more than a decade after the publication of *Portrait,* he seems already to have been recognized as "the Poet Laureate of the Negro Race." Credit for coining the label has long been given to Carl Van Vechten, a white novelist and critic closely associated with the Harlem Renaissance, but direct documentary confirmation of this ascription has yet to be found. Joel Conorroe, in his anthology *Six Americans,* suggests the source may have been Hughes himself.[42] In any case, by the late twenties the honorific was widely enough known that in the black press hostile reviewers of *Fine Clothes to the Jew,* his third collection of poems, could refer to Hughes sardonically as "the poet low-rate."[43] It is entirely possible the term circulated in conversations among the *cognoscenti* of the New Negro movement and their white supporters before it found its way into print. It is intriguing to imagine an oral origin for the phrase; an oral origin would make the phrase's vernacular status that much more evident. It would also serve as a reminder that even the most sophisticated and exclusive of modern literary movements have a vernacular dimension. The Harlem Renaissance was identical to the aggregations of movements that constituted white modernism in being driven by the oral subculture of the salon no less than by the institutional structures of the publishing house, the little magazine, the gallery, and the concert hall. Nor would an oral origin have made the phrase "the Poet Laureate of the Negro Race" particularly unique. To cite only one similar instance: Ernest Hemingway presented *The Sun Also Rises,* the novel that announced his membership in the international Parisian *avant garde,* as if oral in origin. The novel's epigraph is the statement "You are a lost generation," ascribed to "Gertrude Stein, in conversation."

However the term originated, it should be clear by now that "Poet Laureate of the Negro Race" is a designation of extraordinary richness. On the one hand, the phrase can be read as an instance of "signifying," the practice of ironic revision Henry Louis Gates and others have argued is the master trope of African-American tradition.[44] For it clearly appropriates in the name of the black vernacular a Latinate term meant to designate elite literary tradition at its most hegemonic. On the other hand, in this case, the revision does more than simply expose a white dominant form as contingent. This revision consists in naming directly a desire that the mainstream Anglophone literary tradition had long kept half-hidden. The revision achieves its paradoxical subversion precisely by revealing an unacknowledged continuity and claiming that continuity for its own. "Poet Laureate of the Negro Race" proclaims Hughes the best of the African-American tradition, and simultaneously proclaims him the equivalent of the best that white tradition has to offer. It thereby implicitly expresses a desire for the prestige of the more dominant tradition, but only by insisting that the dominant tradition is itself secondary, founded on its own impossible desires—as indeed, as we have just seen, the tradition itself does in some profusion. In suggesting a continuity that connects Langston Hughes to Geoffrey Chaucer, I may seem to be making a very traditional humanist claim: that in essential matters of poetic tradition things do not change. In fact, the claim I want to make is slightly, but crucially, different. I want to claim certain things do not change much. To put the matter more precisely, I am arguing that in order for the specific cultural and political claims inherent in the term "the Poet Laureate of the Negro Race" to become fully legible, they must be read against a notion of poetic authority that, while no less political, extends across a longer temporal span and possesses a wider range of applicability.

"Poet Laureate of the Negro Race" signifies both on the entire length of Anglophone poetic tradition and on the tradition's equally durable drive beyond the poetic. The epithet signifies in the name of a black vernacular culture that Hughes claimed as his own and that traces its origin to itself. This fact points to what is perhaps the phrase's broadest complexity. Most sociolinguists now view African-American Vernacular English as the descendant of a pidgin that captured Africans from different language communities developed in order to communicate with each other and their captors and masters. This pidgin then evolved into a Creole, in part because most slaves had intermittent contact with whites, in part because they needed to communicate with each other in ways that would be unintelligible to whites.[45] The origins of the African-American speech community thus extend back to the seventeenth century for sure, and perhaps even to in the mid-sixteenth, when the first contact with English-speaking slavers occurred.[46] This chronology obviously intersects not only with the traditions of laureation but even more closely with the broader traditions of vernacular self-assertion with which they were intertwined. The English speech community's symbolic announcement of itself as a language of learned culture, a language worthy of laureate poets, is followed by its acquisition of a new vernacular, and a vernacular in the original sense, a language of slaves. Articulated on behalf of the black vernacular, "the Poet Laureate of the Negro Race" reclaims the full length of the black vernacular's long past. Throughout his career, in spite of his deep affinities with the modernist vanguard, Hughes also characteristically imagines the integrity of African-American culture as synonymous with its durability and its longevity. In his very first published poem, "The Negro Speaks of Rivers," the narrating I, having "known rivers ancient as the world and older than the flow of human blood in human veins," successively locates itself at the Euphrates at the dawn of civilization, the Congo, the Nile during ancient Egypt, and the Mississippi "when Abe Lincoln went down to New Orleans."[47]

There is nothing accidental about this interest in the diachronic. Nor does it represent a nostalgia that compromises his vanguardist credentials, as some of his New Critical detractors suggested in the forties and fifties. As the Negro poet laureate, speaking both to his community and for it, he had to be innovative and conservative at once. In contrast to white vanguardists, who could represent their relation to the past as a pure break, Hughes was breaking with a dominant tradition in order to preserve and continue a marginalized one. This fundamental imperative would mean a thorough engagement with African-American vernacular speech and speakers throughout his career. However, this engagement would come as an engagement with African-American vernacular traditions, as a whole, and especially with African-American musical traditions. In part this was because of the centrality of these traditions in African-American culture. But it was also because music offered Hughes a model for imagining the relation between his poetry and his community that placed equal emphasis on both of its two ostensibly dissimilar aspects, political interest and poetic form.

Music defines its formal elements precisely by their movement through time. To highlight the affinities between music and poetry is to highlight the diachronic aspect of poetic form. Thus, using music as a model enables Hughes to imagine the relation between poetry and politics as a specifically temporal one. It also enables him to move beyond the synchronic assumptions that frame the received understandings of the opposition between poetry and "common speech." Those positing this opposition have generally tended to assume that poetry has a level of formal artifice common speech lacks. This assumption forms a basic continuity from Wordsworth through Pound, and from Saussure and Bloomfield up through most sociolinguistics.[48] Indeed, it seems sheer common sense. Nevertheless, its obviousness depends on treating both the individual poem and the everyday utterance in completely synchronic terms—that is, as distinct acts completely contained in their moment of occurrence, however that moment is defined. And it certainly is true that if we understand the moment of a poem's utterance as identical to the time it takes the poet to write it, then the poem definitely seems more purposive, more highly crafted, and under greater control of its producer than the casual utterances of everyday speech. However, if one takes a longer view, then one recognizes that poets are no less constrained by the formal parameters of previous poetic traditions than is everyday speech by the abiding structures of the language from which it issues. By the same token, while an individual speaker's use of a completely arbitrary grammatical form like the zero copula of the African-American vernacular may have no particular significance in itself, a speech community's continued attachment to such forms in the face of pressure from more dominant dialects can convey a rich and complicated significance indeed—as sociolinguists have been at great pains to argue.

Wordsworth and Pound wanted poetry written in common speech because—in spite of their other differences—they both thought poetic artifice made for bad poetry. They both expected poetry to purge itself of artifice by imitating common speech. While Hughes shows himself sympathetic to this view, he also, with his career-long interest in rhyme and lots of other obviously poetic effects, shows himself less hostile to artifice. He approaches the problem in a significantly different fashion. He writes poetry in imitation of African-American speech patterns not only because those patterns make his poetry more authentic but also to show that they are already formally poetic. This is true even in those cases where he seems to be following the Wordsworthian/modernist paradigm most straightforwardly, as in his 1927 volume *Fine Clothes to the Jew*. In this tour de force, "deliberately defining poetic tradition according to the standards of a group often seen as sub-poetic—the black masses," he rarely allows his poetry to move "beyond the range of utterance of common black folk."[49] But even this work is mediated through his interest in the blues, and the evidence of his subsequent career strongly suggests he found subordinating to this particular ideal of common speech too restrictive. Instead, like a more traditional laureate, he establishes the poetic legitimacy of his community and its traditions precisely by elaborating the distinctiveness of his own poetic authority.

ASK YOUR MAMA: A Poem in Quarters

ASK YOUR MAMA: 12 Moods for Jazz, was Hughes's last major poem, and his most experimental.[50] Inspired by free jazz and other postbebop developments in African-American music, the poem returns to the peculiar temporal predicament of a community whose political aspirations are still a dream deferred and ever more frustrated. It makes its musical investments a prominent formal feature. The introductory note begins with the musical transcription of a traditional twelve-bar blues entitled "Hesitation Blues" (an obvious reference to the problem of deferral), which Hughes explains "is the leitmotif for this poem" (475). He suggests the poem be read with jazz accompaniment and prints its lines in all caps with musical directions in italics down the right-hand margin.[51] The music specified ranges from African drums to German lieder, to gospel, blues, bebop, to "very modern jazz" (521). In keeping with the encyclopedic range of the accompaniment, Hughes makes the poem's focus the whole of the African diaspora. He draws the title from the dozens, a verbal game of ritualized insult.

The poem's importance is now generally recognized, at least among African-Americanists. Nevertheless, it is fair to say the poem remains largely unanalyzed. Its general tenor may seem clear, but much of its complex political and poetic vision remains more than half-hidden in the difficulties of its experimental form. Despite a considerable publicity campaign by Hughes and his publisher, Alfred A. Knopf, the initial response by reviewers was decidedly mixed, although less hostile than confused.[52] The poem has received scant critical attention since.[53] A number of reviewers related the poem to the Beats, on the basis of its projected jazz accompaniment. The most perceptive of these noted Hughes had been reading his poetry with music off and on for decades, so that if anything, the Beats were imitating him rather than the other way round. Yet no one seems to have noticed that the work's most important white intertext was not Beat poetry but *The Waste Land* of T. S. Eliot.[54] In a clear parody of Eliot's infamous endnotes to that poem, Hughes ends *ASK YOUR MAMA* with a section entitled "LINER NOTES" and subtitled *"For the Poetically Unhep."* These notes consist of sardonic political glosses of each "mood," and they highlight the intermediate space between learned and vernacular Hughes occupies as a black poet. "Unhep" is originally a black-vernacular term brought to whites through the world of jazz, but Hughes makes hepness specifically poetic, laying claim to his own form of erudition and readjusting the balance between vernacular expression and poetic authority. This engagement with Eliot is crucial, for even now the extreme topicality of the poem's political humor and its continual references to a wide range of crises from the late nineteen fifties and very early sixties may tempt readers to assume the poem can be absorbed by its occasion. To do so, however, would be to miss a fundamental point: that the racial crises suddenly taking center stage at the beginning of the nineteen sixties cannot be understood without understanding the long history that produced them.

ASK YOUR MAMA is a poem about racial segregation in its broadest sense: its past, its present, its cultural and political effects and their persistence. It begins with the juridical segregation of the American South and the Civil Rights Movement, but it moves quickly to the economic segregation in northern cities and returns repeatedly to the hostility of northern white suburbs to upwardly mobile blacks. It also moves just as quickly to the African diaspora and the death throes of European colonialism in Africa itself. Hughes continually breaks segregation down to its elements as a grotesque and nightmarish set of spatial practices horrifically efficacious in spite of their stark illogic and ultimate inability to control completely the geographical divisions they enforce. For Hughes, the most paradoxical feature of this illogic is its apparently inexhaustible persistence. Nearly a century after the abolition of slavery, the South remains legally segregated, segregation persists as a fundamental material and cultural condition in the ostensibly nonsegregated

North, and colonialism hangs on in Africa despite the West's ideological pro-motion of principles of self-determination. The brutal, manifold persistence of segregation is what gives the engagement with Eliot particular poignancy.

The Waste Land is also about a catastrophic historical delay. Eliot draws the figure of the Fisher King from Jessie L. Weston's *From Ritual to Romance,* an anthropological account of medieval romance. While the king languishes interminably with enchanted wounds, his land remains gripped by famine, and Eliot uses this mythic motif to figure Christianity's continuing delay in bringing deliverance to its believers and Western modernity's consequent dis-enchantment with its past. At the time *ASK YOUR MAMA* appeared, Eliot's influence on Anglophone literary culture had reached its apogee, and much of that culture took the spiritual disenchantment adumbrated in *The Waste Land* as its founding historical condition. *ASK YOUR MAMA* attempts to funda-mentally reorient this perception of modernity. The poem takes Eliot's claim of historical paralysis literally, but insists on its materiality, embodied in the paralytic state of current race relations.

This shift also entails a more material understanding of poetry; here Hughes is less interested in poetry's subordination to politics than in the polit-ical materiality of poetic form and in the formal materiality of cultural expres-sion more generally. Part of Eliot's disenchantment in *The Waste Land* is the conviction that poets and poetry have outlived their authority: cut off from the past, the modern poet can do no more than register modernity's gross inadequacy in the face of poetry's traditional forms. Like Petrarch, Chaucer, Dunbar, and the other late medieval and early modern promulgators, Eliot populates *The Waste Land* with the shades of dead *auctores,* but the loss is now nearly absolute. These shades have no exemplary power over the future; they no longer offer the present a resource for reconstructing continuities; they serve only to remind the present of its own irremediable inadequacy. For Hughes, by contrast, black cultural expression constitutes a preeminent form of resistance to the long stasis of racial oppression. With its many catalogs of black artists, *ASK YOUR MAMA* is a kind of mid-twentieth-century *House of Fame* or *Garland of Laurel* for the African-American tradition. While it differs from the *House of Fame* tradition in its emphasis on the living rather than the dead, its single most pivotal figure is arguably Charlie Parker, the jazz saxo-phonist who died in 1955 at the age of thirty-five. His loss preoccupies the final three moods, giving them an appropriately elegiac cast. Moreover, *ASK YOUR MAMA* shares with the *House of Fame* tradition—and late medieval and early modern laureation generally—an overriding interest in the discur-sive power of expressive forms, their capacity to construct and maintain politi-cal continuities. It is ironic that Hughes's resistance to Eliot enables him to recover this aspect of previous Anglophone tradition, since it was this aspect Eliot was most at pains to insist was irrecuperably lost.

Hughes dramatizes his interest in the formal durability of black expressive traditions in the most elemental arrangements of the poem's own form. Twelve, the number of its moods, corresponds both to the dozens and to the twelve bars of the "Hesitation Blues." Moreover, "mood" is itself a formal term, designating either a rhythmic scheme in music or a class of verb inflections in language. Thus this poem, about a crisis in the movement of historical time, thematizes in its structure the measurement of time in both musical and poetic discourse. The poem returns repeatedly to problems of numbering and measure, not only as they relate to cultural expression, but also as they relate to money and property. The moods vary in length from 23 lines to 133, and the poem does not move from mood to mood in any easily discernible narrative sequence. Indeed, one advantage of this experimental form is that it allows Hughes to explore the stasis of race relations without positing some historical teleology that would belie the catastrophic severity of that stasis. With each new mood, we return once more to the poem's premise, and, like melodic themes or chord progressions in a piece of music, the poem's tropes achieve their fullness of meaning not from a continuous narrative development but from continual repetition.

At the same time, while the twelve moods lack sequential development, it is still possible to arrange them in larger units. One can divide the poem in quarters, each quarter associated with a different musical tradition. Over the first three moods, "CULTURAL EXCHANGE," "RIDE, RED, RIDE," and "SHADES OF PIGMEAT," presides the figure of Leontyne Price, an African-American opera singer, that is, a singer whose expressive achievement comes precisely from her mastery of one of European music's most prestigious traditions. The next three moods, "ODE TO DINAH," "BLUES IN STEREO," and "HORN OF PLENTY," offer the figure of Dinah Washington, known as the "Queen of the Blues," whose crossover success brought the blues to commercial white audiences. The next three, "GOSPEL CHA-CHA," "IS IT TRUE," and "ASK YOUR MAMA," invoke the African roots of musics of the African diaspora; and, as I have already noted, the final three, "BIRD IN ORBIT," "JAZZTET MUTED," and "SHOW FARE, PLEASE," offer the figure of Charlie Parker, one of the guiding lights of bebop, whose innovations would also inspire the even more vanguardist versions of jazz that followed.

The notion of the quarter as a numerical division of various sorts recurs throughout the poem. The word "quarter" also occupies the central position in the poem's most important catchphrase. The opening mood, "CULTURAL EXCHANGE," begins:

Négritude

IN THE
IN THE QUARTER
IN THE QUARTER OF THE NEGROES
(477)

This incantatory, repetitive opening uses "QUARTER" to emphasize that the dynamism of linguistic form lies precisely in its abstractness, focusing the reader's attention on the construction of the two successive prepositional phrases. The first line presents language as pure grammatical form; the second adds the referentiality of the noun "QUARTER," but as a reference that is itself largely empty. Thus, by the time we get to the full version of the catchphrase in the third line, we experience its dense ideological import as thoroughly sculpted by the phonological and grammatical forms of its language. Nor does the interdependence between politics and poetry end even here.

"IN THE QUARTER OF THE NEGROES" will recur throughout the poem, orienting its complex cultural geography. Anticipating current notions of the African diaspora, Hughes invokes Negro quarters all over the globe, here initially in the U.S. South, "BY THE RIVER AND THE RAILROAD," then in the suburbs of New York City, and later other prosperous suburbs; Cuba, Martinique, Grenada, Haiti, and nearly everywhere else in the Caribbean; the Congo and other parts of Africa; Harlem, Buffalo, Cincinnati, Chicago, Kansas City, and Paris. The phrase itself is slightly awkward, and suggests a translation from the French, where both _quartier_ as the designation of a section of a city and a prepositional phrase like _des noirs_ instead of a simple attributive would seem more natural and less stilted. No doubt Hughes wants to call attention to the remarkable internationalism of black culture. At various points he resorts to catchphrases in French and Spanish. He may even be paying implicit homage to the Négritude movement, whose founder, Aimé Césaire, he mentions in the poem's tenth mood. But the impression of a French phrase translated into English also highlights the dominant role English plays in this diaspora. Hughes is specifically concerned with the ironies of the postwar situation, the beginnings of the historical moment we now call postcolonial. As African nations were struggling to achieve independence, they looked to African-American artists for cultural leadership, yet in Hughes's words they found themselves "baffled" by "an America that seems to understand so little about its black citizens" and that "pays more attention to Moscow than Mississippi" (527). In this postcolonial moment, English has achieved the status of international master-language, far surpassing that of Latin in the Western Middle Ages. To that master-language, Hughes defiantly proposes the African-American tradition as a central node of an international vernacular.

pun

The other senses of "quarter" enact the power of this vernacular in other ways. Punning on his initial use of the word, Hughes supplements the recurrence of "QUARTER" in "QUARTER OF THE NEGROES" with "quarter" in the original sense of "fraction," and in a specific application of that sense, the twenty-five-cent coin. The pun is often viewed as a use of language dependent on linguistic similarities at their most superficial and meaningless. In fact, the pun is made possible by the long accretion of meaning over time, and it works by reactivating a word's diachronic semantic shifts. "Quarter" came into Middle English from Latin, via Old French. Its subsequent profusion of meaning illustrates the power of vernacularization. Hughes draws on this profusion to interfuse poetically the durability of racial oppression with the tenacity of black resistance. The poem's fourth mood, "ODE TO DINAH," describes the moment of its present as "THIS LAST QUARTER OF CENTENNIAL / 100 YEARS OF EMANCIPATION." Some lines later the quarter as coin dramatizes the economic expropriation of African-American music:

> . . . FAT JUKEBOXES
> WHERE DINAH'S SONGS ARE MADE
> FROM SLABS OF SILVER SHADOWS
> AS EACH QUARTER CLINKS
> INTO A MILLION POOLS OF QUARTERS
> TO BE CARTED OFF BY BRINK'S . . .
>
> (491)

From these two senses of "quarter," the poem moves on to the more general term "number," especially in senses relating to money and property. The next mood, "BLUES IN STEREO," declares in its first line, "YOUR NUMBER'S COMING OUT." The ninth mood, "ASK YOUR MAMA," is full of numbered streets from many American cities and numbers used in games of chance. The poem's final mood, "SHOW FARE, PLEASE," returns to the quarter to assert the inexhaustibility of African-American inventiveness in the face of economic privation:

> DID YOU EVER SEE TEN NEGROES
> WEAVING METAL FROM TWO QUARTERS
> INTO CLOTH OF DOLLARS
> FOR A SUIT OF GOOD-TIME WEARING?
> WEAVING OUT OF LONG-TERM CREDIT
> INTEREST BEYOND CARING?
>
> (525)

Economic relations are no less dependent than poetic tradition on structures of formal measurement. These lines equate improvised games of chance with the assumption of "LONG-TERM CREDIT" and see in each a sort of resistance analogous to cultural expression, in that both are based on the manipulation of form. Yet, these equivalences are by no means triumphalist. The fourth mood links the problem of formal measure to racial oppression's temporal double bind. On the one hand, the time of racial oppression seems never ending, as the promise of progress in race relations is continually betrayed:

> GOT TO WAIT—
> THIS LAST QUARTER OF CENTENNIAL
> GOT TO WAIT
>
> (492)

On the other hand, it moves too quickly, providing it at once the most immediate and most global evidence of racism's destructive power:

> LIVING 20 YEARS IN 10
> BETTER HURRY, BETTER HURRY
> BEFORE THE PRESENT BECOMES WHEN
> AND YOU'RE 50
> WHEN YOU'RE 40
> 40 WHEN YOU'RE 30
> 30 WHEN YOU'RE 20
> 20 WHEN YOU'RE 10
> IN THE QUARTER OF THE NEGROES
> WHERE THE PENDULUM IS SWINGING
> TO THE SHADOW OF THE BLUES,
> EVEN WHEN YOU'RE WINNING
> THERE'S NO WAY NOT TO LOSE.
>
> (492–93)

A pendulum measures the movement of time, but in such a way as to present that movement as repetitive and static. A visual form of measurement driven by gravity, here it is driven by "THE SHADOW OF THE BLUES," the temporal loss itself structured by the African-American tradition's characteristic form for the expression of the loss. But the structuring is attenuated, effected not by the substance of the blues but only by their shadow. At its most material level the temporal loss that gives rise to the blues remains necessarily beyond their reach.

Figures of shadow and shade occur in almost every mood. In contrast to the figures of music and measurement, they are images of visual illusion. They are also elegiac, and even infernal, suggesting a descent to the underworld.[55] The image of the shadow is an image of repetition. Paradoxically, because it is spatial, it is also an image of simultaneity. The image thus figures a repetition that endures, that is inseparable from the thing repeated. The process is self-reproducing and potentially unending. In the eleventh mood, "JAZZTET MUTED," Hughes dramatizes this interminability in an ostentatiously repetitive passage, which also returns to the durability of black resistance:

> IN THE NEGROES OF THE QUARTER
> PRESSURE OF THE BLOOD IS SLIGHTLY HIGHER
> IN THE QUARTER OF THE NEGROES
> WHERE BLACK SHADOWS MOVE LIKE SHADOWS
> CUT FROM SHADOWS CUT FROM SHADE
> IN THE QUARTER OF THE NEGROES
> SUDDENLY CATCHING FIRE
> FROM THE WING TIP OF A MATCH TIP
> ON THE BREATH OF ORNETTE COLEMAN
>
> (521)

Ignored, denied visibility—placed in the shade, as it were—the quarter of the Negroes shadows white society. Not content to remain in the shade, the black shadows move. This shadowy movement produces more shadows. This repetition is a form of resistance, one that is generated from the slenderest of material means—"SHADOWS / CUT FROM SHADOWS" themselves cut from nothing more than the utter darkness signified by "SHADE." The musical cue to this mood reads: *"Bop blues into very modern jazz burning the air eerie like a neon swamp-fire cooled by dry ice until suddenly there is a single ear-splitting piercing flute call"* (521–22). The "eerie" fire "burning" in modern jazz is the "FIRE / . . . /ON THE BREATH OF ORNETTE COLEMAN." Coleman, another saxophonist, was a pioneer of free jazz, a self-consciously vanguardist movement that evolved out of bebop. The fire is "eerie" because, like the Negro blood where this "mood" begins, it is under pressure. Moreover, it is also the product of the "SHADOWS / CUT FROM SHADOWS CUT FROM SHADE," that is, of the tremendous energy of a resistance that has almost no material means of sustenance. These lines conflate the possibility of revolutionary violence with the aesthetic breakthrough of an artistic vanguard, and paradoxically tie them both to the continuities of cultural tradition. The blues are defined by their aesthetic reconfiguration of the social oppression.[56] For

Hughes, the *very modern jazz* emerging out of *bop blues* is tied to its origin by its continuity of political engagement. It is not just that black culture is characterized by moments of explosion; rather, the explosiveness inherent in the culture's social foundation can never be separated from its aesthetic power.

The mood ends by returning to the problem in even more elegiac terms:

> WHERE THE PRESSURE OF THE BLOOD
> IS SLIGHTLY HIGHER—
> DUE TO SMOLDERING SHADOWS
> THAT SOMETIMES TURN TO FIRE
> *HELP ME, YARDBIRD!*
> *HELP ME!*
>
> (522)

This final appeal is simultaneous with the "flute call" of the musical cue. Charlie Parker is the lost laureate. Yet the help Hughes seeks is political as well as poetic. This moment of lament is simultaneously a moment of conjuration and demand, an insistence on the constructive power of elegy, its transformation of loss into continuity. The demand can offer no proof of its efficacy beyond its own absolute urgency. Paradoxically, Hughes's laureation of "YARDBIRD" constructs a political continuity because he speaks in the name of a community to which other forms of political legitimacy have been denied. We return to the question of the poetic authority of a vernacular culture—to the question raised by the poem's title.

The Dozens: Poetry and Aggression

The vernacular is proverbially the mother tongue, the language of the nursery—in Dante's words, "that which children learn from those around them."[57] Dante's commonplace implicitly contains an important political recognition. It gives the vernacular an institutional location, the household, that can be set against the church, Latin's much more prominent institutional location. Moreover, in this opposition between the domestic and the clerical, we can discern an important source of the vernacular's political ambiguity. The household is at once the origin of individual identity and the locus of patriarchal authority. For this reason, in the later Middle Ages the vernacular could, depending on circumstances, serve as the vehicle of either aristocratic interest or individual self-assertion. This ambiguity is also one of the reasons the vernacular's political value can never be reckoned as purely progressive. In *ASK*

*household — but also school —
as institutions of ver-
nacular;
also
black
church*

YOUR MAMA, Hughes's exploration of the dozens enables him to revivify Dante's commonplace and exfoliate its political wisdom. He takes the game's thematization of motherhood literally. He presents motherhood as the crucial mediating category between the public and the private, and the vernacular and the poetic. This enables him to insist that race relations are not only more urgent but also more intimate than commonly imagined.

Through the first three quarters of the poem, he is particularly concerned with the ironies inherent in white culture's profound and unacknowledged psychic dependence on blacks, ironies that express themselves in white naïveté. Through the first nine moods *ASK YOUR MAMA* is offered as a response to a variety of white questions or demands. Only the last of these involves a straightforward exercise of political superiority. In the ninth mood, actually entitled "ASK YOUR MAMA," *"TELL YOUR MA"* is the response to an eviction notice. But in all the other cases, the retort is always a response to naïve attempts at cross-cultural understanding. In "CULTURAL EXCHANGE" (the first mood), one black speaker is asked if he would "RUB OFF" his blackness. In "HORN OF PLENTY" (the sixth mood), a suburban black is asked on his patio where he got his money, and another if he could recommend a maid. In "IS IT TRUE?" (the eighth mood), a third suburban black is asked an unfinished question about sex:

of Dinner

> THEY ASKED ME AT THE PTA
> IS IT TRUE THAT NEGROES—?
> I SAID, ASK YOUR MAMA.
>
> (509)

Confronted with the white myth, this speaker responds with the vernacular wit of the dozens, but in such a way that the irony consists precisely of answering the myth with the reality of miscegenation. That is, absurd enough on its face, the question "IS IT TRUE THAT NEGROES—?" should be rendered even more absurd if read against the long history of forced sexual congress that constituted one of the central and most devastating elements of racial oppression in the United States. These lines come at the very end of the mood. Both this mood and the one before treat the diasporic roots of black vernacular culture ("UNDECIPHERED AND UNLETTERED / UNCODIFIED UNPARSED / IN TONGUES UNANALYZED UNECHOED / UNTAKEN DOWN ON TAPE— / NOT EVEN FOLKWAYS CAPTURED BY MOE ASCH OR ALAN LOMAX NOT YET ON SAFARI" [507]) and the attendant myths of the primitive. These lines also occur just before the directly political use of *"TELL YOUR MA"* at the beginning of the next mood, "ASK

YOUR MAMA." They thus represent a crescendo of sorts, with black speakers confronting whites with the complicity that lies behind their naïveté, culminating in the angry suggestion that sexual pollution is at the heart of this guilt.

With this suggestion, Hughes responds to the social psychologist John Dollard, who published the first extended scholarly analysis of the dozens in the inaugural issue of the psychoanalytic journal *American Imago*.[58] Hughes knew this essay well and corresponded with Dollard while writing *ASK YOUR MAMA*. Dollard suggests the dozens provides an outlet for repressed Oedipal desires: "One must follow Freud exactly at this point and suppose that the accusations made by the speaker represent in most cases repressed wishes of his own." Yet Dollard also takes the subordinate position of blacks as a kind of given and views the significance of the dozens as entirely internal to the black community, "a valve for aggression in a depressed group."[59] By turning the dozens outward, Hughes not only asserts once again the integrity of African-American vernacular expression in the face of white dominance, he also complicates the neat separation Dollard assumes between an ostensibly external category like social group and an ostensibly internal one like repression. Anticipating the critique of some current black feminist scholars, notably Hortense Spillers, Hughes suggests that the internalization of sexual taboos cannot be imagined as prior to the constitution of the domestic sphere, that is, as prior precisely to that sphere whose integrity racial oppression has rendered so problematic. The sexual anxieties put into play by the dozens cannot be fully explained by the ideologies of miscegenation, but they cannot be explained at all without them.[60] Thus, this crescendo at the end of "IS IT TRUE?" by no means constitutes Hughes's last word on the problem. On the contrary, this invocation of a specifically sexual anxiety forms part of a broader analysis of the interdependence between race relations and familial structures.

The first mood, "CULTURAL EXCHANGE," ends with a witty and caustic "DREAM," in which "THE NEGROES / OF THE SOUTH HAVE TAKEN OVER." Hughes imagines as "WHITE MAMMIES" the mothers of leading segregationists Arkansas governor Orville Faubus, Mississippi senator James Eastland, and Alabama governor John Patterson: "DEAR *DEAR* DARLING OLD WHITE MAMMIES— / SOMETIMES EVEN BURIED WITH OUR FAMILY" (480–81). These lines invert one of the stereotypes white racists used to support the ostensible benevolence of segregation. They also remind us that in the segregated South white families depended on black servants to maintain their own internal structure. Thus, this poem, in offering African-American tradition as spanning the gap between the vernacular and the learned, also insists that race spans the opposition between public and

NB miscegenation + vernacular

private. Having exposed segregation's contradictory logic at the heart of the white private sphere, the poem moves on to the structural ruptures racism effects in the black family. In the second mood, "TU ABELA ¿DÓNDE ESTÁ?" (your grandmother, where is she?) becomes a momentary refrain, a muted reminder that the slave trade destroyed intergenerational memories. "ODE TO DINAH" begins with a brief indication of the fracturing of families in the post–Jim Crow migrations to northern cities—"MAMA'S FRUIT-CAKE SENT FROM GEORGIA / CRUMBLES AS IT'S NIBBLED"—and then invokes a more complete devastation:

> TRIBAL NOW NO LONGER PAPA MAMA
> IN RELATION TO THE CHILD
> ONCE YOUR BROTHER'S KEEPER
> NOW NOT EVEN KEEPER TO YOUR CHILD—
> (492)

"BIRD IN ORBIT" also features the problem of generational continuity, with the repeated question "GRANDPA, WHERE DID YOU MEET MY GRANDMA," and Sojourner Truth's lament for her lost children:

> ALL SOLD DOWN THE RIVER.
> *I LOOK AT THE STARS,*
> *AND THEY WONDER WHERE I BE*
> *AND I WONDER WHERE THEY BE*
> (518)

However, what ultimately seems most salient to Hughes about these violent ruptures is less their extreme forms and more the pressure they exert even where they are successfully resisted. The most profound irony in the entire poem occurs in the final mood, "SHOW FARE, PLEASE." Here, the imperative of the title is taken literally, as the mood is dominated by questions a child asks its mother. The questions all center on the child's desire for show fare: "TELL ME, MAMA, CAN I GET MY SHOW / TELL ME FARE FROM YOU?" The motif actually occurs once before in the poem, at a much earlier point. In "ODE TO DINAH," directly after the passage on the breakdown of the family ("TRIBAL NOW NO LONGER"), a child declares, *"I WANT TO GO TO THE SHOW, MAMA,"* and the mother responds, *"NO SHOW FARE, BABY—/ NOT THESE DAYS."* These questions connect the pressures on the family with the white appropriation of black expressive culture and the enmeshment of that culture in an economic system that keeps it a distance

X plen

(far) fare

from its own community. Hughes makes the transmission of this culture and the interchange between mother and child completely interdependent. He thus expands the proverbial transmission of the vernacular from mother to child to include the whole of culture, not just language, and he casts the transmission in political terms by framing it with the socioeconomic predicament out of which domestic relations are produced.

By taking literally the injunction to "ASK YOUR MAMA," the final mood insists on the literal connection between the dozens and its social location. That is, it ties the aesthetic dynamics of the genre to the socioeconomic deprivation of the African-American community and specifically to the vulnerabilities of its familial structures. Hortense Spillers has written that "the dozens takes the assaulted home to the backbone by 'talking about' his mama and daddy."[61] In this final mood, with its plaintive cries of a child whose mother cannot even afford show fare, Hughes takes the dozens home to its social backbone, suggesting its defiance and aggression emerge from its vulnerabilities. Revealing these vulnerabilities does not necessarily undercut the defiance—indeed, in some ways it makes the defiance even more heroic. Rather, this final ironic turn gives a more capacious view of the significance of that defiance, giving us a perspective on the dozens that the dozens could not itself provide. This poem, which at every point announces its allegiance to and dependence upon the dozens and African-American vernacular culture more generally, also makes its own contribution. Without ever ceasing to be vernacular, that contribution is also specifically poetic. Hughes holds the relation between the vernacular and the poetic in suspension, but this judgment is never less historical and political than it is poetic.

The earliest evidence for the tradition of the dozens is a Texas song collected in 1891 by the folklorist Gates Thomas: "Talk about one thing, talk about another; / But ef you talk about me, I'm gwain to talk about your mother."[62] It is fitting this evidence has poetic affinities. Geneva Smitherman suggests the term "dozens" derives from the twelve rhyming couplets that constituted the game in an original folk form.[63] Although typically associated with the catchphrase *"ask your mama,"* or *"your mama,"* in fact the banter can involve insulting any relative and can be employed by women as well as men. Following Dollard, most anthropologists and social scientists have stressed the aggression inherent in the dozens, viewing it as functional adaptation to social subordination. Smitherman and, more recently, Robin D. G. Kelley have stressed its aesthetic character. Kelley in particular objects to all functionalist explanations, arguing that they are reductive and deny the aesthetic specificity of vernacular by casting it as a compensatory response to some form of social dysfunction. He shrewdly observes that the very methods of ethnography necessarily make the dozens appear more ritualistic than they actually are: "white ethnographers seemed oblivious to the fact that their very presence shaped what they observed. Asking their subjects to 'play the dozens' while an interloper records the 'session' with a tape recorder and notepad has the effect of creating a ritual performance for the sake of an audience, of turning spontaneous, improvised verbal exchanges into a formal practice."[64] The point of the improvisation is not aggression: "The pleasure of the dozens is not the viciousness of the insult but the humor, the creative pun, the outrageous metaphor." References to "your mama" are often almost purely generic, "a code signaling the dozens have begun . . . a shift in speech" accessing "a mutable, nameless body of a shared imagination that can be constructed and reconstructed in a thousand different shapes, sizes, colors, and circumstances."[65] Although Kelley does not make this point, the methodological shortcomings of ethnography stem from its overreliance on the synchronic. Not only does it ignore the game's integrity as a vernacular tradition, that "nameless body of shared imagination," it also ignores the personal histories of the individuals involved and their past relations with each other. Ethnography makes both of these forms of diachrony illegible precisely in order to ensure the objectivity of its evidence. Perhaps this explains why many of the best accounts of the dozens come from literary sources. Literature manages diachrony better because it has very different standards of truth.

ASK YOUR MAMA manages a more capacious view of the dozens than even the most sympathetic scholarly accounts like Smitherman's and Kelley's. For—paradoxically—without ever slighting the game's aesthetic appeal, the poem can also celebrate its banal aggressivity in ways foreclosed by their polemical insistence on the aesthetic. The gap is particularly striking in Kelley's case. His highly political argument assumes a rather apolitical notion of the aesthetic, insisting the aesthetic pleasure of the dozens somehow insulates it from its social location. Yet he also draws on the aggressivity of the dozens in order precisely to locate his own argument socially. He casts his book as a defense of the values of African-American urban culture and as a response to social scientists, politicians, and journalists who have attacked these values as dysfunctional. He imagines his title as expressing his response in the terms of that culture, turning the accusation of dysfunction back on the commentators: Yo' Mama's Disfunktional. The bravura of this rhetorical turn owes a good deal to ASK YOUR MAMA, as Kelley explicitly acknowledges, offering three lines from "HORN OF PLENTY" as the epigraph to his introduction. In his critique of previous scholarship, Kelley aspires to the same zone of mixed discourse as Hughes's poem. For this reason, we should view the gap in his analysis as the result of discursive protocols he is struggling against: he draws on

Hughes's legacy in an attempt to move social science beyond its own discursive limits. If his reproduction of that legacy is less than complete, that may be more a sign of the legacy's immensity than his failing. In that legacy we may also glimpse a strength of poetic tradition that enables it to outstrip the synchronic canons of objectivity so important to social science. As one of the earliest accounts of the dozens, *ASK YOUR MAMA* remains the most authoritative. Its experimental form enables it to handle the multiple diachronic contexts for the dozens, and its capacious vision enables it to do justice to the genre's defiant wit, to its resilient abundance of forms, and to the social vulnerabilities that surround it and give it meaning. The poem draws much of its authority from the dozens' aesthetic scope. It is able to translate that scope to its own discourse because that discourse is also aesthetic. It preserves the essential vernacularity of the dozens because it can hold its own relation to vernacularity in a long, always hopeful, suspension.

NOTES

1. John R. Rickford, *African American Vernacular English* (see Further Reading, page 257), 330.

2. I cite here only the work that has had the most influence on my own thinking in this essay. In Middle English studies: Rita Copeland, *Rhetoric, Hermeneutics, and Translation* (see Further Reading); idem, *Pedagogy, Intellectuals, and Dissent in the Later Middle Ages: Lollardy and Ideas of Learning* (Cambridge: Cambridge University Press, 2001); Russell A. Potter, "Chaucer and the Authority of Language: The Politics and Poetics of the Vernacular in Late Medieval England," *Assays* 6 (1991): 73–91; Kathryn Kerby-Fulton and Steven Justice, "Langlandian Reading Circles and the Civil Service in London and Dublin, 1380–1427," *New Medieval Literatures* 1 (1997): 59–83; David Wallace, *Chaucerian Polity: Absolutist Lineages and Associational Forms in England and Italy* (Stanford: Stanford University Press, 1997); Nicholas Watson, "Conceptions of the Word" (see Further Reading): 85–124; idem, "Visions of Inclusion: Universal Salvation and Vernacular Theology in Pre-Reformation England," *Journal of Medieval and Renaissance Studies* 27 (1997): 145–87; Katherine Zieman, "Chaucer's Voys," *Representations* 60 (1997): 70–91; Christopher Cannon, *The Making of Chaucer's English* (see Further Reading); Fiona Somerset, *Clerical Discourse and Lay Audience* (see Further Reading); Jocelyn Wogan-Browne et al., eds., *The Idea of the Vernacular* (see Further Reading). In African-American studies: Houston A. Baker Jr., *Blues, Ideology, and Afro-American Literature* (see Further Reading); Henry Louis Gates Jr., *The Signifying Monkey: A Theory of African-American Literary Criticism* (New York and Oxford: Oxford University Press, 1988); Stephen E. Henderson, "Worrying the Line: Notes on Black American Poetry," in *The Line in Postmodern Poetry*, ed. Robert Joseph Frank and Henry M. Sayre (Urbana: University of Illinois Press, 1988), 60–82; Robert G. O'Meally, "On Burke and the Vernacular: Ralph Ellison's Boomerang of History," in *History and Memory in African-American Culture*, ed. Genevieve Favre and Robert O'Meally (New York: Oxford University Press, 1994), 244–60.

3. Russell Hope Robbins, "Dissent in Middle English Literature: The Spirit of (Thirteen) Seventy-Six," *Medievalia et Humanistica* 9 (1979): 40; cited in Potter, "Chaucer and the Authority of Language," 73.

4. Alison Cornish, "A Lady Asks" (see Further Reading), 166.

5. Watson, "Visions of Inclusion." On the Lollards, see Anne Hudson, *The Premature Reformation: Wycliffite Texts and Lollard History* (Oxford: Oxford University Press, 1988); idem, "Piers Plowman and the Peasants' Revolt: A Problem Revisited," *Yearbook of Langland Studies* 8 (1995): 85–106; Copeland, *Pedagogy;* David Aers and Lynn Staley, *The Powers of the Holy: Religion, Politics, and Gender in Late Medieval English Culture* (University Park: Pennsylvania State University Press, 1996); Paul Strohm, *England's Empty Throne: Usurpation and the Language of Legitimation, 1399–1422* (New Haven and London: Yale University Press, 1998).

6. Arnold Rampersad, *The Life of Langston Hughes; Volume II: 1941–1967: I Dream a Life* (Oxford and New York: Oxford University Press, 1988), 316.

7. Ferdinand de Saussure, *Course in General Linguistics,* ed. Charles Bally and Albert Sechehaye, with the collaboration of Albert Riedlinger, trans. Roy Harris (London: Gerald Duckworth & Co., 1983), 24–25.

8. Leonard Bloomfield, *Language* (New York: Holt, Rinehart & Winston, 1933), 21.

9. Rickford, *African American Vernacular English,* 330.

10. Christopher Cannon, in his excellent new study, *The Making of Chaucer's English,* demonstrates in painstaking detail that Chaucer's borrowings were hardly exclusive to him. Despite Chaucer's long reputation as the great originator, Cannon shows convincingly that in borrowing from Latin Chaucer was following a poetic practice already well established among English poets. While Cannon's findings significantly complicate our view of Chaucer's originality, from a linguistic point of view they also make the problem of learned borrowing more important. For now we are dealing with a widespread cultural phenomenon rather than the innovation of an isolated genius. Moreover, as Cannon points out at some length, the myth of Chaucer as originator itself goes on to acquire a broad cultural significance (179–220).

11. Hans Aarslef, *From Locke to Saussure: Essays on the Study of Language and Intellectual History* (Minneapolis: University of Minnesota Press, 1982), 372–81; Mary Jacobus, *Tradition and Experiment in Wordsworth's "Lyrical Ballads" (1798)* (Oxford: Clarendon Press, 1976), 210–11.

12. William Wordsworth and Samuel Taylor Coleridge, *Lyrical Ballads,* ed. R. L. Brett and A. R. Jones (London: Methuen, 1963; reprint, Cambridge: Cambridge University Press, 1976), 241. Subsequent citations are to this edition. Page numbers are given in the text.

13. Thomas Hoccleve, in the *Regement of Princes* (1410–12). Hoccleve, *Regement,* ed. Frederick Furnivall (London, 1897), line 4978.

14. For a concise survey of representative views, see Richard Foster Jones, *The Triumph of the English Language* (see Further Reading), 171–81.

15. Noam Chomsky, *Aspects of the Theory of Syntax* (Cambridge: MIT Press, 1965); cited in J. K. Chambers, *Sociolinguistic Theory: Linguistic Variation and Its Social Significance* (Oxford and Cambridge, Mass.: Blackwell, 1995), 26.

16. Chambers, *Sociolinguistic Theory,* 15.

17. As Rickford does in part II of *African American Vernacular English,* 155–251. See also the essays in *English in Its Social Contexts,* ed. Tim William Machan and Charles T. Scott (see Further Reading). In the introduction, the editors provide a lucid and extremely useful account of the possibilities for productive exchange between sociolinguistics and historical linguistics.

18. Saussure, *Course in General Linguistics,* 73–74.

19. Baker, *Blues, Ideology,* xii.

20. Ibid., 2.

21. Richard Mulcaster, *Mulcaster's Elementarie,* ed. E. T. Campagnac (Oxford: Clarendon Press, 1925), 180 (originally *The First Part of the Elementaire which entreateth chefelie of the right writing of our English tung* [London: Thomas Vautrouiller, 1582]); cited in Jones, *The Triumph of the English Language,* 193. See also Albert C. Baugh and Thomas Cable, *A History of the English Language,* 3d ed. (London, Boston, Melbourne, and Henley: Routledge & Kegan Paul, 1978), 203–4.

22. Jeffrey Knapp, *An Empire Nowhere: England, America, and Literature from "Utopia" to "The Tempest"* (Berkeley and Los Angeles: University of California Press, 1992), 106–33.

23. Baker, *Blues, Ideology,* xii.

24. Henry Louis Gates Jr. and K. A. Appiah, eds., *Langston Hughes: Critical Perspectives Past and Present* (New York: Amistad, 1993).

25. Henry Louis Gates Jr., Nellie McKay, et al., eds., *The Norton Anthology of African American Literature* (New York: W. W. Norton & Co., 1997), 1254.

26. *New York Daily News,* February 9, 1996, 57.

27. Kevin Young, "Langston Hughes," *New Yorker,* February 8, 1999, 44.

28. For Hughes's own interest in the elegiac, see Jahan Ramazani, *Poetry of Mourning: The Modern Elegy from Hardy to Heaney* (Chicago and London: University of Chicago Press, 1994), 135–75; Larry Scanlon, "'Death Is a Drum': Rhythm, Modernity, and the Negro Poet Laureate," in *Race and the Musical Imagination,* ed. Philip Bohlman and Ronald Radano (Chicago and London: University of Chicago Press, 2000), 510–53; and idem, "News from Heaven: Vernacular Time in Langston Hughes's *Ask Your Mama,*" *Callalloo* 25 (2002): 45–47.

29. Seth Lerer, *Chaucer and His Readers: Imagining the Author in Late Medieval England* (Princeton: Princeton University Press, 1993), and Richard Helgerson, *Self-Crowned Laureates: Spenser, Jonson, Milton, and the Literary System* (Berkeley, Los Angeles, London: University of California Press, 1983), esp. 14–54.

30. William Nelson, *John Skelton, Laureate* (New York: Russell & Russell, 1964), 40–48; Maurice Pollet, *John Skelton: Poet of Tudor England,* trans. John Warrington (Lewisburg: Bucknell University Press, 1970), 10–11; James Anderson Winn, *John Dryden and His World* (New Haven and London: Yale University Press, 1987), 191–92, 208–10. The date for Skelton is an approximation, based on a somewhat ambiguous entry in his personal calendar. No record of the award survives from Oxford itself; the first official confirmation comes from Cambridge, which in 1493 awarded him its own laurel on the basis of his award by Oxford. As Pollett notes, and Nelson explains in more detail, Skelton was not the first to be so honored by Oxford, which made the award to a number of distinguished poets and scholars between 1470 and 1513. See also Lerer, *Chaucer and His Readers,* 161–63.

31. Geoffrey Chaucer, *The Riverside Chaucer,* ed. Larry Benson et al. (Boston: Houghton-Mifflin, 1986), 137.

32. For a much different reading, see Lerer, *Chaucer and His Readers,* 24–34.

33. Francesco Petrarca, *Scritti inediti,* ed. Attilio Hortis (Trieste, 1874), 311, 312; translation mine. I have been guided by Ernest Hatch Wilkins's translation in *Studies in the Life and Works of Petrarch* (Cambridge, Mass.: Mediaeval Academy of America, 1955), 300–313: "cum in ceteris artibus studiis et labore possit ad terminum perverniri in arte poetica secus est in qua nil agitur sine interna quadam et divinitus in animum vatis infusa vi."

34. Petrarca, *Scritti,* 316: "affectus iste animi victor difficultatis illius ex tribus quoque radicibus exoritur, quarum prima est honor reipublice secunda decor proprie glorie tertia calcar aliene industrie."

35. John Lydgate, *Lydgate's Troy Book,* pts. 2 and 3, ed. Henry Bergen (London: Early English Text Society, 1908, 1910; reprint, Millwood, N.Y.: Kraus Reprint Co., 1975), 516–17, lines 4234–43. Cf. Lerer (*Chaucer and His Readers,* 50–51), who reads this passage otherwise than I do.

36. Helgerson, *Self-Crowned Laureates,* 10–11 and passim.

37. Ibid., 11.

38. Ibid., 7.

39. Percy Bysshe Shelley, "A Defense of Poetry," in *Shelley's Prose, or, The Trumpet of a Prophecy,* ed. David Lee Clark (Albuquerque: University of New Mexico Press, 1954), 297.

40. James Joyce, *Portrait of the Artist as a Young Man,* ed. Seamus Deane (New York: Penguin Books, 1993), 85, 220, 275–76.

41. Peter Jones, ed., *Imagist Poetry* (Harmondsworth, Middlesex: Penguin Books, 1972), 135.

42. Conoroe, Joel, ed., *Six Americans: An Anthology* (New York: Vintage Books, 1991), 228.

43. *Chicago Whip*, February 26, 1927. Cited by Arnold Rampersad, "Langston Hughes's Fine Clothes to the Jew," *Callaloo* 9 (1986): 151.

44. Gates, *The Signifying Monkey*. The term is itself vernacular in origin. It is the term by which African-American oral tradition designates its own characteristic set of verbal practices.

45. For a lucid and concise account, see John R. Rickford, "The Question of Prior Creolization in Black English," in *Pidgin and Creole Linguistics,* ed. Albert Valdman (Bloomington and London: Indiana University Press, 1977), 190–221. See also Suzanne Romaine, *Pidgin and Creole Languages* (see Further Reading), 167–72; Geneva Smitherman, *Talkin and Testifyin: The Language of Black America,* 2d ed. (Detroit: Wayne State University Press, 1986); and Walt Wolfram, *Dialects and American English* (Englewood Cliffs, N.J.: Prentice Hall, 1991), 91–116. There are still some adherents to the older view that the African-American acquisition of English can be explained on the basis of existing regional and social dialects. See Edgar W. Schneider, *American Earlier Black English: Morphological and Syntactic Variables* (Tuscaloosa: University of Alabama Press, 1989).

46. Winthrop D. Jordan, *White over Black: American Attitudes Toward the Negro, 1550–1812* (Chapel Hill: University of North Carolina Press, 1968), 58–85.

47. Hughes, 1995, 23.

48. But cf. Rickford, *African American Vernacular English,* 12:

> AAVE use, even at its most vernacular, does not consist simply of stringing together features like those in tables [of phonological and grammatical structures]. What these lists fail to convey is the way skilled AAVE speakers use those features, together with distinctive AAVE words, prosodies and rhetorical/expressive styles, to inform, persuade, attract, praise, celebrate, chastise, entertain, educate, get over, set apart, mark identity, reflect, refute, brag, and do all the varied things for which human beings use language.

49. Rampersad, "Langston Hughes's Fine Clothes to the Jew," 145, 152.

50. A more comprehensive version of my reading in this section can be found in Scanlon, "News from Heaven."

51. There is one extant recording of Hughes reading the poem, on *The Black Verse* (Buddah Records, n.d.). On this recording he reads without accompaniment. (My thanks to my colleague Brent Edwards for alerting me to this recording.)

52. Rampersad, *Life of Langston Hughes,* II:343–44; *Langston Hughes: The Contemporary Reviews,* ed. Tish Dace (Cambridge, New York, and Melbourne: Cambridge University Press, 1997), 40–41, 635–46.

53. Two important recent exceptions: R. Baxter Miller, "Framing and Framed Languages in Hughes's *Ask Your Mama: 12 Moods for Jazz,*" *MELUS* 17, no. 4 (1991–92): 3–13, and José Piedra, "Through Blues," in *Do the Americas Have a Common Literature?* ed. Gustavo Pérez Firmat (Durham, N.C.: Duke University Press, 1990), 107–29.

54. Rampersad (*Life of Langston Hughes,* II:319) seems to have been the first critic to note this connection.

55. This figure also recalls Eliot, and through him the traditions of classical epic. Part I of *The Waste Land* is entitled "The Burial of the Dead," and it concludes with a nightmarish vision of contemporary London:

> Unreal City,
> Under the brown fog of a winter dawn,
> A crowd flowed over London Bridge, so many,
> I had not thought death had undone so many.

T. S. Eliot, *Collected Poems, 1909–1962* (London: Faber & Faber, 1963), 65.

56. Cf. Baker, *Blues, Ideology,* 7.

57. Dante Alighieri, *Literature in the Vernacular (De vulgari eloquentia)*, trans., with an introduction, by Sally Purcell (Manchester: Carcanet New Press, 1981), 15.

58. John Dollard, "The Dozens: The Dialectic of Insult," *American Imago* 1 (1939): 3–25.

59. Ibid., 25, 22.

60. Hortense Spillers, "Mama's Baby, Papa's Maybe: An American Grammar Book," *Diacritics* 17 (1987): 65–81; idem, "'All the Things You Could Be by Now, If Sigmund Freud's Wife Was Your Mother': Psychoanalysis and Race," *boundary 2* 23 (1996): 75–141. See also Cheryl Wall, "Sifting Legacies in Lucille Clifton's Generations," *Contemporary Literature* 40 (1999): 554–74.

61. Spillers, "All the Things," 140.

62. Cited by Lawrence W. Levine, *Black Culture and Black Consciousness: Afro-American Folk Thought from Slavery to Freedom* (Oxford, London, and New York: Oxford University Press, 1977), 352.

63. Smitherman, *Talkin and Testifyin,* 131–32.

64. Robin D. G. Kelley, *Yo' Mama's DisFUNKtional! Fighting the Culture Wars in Urban America* (Boston: Beacon Press, 1997), 33.

65. Ibid., 34.

FURTHER READING

Listed here is a small selection of books and articles, mostly cited in this volume, that are foundational for the study of medieval and postmedieval vernacularity and language theory or that describe particular literatures and languages discussed in this volume.

Aers, David. *"Vox populi* and the Literature of 1381." In Wallace, *Cambridge History,* 432–53.

Ahmad, Aijaz. *In Theory: Classes, Nations, Literatures.* London: Verso, 1992.

Anderson, Benedict. *Imagined Communities: Reflections on the Origin and Spread of Nationalism.* London: Verso, 1991.

Aston, Margaret. "Wycliffe and the Vernacular." In *Faith and Fire: Popular and Unpopular Religion, 1350–1600,* 27–72. London: Hambledon, 1993.

Baker, Houston A., Jr. *Blues, Ideology, and Afro-American Literature: A Vernacular Theory.* Chicago: University of Chicago Press, 1984.

Beer, Jeanette, ed. *Translation Theory and Practice in the Middle Ages.* Kalamazoo: Medieval Institute Publications, Western Michigan University, 1997.

Biddick, Kathleen. *The Shock of Medievalism.* Durham, N.C.: Duke University Press, 1998.

Bonner, Anthony. "Ramon Llull: Autor, Autoritat i Illuminat." In *Actes de l'Onzè Col·loqui Internacional de Llengua i Literatura Catalanes, Palma (Mallorca) 8–12 de septembre de 1997.* Barcelona, 1998.

Brown, Fahamisha Patricia. *Performing the Word: African American Poetry as Vernacular Culture.* New Brunswick, N.J.: Rutgers University Press, 1999.

Cannon, Christopher. *The Making of Chaucer's English: A Study of Words.* Cambridge: Cambridge University Press, 1998.

Chaurand, Jacques, ed. *Nouvelle histoire de la langue française.* Paris: Seuil, 1999.

Clanchy, Michael. *From Memory to Written Record: England, 1066–1307.* Oxford: Basil Blackwell, 1979. (2d ed., Oxford: Basil Blackwell, 1993.)

Close, Elizabeth. *The Development of Modern Rumanian: Linguistic Theory and Practice in Muntenia, 1821–1838.* London: Oxford University Press, 1974.

Cohen, Jeffrey Jerome, ed. *The Postcolonial Middle Ages.* New York: St. Martin's Press, 2000.

Constable, Giles. "The Language of Preaching in the Twelfth Century." *Viator* 25 (1994): 134–42. (Reprinted in *Culture and Spirituality in Medieval Europe,* 131–52. Aldershot: Variorum, 1996.)

Copeland, Rita. "Rhetoric and Vernacular Translation in the Middle Ages." *Studies in the Age of Chaucer* 9 (1987): 41–75.

———. *Rhetoric, Hermeneutics, and Translation in the Middle Ages: Academic Traditions and Vernacular Texts.* Cambridge: Cambridge University Press, 1991.

Cornish, Alison. "A Lady Asks: The Gender of Vulgarization in Late Medieval Italy." *Proceedings of the Modern Language Association* 115 (2000): 166–80.

Curtius, Ernst Robert. *European Literature and the Latin Middle Ages.* Translated by Willard R.

Trask. Princeton: Princeton University Press, 1990. (Originally published in German, 1953.)

Das Gupta, Jyitirindra. *Language Conflict and National Development: Group Politics and National Language Policy in India*. Berkeley and Los Angeles: University of California Press, 1985.

Dembowski, Peter. "Learned Latin Treatises in French: Inspiration, Plagiarism, and Translation." *Viator* 17 (1986): 255–69.

Eco, Umberto. *The Search for the Perfect Language*. Oxford: Basil Blackwell, 1995.

Fishman, Joshua. *Language and Nationalism*. Rowley, Mass.: Newbury House Publishers, 1972.

Green, Richard Firth. *A Crisis of Truth: Literature and Law in Medieval England*. Philadelphia: University of Pennsylvania Press, 1999.

Hahn, Thomas. "Early Middle English." In Wallace, *Cambridge History*, 61–91.

Hames, Harvey. *The Art of Conversion: Christianity and Kabbalah in the Thirteenth Century*. Leiden: Brill, 2000.

Hicks, Eric, ed. *Le débat sur le Roman de la rose*. Paris: Champion, 1977.

Hudson, Anne. "Lollardy: The English Heresy?" *Studies in Church History* 18 (1982): 261–83. (Reprinted in Hudson, *Lollards and Their Books*, 141–63. London: Hambledon, 1985.)

———. "Wyclif and the English Language." In *Wyclif in His Times*, edited by Anthony Kenny, 85–103. Oxford: Clarendon Press, 1986.

Jones, Richard Foster. *The Triumph of the English Language: A Survey of Opinions Concerning the Vernacular from the Introduction of Printing to the Restoration*. Stanford: Stanford University Press, 1953.

Judy, Ronald A. T. *(Dis)Forming the American Canon: African-Arabic Slave Narratives and the Vernacular*. Minneapolis: University of Minnesota Press, 1993.

Justice, Steven. *Writing and Rebellion: England in 1381*. Berkeley and Los Angeles: University of California Press, 1994.

King, Christopher. *One Language, Two Scripts: The Hindi Movement in Nineteenth-Century North India*. Delhi: Oxford University Press, 1994.

Lodge, R. Anthony. *French: From Dialect to Standard*. London: Routledge, 1993.

Lusignan, Serge. "Langue française et société du XIIIe au IVe siècle." In *Nouvelle histoire de la langue française*, edited by Jacques Chaurand, 93–143. Paris: Seuil, 1999.

———. *Parler vulgairement: Les intellectuels et la langue française au XIIIe et XIVe siècles*. 2d ed. Paris: Vrin, 1987.

Machan, Tim William, and Charles T. Scott, eds. *English in Its Social Contexts*. New York: Oxford University Press, 1992.

Minnis, Alastair J. *Magister Amoris: The Roman de la Rose and Vernacular Hermeneutics*. Oxford: Clarendon, 2001.

———. *Medieval Theory of Authorship: Scholastic Literary Attitudes in the Later Middle Ages*. 2d ed. Philadelphia: University of Pennsylvania Press, 1988.

Petrucci, Armando. *Writers and Readers in Medieval Italy: Studies in the History of Written Culture*. Translated by Charles M. Radding. New Haven: Yale University Press, 1995.

Rickford, John R. *African American Vernacular English: Features, Evolution, Educational Implications*. Oxford: Basil Blackwell, 1999.

Romaine, Suzanne. *Pidgin and Creole Languages*. London: Longman, 1988.

Sanders, Willy. *Sachsensprache, Hansesprache, Plattdeutsch: Sprachgeschichtliche Grundzüge des Niederdeutschen*. Göttingen: Vandenhoeck & Ruprecht, 1982.

Schenker, Alexander, and Edward Stankiewicz, eds. *The Slavic Literary Languages*. New Haven: Yale Concilium on International and Area Studies, 1980; distributed by Slavica, Columbus, Ohio.

Sisam, Kenneth. *Studies in the History of Old English Literature*. Oxford: Clarendon, 1953.

Somerset, Fiona. *Clerical Discourse and Lay Audience in Late Medieval England.* Cambridge: Cambridge University Press, 1998.

Spencer, Helen Leith. *English Preaching in the Late Middle Ages.* Oxford: Clarendon, 1993.

Stone, Gerald, and Dean Worth, eds. *The Formation of the Slavonic Literary Languages.* Columbus, Ohio: Slavica, 1985.

Thomas, George. *Linguistic Purism.* London: Longman, 1991.

Turville-Petre, Thorlac. *England the Nation.* Oxford: Clarendon, 1996.

Viswanathan, Gauri. *Masks of Conquest: Literary Studies and British Rule in India.* New York: Columbia University Press, 1989.

van den Branden, L. *Het streven naar verheerlijking, zuivering en opbouw van het Nederlands.* Gent, 1956.

Van der Wal, Marijke. *De moedertaal centraal: Standaardisatie-aspecten in de Nederlanden omstreeks 1650.* The Hague: Sdu, 1995.

Van der Wal, Marijke (in cooperation with Cor van Bree). *Geschiedenis van het Nederlands.* Zutphen, 1992.

Wallace, David, ed. *The Cambridge History of Medieval English Literature.* Cambridge: Cambridge University Press, 1999.

Watson, Nicholas. "Censorship and Cultural Change in Late-Medieval England: Vernacular Theology, the Oxford Translation Debate, and Arundel's Constitutions of 1409." *Speculum* 70 (1995): 822–66.

———. "Conceptions of the Word: The Mother Tongue and the Incarnation of God." *New Medieval Literatures* 1 (1997): 85–124.

Welliver, Warman. *Dante in Hell: The "De Vulgari Eloquentia": Introduction, Text, Translation, Commentary.* Ravenna: Longo Editore, 1981.

Wogan-Browne, Jocelyn, Nicholas Watson, Andrew Taylor, and Ruth Evans, eds. *The Idea of the Vernacular: An Anthology of Middle English Literary Theory, 1280–1520.* University Park: Pennsylvania State University Press, 1999.

Wright, Roger. *Late Latin and Early Romance in Spain and Carolingian France.* Liverpool: Francis Cairns, 1982.

Zink, Michel. *La prédication en langue romane avant 1300.* Paris: Editions Honoré Champion, 1976.

FIONA SOMERSET is Associate Professor of English at Duke University (formerly Associate Professor of English, University of Western Ontario). As well as numerous articles on Chaucer, Langland, Lydgate, Wycliffism, and late medieval English Latinity and vernacularity, and editor of four Wycliffite dialogues (forthcoming from the Early English Text Society), she is author of *Clerical Discourse and Lay Audience in Late Medieval England* (Cambridge, 1998) and co-editor, with Jill Havens and Derrick Pitard, of *Lollards and Their Influence in Later Medieval England* (Brewer, 2003). She is associate editor of the *Yearbook of Langland Studies* and a member of the executive committee of the Lollard Society, organizing its very popular sessions each year at Kalamazoo.

NICHOLAS WATSON is Professor in the Department of English and American Literature and Language at Harvard University (formerly Professor of English, University of Western Ontario). Besides writing articles on Middle English mysticism, vernacular theology and poetry, and editing the *Liber visionum* of John of Morigny (with Claire Fanger) and *The Writings of Julian of Norwich* (with Jacqueline Jenkins) (both forthcoming), he is author of *Richard Rolle and the Invention of Authority* (Cambridge, 1991); editor of *Richard Rolle's Emendatio Vitae* (Toronto, 1995); co-editor and translator (with Anne Savage) of *Anchoritic Spirituality: "Ancrene Wisse" and Associated Works* (Paulist Press, 1991); and co-editor (with Jocelyn Wogan-Browne, Andrew Taylor, and Ruth Evans) of *The Idea of the Vernacular: An Anthology of Middle English Literary Theory, 1280–1520* (Penn State, 1999).

GRETCHEN V. ANGELO is Assistant Professor of Modern Languages at California State University, Los Angeles, and author of several articles on Old and Middle French literature.

NANDI BHATIA is Associate Professor of English at the University of Western Ontario, where she teaches postcolonial literature and theory. She has published articles in the field of postcolonial studies in various journals and book collections and a book, *Acts of Authority/Acts of Resistance: Theatre and Politics in Colonial and Postcolonial India* (Michigan, 2003).

CHARLES F. BRIGGS is Associate Professor of History at Georgia Southern University and author of *Giles of Rome's "De Regimine Principum": Reading and Writing Politics at Court and University, c. 1275–c. 1525* (Cambridge, 1999). He is currently researching the Latin and vernacular reception of Aristotelian moral philosophy.

JACK FAIREY is a Ph.D. candidate studying nineteenth-century Ottoman and Balkan history at the University of Toronto's Department of History. He is currently completing a dissertation titled "International Diplomacy, Ecclesiastical Reform, and the Orthodox Church in the Ottoman Empire During the Reign of Sultan Abdülmecid, 1839–1861."

HARVEY HAMES received his Ph.D. in history from Cambridge and is Associate Professor of History at Ben Gurion University, Beersheba, Israel. He is author of *The Art of Conversion: Christianity and Kabbalah in the Thirteenth Century* (Brill, 2000), and his interests include medieval polemics, Kabbalah, and philosophy, particularly in the western Mediterranean world.

JEROEN JANSEN is a research fellow of the Universiteit van Amsterdam, Netherlands (Ph.D., Dutch literature, Universiteit van Amsterdam, 1995). He has published on rhetoric and literary criticism from the sixteenth to the eighteenth centuries and on Dutch literature of the same period, including *Decorum: Observaties over de literaire gepastheid in de renaissancistische poëtica* (Verloren, 2001).

SARA S. POOR is Assistant Professor at Princeton University (formerly at Stanford University) and author of a study of Mechthild of Magdeburg, *Gender and the Making of Textual Authority: Mechthild of Magdeburg and Her Book* (Pennsylvania, forthcoming), as well as several articles on Mechthild and other topics.

WILLIAM ROBINS is Associate Professor of English, University of Toronto, and author of a forthcoming study and edition of Antonio Pucci's *Queen of the Orient* (Toronto), besides many articles on late antiquity, the Middle Ages, and the early sixteenth century.

LARRY SCANLON is Professor of English at Rutgers University. Besides many articles, he is author of *Narrative, Authority, and Power: The Medieval Exemplum and the Chaucerian Tradition* (Cambridge, 1994), and has enjoyed a distinguished recent career as editor of *Studies in the Age of Chaucer*.

ANDREW TAYLOR is Associate Professor of English at the University of Ottawa. He is the author of *Textual Situations: Three Medieval Manuscripts and*

Their Readers (2002) and co-editor (with Jocelyn Wogan-Browne, Nicholas Watson, and Ruth Evans) of *The Idea of the Vernacular: An Anthology of Late Middle English Literary Theory, 1280–1520* (1999) and (with David Townsend) of *The Tongue of the Fathers: Gender and Ideology in Medieval Latin* (1998). His current research focuses on late medieval aristocratic reading in England.

CLAIRE M. WATERS is Assistant Professor of English at the University of California, Davis. She has written several articles on medieval religious literature, including saints' lives, and her book on the role of embodiment in preaching, *Angels and Earthly Creatures: Preaching, Performance, and Gender in the Later Middle Ages* (University of Pennsylvania Press, 2003).

MEG WORLEY is the Associate Director of the Stanford Humanities Laboratory and a lecturer in the Departments of Comparative Literature and English at Stanford.

Index

Acciaioli, Alamanno, 130 n. 13
   Cronaca, 120–21
Acharya, P. B., *The Tragicomedies of Shakespeare, Kalidasa, and Bhavabhuti,* 213
Adam, 1, 2, 13, 43, 54 n. 2
Adamic language, 1–13, 16, 165
Adelung, Johann C., 181
Ælfric, 25–26
Aers, David, 150
Africa, 15, 239, 242. *See also* Egypt, Tunis
African-American, xi, 1, 8, 164, 220–56
Agrippa, Cornelius, 12 nn. 3, 7
Ahmad, Aziz, 212
Ainsworth, Peter, 143 n. 19, 144 n. 44
Alabama, 248
Albania, 184
Albert of Bavaria, 134
Albertus Magnus, 104
Alecsandri, Vasile, 188, 189, 196–97 n. 50, 197 n. 54
   Poesii populare, 192
Alemannic, 60, 64. *See also* German
Alexis, Saint, 74
Alice of Louth, 128
Allahabad, 203, 216 n. 29
Al-Mustansir, 46
America, 164. *See also* Canada; United States
American Heritage Dictionary, 220
American South, 239–40, 242
Amiens, 137
Amsterdam, 167, 172
   chamber of rhetoric, 170, 171
Anderson, Benedict, *Imagined Communities,* 159
Anderson, Elizabeth A., 78 n. 42
Anderson, John, 21, 28 n. 11
Angelo, Gretchen, xiii, 8, 81–82, 83, 85–98
angels, 1–8
Angevin, 23. *See also* French
Anglo-Norman, xi, 23, 24, 26, 160, 162. *See also* French

Anjuman Taraqqui-e-Urdu, 212
Anti-Bonjourists. *See* Bonjourists
Antwerp, 166, 167
Apollo, 6
Apollonius, 2–8, 12 n. 5
Appiah, Anthony, 228
Aquinas, Thomas, 3, 103, 104
   Summa theologica, 13 n. 10, 107
Aquitaine, 140, 141
Arabic, 11, 13 n. 12, 43, 46, 51, 53, 100. *See also* Greco-Arabic
"Arabic mode of speech," 52, 56 n. 38
Aragon, 43, 55 n. 22, 56 n. 43
Aristotle, 6, 44, 100–108
   Economics (pseudo-Aristotle), 103
   Nicomachean Ethics, 102, 103, 107. *See also* Grosseteste, Robert; Oresme, Nicole
   Parvi flores (compilation), 103
   Politics, 102. *See also* William of Moerbeke
   Posterior Analytics, 106–7
   Rhetoric, 104. *See also* Giles of Rome
Arkansas, 248
Arn, Mary-Jo, 144 n. 41
Arrouaise, Augustinian monastery of, 23
Ars. See Llull, Ramon
Ars notoria, 1–13, 165
Arthur, King, 35, 230
Artois, 137
Arundel, Thomas, 156 n. 21
   Constitutions, 81, 84, 145–57
Arya Samaj. *See* Hindi
Aryan, 163, 164, 210
Asachi, Gheorghe, 187
Asiatic Journal, 206
Asiatic Society, 206
Aston, John, 147
ASTRA, 191, 197 n. 59
Athens, 6, 128, 161
auctoritas, auctores, 6, 87, 93, 100, 101, 163, 165, 240